*Vest Pocket*
# Dictionary

### 1992
### Revised Edition

Walter C. Kidney, Editor

Prepared under the direction of
Laurence Urdang

**THOMAS NELSON PUBLISHERS**
Nashville • Camden • Kansas City

**Revised Edition 1992**

Copyright © 1978, 1985, 1992 by Thomas Nelson Inc., Publishers

All rights reserved. No part of this book may be used or reproduced in any manner whatsoever without written permission of the publisher. Printed in the United States of America.

### Library of Congress
### Cataloging-in-Publication Data

Webster's vest pocket dictionary / Walter C. Kidney, editor ; prepared under the direction of Laurence Urdang.
— Rev. ed.
    p.    cm.
  ISBN 0-8407-6822-2 (pb)
  1. English language—Dictionaries.
I. Kidney, Walter C.
PE1628.W567  1992
423—dc20                                      91–37335
                                                    CIP

1 2 3 4 5 — 96 95 94 93 92

# A

**A, a,** *n.* first letter of the English alphabet.

**a,** *indef. art.* 1. one. 2. any single.

**a·ban'don,** *v.t.* 1. leave permanently. 2. give up. —**a·ban'don·ment,** *n.*

**a·ban'doned,** *adj.* without self-restraint; shameless.

**a·bash',** *v.t.* embarrass; shame.

**a·bate',** *v.t., v.i.,* lessen, diminish. —**a·bate'ment,** *n.*

**ab'bess,** *n.* nun directing a convent.

**ab'bey,** *n., pl.* **ab'beys.** monastery or convent.

**ab'bot,** *n.* monk directing a monastery.

**ab·bre'vi·ate',** *v.t.* shorten to essentials. —**ab·bre'vi·a'tion,** *n.*

**ab'di·cate',** *v.t.* give up, as office or power. —**ab'di·ca'tion,** *n.*

**ab'do·men,** *n.* 1. part of the human body between the chest and hip. 2. part of an animal body in a similar location. —**ab·dom'i·nal,** *adj.*

**ab·duct',** *v.t.* carry away, esp. by force.

**ab''er·ra'tion,** *n.* deviation from what is considered normal.

**a·bet',** *v.t.* aid or encourage. —**a·bet'tor, a·bet'ter,** *n.*

**a·bey'ance,** *n.* suspension of activity.

**ab·hor',** *v.t.* regard with horror or disgust. —**ab·hor'rence,** *n.* —**ab·hor'rent,** *adj.*

**a·bide',** *v.i.* 1. remain. 2. dwell. —*v.t.* 3. wait for. 4. *Informal.* tolerate.

**a·bid'ing,** *adj.* enduring; steadfast.

**a·bil'i·ty,** *n., pl.* **-ties.** 1. power. 2. talent; aptitude.

**ab·ject',** *adj.* 1. downcast. 2. contemptible.

**ab·jure',** *v.t.* renounce formally. —**ab''ju·ra'tion,** *n.*

**a·blaze',** *adv., adj.* afire.

**a'ble,** *adj.,* **abler, ablest.** 1. with the power to do a certain thing. 2. competent. —**a'bly,** *adv.*

**ab·nor'mal,** *adj.* not normal. —**ab''nor·mal'i·ty,** *n.*

**a·board',** *adv.* 1. onto a ship, train, etc. —*prep.* 2. on a ship, train, etc.; on board.

**a·bode',** *n.* home; dwelling.

**a·bol'ish,** *v.t.* do away with. —**ab''o·li'tion,** *n.*

**a·bom'in·a·ble,** *adj.* disgusting; loathsome.

**a·bom'in·ate'',** *v.t.* hate or loathe. —**a·bom'in·a'tion,** *n.*

**ab''o·rig'i·nal,** *adj.* primitive; original.

**a''bo·rig'in·e,** *n.* original inhabitant, esp. a savage.

**a·bor'tion,** *n.* termination of pregnancy before full development of a fetus.

**a·bor'tive,** *adj.* (of a hope or attempt) frustrated at an early stage.

**a·bound',** *v.i.* to have or offer something in abundance.

**a·bout',** *prep.* 1. concerning; regarding. 2. around. 3. on the point of. —*adv.* 4. nearly; approximately.

**a·bove',** *prep.* 1. higher than. 2. greater than. —*adv., adj.* 3. to or in a higher place. 4. in a previous part of a text.

**a·bove'board'',** *adj., adv.* without deception or disguise.

**a·breast',** *adv., adj.* side by side.

**a·bridge',** *v.t.* shorten; abbreviate. —**a·bridg'ment,** *n.*

**a·broad',** *adv., adj.* outside one's own country.

**a·brupt',** *adj.* 1. sudden. 2. steep. —**ab·rupt'ness,** *n.*

**ab'scess,** *n.* area filled with pus.

**ab·scond',** *v.i.* leave secretly and hurriedly.

**ab·sent',** *adj.* (ab'sənt) not present. —*v.t.* (ab sent') remove. —**ab'sence,** *n.*

**ab''sen·tee',** *n.* absent person. —**ab''sen·tee'ism,** *n.*

**ab'sent-mind'ed,** *adj.* not paying attention.

**ab'so·lute',** *adj.* 1. perfect. 2. pure; unqualified. —**ab''so·lute'ly,** *adv.*

**ab·solve',** *v.t.* free from blame or guilt. —**ab''so·lu'tion,** *n.*

**ab·sorb',** *v.t.* take in, as a fluid. —**ab·sorb'ent,** *adj., n.* —**ab·sorp'tion,** *n.*

**ab·stain',** *v.i.* refrain. —**ab'sti·nent,** *adj.*

**ab·ste'mi·ous,** *adj.* abstaining from excess.

**ab·stract',** *adj.* (ab'strakt) 1. nonmaterial; non-specific. —*n.* 2.

summary; abridgment. —v.t. (abstrakt') 3. remove, esp. in a theft. —ab·strac'tion, n.

ab·struse', adj. hard to understand.

ab·surd', adj. nonsensical. —ab·surd'ly, adv. —ab·surd'i·ty, n.

a·bun'dance, n. great supply. —a·bun'dant, adj.

a·buse', v.t. (ə byo͞oz') 1. use or treat wrongly. —n. (ə byo͞os') 2. wrong use or treatment. —a·bus'ive, adj.

a·but', v.i. meet at an edge or end; border.

a·byss', n. great depth; chasm.

ac''a·dem'ic, adj. pertaining to scholarship.

a·cad'e·my, n. 1. school. 2. cultural organization.

ac·cede', v.i. consent.

ac·cel'er·ate', v.t., v.i. increase in speed. —ac·cel'er·a'tion, n.

ac·cel'er·a''tor, n. vehicle speed control.

ac·cent, n. (ak'sent) 1. emphasis. —v.t. (ak sent') 2. emphasize; stress.

ac·cen'tu·ate', v.t. emphasize; stress.

ac·cept', v.t. receive or take willingly. —ac·cept'a·ble, adj. —ac·cept'ance, n.

ac'cess, n. means or way of approach.

ac·ces'si·ble, adj. readily approached or reached.

ac·ces'so·ry, n., pl. -ries. 1. additional working part, decorative object, etc. 2. companion in a crime.

ac'ci·dent, n. unexpected event, usually undesirable. —ac''ci·den'tal, adj.

ac·claim', v.t. 1. applaud; cheer. —n. 2. applause. —ac''cla·ma'tion, n.

ac'cli·mate'', v.t. accustom to a new environment. Also, ac·clim'a·tize''.

ac·com'mo·date'', v.t. 1. provide with food, lodging, etc. 2. adjust to existing conditions. —ac·com'mo·da'tion, n. —ac·com'mo·dat''ing, adj.

ac·com'mo·da'tions, n., pl. lodgings, esp. temporary ones.

ac·com'pa·ni·ment, n. something used with another thing; accessory.

ac·com'pa·ny, v.t. travel with.

ac·com'plice, n. associate in crime.

ac·com'plish, v.t. succeed in doing. —ac·com'plish·ment, n.

ac·cord', n. agreement; harmony. —ac·cord'ance, n.

ac·cord'ing·ly, adv. therefore.

ac·cor'di·on, n. reed instrument with keyboard and bellows.

ac·cost', v.t. approach and catch the attention of.

ac·count', v.t. 1. regard as. —v.i. 2. account for, a. explain or interpret. b. justify. c. be condemned or punished for. —n. 3. story; narrative. 4. explanation. 5. justification. 6. importance. 7. set of business transactions involving one client or customer. 8. business record.

ac·count'a·ble, adj. answerable; responsible.

ac·cred'it, v.t. certify as competent or valid. —ac·cred''it·a'tion, n.

ac·crue', v.i. be added, esp. in a regular way. —ac·cru'al, n.

ac·cu'mu·late', v.t., v.i. gather; collect. —ac·cu'mu·la'tion, n.

ac'cu·rate, adj. correct; truthful. —ac'cu·ra·cy, ac'cu·rate·ness, n.

ac·curs'ed', adj. 1. under a curse. 2. damnable.

ac·cu'sa·tive, n. grammatical case for direct object of verb. —ac·cu'sa·tive, adj.

ac·cuse', v.t. denounce; blame. —ac·cus'er, n. —ac''cu·sa'tion, n.

ac·cus'tom, v.t. cause to become used to something.

ac·cus'tomed, adj. usual; customary.

ace, n. playing card with one pip.

ache, v.i. 1. suffer dull pain. —n. 2. dull pain.

a·chieve', v.t. succeed in reaching, finishing, or fulfilling. —a·chieve'ment, n.

ac'id, n. 1. chemical compound reacting with base to form salt. —adj. 2. pertaining to acids. 3. sour. —a·cid'i·ty, n.

ac·knowl'edge, v.t. 1. admit as true or valid. 2. show appreciation or gratitude for.

ac'me, n. summit.

ac'o·lyte, n. priest's assistant; altar boy.

a'corn, n. nut of an oak tree.

a·cous'tic, adj. pertaining to transmission or reception of sound through air, etc.

**a·cous'tics**, *n.* science of transmission of sound through air, etc.

**ac·quaint'**, *v.t.* 1. make known. 2. make familiar. —**ac'quain'tance**, *n.*

**ac''qui·esce'**, *v.i.* consent or comply. —**ac''qui·es'cence**, *n.*

**ac·quire'**, *v.t.* obtain; get.

**ac''qui·si'tion**, *n.* act or instance of acquiring.

**ac·quis'i·tive**, *adj.* greedy, grasping.

**ac·quit'**, *v.t.* release from blame or detention. —**ac·quit'tal**, *n.*

**a'cre**, *n.* land area equal to 43,560 square feet or 4,047 square meters. —**a'cre·age**, *n.*

**ac'ri·mo'ny**, *n.* harshness of manner or expression. —**ac''ri·mo'ni·ous**, *adj.*

**ac'ro·bat''**, *n.* gymnastic entertainer, esp. one performing high above the ground.

**ac''ro·nym**, *n.* word formed from the initial letters of a phrase or title, as *NASA*.

**a·cross'**, *prep.* 1. from one side to the other of. 2. on the other side. —*adv.* 3. from one side to the other.

**act**, *n.* 1. something done. 2. law. 3. one of the main divisions of a play, etc. —*v.i.* 4. do something. 5. conduct oneself. 6. perform in a play or plays.

**act'ing**, *n.* 1. the profession of one who performs in plays. —*adj.* 2. performing a specified function for the time being.

**ac'tion**, *n.* 1. state of being active. 2. something done.

**ac'ti·vate'**, *v.t.* cause to be active. —**ac''ti·va'tion**, *n.*

**ac'tive**, *adj.* 1. performing actions. 2. having an effect.

**ac·tiv'i·ty**, *n., pl.* **-ties**. action, esp. one of a number performed in a sequence.

**ac'tor**, *n.* man performing in plays. Also, *fem.,* **ac'tress**.

**ac'tu·al**, *adj.* really existing. —**ac''tu·al'i·ty**, *n.*

**ac'tu·al·ly** *adv.* really.

**a·cu'men**, *n.* sharpness of mind.

**a·cute'**, *adj.* sharp. —**a·cute'ness**, *n.*

**ad'age**, *n.* old saying.

**ad'a·mant**, *adj.* unyielding.

**a·dapt'**, *v.t.* change to suit conditions. —**a·dapt'a·ble**, *adj.* —**a''dap·ta'tion**, *n.*

**add**, *v.t.* 1. join to another or oth-

ers. 2. compute as a total. —*v.i.* 3. constitute an addition. —**ad·di'tion**, *n.* —**ad·di'tion·al**, *adj.*

**ad·dict'**, *v.t.* (a dikt') 1. make dependent on a drug, etc. —*n.* (a' dikt) 2. addicted person.

**ad·dress'**, *v.t.* (a dres', or for 2, ad'res), *n.* 1. speech; oration. 2. location of a business, residence, etc. —*v.t.* 3. speak to formally. 4. direct as a message. —**ad''dress·ee'**, *n.*

**ad·e·noid''**, *n.* normal growth in the throat behind the nose.

**a·dept'**, (a dept') *adj.* skilled.

**ad'e·quate**, *adj.* suitable or sufficient. —**ad'e·qua·cy**, *n.*

**ad·here'**, *v.i.* cling. —**ad·her'ent**, *adj.* —**ad·her'ence**, **ad·he'sion**, *n.* —**ad·he'sive**, *adj., n.*

**ad''-hoc''** *adj.* for one special purpose.

**a·dieu'** (ə dyoe', a dyōō'), *interj., n., pl.* **-dieux**. *French.* goodbye.

**ad·ja'cent**, *adj.* near or adjoining.

**ad·jec'tive**, *n.* word qualifying a noun.

**ad·join'**, *v.t.* be next to.

**ad·journ'**, *v.t.* suspend operations of (a meeting, court, etc.). —*v.i.* 2. suspend operations. —**ad·journ'ment**, *n.*

**ad'junct**, *n.* something added.

**ad·jure'**, *v.t.* 1. command formally. 2. request solemnly.

**ad·just'**, *v.t.* 1. cause to fit or function properly. 2. settle. —*v.i.* 3. adapt oneself. —**ad·just'er**, **ad·just'or**, *n.* —**ad·just'ment**, *n.*

**ad·min'is·ter**, *v.t.* 1. direct or manage. 2. give, esp. according to prescribed rules.

**ad·min''is·tra'tion**, *n.* act or process of administering. —**ad·min'is·tra'tive**, *adj.* —**ad·min'is·tra'tor**, *n.*

**ad'mi·ral**, *n.* naval officer of the highest rank.

**ad·mire'**, *v.t.* regard with great respect or pleasure. —**ad'mir·a·ble**, *adj.* —**ad''mi·ra'tion**, *n.* —**ad·mir'er**, *n.*

**ad·mis'si·ble**, *adj.* 1. proper for admission. 2. allowable.

**ad·mis'sion**, *n.* 1. act or instance of admitting. 2. confession.

**ad·mit'**, *v.t.* 1. allow to enter. 2. confess or concede. —**ad·mit'tance**, *n.*

**ad·mix'ture**, *n.* something added to a mixture.

**ad·mon'ish**, *v.t.* 1. urge, esp. as a

warning. 2. reproach. —**ad''mo·ni'tion**, *n.*

**ad'o·les'cence**, *n.* youth between puberty and physical maturity. —**ad''o·les'cent**, *adj., n.*

**a·dopt'**, *v.t.* take as one's own. —**a·dop'tion**, *n.*

**a·dore'**, *v.t.* worship. —**a''do·ra'·tion**, *n.* —**a·dor'a·ble**, *adj.*

**a·dorn'**, *v.t.* decorate. —**a·dorn'·ment**, *n.*

**a·drift'**, *adj., adv.* drifting.

**a·droit'**, *adj.* clever.

**ad''u·la'tion**, *n.* excessive praise or respect.

**a·dult'**, *n.* 1. physically mature person or animal. —*adj.* 2. physically mature.

**a·dul'ter·ate''**, *v.t.* add undesirable ingredients to.

**a·dul'ter·y**, *n., pl.* **-ies**. infidelity of a spouse.

**ad·vance'**, *v.t.* 1. move forward. 2. suggest for consideration. 3. pay before earned. —*v.i.* 4. move forward. —*n.* 5. motion forward. 6. sum to be repaid in money or work. —*adj.* 7. early. —**ad·vance'·ment**, *n.*

**ad·van'tage**, *n.* more favorable situation. —**ad''van·ta'geous**, *adj.*

**ad'vent**, 1. arrival. 2. Advent, a. coming of Christ. b. period before Christmas.

**ad·ven'ture**, *n.* risky undertaking. —**ad·ven'tur·er**, *n.* —**ad·ven'·tur·ous**, *adj.*

**ad'verb**, *n.* Grammar. word modifying a verb. —**ad·ver'bi·al**, *adj.*

**ad'ver·sar''y**, *n., pl.* **-saries**. opponent or enemy.

**ad·verse'**, *adj.* opposing or unfavorable.

**ad·ver'si·ty**, *n., pl.* **-ties**. difficulty or misfortune.

**ad'ver·tise''**, *v.t.* call attention to in order to elicit a public response. —**ad''ver·tis'er**, *n.* —**ad''ver·tise'ment**, *n.* —**ad''ver·tis'ing**, *n.*

**ad·vice'**, *n.* opinion urging choice or rejection of a course of action.

**ad·vis'a·ble**, *adj.* to be advised; desirable.

**ad·vise'**, *v.t.* urge to choose or reject a course of action. —**ad·vis'·er**, **ad·vi'sor**, *n.*

**ad'vo·cate**, *n.* (ad'və kət) 1. person arguing one side of a dispute, esp. a lawyer. —*v.t.* (ad'və kāt'')

2. to argue in favor of. —**ad'vo·ca·cy**, *n.*

**aer'ate**, *v.t.* expose to air.

**aer'i·al**, *adj.* 1. in or of the air. 2. pertaining to aviation. —*n.* 3. antenna for sending or receiving radio waves.

**ae·ro''bics**, *n.* exercises to strengthen circulation and respiration.

**aer''o·nau'tics**, *n.* science of flying.

**aer''o·sol**, *n.* liquid applied by spraying from a pressurized container.

**aer'o·space''**, *n.* all space, including the earth's atmosphere.

**aes·thet'ic** (es thet'ik), *adj.* 1. pertaining to beauty. 2. sensitive to art or beauty. —*n.* 3. **aesthetics**, study of art or beauty.

**a·far'**, *adv.* at a great distance.

**af'fa·ble**, *adj.* cordial; pleasant.

**af·fair'**, *n.* 1. business matter. 2. event. 3. amorous relationship.

**af·fect'**, *v.t.* have influence on.

**af''fec·ta'tion**, *n.* pretentious mannerism.

**af·fect'ed**, *adj.* 1. characterized by affectation. 2. moved emotionally.

**af·fec'tion**, *n.* love.

**af·fec'tion·ate**, *adj.* loving.

**af''fi·da'vit**, *n.* sworn written statement.

**af·fil'i·ate''**, *v.t.* combine, as independent businesses for mutual benefit.

**af·fin'i·ty**, *n., pl.* **-ties**. attraction.

**af·firm'**, *v.t.* 1. state emphatically. 2. confirm; ratify. —**af·fir'ma'·tion**, *n.* —**af·fir'ma·tive**, *adj.*

**af·fix'**, *v.t.* attach.

**af·flict'**, *v.t.* trouble. —**af·flic'·tion**, *n.*

**af'flu·ent**, *adj.* prosperous. —**af'·flu·ence**, *n.*

**af·ford'**, *v.t.* 1. have enough money or other resources. 2. supply; provide.

**af'fray**, *n.* fight.

**af·front'**, *v.t.* 1. insult or challenge openly. —*n.* 2. open insult or challenge.

**a·fire'**, *adv., adj.* on fire. Also, **a·flame'**.

**a·fraid'**, *adj.* full of fear.

**aft**, *adv., adj. Nautical.* toward or at the stern.

**af'ter**, *prep.* 1. behind. —*adv.* 2. later.

**af·ter·math''**, *n.* consequence, usually unfavorable.

**af''ter·noon'**, *n.* period after noon and before evening.

**af·ter·ward**, *adv.* later. Also, **af'ter·wards.**

**a·gain'**, *adv.* once more.

**a·gainst'**, *prep.* 1. toward or into contact with. 2. opposed or hostile to.

**age**, *n.* 1. remoteness in time of birth or origin. —*v.i.* 2. become old.

**a'ged**, *adj.* old.

**age''is·m**, *n.* discrimination against the elderly.

**age'less**, *adj.* unaffected by time or age.

**a'gen·cy**, *n., pl.* **-cies.** 1. office handling business for others. 2. active force.

**a·gen'da** (ə jen'də), *n., pl.* business matters to be dealt with.

**a'gent**, *n.* person handling business for others.

**ag·gra·vate''**, *v.t.* 1. make worse. 2. annoy. —**ag''gra·va'tion,** *n.*

**ag'gre·gate**, *adj.* 1. total; collective. —*n.* 2. sum; total. —**ag''gre·ga'tion,** *n.*

**ag·gres'sion**, *n.* hostile act or policy. —**ag·gres'sor,** *n.*

**ag·gres'sive**, *adj.* 1. disposed to commit aggressions. 2. forceful, as in business.

**a·ghast'**, *adj.* horrified.

**a·gile'**, *adj.* nimble; deft. —**a·gil'i·ty,** *n.*

**ag'i·tate''**, *v.t.* 1. shake violently. 2. disturb emotionally. —**a'gi·ta'tion,** *n.*

**ag·nos'tic**, *n.* person regarding the existence of God as unknowable.

**a·go'**, *adj., adv.* in the past.

**a·go'ny**, *n., pl.* **-ies.** intense suffering.

**a·gree'**, *v.i.* 1. consent or promise. 2. be of the same opinion. 3. be harmonious or in accord. 4. match exactly. —*v.t.* 5. concede as true. —**a·gree'ment,** *n.*

**a·gree'a·ble**, *adj.* pleasant. —**a·gree'a·bly,** *adv.*

**ag'ri·cul'ture**, *n.* science or occupation of farming. —**ag''ri·cul'tur·al,** *adj.*

**a·head'**, *adv., adj.* in front.

**aid**, *n., v.* help.

**AIDS**, acquired immune deficiency syndrome.

**ail**, *v.t.* distress or sicken. —**ail'ment,** *n.*

**aim**, *v.t.* 1. point, as for shooting. —*v.i.* 2. point a gun, etc. —*n.* 3. act of pointing a gun, etc. 4. intention or goal.

**aim'less**, *adj.* without a goal or purpose.

**air**, *n.* 1. gas compound surrounding the earth. —*v.t.* 2. ventilate.

**air conditioning**, treatment of air to control purity, temperature, and humidity. —**air'con·di''tion,** *v.t.*

**air'craft**, *n., pl.* **-craft.** flying craft.

**air'line**, *n.* company operating regularly scheduled aircraft flights. —**air'lin''er,** *n.*

**air'plane**, *n.* heavier-than-air flying craft with wings.

**air'port''**, *n.* airfield with terminal, storage, and service buildings.

**air'tight'**, *adj.* preventing passage of air.

**air'y**, *adj.,* **airier, airiest.** open to air or breeze.

**aisle** (īl), *n.* 1. passageway, esp. among seats as in a theater. 2. a division of a church, esp. between pillars.

**a·jar'**, *adj., adv.* partly open, as a door.

**a·kin'**, *adj.* of the same family.

**a·larm'**, *n.* 1. emergency signal. —*v.t.* 2. startle or frighten.

**al·bi'no**, *n., pl.* **-nos.** person or animal without skin pigmentation.

**al'bum**, *n.* blank book.

**al'co·hol'**, *n.* colorless liquid used as fuel, intoxicant, etc.

**al''co·hol'ic**, *adj.* 1. pertaining to alcohol. —*n.* 2. person addicted to alcohol.

**al'cove**, *n.* place set back from a larger adjoining space.

**ale**, *n.* strong beerlike drink.

**a·lert'**, *adj.* 1. watchful. —*v.t., n.* 2. alarm.

**al'fal·fa**, *n.* fodder plant.

**al'ge·bra**, *n.* mathematical system based on symbols, not numbers. —**al''ge·bra'ic,** *adj.*

**al'i·as**, *adv.* otherwise known as.

**al'i·bi**, *n., pl.* **-bis.** legal plea of absence from the scene of a crime.

**al'i·en**, *adj.* 1. from outside; foreign. —*n.* 2. foreigner.

**al'i·en·ate''**, *v.t.* 1. deprive someone of. 2. act so as to lose the friendship of.

**a·lign'** (ə līn'), *v.t.* line up.

**a·like'**, *adj.* 1. of the same kind or form. —*adv.* 2. in the same way.

**a·live'**, *adj.* living.

**al·ka·li'**, *n., pl.* **-lis.** acid-neutralizing chemical. —**al'ka·line''**, *adj.*

**all**, *adj.* 1. every. —*n.* —*pron.* 2. everything or everybody.

**al·lay'**, *v.t.* calm or soothe.

**al·lege'**, *v.t.* assert, esp. without proof. —**al''le·ga'tion**, *n.*

**al·le'giance**, *n.* loyalty.

**al'le·go''ry**, *n., pl.* **-ies.** story or display using symbols.

**al·ler'gy**, *n., pl.* **-gies.** excessive sensitivity to some substance.

**al·le'vi·ate'**, *v.t.* relieve; mitigate.

**al·ley**, *n., pl.* **-leys.** narrow service street.

**al·li'ance**, *n.* 1. combination of independent nations, etc. 2. organization or club.

**al·lied'**, *adj.* 1. joined in an alliance. 2. closely related.

**al'li·ga·tor**, *n.* broad-snouted reptile of the southeastern U.S.

**al'lo·cate''**, *v.t.* assign or allot.

**al·lot'**, *v.t.* 1. distribute to sharing parties. 2. assign. —**al·lot'ment**, *n.*

**al·low'**, *v.t.* 1. permit. 2. give or grant. 3. grant to be true. —**al·low'a·ble**, *adj.* —**al·low'ance**, *n.*

**al·loy'**, *n.* (al loi') 1. mix. —*n.* (al'loi) 2. metal or metals with admixtures.

**al·lude'**, *v.i.* make reference to. —**al·lu'sion**, *n.*

**al·lure'**, *v.t.* 1. attract temptingly. —*n.* 2. quality of attraction or temptation.

**al·ly'**, *v., n., pl.* **-lies.** *v.t., v.i.* 1. unite for a common purpose. —*n.* 2. person, country, etc. joined in an alliance.

**al'ma·nac''**, *n.* annual publication including a calendar and diverse useful information.

**al·might'y**, *adj.* 1. totally powerful. —*n.* 2. **the Almighty**, God.

**al'mond**, *n.* edible nut from a tree.

**al'most**, *adv.* nearly.

**alms** (ahms), *n., pl.* **alms.** charitable gift or money.

**a·loft'**, *adv., adj.* up high.

**a·lone'**, *adj. adv.* by oneself or itself.

**a·long'**, *prep.* 1. in the lengthwise direction of. —*adv.* 2. steadily forward or into the future.

**a·long'side''**, *prep.* beside.

**a·loof'**, *adv.* 1. at some distance. —*adj.* 2. showing no interest or concern.

**a·loud'**, *adv.* loudly.

**al'pha·bet''**, *n.* all the letters of a language in a customary order. —**al''pha·bet'i·cal**, *adj.* —**al'pha·bet·ize''**, *v.t.*

**al·read'y**, *adv.* before a stated time.

**al'so**, *adv.* additionally.

**al'tar**, *n.* block or table used for religious ceremonies.

**al'ter**, *v.t., v.i.* change. —**al''ter·a'tion**, *n.*

**al·ter·nate'**, *v.i.* (ahl'tər nāt') 1. act, appear, etc. in turns. —*v.t.* 2. employ in turns. —*adj.* (ahl'tər nat) 3. acting, appearing, etc. in turns.

**al·ter'na·tive''**, *n.* 1. other choice. —*adj.* 2. available as another choice.

**al·though'**, *conj.* even though.

**al'ti·tude**, *n.* height, esp. when considerable.

**al'to**, *n.* musical range between soprano and tenor.

**al''to·geth'er**, *adv.* 1. completely. 2. in general.

**al'tru·ism**, *n.* concern for others, not oneself.

**a·lu'mi·num**, *n.* lightweight metal.

**a·lum'nus**, *n., pl.* **-ni.** school graduate. Also, *fem.,* **a·lum'na**, *pl.* **-nae.**

**al'ways**, *adv.* 1. forever. 2. continually.

**a·mal'gam·ate''**, *v.t., v.i.* form into a combination or mixture.

**a·mass'**, *v.t.* gather.

**am'a·teur**, *n.* non-professional participant.

**a·maze'**, *v.t.* stun with surprise. —**a·maz'ing**, *adj.* —**a·maze'ment**, *n.*

**am·bas'sa·dor**, *n.* senior diplomat.

**am'ber**, *n.* fossil resin.

**am·big'u·ous**, *adj.* having more than one possible meaning. —**am''bi·gu'i·ty**, *n.*

**am·bi'tion**, *n.* 1. strong desire for success. 2. thing whose attainment is strongly desired. —**am·bi'tious**, *adj.*

**am'ble**, *v.i.* move easily and slowly.

**am'bu·lance**, *n.* vehicle for the sick.

**am'bush**, *n., v.t.* attack from a concealed position.

**a·mel'io·rate''**, *v.t.* improve.

**a·men'a·ble**, *adj.* agreeable.

**A**
**B**

**a·mend'**, *v.t.* 1. alter. 2. improve. —**a·mend'ment**, *n.*

**a·men'i·ty**, *n., pl.* **-ties.** something agreeable or polite.

**ame'thyst**, *n.* violet quartz or corundum.

**a'mi·a·ble**, *adj.* creating friendly feelings.

**a'mi·ca·ble**, *adj.* without hostility or resentment.

**a·mid'**, *prep.* among. Also, **a·midst'.**

**a·miss'**, *adj.* not right. —*adv.* 2. not in the right way.

**am'i·ty**, *n.* friendship.

**am·mo'ni·a**, *n.* pungent, water-soluble gas.

**am'mu·ni'tion**, *n.* projectiles, together with their charges of gunpowder, etc. fired esp. from guns.

**am·ne'sia**, *n.* loss of memory.

**am·nes'ty**, *n., pl.* **-ties.** general pardon by a government, esp. for political crimes.

**a·mong'**, *prep.* surrounded closely by. Also, **a·mongst'.**

**am'or·ous**, *adj.* loving.

**a'mor·tize"**, *v.t.* pay off gradually.

**a·mount'**, *n.* 1. total. 2. quantity. —*v.i.* 3. add up.

**am'pere'**, *n.* unit for measuring electric current.

**am·phib'i·an**, *n.* 1. animal able to live on land and water. —*adj.* 2. Also, **am·phib'i·ous.** able to live on land and water.

**am'phi·the"a·ter**, *n.* arena or stadium with tiers of seats surrounding the central area. Also, **am'phi·the'a·tre.**

**am'ple**, *adj.*, **ampler, amplest.** 1. copious. 2. sufficient.

**am'pli·fy"**, *v.t.* 1. increase in size. 2. increase in strength, as an electronic signal.

**am'pu·tate"**, *v.t.* remove, as a limb of a body.

**a·muse'**, *v.t.* 1. be funny to. 2. entertain. —**a·muse'ment**, *n.*

**an**, *indef. art.* variant of *a*, used when the following word begins with a vowel.

**a·nach'ron·ism**, *n.* something outside its proper historical period.

**an"a·log**, *n.* represented by physical variables.

**a·nal'o·gy**, *n., pl.* **-gies.** comparison of an unfamiliar thing to a more familiar one. —**a·nal'o·gous,** *adj.*

**a·nal'y·sis**, *n., pl.* **-ses.** separa-

tion into component parts. —**an'a·lyst,** *n.* —**an"a·lyt'ic, an"a·lyt'ic·al,** *adj.* —**an'a·lyze",** *v.t.*

**an·ar'chy**, *n.* 1. society without rulers. 2. political or organizational chaos.

**a·nat'o·my**, *n.* 1. study of the composition of animals and plants. 2. composition of an animal or plant.

**an"ces·tor**, *n.* forebear; one from whom a person descends. Also, *fem.* **an"ces·tress.** —**an"ces·try,** *n.*

**an'chor**, *n.* 1. device for mooring a ship or boat. —*v.i.* 2. secure by anchor.

**an·cho'vy**, *n., pl.* **-vies.** tiny, salty, herringlike fish.

**an'cient**, *adj.* 1. of the oldest period of human history. 2. very old.

**and,** *conj.* along with.

**an'ec·dote",** *n.* true short story.

**a·ne'mi·a**, *n.* shortage of hemoglobin or red cells in the blood. —**a·ne'mic,** *adj.*

**an"es·the'sia**, *n.* lack of sensation induced by a gas or drug. —**an"es·thet'ic,** *adj.*, *n.*

**a·new'**, *adv.* once more.

**an'gel**, *n.* messenger or attendant of God.

**an'ger**, *n.* 1. strong annoyance. —*v.t.* 2. make angry.

**an'gle**, *n.* 1. divergence of two lines or surfaces that meet. —*v.i.* 2. fish. 3. *Informal.* use stratagems for personal gain.

**An'glo-Sax'on**, *n.* person descended from the Angles and Saxons in England.

**an'gry**, *adj.* **-grier, -griest.** seriously annoyed.

**an'guish**, *n.* intense suffering.

**an'gu·lar**, *adj.* having angles.

**an'i·mal**, *n.* 1. living thing other than a plant or bacterium. 2. any such thing other than a human being. —*adj.* 3. pertaining to animals.

**an'i·mate**, *v.t.* 1. give life to. 2. make lively. —**an"i·ma'tion,** *n.*

**an"i·mos'i·ty**, *n., pl.* **-ties.** hostility.

**an'kle**, *n.* joint between the foot and the leg.

**an'nals**, *n., pl.* historical records.

**an·nex'**, *v.t.* (an neks') 1. join to a larger existing part. —*n.* (an'neks) 2. a part so joined. —**an"nex·a'tion,** *n.*

**an·ni'hil·ate"**, *v.t.* destroy utterly.

**an"ni·ver'sar·y**, *n., pl.* **-ries.** same day of the year as that on which something occurred.

**an'no·tate"**, *v.t.* explain or elaborate with notes.

**an·nounce'**, *v.t.* make known, esp. publicly. **—an·noun'cer**, *n.* **—an·nounce'ment**, *n.*

**an·noy'**, *v.t.* trouble, esp. so as to provoke dislike. **—an·noy'ance**, *n.*

**an'nu·al**, *adj.* 1. yearly. **—n.** 2. something published once a year.

**an·nu'i·ty**, *n., pl.* **-ties.** annual income bought from an insurance company.

**an·nul'**, *v.t.* make legally void.

**a·noint'**, *v.t.* put oil, etc. on as part of a ceremony of consecration.

**a·nom'a·ly**, *n., pl.* **-lies.** something inconsistent or abnormal.

**a·non'y·mous**, *adj.* written or spoken by someone whose name is unknown or unpublished.

**an·oth'er**, *adj.* 1. one more. 2. different.

**an'swer**, *n.* 1. reply to a question. **—v.t.** 2. reply to.

**an'swer·a·ble**, *adj.* 1. able to be answered. 2. accountable; responsible.

**ant**, *n.* small social insect.

**an·tag'o·nism**, *n.* hostility. **—an·tag'o·nist**, *n.* **—an·tag'o·nis"tic**, *adj.* **—an·tag'o·nize"**, *v.t.*

**Ant·arc'tic**, *n.* 1. southernmost zone of the earth. **—adj.** 2. pertaining to this zone.

**an"te·ce'dent**, *adj.* 1. coming before. **—n.** 2. something coming before.

**an'te·lope"**, *n.* deerlike animal.

**an·ten'na**, *n., pl.* **-nae** (for one), **-nas** (for 2). 1. feeler on the head of an insect. 2. aerial; conductor for sending or receiving radio waves.

**an·te'ri·or**, *adj.* previous.

**an'te·room"**, *n.* room preceding a major room.

**an'them**, *n.* hymnlike song.

**an·thol'o·gy**, *n.* book of literary selections.

**an'thra·cite"**, *n.* hard coal.

**an"thro·pol'o·gy**, *n.* study of mankind. **—an"thro·pol'o·gist**, *n.*

**an·ti·bod'y**, *n., pl.* **-ies.** blood ingredient that fights foreign substances, e.g. bacteria.

**an'tic**, *n.* ridiculous or peculiar action.

**an·tic'i·pate"**, *v.t.* 1. look forward to, esp. with pleasure. 2. use forethought to deal with. 3. predict. **—an·tic"i·pa'tion**, *n.*

**an"ti·cli'max**, *n.* disappointment of increasing expectations.

**an'ti·dote"**, *n.* substance to counteract a poison.

**an'ti·quat"ed**, *adj.* obsolete.

**an·tique'**, *n.* 1. old manufactured object, esp. a valuable one. **—adj.** 2. ancient.

**an·tiq'ui·ty**, *n., pl.* **-ties.** 1. ancient times. 2. something antique.

**an"ti·sep'tic**, *n.* 1. substance for destroying harmful bacteria. **—adj.** 2. destroying harmful bacteria.

**an"ti·so'cial**, *adj.* hostile to society.

**an"ti·tox'in**, *n.* substance for counteracting plant, animal, or bacterial toxin.

**ant'ler**, *n.* horn of a deer, moose, etc.

**an'vil**, *n.* object on which iron, etc. is rested while being hammered.

**anx·i·e·ty**, *n., pl.* **-ies.** 1. fear of possible harm. 2. eagerness to act. **—anx'ious**, *adj.*

**an'y**, *adj.* 1. someone, as readily as all others. 2. every. **—n.** 3. any person or persons.

**an'y·bod"y**, *pron.* some one person, as readily as all others. Also, **an'y·one".**

**an'y·how"**, *adv.* 1. in any way. 2. whatever the situation is. Also, **an'y·way".**

**an'y·thing"**, *pron.* 1. some one thing, as readily as all others. **—n.** 2. something, whatever or how much it may be.

**an'y·where"**, *adv.* in any or into any place. Also, **an'y·place".**

**a·part'**, *adv.* 1. to pieces. 2. separately.

**a·part'ment**, *n.* series of rooms forming a separate dwelling in a building.

**ape**, *n.* 1. large animal of the monkey family. **—v.t.** 2. imitate.

**ap'er·ture**, *n.* opening.

**a'pex**, *n.* peak.

**aph'o·rism**, *n.* brief statement of a truth.

**a·piece'**, *adv.* for each.

**a·pol'o·get'ic**, *adj.* confessing oneself to be at fault.

**a·pol'o·gize''**, v.i. confess oneself to be at fault and seek forgiveness.

**a·pol'o·gy**, n., pl. **-gies.** 1. confession of a fault in search of forgiveness. 2. statement defending one's actions, etc.

**apo·plex'y**, n. bursting of blood vessel with consequent loss of bodily function.

**a·pos'tle**, n. one of the twelve disciples of Christ sent to preach.

**ap·pall'**, v.t. put in a state of horror or fear.

**ap''pa·ra'tus**, n. instruments, etc. required for an experiment, job, etc.

**ap·par'el**, n. clothes.

**ap·par'ent**, adj. 1. clear; obvious. 2. as judged from appearances.

**ap''pa·ri'tion**, n. ghost or phantom.

**ap·peal'**, n. 1. request for help, mercy, etc. 2. request for reconsideration. 3. attractiveness. —v.t. 4. request to have reconsidered. —v.i. 5. make an appeal. 6. have appeal.

**ap·pear'**, v.i. 1. come into sight. 2. seem. —**ap·pear'ance**, n.

**ap·pease'**, v.t. satisfy when hostile or demanding. —**ap·pease'ment**, n.

**ap·pend'**, v.t. add; join. —**ap·pend'age**, n.

**ap''pen·dec'to·my**, n., pl. **-ies.** surgical removal of an appendix.

**ap·pen''di·ci'tis**, n. inflammation of the appendix.

**ap·pen'dix**, n., pl. **-dixes, -dices.** 1. supplementary portion at the end of a book, etc. 2. blind branch of the intestine.

**ap·pe·tite''**, n. desire, as for food. —**ap''pe·tiz''er**, n. —**ap''pe·tiz''ing,** adj.

**ap·plaud'**, v.t. show approval of, as by applause.

**ap·plause'**, n. indications of approval of a dramatic performance, etc.

**ap''ple**, n. common, crisp fruit, generally red or green.

**ap·pli'ance**, n. machine, etc., esp. for home use.

**ap'pli·ca·ble**, adj. able to be applied.

**ap·ply'**, v.t. 1. place, as on an object or surface. —v.i. 2. make a formal request. —**ap''pli·ca'tion,** n. —**ap'pli·cant,** n.

**ap·point'**, v.t. 1. choose and designate. 2. provide; furnish.

**ap·point'ment**, n. 1. meeting at a stated time. 2. selection, as for public office.

**ap·por'tion**, v.t. divide into shares.

**ap·praise'**, v.t. estimate the value of.

**ap·pre'ci·a·ble**, adj. 1. sufficient to be noted. 2. worthy of note; considerable.

**ap·pre'ci·ate''**, v.t. 1. be grateful for. 2. value truly. —**ap·pre''ci·a'tion,** n.

**ap''pre·hend'**, v.t. 1. fear. 2. understand. 3. capture and arrest. —**ap''pre·hen'sion,** n.

**ap''pre·hen'sive**, adj. fearful.

**ap·pren'tice**, n. assistant learning a trade.

**ap·prise'**, v.t. inform; notify.

**ap·proach'**, v.t. 1. come close to. 2. propose business to. —v.i. 3. come close. —n. 4. act or instance of coming close. 5. manner of taking action.

**ap·proach'a·ble**, adj. willing to be talked with.

**ap''pro·ba'tion**, n. approval.

**ap·pro'pri·ate**, adj. (ap pro'pri ət) 1. suitable. —v.t. (ap pro'pri āt'') 2. reserve for a purpose, as money. 3. take for oneself. —**ap·pro''pri·a'tion,** n.

**ap·prove'**, v.t. 1. state to be good or suitable. 2. think favorably of. —**ap·prov'al,** n.

**ap·prox'i·mate**, adj. (ap prox'i mət) 1. reasonably accurate but not precise. —v.t. (ap prox'i māt'') 2. amount to as an approximate figure, etc. —**ap·prox'i·mate·ly,** adv. —**ap·prox''i·ma'tion,** n.

**a'pri·cot''**, n. orange-colored peachlike fruit.

**a'pron**, n. covering worn over a dress or trouser front when working.

**ap·ro·pos'** (ap''rə pō''), adv. 1. apropos of, with regard to. —adj. 2. to the point; relevant.

**apt**, adj. 1. displaying a tendency. 2. likely. 3. able; intelligent.

**ap'ti·tude''**, n. talent or ability.

**a·quar'i·um**, n. tank, bowl, etc., usually with glass walls, used for displaying live fish, etc.

**a·quat'ic**, adj. of the water.

**aq'ue·duct**, n. engineering structure for conducting water.

**ar'a·ble**, adj. good for producing crops.

**ar·bit·er**, *n.* judge of controversial matters.

**ar·bi·trar''y**, *adj.* admitting no discussion or complaint.

**ar·bi·trate'**, *v.t.* adjudicate after hearing disputants. —**ar''bi·tra'tion**, *n.* —**ar'bi·tra''tor**, *n.*

**ar·bor**, *n.* shaded walk or garden.

**arc**, *n.* segment of a circle.

**ar·cade'**, *n.* **1.** row of arches. **2.** covered walk, esp. one between shops.

**arch**, *n.* curved structure resisting compressive forces.

**ar''chae·ol'o·gy**, *n.* archeology.

**ar·cha'ic**, *adj.* out of date.

**arch'bi'shop**, *n.* superior bishop.

**arch'er**, *n.* user of a bow and arrow. —**arch'er·y**, *n.*

**ar'chi·tect''**, *n.* designer of buildings.

**ar'chi·tec''ture**, *n.* art of designing buildings. —**ar''chi·tec'tur·al**, *adj.*

**ar·chives'**, *n.*, *pl.* official records.

**Arc'tic**, *n.* **1.** northernmost zone of the earth. —*adj.* **2.** pertaining to this zone.

**ar'dent**, *adj.* eager.

**ar'dor**, *n.* eagerness; zeal.

**ar'du·ous**, *adj.* difficult or tedious.

**ar'e·a**, *n.* **1.** surface measure. **2.** region.

**a·re'na**, *n.* large space for athletic contests and spectators.

**ar·gue'**, *v.i.* express a difference or differences of opinion. —**ar'gu·ment**, *n.*

**ar''gu·men'ta·tive**, *adj.* given to argument or quarreling.

**a'ri·a**, *n.* song, as in an opera.

**a'rid**, *adj.* dry.

**a·rise'**, *v.i.* **1.** get up. **2.** happen.

**ar''is·toc'ra·cy**, *n.*, *pl.* -**cies.** small hereditary or select class. —**a·ris'to·crat**, *n.* —**a·ris''to·crat'ic**, *adj.*

**a·rith'me·tic**, *n.* calculation with numerals.

**ark**, *n.* **1.** vessel of Noah. **2.** wooden chest.

**arm**, *n.* **1.** upper human limb. —*v.t.* **2.** equip with weapons.

**arm''a·ment**, *n.* weapons with which a ship, airplane, etc. is equipped.

**arm'chair''**, *n.* chair with arm supports.

**ar'mi·stice**, *n.* suspension of hostilities; truce.

**ar'mor**, *n.* material, usually metal,

protecting against weapons and missiles. —**ar'mored**, *adj.*

**ar'mor·y**, *n.*, *pl.* -**ies** building for military activities and equipment storage.

**arm'pit''**, *n.* area beneath the arm at the shoulder.

**ar'my**, *n.*, *pl.* -**mies.** land military force.

**a·ro'ma**, *n.* scent; odor. —**ar'o·mat'ic**, *adj.*

**a·round'**, *prep.* **1.** on all sides of. —*adv.* **2.** on all sides. **3.** *Informal.* nearby.

**a·rouse'**, *v.t.* **1.** awaken. **2.** call into activity.

**ar·raign'**, *v.t.* bring to court as a defendant.

**ar·range'**, *v.t.* **1.** put in order. —*v.i.*, *v.i.* **2.** plan; prepare. —**ar·range'ment**, *n.*

**ar·ray'**, *v.t.* **1.** arrange. —*n.* **2.** order or arrangement.

**ar·rears'**, *n.*, *pl.* things overdue, esp. payments.

**ar·rest'**, *v.t.* **1.** seize because of the commission of a crime. **2.** stop. —*n.* **3.** act or instance of arresting.

**ar·rive'**, *v.i.* **1.** come to a place. **2.** happen. —**ar·riv'al**, *n.*

**ar'ro·gant**, *adj.* proud and insolent. —**ar'ro·gance**, *n.*

**ar'row**, *n.* missile shot from a bow.

**ar'se·nal**, *n.* place for making or storing weapons.

**ar·se'nic**, *n.* silvery-white poisonous chemical element.

**ar'son**, *n.* crime of burning buildings, etc.

**art**, *n.* **1.** activity of creating things that arouse the emotions through one or more senses. **2.** things so created. **3.** skill or profession. **4.** cunning.

**ar'ter·y**, *n.*, *pl.* -**ies. 1.** major blood vessel. **2.** main line of travel or communication. —**ar·te'ri·al**, *adj.*

**art'ful**, *adj.* cunning.

**ar·thri'tis**, *n.* inflammation of a joint of the body.

**ar'ti·choke''**, *n.* edible flower head of thistlelike plant.

**ar'ti·cle**, *n.* object for use.

**ar·tic'u·late**, *adj.* (ahr tik'yoo lat) **1.** readily understood. —*v.t.* (ahr tik'yoo lāt'') **2.** express clearly. **3.** assemble with joints. —**ar·tic''u·la'tion**, *n.*

**ar'ti·fice**, *n.* **1.** cunning. **2.** cunning action.

**ar″ti·fi′cial,** *adj.* manufactured, esp. in imitation. —**ar″ti·fi′cial·i′ty,** *n.*

**ar·til′ler·y,** *n.* guns or other devices for shooting large missiles.

**ar·ti·san,** *n.* craftsman.

**art′ist,** *n.* practitioner of an art. —**ar·tis′tic,** *adj.* —**ar′tist·ry,** *n.*

**art′less,** *adj.* unaffected; natural.

**as,** *adv.* 1. equally. 2. for example. 3. if and when. —*conj.* 4. equally to. 5. in the manner that. 6. while. 7. because; since. 8. though.

**as·bes′tos,** *n.* fibrous mineral used in fireproofing.

**as·cend′,** *v.t.,v.i.* climb or rise. —**as·cent′,** *n.*

**as·cer′tain,** *v.t.* find out.

**as·cet′ic,** *adj.* 1. without pleasure or self-indulgence. —*n.* 2. one who lives an ascetic life.

**as·cribe′,** *v.t.* relate to a supposed cause. —**as·crip′tion,** *n.*

**ash,** *n.,* *pl.* **ashes.** 1. remainder of something not fully burnt. 2. tree of the olive family. —**ash′tray″,** *n.*

**a·shamed′,** *adj.* feeling shame.

**a·shore′,** *adj.,adv.* on or onto the shore.

**a·side′,** *adv.* 1. at or to the side. 2. apart.

**ask,** *v.t.* 1. seek to know. 2. seek, as a favor.

**a·sleep′,** *adj.,adv.* in or into a state of sleep.

**as·par′a·gus,** *n.* plant with edible shoots.

**a″spar′tame,** *n.* a synthetic sweetener.

**as′pect,** *n.* 1. way of interpreting or understanding something. 2. appearance or manner.

**as·per′sion,** *n.* hostile or accusing remark.

**as′phalt,** *n.* black tarlike material.

**as·phyx′i·ate″,** *v.t.* harm through deprivation of oxygen.

**as·pire′,** *v.i.* have ambitious intentions. —**as″pi·ra′tion,** *n.* —**as′pir·ant,** *n.*

**as·pi′rin,** *n.* white crystalline drug used to relieve minor pain and fever.

**ass,** *n.* donkey.

**as·sail′,** *v.t.* attack. —**as·sail′ant,** *n.*

**as·sas′sin,** *n.* murderer, esp. of a statesman. —**as·sas′sin·ate″,** *v.t.* —**as·sas″sin·a′tion,** *n.*

**as·sault′,** *n.,v.t.* attack.

**as·say′,** *n.* 1. chemical evaluation, as of an ore. —*v.t.* 2. perform an assay upon.

**as·sem′ble,** *v.t.,v.i.* gather. —**as·sem′blage,** **as·sem′bly,** *n.*

**as·sent′,** *v.i.* 1. agree; consent. —*n.* 2. agreement; consent.

**as·sert′,** *v.t.* 1. declare. 2. claim. —**as·ser′tion,** *n.* —**as·ser′tive,** *adj.*

**as·sess′,** *v.t.* evaluate. —**as·ses′sor,** *n.*

**as′set,** *n.* something contributing to a profit or advantage.

**as·sid′u·ous,** *adj.* devoted to a task.

**as·sign′,** *v.t.* 1. give out as a task or responsibility. 2. appoint. 3. transfer possession or enjoyment of. —**as·sign′ment,** *n.* —**as·sign′a·ble,** *adj.*

**as·sim′i·late″,** *v.t.* 1. absorb. 2. make like some larger entity. —**as·sim″i·la′tion,** *n.*

**as·sist′,** *v.t.* help in a task or occupation. —**as·sist′ant,** *n.* —**as·sist′ance,** *n.*

**as·so·ci·ate′,** *v.t.,v.i.* (as so′shē·āt) 1. join in a social or business relationship. —*v.t.* 2. connect in one's mind. —*n.* (as so′shē·at) 3. someone or something so joined. —**as·so″ci·a′tion,** *n.*

**as·sort′,** *v.t.* classify. —**as·sort′ment,** *n.*

**as·sort′ed,** *adj.* of various kinds.

**as·suage′** (as swāj′), *v.t.* relieve, as suffering.

**as·sume′,** *v.t.* 1. suppose without knowing. 2. take upon oneself.

**as·sump′tion,** *n.* 1. act or instance of assuming. 2. **the Assumption,** ascent of the Virgin Mary to heaven, celebrated August 15.

**as·sure′,** *v.t.* 1. state emphatically. 2. convince. 3. make certain or safe. 4. reassure. —**as·sur′ance,** *n.* —**as·sured′,** *adj.*

**as′ter·isk,** *n.* a sign, *, used for footnote references, etc. in print.

**asth′ma,** *n.* respiratory disorder.

**a·stig′ma·tism,** *n.* eye defect which causes imperfect focusing.

**as·ton′ish,** *v.t.* surprise greatly. —**as·ton′ish·ment,** *n.*

**as·tound′,** *v.t.* surprise very greatly.

**a·stray′,** *adv.,adj.* away from guidance or control.

**a·strin″gent,** *adj.* 1. constrictive,

styptic. —n. 2. substance which causes contraction of body tissues.

as·trol′o·gy, n. study of stars and planets as influences on events.

as′tro·naut″, n. person exploring or traveling through outer space.

as·tron′o·my, n. study of planets, stars, etc. and space.

as·tute′, adj. shrewd.

a·sy′lum, n. home for persons needing protection, e.g. the insane.

at, prep. in, on, or near (used to specify time, place, or rate.)

a′the·ism, n. belief that no god exists.

ath′lete″, n. a person who engages in athletics.

ath·let′ics, n., pl. sports involving vigorous bodily exercise. —ath·let′ic, adj.

at′las, n. book of maps.

at′mos·phere″, n. air closest to the earth. —at″mos·pher′ic, adj.

at′oll, n. ring of coral islands or reefs.

a′tom, n. smallest unit constituting a distinct chemical element. —a·tom′ic, adj.

at·om·iz″er, n. device creating a fine spray.

a·tone′, v.i. make right or show regret for a wrong one has done. —a·tone′ment, n.

a·tro′cious, adj. 1. vicious; outrageous. 2. wretchedly bad. —a·troc′i·ty, n.

a″tro·phy, n. 1. a wasting away. —v.i., v.t. 2. to waste away.

at·tach′, v.t. 1. fasten to something. 2. bind by ties of affection. —at·tach′ment, n.

at″ta·ché′, n. special member of an embassy staff.

at·tack′, v.t. 1. act against with physical violence, harsh words, etc. —n. 2. act or manner of attacking.

at·tain′, n. arrive at. —at·tain′a·ble, adj. —at·tain′ment, n.

at·tempt′, v.t., n. try.

at·tend′, v.t. 1. be present at. 2. accompany. 3. care for. —at·ten′dance, n.

at·tend′ant, n. 1. minor assistant. —adj. 2. accompanying.

at·ten′tion, n. 1. heed. 2. care, esp. medical care.

at·ten′tive, adj. paying heed or care.

at·ten′u·ate″, v.t. 1. thin. 2. weaken or dilute.

at·test′, v.t. bear witness; certify.

at′tic, n. unfinished floor space beneath the roof of a house.

at·tire′, v.t. 1. dress, esp. showily. —n. 2. clothes, esp. showy ones.

at′ti·tude″, n. 1. opinion or feeling. 2. posture.

at·tor′ney, n., pl. -eys. lawyer.

at·tract′, v.t. pull towards oneself. —at·trac′tion, n. —at·trac′tive, adj.

at·trib·ute′, v.t. (ət trib′yŏŏt) 1. name something as the cause for. —n. (at′trib yŏŏt) 2. distinguishing quality or feature. —at″tri·bu′tion, n.

auc′tion, n. 1. public sale to the highest bidder for each item. —v.t. 2. sell at an auction. —auc″tion·eer′, n.

au·da′cious, adj. daring. —au·dac′i·ty, n.

au′di·ble, adj. able to be heard. —au′di·bly, adv. —au″di·bil′i·ty, n.

au′di·ence, n. 1. group attending a play, concert, lecture, etc. 2. persons reached by a book, etc. 3. formal interview.

au′di·o″, adj. pertaining to electronic reproduction of sound.

au′dit, v.t. 1. examine financial accounts. —n. 2. examination of financial accounts. —au′di·tor, n.

au·di′tion, n. trial of ability for an actor, musician, etc.

au″di·to′ri·um, n. room for an audience.

aug·ment′, v.t. add to.

aunt, n. sister of a father or mother, or wife of an uncle.

au′ra, n. quality emanating from a particular place or person.

aus·pi′cious, adj. favorable; promising.

aus·tere′, adj. severe in manner. —aus·ter′i·ty, n.

au·then′tic, adj. true or genuine. —au″then·tic′i·ty, n.

au·then′ti·cate″, v.t. prove the authenticity of.

au′thor, n. creator, esp. of a written work. Also, fem., au′thor·ess.

au·thor″i·tar′i·an, adj. characterized by excessive show or use of authority.

au·thor′i·ta″tive, adj. having authority.

au·thor′i·ty, n., pl. -ties. 1. official power. 2. expert.

**au'thor·ize**, v.t. give official consent to. —**au'thor·i·za'tion**, n.

**au'to·bi·og'ra·phy**, n., pl. -ies. story of one's own life.

**au·toc'ra·cy**, n., pl. -cies. government by one absolute ruler. —**au'to·crat**, n.

**au'to·graph'**, n. one's name in one's handwriting.

**au'to·mat'ic**, adj. controlled by machinery, etc. rather than humans.

**au'to·ma'tion**, n. replacement of human beings as controlling elements by automatic devices.

**au'to·mo·bile'**, n. self-propelled passenger vehicle.

**au'to·mo'tive**, adj. pertaining to self-propelled road vehicles.

**au·ton'o·my**, n. self-government. —**au·ton'o·mous**, adj.

**au·top'sy**, n., pl. -sies. examination of a corpse to determine the cause of death.

**au'tumn**, n. season between summer and winter.

**aux·il'ia·ry**, adj. serving to assist.

**a·vail'**, v.i. 1. be of help or use. —n. 2. advantage or benefit.

**a·vail'a·ble**, adj. able to be used or acquired.

**av'a·lanche''**, n. sudden descent down a slope of a mass of snow, rock, etc.

**av'a·rice**, n. greed. —**av''a·ri'cious**, adj.

**a·venge'**, v.t. take revenge for.

**av'e·nue''**, n. 1. major street. 2. approach road.

**av'er·age**, n. 1. number representing the sum of a group of added figures divided by the number of figures. —adj. 2. typical.

**a·verse'**, adj. opposed; reluctant.

**a·ver'sion**, n. strong dislike.

**a''vi·a'tion**, n. practice of flying aircraft.

**a'vi·a'tor**, n. person who flies aircraft. Also, fem., **a''vi·a'trix**.

**a'vid**, adj. eager. —**a·vid'i·ty**, n.

**av''o·ca'tion**, n. spare-time pursuit; hobby.

**a·void'**, v.t. keep oneself away or safe from. —**a·void'a·ble**, adj. —**a·void'ance**, n.

**av''oir·du·pois'**, n. system of weights using a pound of 16 ounces.

**a·vow'**, v.t. confess. —**a·vow'al**, n.

**a·wait'**, v.t. wait for.

**a·wake'**, v.t., v.i. 1. Also, **a·wak'en**, wake. —adj. 2. not asleep.

**a·ward'**, v.t. 1. bestow, as a prize, favor, etc. —n. 2. something awarded.

**a·ware'**, adj. conscious or perceptive.

**a·way'**, adv. 1. to or in another place or direction. 2. from a place.

**awe**, n. overwhelming respect, reverence, etc.

**aw'ful**, adj. bad.

**a·while'**, adv. for a while.

**awk'ward**, adj. 1. clumsy. 2. embarrassing.

**awn'ing**, n. device for shading windows, porches, etc. usually made of canvas.

**a·wry'**, adv., adj. not right.

**ax**, n., pl. axes. broad-bladed chopping tool. Also, **axe**.

**ax'i·om**, n. statement accepted as a basic truth.

**ax'is**, n., pl. axes. line on which something is centered or rotates.

**ax'le**, n. shaft on which a wheel turns.

**ay''a·tol'lah**, n. Shi'ite Muslim religious leader.

**az'ure**, n. sky blue.

# B

**B, b**, n. second letter of the English alphabet.

**bab'ble**, v.t., v.i. 1. speak unclearly or meaninglessly. —n. 2. unclear or meaningless spoken words or sounds.

**ba·boon'**, n. large monkey.

**ba'by**, n., pl. -bies. 1. very young child. 2. infantile person. —v.t. 3. treat with excessive care or indulgence. —**ba'by·ish**, adj. —**ba'by·hood**, n.

**bach'e·lor**, n. 1. unmarried man. 2. person holding the lowest academic degree.

**back**, n. 1. part of a person opposite the face. 2. side of an object opposite that usually faced; rear. —adj. 3. at the rear. 4. related to

the past. **5.** toward the rear.
—**back′ing,** n.

**back′bone,** n. spine.

**back′ground,** n. area at the rear of a scene.

**back′ward,** adv. Also, **back′-wards. 1.** toward the rear. —adj. **2.** toward the rear or the past. —**back′ward·ly,** adv. —**back′-ward·ness,** n.

**ba′con,** n. cured meat from the back and sides of a hog.

**bac·te′ri·a,** n., pl. of **bacterium.** microscopic vegetable organism.

**bad,** adj., **worse, worst.** unfavorable, evil, or unacceptable.

**baf′fle,** v.t. confuse.

**bag,** n. flexible container open at one end.

**bag′gage,** n. containers for things taken on a journey.

**bag′gy,** adj. irregularly bulging.

**bail,** n. **1.** security for temporary release of a prisoner. **2.** suspension handle.

**bait,** n. something used as an attraction in trapping or fishing.

**bake,** v.t., v.i. cook or harden with dry heat.

**bak′er·y,** n., pl. **-eries.** place for baking food made with flour, etc.

**bal′ance,** n. **1.** state of rest due to equal leverage around a point or line. **2.** remainder from a subtraction. —v.t. **3.** put in balance. —v.i. **4.** come into or be in balance.

**bal′co·ny,** n., pl. **-nies.** floor area projecting from a building.

**bald,** adj. without hair.

**bale,** n. large compressed or tied bundle.

**bale′ful,** adj. hostile; evil.

**balk** (bawk), v.i. **1.** refuse to act. **2.** be daunted.

**ball,** n. **1.** evenly rounded object; sphere. **2.** an entertainment of dancing.

**bal′lad,** n. **1.** narrative song or poem. **2.** sentimental song.

**bal·let** (bal lā′), n. entertainment by dancers, esp. one acting out a story.

**bal·loon′,** n. baglike lighter-than-air vehicle with no engine or steering mechanism.

**bal′lot,** n. **1.** paper for indicating a vote. **2.** collective vote for a candidate, proposal, etc.

**ball′room,** n. room for social dancing.

**balm** (bahm), n. healing or soothing substance.

**balm′y,** adj., **balmier, balmiest.** soothing or refreshing.

**bal′us·ter,** n. columnlike support for a railing.

**bal′us·trade″,** n. railing supported by balusters.

**bam·boo″,** n. tall tropical grass with hollow woodlike stems.

**ban,** v.t. **1.** forbid. —n. **2.** act or instance of forbidding.

**ba′nal,** adj. boringly ordinary.

**ba·nan′a,** n. **1.** treelike tropical plant **2.** fruit from this plant.

**band,** n. **1.** strip of binding material. **2.** stripe. **3.** group of wind and percussion musicians. **4.** informal group, esp. of armed persons. —v.t. **5.** mark with bands. —v.i. **6.** gather or unite. —**band′mas″-ter,** n. —**bands′man,** n. —**band′-stand″,** n.

**band′age,** n. **1.** strip of cloth, etc., esp. for covering a wound. —v.t. **2.** tie with a bandage.

**ban·dan′na,** n. printed cloth for the head or neck. Also, **ban·dan′-a.**

**ban′dit,** n. armed robber.

**bane′ful,** adj. destructive.

**bang,** n. **1.** loud noise, as from an explosion or collision. —v.i. **2.** make a loud noise. —**bang′ish ment,** n.

**ban′ish,** v.t. drive away; exile.

**ban′ister,** n. stair railing.

**bank,** n. **1.** shore of a river or lake. **2.** slope organization for the saving and lending of money.

**bank′er,** n. proprietor or officer of a bank.

**bank′rupt″,** adj. unable to pay debts.

**ban′ner,** n. flag.

**ban′quet,** n. formal dinner or luncheon.

**ban′tam,** adj. miniature; tiny.

**ban′ter,** n. **1.** teasing. —v.i. **2.** exchange teasing remarks.

**bap′tism,** n. rite of initiation, as into a church. —**bap·tis′mal,** adj.

**bap·tize′,** v.t. initiate into a church, esp. by sprinkling with or immersion in water.

**bar,** n. **1.** long round object, used in an enclosure, as a lever, etc. **2.** drinking place. —v.t. **3.** exclude.

**barb,** n. sharp projection.

**bar·bar′i·an** (bahr be′ ən), n. uncivilized person; savage.

**bar·bar·ous** (bahr´bə rəs), *adj.* 1. cruel. 2. uncivilized.

**bar´be·cue**, *n.* 1. to cook outdoors over an open fire. 2. fireplace or grill used for cooking outdoors. 3. meal cooked over an open fire. 4. meat cooked and basted with sauce.

**barbed**, *adj.* 1. having sharp projections. 2. harsh, as a remark; caustic.

**bare**, *adj.*, **barer, barest**, *adj.* 1. uncovered or unconcealed. —*v.t.* 2. strip of covering or concealment.

**bare´ly**, *adv.* by the smallest possible amount.

**bar´gain**, *n.* 1. business agreement. 2. advantageous purchase. —*v.i.* 3. reach or attempt to reach a business agreement.

**barge**, *n.* 1. slow freight-carrying boat. 2. ceremonial boat carrying royalty, etc. —*v.i.* 3. **barge in**, *Informal.* intrude.

**bar´i·tone´´**, *n.* musical range between tenor and bass.

**bark**, *n.* 1. short utterance of a dog. 2. covering of the stem of a tree or shrub. 3. sailing vessel square-rigged on all but the last of three or more masts. —*v.i.* 4. utter a bark.

**bar´ley**, *n.* grass with edible grain.

**barn**, *n.* building for crop storage, keeping of cows, etc.

**bar´na·cle**, *n.* shellfish that clings to ship bottoms, etc.

**ba·rom´e·ter**, *n.* device for measuring atmospheric pressure and thus foretelling weather changes. —**bar´o·met´ric, bar´´o·met´ri·cal**, *adj.*

**bar´rack**, *n.* Usually, **barracks**, dormitory for soldiers.

**bar·rage** (bar rahz´), *n.* defensive barrier of artillery fire, captive balloons, etc.

**bar´rel**, *n.* container, usually wood, with circular ends and bulging sides.

**bar´ren**, *adj.* 1. unable to support plant life. 2. unable to bear children.

**bar´ri·cade´´**, *n.* 1. obstruction, as to military advance. —*v.t.* 2. defend or shut off with a barricade.

**bar´ri·er**, *n.* obstruction.

**bar´ter**, *n.*, *v.t.*, *v.i.* trade with goods or services alone.

**base**, *n.* 1. part on which a thing

rests or stands. 2. basis. —*v.t.* 3. give a basis or foundation to. —*adj.* 4. contemptible.

**base´ball´´**, *n.* 1. game played in a diamond-shaped field with a batted ball. 2. ball used in this game.

**base´ment**, *n.* lowermost part of a building.

**bash´ful**, *adj.* shy.

**bas´ic**, *adj.* most important or significant; essential.

**ba´sin**, *n.* 1. shallow bowl for liquids. 2. bowl.

**ba´sis**, *n.*, *pl.* **-ses** something on which a thing depends.

**bas´ket**, *n.* container of woven wood, wire, etc.

**bas´ket·ball´´**, *n.* game in which a ball is tossed over a hoop into a suspended net.

**bass**, *n.* lowermost musical range.

**bas´tard**, *n.* 1. person born out of wedlock. —*adj.* 2. not authentic.

**baste**, *v.t.* 1. sew temporarily. 2. cover with juices, etc. while cooking.

**bat**, *n.* 1. club used for striking a ball, as in baseball or cricket. 2. nocturnal flying mammal.

**batch**, *n.* quantity of material prepared or gathered at one time.

**bath**, *n.*, *pl.* **baths**. complete washing or immersion. —**bath´room´**, *n.* —**bath´tub´**, *n.*

**bathe**, *v.i.* 1. take a bath. —*v.t.* 2. give a bath to.

**bath´robe´**, *n.* robe used before and after bathing.

**ba´ton´**, *n.* staff used for directing musicians, as a badge of office, etc.

**bat·tal´ion**, *n.* subdivision of a military division.

**bat´ter**, *v.t.* 1. hit or attack repeatedly. —*n.* 2. person who bats. 3. cake mixture.

**bat´ter·y**, *n.*, *pl.* **-ies.** *n.* 1. device for storing electricity. 2. group of cannon used together.

**bat´tle**, *n.* 1. major military encounter. —*v.t.*, *v.i.* 2. fight. —**bat´tle·field´´**, *n.*

**bat´tle·ship´´**, *n.* warship with heavy guns and armor.

**bay**, *n.* 1. distinct area of a wall. 2. broad inlet, esp. of a sea. 3. **at bay**, a. unable to escape. b. unable to attack. —*v.i.* 4. give prolonged bark.

**bay´o·net´´**, *n.* sharp thrusting weapon attached to a gun muzzle.

**ba·zaar´**, *n.* 1. Near Eastern

salesplace. 2. temporary sale, esp. for charity.

**beach**, *n.* flat shore, esp. a sandy one.

**bea'con**, *n.* elevated signal light.

**bead**, *n.* 1. small decorative ball. 2. small drop.

**beak**, *n.* pointed mouth, esp. of a bird.

**beam**, *n.* 1. horizontal structural member. 2. shaft of light —*v.i.* 3. shine.

**bean**, *n.* any of various edible seeds.

**bear**, *v.t.* 1. carry. 2. endure. 3. suffer. 4. give birth to. —*n.* 5. large shaggy mammal.

**beard**, *n.* hair on the lower jaw, etc.

**bear'ing**, *n.* 1. posture or attitude. 2. support for a rotating part.

**beast**, *n.* 1. large animal. 2. cruel or uncouth person.

**beat**, *v.t.* 1. hit with force. 2. win against. 3. move vigorously back and forth, as arms or wings. —*v.i.* 4. throb, as the heart. —*n.* 5. marked rhythm.

**beat'ing**, *n.* 1. act or instance of hitting, esp. a person or animal. 2. defeat.

**beau**, *n., pl.* **beaus, beaux.** suitor.

**beau'ti·ful**, *adj.* having beauty.

**beau'ti·fy'**, *v.t.* make beautiful.

**beau'ty**, *n., pl.* **-ties.** quality sensed in that which is for perfect harmony.

**bea'ver**, *n.* broad-tailed, dam-building rodent.

**be·cause'**, *conj.* 1. for the reason that. 2. **because of**, as a result of.

**beck'on**, *v.i.* 1. make a summoning gesture. —*v.t.* 2. summon with a gesture.

**be·come'**, *v.i.* come to be as specified.

**be·com'ing**, *adj.* suitable; seemly.

**bed**, *n.* 1. object to lie upon. 2. layer of surface soil, as for flowers. —*v.t.* 3. put into a bed. —**bed'room'**, *n.* —**bed'spread'**, *n.*

**bed'clothes'**, *n., pl.* sheets, covers, etc. for a bed.

**bed'stead'**, *n.* framework for bedding.

**bee**, *n.* four-winged, pollen-gathering insect. —**bee'hive'**, *n.* —**bees' wax'**, *n.*

**beech**, *n.* hardwood tree.

**beef**, *n.* meat from cows, steers, etc.

**bee'line''**, *n.* straight route.

**beer**, *n.* drink of fermented malt, hops, etc.

**beet**, *n.* plant with an edible root.

**bee'tle**, *n.* insect with hard wings.

**be·fall'**, *v.i.* happen.

**be·fit'**, *v.t.* be suitable to.

**be·fore'**, *prep.* 1. at an earlier time than. 2. in front of. —*adv.* 3. at an earlier time. —*conj.* 4. earlier than the time that something happens.

**be·fore'hand'**, *adv.* in advance.

**be·friend'**, *v.t.* act as a friend to.

**beg**, *v.t., v.i.* ask as a favor.

**beg'gar**, *n.* person who asks strangers for his livelihood.

**be·gin'**, *v.t., v.i.* start; commence.

**be·gin'ner**, *n.* 1. person who begins. 2. completely inexperienced person.

**be·grudge'**, *v.t.* resent another's having or receiving.

**be·guile'**, *v.t.* 1. charm. 2. while away pleasantly.

**be·half'**, *n.* **in** or **on behalf of, a.** in the name of. **b.** in support of.

**be·have'**, *v.t.* 1. conduct oneself properly —*v.i.* 2. conduct in a specified way. —**be·hav'ior**, *n.*

**be·hest'**, *n.* command; urging.

**be·hind'**, *prep.* 1. at the rear of. —*adv.* 2. at the rear.

**be·hold'**, *v.t.* see; look at.

**be'ing**, *n.* 1. existence. 2. essential nature. 3. something alive.

**be·lat'ed**, *adj.* later than expected or desirable.

**belch**, *v.i.* 1. emit stomach gas through the mouth. —*n.* 2. act or instance of belching.

**bel'fry** (bel'frē), *n., pl.* **-fries.** tower or turret for bells.

**be·lie'**, *v.t.* 1. represent deceptively. 2. prove as false.

**be·lieve'**, *v.t.* 1. accept as true or truthful. —*v.i.* 2. have faith. —**be·lief'**, *n.* —**be·liev'er**, *n.* —**be·liev'able**, *adj.*

**be·lit'tle**, *v.t.* treat as of minor importance.

**bell**, *n.* hollow instrument, usually metal, that sounds when struck.

**bel'li·cose'**, *adj.* warlike.

**bel·lig'er·ent**, *adj.* 1. eager to fight. 2. at war. —*n.* 3. nation, etc. at war. —**bel·lig'er·ence**, *n.*

**bel'low**, *v.t., v.i.* 1. shout or roar. —*n.* 2. **bellows**, device for pumping air to a hearth.

**bel'ly**, *n.* stomach.

**be·long'**, *v.i.* 1. be property. 2. be a member, citizen, etc. of something. 3. be appropriate.

**be·long'ings**, *n., pl.* possessions.

**be·lov'ed**, *adj.* 1. loved. —*n.* 2. loved one.

**be·low'**, *prep.* 1. lower than; under. 2. inferior in worth or amount to. —*adv., adj.* 3. to or in some lower place.

**belt**, *n.* 1. strap worn around the waist, over the chest, etc. 2. long, narrow region, road, etc.

**be·moan'**, *v.t.* lament.

**bench**, *n.* 1. broad seat or stool. 2. massive worktable.

**bend**, *v.t.* 1. form as a curved or angled shape, esp. by force. —*v.i.* 2. bow or stoop. —*n.* 3. curve, as in a road or river.

**be·neath'**, *prep.* 1. under. —*adj., adv.* 2. underneath.

**ben'e·dic'tion**, *n.* blessing.

**ben'e·fac'tor**, *n.* conferer of benefactions. Also, *fem.,* **ben'·e·fac'tress.**

**be·nef'i·cent**, *adj.* doing good.

**ben'e·fi'cial**, *adj.* useful; advantageous.

**ben'e·fi'ci·ar·y**, *n., pl.* **-aries.** enjoyer of a benefit.

**ben'e·fit**, *n.* 1. advantage. —*v.t.* 2. be of advantage to.

**be·nev'o·lent**, *adj.* kindly; well-intentioned. —**be·nev'o·lence,** *n.*

**be·nign'**, *adj.* 1. friendly; well-intentioned. 2. *Medicine.* not malignant.

**be·queath'**, *v.t.* transfer to heirs. —**be·quest',** *n.*

**be·rate'**, *v.t.* scold.

**be·reave'**, *v.t.* 1. leave sorrowful, esp. by dying. 2. deprive; strip. —**be·reave'ment,** *n.*

**ber'ry**, *n., pl.* **-ries.** juicy cover for a seed or seeds.

**berth**, *n.* shelflike bed.

**be·seech'**, *v.t.* request earnestly.

**be·set'**, *v.t.* harass.

**be·side'**, *prep.* 1. at the side of. 2. compared with.

**be·sides'**, *adv.* 1. in addition; else. —*prep.* 2. in addition to; other than.

**be·siege'**, *v.t.* lay siege to.

**best**, *adj.* 1. superlative of *good.* 2. major; greater. —*adv.* 3. superlative of *well.* 4. that which is best. 5. one's utmost.

**bes'ti·al**, *adj.* savage.

**be·stow'**, *v.t.* give or grant. —**be·stow'al,** *n.*

**bet**, *n.* 1. guess on the unpredictable outcome of an event, made to gain money, etc. —*v.t.* 2. put up to back one's bet.

**be·tray'**, *v.t.* 1. be treacherous to. 2. reveal, as a secret. —**be·tray'al,** *n.*

**be·troth'al**, *n.* engagement to marry.

**bet'ter**, *adj.* 1. comparative of *good.* 2. major; greater. —*adv.* 3. comparative of *well.* —*n.* 4. social superior.

**bet'ter·ment**, *n.* improvement.

**be·tween'**, *prep.* 1. with two specified persons or things, one on each side. 2. involving or relating two persons or things. 3. as a result of two specified causes.

**bev'el**, *n.* 1. outer edge formed as a diagonal. —*v.t.* 2. form as such a diagonal.

**bev'er·age**, *n.* something to drink other than water.

**be·ware'**, *v.i.* 1. be cautious. —*v.t.* 2. be cautious of.

**be·wil'der**, *v.t.* confuse, esp. with surprise. —**be·wil'der·ment,** *n.*

**be·witch'**, *v.t.* cast a spell on.

**be·yond'**, *prep.* 1. on the far side of. 2. too late or advanced for. —*adv.* 3. further away.

**bi·an'nu·al**, *adj.* twice a year. —**bi·an'nu·al·ly,** *adv.*

**bib**, *n.* apronlike cloth to catch dribbles.

**bib'li·og'ra·phy**, *n., pl.* **-phies.** list of books, articles, etc. used, recommended, or in existence.

**bib'u·lous**, *adj.* fond of alcoholic beverages.

**bick'er**, *v.i.* quarrel about trifles.

**bi'cy·cle**, *n.* two-wheeled vehicle for a balancing rider. —**bi'cy·clist, bi'cy·cler,** *n.*

**bid**, *n.* 1. offer to fulfill a contract for a stated sum. —*v.t.* 2. command or ask.

**big**, *adj.,* **bigger, biggest.** 1. great in size or amount. 2. important.

**big'a·my**, *n.* marriage to two spouses in a single period. —**big'a·mist,** *n.*

**big'ot**, *n.* person with strong, intolerant, unreasoning attitudes. —**big'ot·ry,** *n.* —**big'ot·ed,** *adj.*

**bi·lat'er·al**, *adj.* 1. involving two sides or factions. 2. reciprocal; mutual.

**bil'ious**, *adj.* ill-tempered.

**bill**, *n.* 1. itemized list or statement. 2. piece of paper currency. 3.

beak of a bird. —*v.t.* **4.** request payment from in writing.

**bill′board″,** *n.* large board for advertising posters.

**bil′let,** *n.* **1.** job; position. **2.** order to house a soldier. —*v.t.* **3.** house with such an order.

**bill′fold″,** *n.* wallet.

**bil′liards,** *n.* game using hard balls propelled by a cue.

**bil′lion,** *n.* *U.S.* thousand million.

**bill of fare,** menu.

**bil′low,** *n.* **1.** swelling mass, as of water or smoke. —*v.i.* **2.** appear in billows.

**bi·month′ly,** *adj.* every two months.

**bin,** *n.* large container for loose storage or display.

**bi′na·ry,** *adj.* of or pertaining to the mathematical base 2.

**bind,** *v.t.* **1.** tie or fasten together. **2.** obligate. —**bind′er,** *n.* —**bind′ing,** *n.*

**bin·oc′u·lar,** *n.* **1.** binoculars, twin telescopelike glasses, one for each eye. —*adj.* **2.** pertaining to both eyes.

**bi′′o·chem′is·try,** *n.* study of life processes as an aspect of chemistry.

**bi·og′ra·phy** *n., pl.* -**phies.** story of a person's life or career. —**bi′′o·graph′i·cal,** *adj.* —**bi·og′ra·pher,** *n.*

**bi·ol′o·gy,** *n.* study of animals and plants. —**bi′′o·log′i·cal,** *adj.* —**bi·ol′o·gist,** *n.* —**bi′′o·phys′i·cist,** *n.*

**bi·o′′nics,** *n.* the study of living systems for application to mechanical or electronic systems.

**birch,** *n.* hardwood tree with smooth bark.

**bird,** *n.* warm-blooded, feathered, flying animal.

**birth,** *n.* **1.** emergence from a womb, egg, etc. **2.** heredity. **3.** origin or beginning. —**birth′mark″,** *n.* —**birth′place″,** *n.* —**birth′rate″,** *n.* —**birth′right″,** *n.*

**birth′day″,** *n.* anniversary of one's birth.

**bis′cuit,** *n., pl.* -**cuits, -cuit. 1.** small, hard-baked cookie or cracker. **2.** breadlike lump eaten esp. with gravy.

**bi′sect″,** *v.t.* divide in two parts, esp. equal ones.

**bish′op,** *n.* clergyman overseeing a number of local churches or parishes. —**bish′op·ric,** *n.*

**bi′son,** *n.* shaggy, large North American mammal.

**bit,** *n.* **1.** small piece or amount. **2.** boring tool. **3.** metal mouthpiece for controlling a horse. **4.** (computers) one binary digit or piece of data.

**bitch,** *n.* female dog.

**bite,** *v.t.* **1.** close one's jaws firmly upon. —*n.* **2.** wound from being bitten.

**bit′ing,** *adj.* wounding to the feelings.

**bit′ter,** *adj.* **1.** harsh-tasting. **2.** causing much suffering. **3.** extremely resentful. —**bit′ter·ness,** *n.*

**bi′valve″,** *n.* mollusk with two hinged shells.

**bi·week′ly,** *adj., adv.* every two weeks.

**bi·zarre′,** *adj.* odd; grotesque.

**black,** *n.* **1.** perfectly dark color, opposite to white in shading. **2.** person of central African descent; negro. —*adj.* **3.** of the color black.

**black′ber″ry,** *n., pl.* -**ries.** dark berry of various types of bramble.

**black′bird″,** *n.* bird whose male has black plumage.

**black′board″,** *n.* board of slate or other material for writing on with chalk.

**black′en,** *v.t.* **1.** make black. **2.** defame.

**black′mail′,** *n.* **1.** extortion by threats, esp. to reveal harmful information. —*v.t.* **2.** practice blackmail on.

**black market,** unlawful system for selling legally restricted goods.

**black′out″,** *n.* **1.** putting-out of lights, as in a play or during an air raid. **2.** sudden loss of consciousness.

**black′smith″,** *n.* person who forges iron by hand.

**blad′der,** *n.* **1.** sac for collecting and discharging body fluids. **2.** any of various bags for air or liquid.

**blade,** *n.* **1.** metal part with a cutting edge or point. **2.** leaf, esp. of grass.

**blame,** *v.t.* **1.** accuse for a fault. —*n.* **2.** responsibility.

**blanch,** *v.t., v.i.* turn pale or white.

**blank,** *adj.* **1.** free of marks, as paper. —*n.* **2.** blank piece of paper.

**blank′et,** *n.* warm bedcover.

**blas·pheme′,** *v.t.* speak sacrilegiously of. —**blas·phem'er**, n. —**blas'phem·y**, n. —**blas'phem·ous**, adj.

**blast**, v.t. 1. shatter, as with lightning or explosives. —n. 2. explosion or explosive force. 3. violent rush of air.

**bla'tant**, adj. shamelessly obvious.

**blaze**, —v.i. 1. burn brightly. —n. 2. bright fire.

**bleach**, v.t., v.i. 1. make or become light in color. —n. 2. something used for bleaching.

**bleak**, adj. barren and gloomy.

**bleed**, v.i. 1. lose blood. —v.t. 2. cause to lose blood.

**blem'ish**, n. 1. skin flaw. 2. flaw or defacement. —v.t. 3. make or form a blemish upon.

**blend**, v.t. 1. mix. —n. 2. mixture.

**bless**, v.t. 1. invoke divine favor for. 2. confer happiness upon. —**bles'sed**, adj.

**bles'sing**, n. 1. invocation of divine favor. 2. favorable event or circumstance.

**blight**, n. 1. plant disease. 2. deterioration.

**blind**, adj. 1. without eyesight. —v.t. 2. make blind. —**blind'ness**, n.

**blind'fold''**, n. 1. device to prevent a person temporarily from seeing. —v.t. 2. put a blindfold on.

**blink**, v.i. wink repeatedly.

**bliss**, n. intense, tranquil happiness. —**bliss'ful**, adj.

**blis'ter**, n. 1. raised area of skin enclosing watery matter. —v.t., v.i. 2. form blisters on.

**blithe**, adj. cheerful.

**bliz'zard**, n. heavy storm of snow and wind.

**bloat**, v.t. swell abnormally.

**bloc**, n. group of organizations or persons united in a common interest.

**block**, n. 1. thick, short piece of material. 2. urban area bounded by streets. —v.t. 3. obstruct.

**block·ade'**, n. 1. barrier to navigation, created by warships, etc. —v.t. 2. impose such a barrier on.

**blond**, adj. 1. having light hair and skin. —n. 2. blond person. Also, fem., **blonde**.

**blood**, n. 1. fluid in the arteries of animals. 2. lineage.

**blood'hound''**, n. large hound tracking by scent.

**blood'shed''**, n. killing.

**blood'shot''**, adj. reddened from broken veins, as the eyes.

**blood'thirst''y**, adj. eager to kill.

**blood'y**, adj., -ier, -iest. 1. covered with blood. 2. involving much bloodshed.

**bloom**, v.i. 1. put forth flowers. —n. 2. flower.

**blos'som**, n. 1. flower, esp. of a fruit. —v.i. 2. put forth blossoms.

**blot**, n. 1. stain, as from ink. —v.t. 2. stain.

**blouse**, n. loose shirt.

**blow**, v.i. 1. move, as wind. 2. exhale with force. —v.t. 3. drive with wind or breath. 4. cause to sound with the breath, as a horn. —n. 5. stroke, as with a fist or club.

**blow'out''**, n. break of an automobile tire.

**blow'torch''**, n. lamp for burning or melting.

**blub'ber**, n. 1. whale fat. —v.i. 2. weep noisily.

**blue**, n. 1. primary color, that of a clear sky. —adj. 2. of the color blue.

**blue'ber''ry**, n., pl. -ries. shrub with blue-black berries.

**blue'print''**, n. 1. photographic reproduction of a measured drawing, appearing as white on blue. 2. any plan or project.

**bluff**, v.i. 1. deceive with an air of frankness or assurance. —adj. 2. frank or abrupt in manner. 3. rising steeply. —n. 4. steep cliff or ridge.

**blun'der**, n. 1. avoidable error. —v.i. 2. make such an error.

**blunt**, adj. 1. with a dull edge. 2. plain-spoken.

**blur**, v.t. 1. cause to lose sharpness or clarity. —v.i. 2. become indistinct. —n. 3. something that blurs; smear.

**blush**, v.i. 1. become red in the face with embarrassment or anger. —n. 2. redness in the face.

**blus'ter**, v.i. 1. roar, as the wind. 2. pretend rage, bravery, etc.

**boar**, n. 1. ungelded male pig. 2. wild hog.

**board**, n. 1. long, flat piece of wood. 2. meals as part of one's accommodations. 3. administrative group. —v.t. 4. go on or onto, as a ship. —**board'er**, n.

**boast**, v.i. 1. talk to excess about one's merits or accomplishments.

—*n.* **2.** boasting remark. —**boast'-ful**, *adj.*

**boat**, *n.* small vessel or craft.

**bob**, *v.t.* **1.** cut in a short hairdo. —*v.i.* **2.** sink, then rise again quickly. —*n.* **3.** short hairdo.

**bod'i·ly**, *adj.* pertaining to the body.

**bod'y**, *n., pl.* -**ies**. *n.* **1.** physical part of a man or animal. **2.** group or organization.

**bod'y·guard''**, *n.* person or group protecting against attack.

**bog**, *n.* **1.** marshy or spongy area. —*v.t.*, *v.i.* **2.** sink into a bog. **3.** slow or halt, as in accomplishing something.

**bo'gus**, *adj.* false.

**boil**, *v.t.* **1.** heat in water that bubbles from being heated. **2.** heat to bubbling. —*v.i.* —*n.* **3.** inflamed, pus-filled swelling.

**boil'er**, *n.* container for making steam or heating water.

**bois'ter·ous**, *adj.* **1.** rowdy. **2.** stormy.

**bold**, *adj.* daring. —**bold'ness**, *n.*

**bol'ster**, *n.* **1.** long pillow. —*v.t.* **2.** prop up.

**bolt**, *n.* **1.** fastener with a thread; screw. **2.** sliding device for securing a door, etc. **3.** stroke of lightning. **4.** sudden dash. —*v.t.* **5.** fasten or secure with a bolt. —*v.i.* **6.** flee or start suddenly.

**bomb**, *n.* **1.** explosive or incendiary device. —*v.t.* **2.** destroy or attack with bombs.

**bom·bard'**, *v.t.* attack with bombs or shells. —**bom·bard'ment**, *n.*

**bom'bast**, *n.* grandiose, empty language. —**bom·bas'tic**, *adj.*

**bomb'er**, *n.* military plane for dropping bombs.

**bomb'shell''**, *n.* **1.** bomb. **2.** someone or something sensational.

**bona fide** (bō'nə fīd'', bō'nə fē'-dä), in good faith.

**bon'bon''**, *n.* piece of candy.

**bond**, *n.* **1.** something that binds. **2.** business obligation. **3.** certificate of money lent at interest to an organization.

**bond'age**, *n.* servitude.

**bone**, *n.* **1.** part of a skeleton. —*v.t.* **2.** remove the bones from.

**bon'fire''**, *n.* large outdoor fire.

**bon'net**, *n.* woman's cloth hat with a chin strap.

**bo'nus**, *n., pl.* -**nuses**. payment in addition to that customary.

**bon'y**, *adj.* -**ier**, -**iest**. with bones much in evidence.

**book**, *n.* **1.** long piece of writing, etc., published or kept as a distinct entity. **2. books**, business accounts. —*v.t.* **3.** record. —**book'-case''**, *n.* —**book'keep''er**, *n.* —**book'let**, *n.* —**book'shelf''**, *n.* —**book'shop''**, **book'store''**, *n.*

**boom**, *n.* **1.** loud, deep, hollow sound. **2.** flurry of business or industrial activity. —*v.i.* **3.** make a booming noise.

**boon**, *n.* favor or blessing.

**boor**, *n.* uncouth person. —**boor'ish**, *adj.*

**boost**, *v.t.* **1.** lift from below. **2.** add to the power of. —*n.* **3.** act or instance of boosting.

**boot**, *n.* **1.** shoe with tall sides. —*n.*, *v.t.* **2.** kick. —*v.t.* **3.** (computers) to load operating system software.

**booth**, *n.* small shelter or enclosure.

**bor'der**, *n.* **1.** edge. —*v.i.* **2. border on**, adjoin. —**bor'der·line''**, *n.*

**bore**, *v.t.*, *v.i.* **1.** penetrate with a rotating movement. —*v.t.* **2.** dig by boring. **3.** weary by being uninteresting. **4.** uninteresting person or thing. —**bore'dom**, *n.*

**bor'ough**, *n.* incorporated town.

**bor'row**, *v.t.* take and later return.

**bos'om**, *n.* **1.** human breast, esp. as the seat of emotion. **2.** midst.

**boss**, *n.* employer or manager.

**bos'sy**, *adj. Informal.* domineering.

**bot'a·ny**, *n.* study of plants.

**both**, *adj.*, *pron.* **1.** one and the other. —*conj.*, *adv.* **2.** equally.

**both'er**, *v.t.* **1.** annoy or worry. —*n.* **2.** source of annoyance or worry. —**both'er·some**, *adj.*

**bot'tle**, *n.* container, usually glass and with a stoppable narrow outlet, for liquids and gases.

**bot'tom**, *n.* lowermost part.

**bou·doir''**, *n.* woman's private sitting room.

**bough**, *n.* limb of a tree.

**bouil·lon** (bool'yən), *n.* clear broth.

**boul'der**, *n.* large, rounded stone.

**bounce**, *v.i.* jump in a new direction after striking a hard surface.

**bound**, *v.i.* **1.** jump. **2.** bounce. —*v.t.* **3.** adjoin or determine the boundaries of. —*n.* **4.** act or instance of jumping or bouncing. **5. bounds**, limits. —*adj.* **6.** tied or joined. **7.** obligated. **8.** certain. **9.** headed for a specified goal.

**bound'a·ry,** *n., pl.* **-ries.** border of an area of land.

**bou·quet',** *n.* **1.** bunch or arrangement of flowers. **2.** aroma of wine.

**bour·geois** (boŏr"zhwah), *n., pl.* **-geois,** *n.* **1.** member of the bourgeoisie. —*adj.* **2.** pertaining to the bourgeoisie.

**bour·geoi·sie** (boŏr"zhwah zē'), *n., sing.* or *pl.* social class of merchants, businessmen, professionals, clerks, etc.; middle class.

**bout,** *n.* fight or contest.

**bow,** *n.* **1.** springy length of wood for shooting arrows. **2.** length of wood for playing various stringed instruments. **3.** Also, **bow knot,** knot with two loops. **4.** front part of a ship, etc. **5.** forward bend of the upper body as a mark of respect or acceptance. —*v.i.* **6.** bend the upper body forward. **7.** agree or submit.

**bow'el,** *n.* intestine.

**bowl,** *n.* **1.** deep, wide-topped container. —*v.t.* **2.** roll with an underhanded motion.

**box,** *n.* **1.** container, usually rectangular and with a lid. **2.** compartment suggesting this in form. —*v.t.* **3.** put into a box. **3.** have a fistfight with.

**boy,** *n.* young male. —**boy'hood',** *n.* —**boy'ish,** *adj.*

**boy'cott,** *n.* **1.** refusal to deal or associate with a person or persons in order to coerce them. —*v.t.* **2.** practice a boycott on.

**brace,** *v.t.* **1.** stiffen. —*n.* **2.** stiffening device.

**brace'let,** *n.* decorative armband.

**brack'et,** *n.* **1.** brace for a corner. —*v.t.* **2.** support with brackets.

**brag,** *v.i.* **1.** boast. —*n.* **2.** boasting talk.

**braid,** *n.* **1.** interweaving of three strands of fiber. —*v.t.* **2.** make into a braid.

**brain,** *n.* organ of thought, control of actions, etc. —**brain'y,** *adj.*

**brake,** *n.* **1.** device for slowing or stopping machinery. —*v.t., v.i.* **2.** slow down or stop with a brake.

**brake'man,** *n.* assistant to a railroad conductor.

**bran,** *n.* grain husks separated from flour in milling.

**branch,** *n.* woodlike extension from the body of a tree, etc.

**brand,** *n.* **1.** identifying mark or symbol of a company's merchandise. **2.** identifying mark burned into hide or skin. —*v.t.* **3.** put a brand on.

**bran'dish,** *v.t.* wave, as a sword or club.

**bran'dy,** *n.* distilled grape or other wine.

**brash,** *adj.* **1.** hot-headed. **2.** noisy and uncouth.

**brass,** *n.* alloy of copper and zinc.

**brat,** *n.* ill-behaved child.

**bra·va'do,** *n.* false courage or confidence.

**brave,** *adj.* **1.** courageous. —*v.t.* **2.** encounter defiantly. —**brav'er·y, brave'ness,** *n.*

**brawl,** *n.* noisy fight.

**brawn,** *n.* muscular strength.

**bra'zen,** *adj.* **1.** made of brass. **2.** shameless.

**breach,** *n.* opening broken through.

**bread,** *n.* food of baked flour, water, etc.

**breadth,** *n.* width.

**break,** *v.t.* **1.** force to divide into pieces. **2.** put out of repair. —*n.* **3.** act or instance of breaking. —**break'age,** *n.* —**break'a·ble,** *adj.*

**break''danc·ing,** *n.* style of dancing characterized by acrobatic spins and robotic movement.

**break'down',** *n.* failure of health or operation.

**break'fast,** *n.* morning meal.

**break'neck'',** *adj.* reckless, as speed.

**break'wa''ter,** *n.* wall for breaking the force of waves.

**breast,** *n.* **1.** upper forward part of the body. **2.** woman's milk-secreting gland.

**breath,** *n.* air going into and out of the lungs.

**breathe,** *v.i.* move air into and out of the lungs.

**breath'tak''ing,** *adj.* astonishing or exciting.

**breed,** *v.t.* **1.** give birth to. **2.** raise, as animals. —*n.* **3.** strain, as of animals. —**breed'er,** *n.*

**breed'ing,** *n.* manners or character.

**breeze,** *n.* light wind.

**brev'i·ty,** *n.* briefness.

**brew,** *v.t.* **1.** make by any of various means, as beverages or other liquids. —*n.* **2.** something brewed. —**brew'er,** *n.*

**brew'er·y,** *n., pl.* **-ies.** place for brewing malt beverages.

**bribe,** *v.t.* 1. pay to abuse a position of trust. —*n.* 2. payment offered for this. —**brib'er·y,** *n.*

**brick,** *n.* oblong object of baked or unbaked clay, etc., used in construction.

**bride,** *n.* woman at the time of her wedding. —**brid'al,** *adj.* —**brides' maid''**, *n.*

**bride'groom'',** *n.* man at the time of his wedding.

**bridge,** *n.* 1. structure for crossing a stream, valley, etc. —*v.t.* 2. cross with or as with a bridge.

**bri'dle,** *n.* harness for a horse's head.

**brief,** *adj.* short or concise.

**brief'case'',** *n.* handle-held case for business papers.

**bri·gade'',** *n.* military unit formed of battalions.

**brig'a·dier general,** military officer between a colonel and a major general. Also, **brig''a·dier'.**

**bright,** *adj.* 1. shedding or reflecting much light. 2. intelligent or mentally active. —**bright'en,** *v.t., v.i.*

**bril'liant,** *adj.* very bright. —**bril' liance, bril'lian·cy,** *n.*

**brim,** *n.* rim.

**brine,** *n.* salty water.

**bring,** *v.t.* carry or escort to a place.

**brink,** *n.* edge or verge.

**brisk,** *adj.* 1. lively and abrupt. 2. forceful, as the wind.

**bris'tle,** *n.* 1. stiff hair, as on a pig. —*v.i.* 2. stand up stiffly.

**brit'tle,** *adj.* easily shattered.

**broad,** *adj.* wide. —**broad'en,** *v.t., v.i.*

**broad'cast'',** *v.t.* 1. send by radio or television. —*n.* 2. radio or television program.

**broad'-mind''ed,** *adj.* not strict or opinionated.

**bro·chure',** *n.* pamphlet.

**broil,** *v.t.* cook with direct heat from a fire, etc.

**broke,** *adj. Informal.* without money; bankrupt.

**brok'en,** *adj.* past participle of *break,* used adjectivally.

**brok'er,** *n.* agent for buying and selling. —**brok'er·age,** *n.*

**bron'co,** *n., pl.* **-cos.** wild or half-wild horse of the West. Also, **bron'cho.**

**bron'to·saur''us,** *n.* large herbivorous dinosaur.

**bronze,** *n.* alloy of copper and tin.

**brooch,** *n.* large ornamental pin.

**brood,** *n.* 1. group of children or baby chickens. —*v.i.* 2. worry or sulk at length.

**broom,** *n.* bundle of straws, etc. attached to a stick and used for sweeping. —**broom'stick'',** *n.*

**broth,** *n.* soup from boiled meat.

**broth'el,** *n.* house of prostitution.

**broth'er,** *n.* 1. son of one's father. 2. fellow-human as an object of love, etc. —**broth'er·hood,** *n.* —**broth'er·ly,** *adj.*

**broth'er-in-law'',** *n., pl.* **broth'ers-in-law''.** 1. brother of a spouse. 2. husband of a sister or sister-in-law.

**brow,** *n.* 1. eyebrow. 2. forehead.

**brown,** *n.* color combining red, yellow, and black.

**browse,** *v.i.* look idly through things for sale.

**bruise,** *v.t.* 1. injure the skin or surface of with a blow or pressure. —*n.* 2. mark made by bruising.

**bru·net',** *n.* person with dark hair, esp. when with dark eyes. Also, *fem.,* **bru·nette'.**

**brush,** *n.* 1. device for cleaning, painting, etc. consisting of bristles on a handle. —*v.t.* 2. apply a brush to.

**brusque,** *adj.* abrupt in manner.

**bru'tal,** *adj.* extremely cruel or harsh. —**bru·tal'i·ty,** *n.*

**bru'tal·ize,** *v.t.* 1. make brutal. 2. treat brutally.

**brute,** —*n.* 1. beast. 2. brutal person.

**bub'ble,** *n.* 1. void or body of gas surrounded by a liquid. —*v.i.* 2. give off bubbles.

**buck,** *n.* 1. grown male deer, goat, etc. —*v.t.* 2. oppose with force.

**buck'et,** *n.* open watertight container.

**buck'le,** *n.* 1. fastener for two ends of a belt, etc. —*v.t.* 2. fasten with a buckle. 3. cause to bulge or bend, as sheet metal.

**buck'wheat'',** *n.* wheat with triangular seeds.

**bud,** *n.* 1. swelling from which a flower, leaf, etc. grows. —*v.i.* 2. put forth such swellings.

**budge,** *v.t., v.i.* move by or because of force.

**budg'et,** *n.* allotment of money, time, etc. for various purposes.

**buf'fa·lo'',** *n., pl.* **-loes.** 1. any of

various wild oxen. **2.** American bison.

**buf´fer,** *n.* something that prevents or lessens the shocks of collision.

**buf´fet** (baf fā´), *n.* sideboard.

**bug,** *n.,* *v.t.* **bugged, bug´ging.** *n.* **1.** insect. **2.** (computers) an error in programming. *v.t.* **3.** *Informal.* **a.** plant listening devices in. **b.** pester.

**bu´gle,** *n.* trumpetlike brass instrument.

**build,** *v.t.* assemble, as a structure.

**build´ing,** *n.* habitable construction.

**bulb,** *n.* **1.** any of various underground plant stems, roots, or buds. **2.** something swelling toward the end.

**bulge,** *n.* **1.** swelling. —*v.i.* **2.** swell.

**bulk,** *n.* **1.** size or weight. **2.** greater or principal part. —**bulk´y,** *adj.*

**bull,** *n.* male ox, elephant, etc.

**bull´dog´´,** *n.* small, heavy-built fighting dog.

**bul´let,** *n.* pointed projectile from a firearm.

**bul´le·tin,** *n.* announcement, esp. of news.

**bul´ly,** *n.,* *pl.* **-lies,** *n.* **1.** person who injures or threatens weaker persons. —*v.t.* **2.** act as a bully toward.

**bul´wark,** *n.* defensive wall or barrier.

**bum,** *n.* **1.** poor person who refuses to work. —*v.i.* **2.** live as a bum.

**bum´ble·bee´´,** *n.* yellow- and black bee.

**bump,** *v.t.* **1.** collide with, esp. not violently. —*v.i.* **2.** bump into, collide with. —*n.* **3.** act or instance of bumping or of being bumped.

**bump´er,** *n.* device to receive the shock of collisions.

**bun,** *n.* small baked roll.

**bunch,** *n.* small cluster.

**bun´dle,** *n.* group of things bound or wrapped together.

**bun´gle,** *v.t.* do or act stupidly.

**bunk,** *n.* flat frame serving as a bed, esp. in barracks, camps, or ships.

**bun´ting,** *n.* cloth for making flags or flaglike decorations.

**buoy,** *n.* **1.** floating signal or marker. **2.** life preserver.

**buoy´ant,** *adj.* cheerful or optimistic.

**bur´den,** *n.* **1.** heavy load. —*v.t.* **2.**

put a load upon. —**bur´den·some,** *adj.*

**bu´reau,** *n.,* *pl.* **-reaus, -reaux. 1.** official agency or department. **2.** chest of drawers.

**bu·reau·cra·cy,** (byo͞o rah´kra sē), *n.,* *pl.* **-cies.** government by officials.

**bur´glar,** *n.* person who breaks into buildings, esp. to steal. —**bur´gla·ry,** *n.*

**bur´i·al,** *n.* burying of the dead.

**bur·lesque´,** *n.* **1.** sexually allusive vaudeville. **2.** satirical parody.

**bur´ly,** *adj.,* **-lier, -liest.** big and strong.

**burn,** *v.t.* **1.** use as fuel. **2.** damage with heat. —*v.i.* **3.** be on fire. **4.** give out light or heat. —*n.* **5.** burned place.

**burn´er,** *n.* device for applying intense heat.

**burn´´out,** *n.* lethargy resulting from excess stress.

**bur´row,** *n.* **1.** hole of a digging animal. —*v.i.* **2.** dig deep holes.

**burst,** *v.i.* **1.** be torn apart, as from pressure. —*v.t.* **2.** cause to be torn apart. —*n.* **3.** act or instance of bursting.

**bury,** *v.t.* put under earth or other material.

**bus,** *n.,* *pl.* **-es, -ses,** *v.t.* **-ed** or **-sed, -ing** or **-sing.** *n.* **1.** vehicle for many passengers. **2.** (computers) a circuit for connecting two components. —*v.t.* **3.** transport by bus.

**bush,** *n.* low, spreading woody plant.

**bush´el,** *n.* dry measure of 4 pecks or 32 quarts.

**bus´i·ly,** *adv.* in a busy manner.

**busi´ness,** *n.* **1.** type of work or commerce. **2.** commerce. —**busi´ness·man,** *n* —**busi´ness·wom´´-an,** *n.*

**busi´ness·like´´,** *adj.* efficient.

**bust,** *n.* **1.** head, neck, and upper part of the chest. —*v.t.,* *v.i.* **2.** *Informal.* break or burst.

**bus´tle,** *n.* activity, as of a crowd.

**bus´y,** *adj.,* **-ier, -iest.** with much to do. **2.** in action or use.

**but,** *prep.* **1.** except for. —*conj.* **2.** and yet. **3.** on the other hand.

**butch´er,** *n.* slaughterer or seller of meat.

**butt,** *n.* **1.** thick end. **2.** remnant of a smoked cigarette or cigar. **3.** target. **4.** act or instance of butting. —*v.t.* **5.** ram with the head.

**but'ter,** *n.* solid product made from churned cream.

**but'ter·fly',** *n., pl.* **-flies.** slender-bodied four-winged insect.

**but'ter·milk',** *n.* liquid remaining after butter is made of cream.

**but'tocks,** *n., pl.* part on which one sits.

**but'ton,** *n.* 1. broad object passed through holes or loops in cloth as a fastener. 2. object pushed to operate a control mechanism.

**but'tress,** *n.* 1. heavy mass resisting a thrust, as that of an arch. —*v.t.* 2. give stability or support to.

**buy,** *v.t.* get in return for money.

**buzz,** *v.i.* 1. make a deep, rough hum. —*n.* 2. hum of this sort.

**buz'zard,** *n.* 1. type of slow hawk. 2. type of vulture.

**by,** *prep.* 1. close to. 2. in measures or units of. 3. not later than. —*adv.* 4. aside. 5. past. —**by'stand''er,** *n.*

**by'line,** *n.* printed line identifying author of news story, article, etc.

**byte,** *n.* (computers) a group of eight bits of data.

# C

**C, c,** *n.* third letter of the English alphabet.

**cab,** *n.* 1. chauffeured vehicle for hire. 2. shelter for the operator of a locomotive, etc.

**cab·a·ret** (kab'' rā''), *n.* restaurant with musical entertainment.

**cab'bage,** *n.* vegetable with a head of thick leaves.

**cab'in,** *n.* 1. primitive house. 2. passenger room as on a ship or aircraft.

**cab'i·net,** *n.* 1. boxlike piece of furniture. 2. body of officials reporting to a head of state.

**ca'ble,** *n.* 1. heavy rope. 2. cablegram. —*v.t.* 3. send a cablegram to.

**ca'ble·gram'',** *n.* transoceanic telegraph message.

**cack'le,** *v.i.* make henlike noises.

**cac'tus,** *n., pl.* **-tuses, -ti.** prickly desert plant.

**ca·dav'er,** *n.* corpse. —**ca·dav'er·ous,** *adj.*

**ca'dence,** *n.* 1. rise and fall of a speaking voice. 2. marching rhythm.

**ca·det',** *n.* military student.

**ca·fe** (ka fā'), *n.* small restaurant. Also **ca·fé'.**

**caf''e·te'ri·a,** *n.* self-service restaurant.

**caf·feine',** *n.* stimulant in coffee or tea.

**cage,** *n.* openwork structure for confinement.

**ca·jole',** *v.t.* coax or wheedle.

**cake,** *n.* sweetened piece of baked dough.

**ca·lam'i·ty,** *n., pl.* **-ties.** disaster.

**cal'cu·late'',** *v.t.* ascertain through rational means. —**cal''cu·la'tion,** *n.*

**cal'cu·lus,** *n.* method used in higher mathematics.

**cal'dron,** *n.* large kettle.

**cal'en·dar,** *n.* printed object or device for determining the day of the month, etc.

**calf,** *n., pl.* **calves.** young cow or bull.

**cal'i·ber,** *n.* diameter of a bullet, gun bore, etc.

**cal'i·co'',** *n., pl.* **-coes, -cos.** printed cotton.

**cal'i·per,** *n.* device for measuring outside or inside diameters. Also, **cal'i·pers.**

**call,** *v.t.* 1. utter loudly. 2. summon. 3. telephone. —*n.* 4. act or instance of calling.

**cal·lig''ra·phy,** *n.* handwriting, penmanship, often ornamental.

**call''ing,** *n.* vocation.

**cal'lous,** *adj.* insensitive to the sufferings of others.

**cal'low,** *adj.* immature or inexperienced.

**cal'lus,** *n., pl.* **-luses.** hard thickening on the skin.

**calm,** *adj.* 1. undisturbed. —*n.* 2. state of quiet. —*v.t.* 3. make quiet or tranquil.

**cal'o·rie,** *n.* unit of heat measurement.

**cam'bric,** *n.* fine linen or cotton.

**cam'cor·der,** *n.* combined portable video camera and recorder.

**cam'el,** *n.* desert animal storing water in one or two humps.

**cam'e·o,** *n., pl.* **-os.** gem of contrasting layers of stone.

**C**
**D**

**cam'er·a,** n. boxlike device for taking photographs, shooting movie film, etc.

**cam·ou·flage (kam'ə flahzh''),** n. paintwork, etc. making something hard to see or interpret.

**camp,** n. 1. temporary residence in the open. —v.i. 2. establish or live in a camp.

**cam·paign',** n. 1. series of operations to attain a planned goal. —v.i. 2. act in a campaign.

**cam'phor,** n. aromatic crystalline substance.

**cam'pus,** n., pl. -puses. open area of lawn and trees, esp. the grounds of a school.

**can,** v.i. 1. be able or know how to. 2. preserve in sealed cans or jars. —n. 3. cylindrical container, esp. of sheet metal.

**ca·nal',** n. artificial waterway.

**ca·nar'y,** n., pl. -ies. yellow songbird.

**can'cel,** v.t. cover with marks, esp. in order to invalidate. —**can'cel·la'tion,** n.

**can'cer,** n. spreading malignant tumor. —**can'cer·ous,** adj.

**can''de·la'brum,** n., pl. -bra. branched candlestick.

**can'did,** adj. frank. —**can'dor,** n.

**can'di·date'',** n. competitor for public office, an honor, etc. —**can'di·da·cy,** n.

**can'dle,** n. cylinder of wax, etc. with a central wick for burning.

**can'dle·stick'',** n. holder for candles.

**can'dy,** n., pl. -dies. flavored sweet.

**cane,** n. 1. hollow, jointed plant stalk. 2. stick held while walking.

**ca'nine,** adj. pertaining to dogs.

**can'is·ter,** n. small storage can used in a kitchen.

**can'ker,** n. ulcerous sore.

**can'ni·bal,** n. person or animal that eats its own kind.

**can'non,** n., pl. -nons, -non. heavy gun.

**can·not',** v.i. can not.

**can'ny,** adj. -nier, -niest. shrewd.

**ca·noe (kə nōō'),** n. narrow paddled boat.

**can'on,** n. 1. basic principle or law. 2. official list of writings.

**can'on·ize'',** v.t. declare to be a saint.

**can'o·py,** n., pl. -pies. light, rooflike covering supported by poles.

**cant,** n. hypocritical jargon.

**can·teen',** n. portable container for water.

**can'vas,** n. tightly woven heavy cloth of hemp, cotton, etc.

**can'vass,** v.t., v.i. solicit for votes, opinions, sales orders, etc.

**can'yon,** n. narrow, deep valley.

**cap,** n. soft, close-fitting hat.

**ca'pa·ble,** adj. competent. —**ca''pa·bil'i·ty,** n.

**ca·pa'cious,** adj. spacious.

**ca·pac'i·ty,** n., pl. -ties. 1. ability to contain a quantity of material, number of persons, etc. 2. loosely, capability.

**cape,** n. 1. cloak. 2. projection of land seaward.

**ca'per,** v.i. 1. leap about playfully. —n. 2. playful leap.

**cap'i·tal,** n. 1. location of a national or state government. 2. money for investing or lending.

**cap'i·tal·ism,** n. economic system based on investment or lending at interest of privately owned money. —**cap'i·tal·ist,** n. —**cap''i·tal·is'tic,** adj.

**cap'i·tol,** n. legislative building.

**ca·pit'u·late,** v.i. cease to fight or resist.

**ca·price',** n. whim or whimsy. —**ca·pri'cious,** adj.

**cap·size',** v.t., v.i. overturn, as a boat.

**cap'sule,** n. sealed container.

**cap'tain,** n. 1. military or naval officer. 2. master of a ship. 3. leader.

**cap'tion,** n. title, explanation, etc. for a printed picture.

**cap'tious,** adj. argumentative or fault-finding.

**cap'ti·vate'',** v.t. fascinate, as with charm.

**cap'tive,** n. captured person or animal. —**cap·tiv'i·ty,** n.

**cap'tor,** n. person who takes a captive.

**cap'ture,** v.t. 1. prevent from fleeing, fighting, etc. by force. 2. express through art or speech. —n. 3. act or instance of capturing.

**car,** n. automobile.

**car·a·mel,** n. burnt sugar, used as a flavor or color.

**car'at,** n. 1. unit of 200 milligrams for weighing gems. 2. karat.

**car'a·van'',** n. group of travelers, beasts of burden, etc. in a desert.

**car'bine,** n. 1. short-barreled rifle. 2. light automatic military rifle.

**car′bon,** *n.* nonmetallic element found in organic compounds.

**car′bun·cle,** *n.* **1.** subcutaneous inflammation. **2.** type of gem.

**car′bu·ret′or,** *n.* device for making explosive mixtures of air and gasoline.

**car′cass,** *n.* dead animal body.

**card,** *n.* **1.** stiff paper bearing writing, etc. **2. cards,** game played with cards.

**card′board″,** *n.* thick, papery sheeting.

**car′di·ac″,** *adj.* pertaining to the heart.

**car′di·nal,** *n.* **1.** Roman Catholic ecclesiastic second to the pope. **2.** red American songbird. —*adv.* **3.** primary.

**care,** *n.* **1.** responsibility. **2.** charge or protection. **3.** worry. —*v.i.* **4.** feel affection.

**care′ful,** *adj.* **1.** cautious. **2.** with attention to accuracy.

**care′less,** *adj.* not properly careful.

**ca·ress′,** *v.t.* **1.** touch lightly and affectionately. —*n.* **2.** gesture or touch indicating affection.

**car′go,** *n., pl.* **-goes, -gos.** freight

**car′i·ca·ture′,** *n.* **1.** exaggerated rendering of a person's peculiarities. —*v.t.* **2.** render in caricature.

**car′nage,** *n.* slaughter.

**car′nal,** *adj.* pertaining to the body or its appetites.

**car′ni·val,** *n.* fair with entertainments.

**car′ni·vore″,** *n.* flesh-eating animal or plant. —*car·niv′o·rous, adj.*

**car′ol,** *n.* **1.** song of praise, esp. at Christmas. —*v.i., v.t.* **2.** sing exuberantly.

**ca·rouse′,** *v.i.* drink together boisterously.

**car′pen·ter,** *n.* builder in wood.

**car′pet,** *n.* cloth floor covering.

**car′port,** *n.* open-ended shelter for an automobile.

**car′riage,** *n.* **1.** large animal-drawn passenger vehicle. **2.** any of various moving and carrying devices. **3.** posture.

**car′ri·er,** *n.* **1.** thing or person that carries. **2.** aircraft carrier.

**car′rot,** *n.* vegetable with an edible orange root.

**car′rou·sel,** *n.* merry-go-round.

**car′ry,** *v.t.* **1.** support or suspend. **2.** take the weight of and move. —*v.i.* **3.** be transmitted.

**cart,** *n.* small wagon.

**car·tel′,** *n.* monopolistic association of businesses.

**car′ti·lage,** *n.* tough, elastic skeletal tissue.

**car′ton,** *n.* cardboard box.

**car·toon′,** *n.* amusing or satirical drawing.

**car′tridge,** *n.* unit of ammunition for a handgun, rifle, etc.

**carve,** *v.t.* **1.** form by cutting parts from. **2.** cut into parts, as meat.

**case,** *n.* **1.** box. **2.** instance.

**cash,** *n.* **1.** money as opposed to checks, etc. —*v.t.* **2.** exchange for money, as a check or coupon.

**cash·ier′,** *n.* person in charge of cash in a bank, etc.

**cas′ing,** *n.* outer cover.

**ca·si′no,** *n., pl.* **-nos. 1.** place for dances, entertainments, etc. **2.** place for gambling.

**cask,** *n.* barrel for liquids.

**cas′ket,** *n.* ornate coffin.

**cas′se·role″,** *n.* **1.** dish for baking. **2.** food baked in such a dish.

**cas·sette′,** *n.* a compact, ready-to-use case containing audio or video tape.

**cast,** *v.t.* **1.** throw. **2.** form in a mold. —*n.* **3.** act or instance of casting. **4.** group performing a play, etc.

**caste,** *n.*, rigid social division, esp. in India.

**cas′ti·gate″,** *v.t.* rebuke severely.

**cas′tle,** *n.* heavily fortified residence.

**cas′u·al,** *adj.* **1.** occurring by chance. **2.** relaxed.

**cas·u·al′ty,** *n., pl.* **-ties.** victim of an accident or military action.

**cat,** *n.* small, furry, four-footed animal.

**cat′a·clysm,** *n.* sudden, drastic change.

**cat′a·comb″,** *n.* underground passage with burial places.

**cat′a·log″,** *n.* list of things acquired, to be sold, etc. Also, **cat′a·logue″.**

**cat′a·pult″,** *n.* machine for hurling missiles, launching airplanes, etc.

**cat′a·ract″,** *n.* **1.** large waterfall. **2.** opacity in the eye causing blindness.

**ca·tarrh′,** *n.* inflammation of mucous membranes in the nose or throat.

**ca·tas′tro·phe,** *n.* major disaster.

**catch,** *v.t.* **1.** capture or seize. —*v.i.*

2. become caught or entangled. —*n.* 3. act or instance of catching.

**cat·e·chism** (kat'ə kism), *n.* set of questions and answers, esp. on religious doctrine.

**cat''e·gor'i·cal**, *adj.* pertaining to categories.

**cat'e·go''ry**, *n., pl.* -ries. classification

**ca'ter**, *v.i.* supply food, drink, tableware, etc. to parties for a fee.

**cat'er·pil''lar**, *n.* crawling larva of a butterfly, moth, etc.

**ca·thar'tic**, *n.* 1. medicine for clearing the bowels. —*adj.* 2. pertaining to cathartics.

**ca·the'dral**, *n.* church in which a bishop normally officiates.

**cath'o·lic**, *adj.* 1. universal. 2. **Catholic**, pertaining to the Roman Catholic Church. —**Ca·thol'i·cism**, *n.*

**cat'tle**, *n., pl.* cows, bulls, etc.

**cau''li·flow''er**, *n.* edible white head of a vegetable of the cabbage family.

**cause**, *n.* 1. something to which a later event or condition is attributed. 2. goal or purpose, esp. political or religious. —*v.t.* 3. be the cause of.

**caus'tic**, *adj.* 1. burning. 2. bitterly sarcastic.

**cau'ter·ize''**, *v.t. Medicine.* burn or sear, as the flesh of a wound, to seal it.

**cau'tion**, *n.* 1. care, as to avoid danger. 2. warning. —*v.t.* 3. warn.

**cau'tious**, *adj.* careful to avoid danger.

**cav'al·cade''**, *n.* procession, esp. on horseback.

**cav'al·ry**, *n., pl.* -ries. *n.* 1. fighting force on horseback. 2. fighting force in motor vehicles.

**cave**, *n.* covered opening in the earth.

**cav'ern**, *n.* spacious cave.

**cav'i·ty**, *n., pl.* -ities. hollow place.

**cease**, *v.i., v.t., n.* stop.

**ce'dar**, *n.* type of fragrant pine.

**cede**, *v.t.* yield possession of.

**ceil'ing**, *n.* 1. structure or surface forming the upper part of a room, etc. 2. upper limit.

**cel'e·brate''**, *v.t.* 1. perform ritually. 2. mark or commemorate with festivity. 3. do honor to. —*v.i.* 4. have festivities. —**cel''e·**

bra'tion, *n.* —**cel'e·brat''ed**, *adj.*

**ce·leb'ri·ty**, *n., pl.* -ties. 1. fame. 2. currently famous person.

**cel'er·y**, *n.* plant with edible leaf stalks.

**ce·les'tial**, *adj.* pertaining to heaven or outer space.

**cel'i·bate''**, *n.* 1. unmarried person. —*adj.* 2. pertaining to celibates or celibacy. —**cel'i·ba·cy**, *n.*

**cell**, *n.* habitable space in a prison, monastery, etc.

**cel'lar**, *n.* basement.

**cel'lo·phane''**, *n.* transparent wrapping material.

**cel·lo** (tshel'lō), *n., pl.* -los. large bowed stringed instrument.

**Cel'lu·loid''**, *n. Trademark.* plastic made from nitrocellulose and camphor.

**ce·ment'**, *n.* 1. mixture of burned lime and clay, used for building. —*v.t.* 2. join with cement.

**cem'e·ter''y**, *n., pl.* -ies. area of land for burying the dead.

**cen'sor**, *n.* person who eliminates unauthorized material from writings, etc. —**cen'sor·ship''**, *n.*

**cen'sure**, *n.* rebuke or condemnation.

**cen'sus**, *n.* counting and analysis of population, etc.

**cent**, *n.* hundredth part of a dollar.

**cen·ten'ni·al**, *adj.* 1. pertaining to or marking a period of 100 years. —*n.* 2. hundredth anniversary.

**cen'ter**, *n.* 1. point or area equidistant from all outer points. 2. place of concentration.

**cen'ti·grade''**, *adj.* pertaining to a system of temperature measurement in which the range between the freezing and boiling points of water is 100 degrees; Celsius.

**cen'tral**, *adj.* located at the center.

**cen'tral·ize''**, *v.t.* place at a center.

**cen'tu·ry**, *n., pl.* -ries. period of 100 years.

**ce·ram'ic**, *n.* 1. **ceramics**, making of objects from baked clay or similar materials. 2. pertaining to ceramics.

**ce're·al**, *n.* 1. grain used as food. 2. food manufactured from such grain.

**cer'e·bral**, *adj.* reasoned rather than felt.

**cer″e·mo′ni·al**, *adj.* **1.** formal. —*n.* **2.** ceremony.

**cer′e·mo″ny**, *n.*, *pl.* **-nies.** ordered set of actions for a formal occasion. —**cer″e·mo′ni·ous**, *adj.*

**cer′tain**, *adj.* **1.** without doubt. **2.** without error. —**cer′tain·ty**, *n.*

**cer·tif′i·cate**, *n.* document that certifies.

**cer′ti·fy″**, *v.t.* declare formally to be competent, valid, true, etc. —**cer″ti·fi·ca′tion**, *n.*

**ces·sa′tion**, *n.* stop.

**cess′pool″**, *n.* receptacle for plumbing wastes.

**chafe**, *v.t.* **1.** wear by rubbing. —*v.i.* **2.** become restless and annoyed.

**cha·grin′**, *n.* embarrassment at failure or disappointment.

**chain**, *n.* **1.** flexible length formed of connected pieces. —*v.t.* **2.** fasten with a chain.

**chain reaction**, series of reactions each caused by one immediately previous.

**chair**, *n.* seat with a back.

**chair′man**, *n.* person who presides over a meeting.

**cha·let′** (sha lā′), *n.* Swiss farmhouse with a low, jutting roof.

**chal′ice**, *n.* wine goblet used in religious communions.

**chalk**, *n.* soft white limestone. —**chalk′y**, *adj.*

**chal′lenge**, *v.t.* **1.** call upon to fight, compete, or act bravely. —*n.* **2.** act or instance of challenging.

**cham′ber**, *n.* room, esp. a bedroom.

**cha·me·le·on** (kə mē′lē ən), *n.* lizard able to change the color of its skin.

**cham·pagne** (sham pān′), *n.* sparkling white wine, originally from northern France.

**cham′pi·on**, *n.* **1.** person who fights on another's behalf. **2.** athlete winning or getting first place in a series of competitions. —**cham′pi·on·ship″**, *n.*

**chance**, *n.* **1.** possibility of becoming, doing, or getting something desired. **2.** the unpredictable. —*adj.* **3.** accidental.

**chanc′y**, *adj.*, **-ier, -iest.** risky or uncertain.

**chan″de·lier′**, *n.* lighting fixture suspended from a ceiling.

**change**, *v.t.* **1.** make into a different form. **2.** give up one for the other, as articles of clothing, vehicles, etc. **3.** give lower denominations of money in exchange for. —*v.i.* **4.** become different. —*n.* **5.** act or instance of changing.

**chan′nel**, *n.* **1.** deeper part of a watercourse. **2.** *Television and radio.* frequency band. —*v.t.* **3.** send through or as through a channel.

**chant**, *n.* **1.** heavily rhythmical song or speech. —*v.t.* **2.** sing or utter in a chant.

**cha·os** (kā′os), *n.* utter disorder. —**cha·ot′ic**, *adj.*

**chap**, *v.t.*, *v.i.* roughen or crack, as the skin or lips.

**chap′el**, *n.* minor church.

**chap′lain**, *n.* clergyman employed by an institution, military force, etc.

**chap′ter**, *n.* **1.** division of a book. **2.** local branch of an association.

**char**, *v.t.*, *v.i.* burn on the surface.

**char′ac·ter**, *n.* **1.** personality. **2.** moral strength. **3.** person as judged by his actions. **4.** reputation.

**char″ac·ter·is′tic**, *adj.* **1.** typical. —*n.* **2.** typical or distinguishing quality.

**char′ac·ter·ize″**, *v.t.* give characteristics to.

**char′coal″**, *n.* wood partially burned in the absence of air.

**charge**, *v.t.* **1.** supply or load. **2.** electrify. **3.** make responsible. **4.** require payment. **5.** move swiftly in an attack. —*n.* **6.** act or instance of charging.

**char′i·ot**, *n.* two-wheeled horse-drawn vehicle.

**char′i·ta·ble**, *adj.* kindly.

**char′i·ty**, *n.*, *pl.* **-ties. 1.** love for mankind. **2.** generosity to the needy. **3.** organization for helping the needy.

**char·la·tan** (shahr′lə tən), *n.* perpetrator of frauds.

**charm**, *n.* **1.** attractive or delightful quality. **2.** magic spell. —*v.t.* **3.** exercise charm or a charm upon.

**chart**, *n.* **1.** map, esp. for navigation. **2.** graph or table.

**char′ter**, *n.* **1.** license or franchise. —*v.t.* **2.** grant a charter to. **3.** hire, as for a trip.

**char′y**, *adj.*, **-ier, -iest. 1.** cautious. **2.** sparing.

**chase**, *v.t.* **1.** go after to overtake or

capture. 2. drive away. —n. 3. pursuit.

**chasm** (kaz'm), n. abyss.

**chas·sis** (shas'ē, chas'ē), n., pl. -**sis**. frame and running gear of an automobile, not including the engine.

**chaste**, adj. 1. pure, esp. of sexual desire or activity. 2. tastefully restrained. —**chas'ti·ty,** n.

**chas'ten**, v.t. correct or subdue, esp. by punishment or scolding.

**chas·tise'**, v.t. punish or scold.

**chat**, n. 1. light, informal conversation. —v.i. 2. have such a conversation.

**chat'ter**, v.i. 1. make rapid sounds with the voice. —n. 2. chattering noise.

**chauf·feur'**, n. person hired to drive an automobile.

**cheap**, adj. 1. low in price. 2. low in worth. —**cheap'en,** v.t., v.i.

**cheat**, v.t. 1. deceive, esp. for money. —n. 2. deception.

**check**, n. 1. precaution. 2. inspection. 3. halt or frustration. 4. halt or restrain. 5. verify or investigate.

**check'er**, n. 1. **checkers, a.** pattern of squares in alternating colors. **b.** game played on a board with this pattern. 2. disk used in playing checkers.

**check'mate''**, n. Chess. inevitable capture of a king.

**check'up''**, n. medical examination.

**cheek**, n. side of the face below the eye.

**cheer**, n. 1. happiness. 2. shout of delight, encouragement, etc. —v.i. 3. shout cheers. —**cheer'ful,** adj.

**cheese**, n. food made from milk curds.

**cheese'cake''**, n. cake made with cheese.

**chef**, n. cook, esp. a supervising cook.

**chem'i·cal**, adj. 1. pertaining to, or produced or operated by, chemistry. —n. 2. substance produced by or used in chemistry.

**chem'is·try**, n. study of substances and their production or conversion. —**chem'ist,** n.

**cher'ish**, v.t. regard as dear or precious.

**cher'ry**, n., pl. -**ries**. tree bearing a small, red fruit.

**cher'ub**, n., pl. -**ubs, -ubim**. angel often shown as a chubby, winged child.

**chess**, n. game played on a checkerboard with 16 pieces on each of two sides. —**chess'board'',** n. —**chess'man,** n.

**chest**, n. 1. any of various boxlike containers for storage. 2. part of the body within the ribs.

**chest'nut**, n. tree of the beech family with an edible nut.

**chev'ron**, n. sign like a V or inverted V, used for military insignia, heraldry, etc.

**chew**, v.t. reduce with the teeth, as for swallowing. —**chew'y,** adj.

**chic**, n. elegance; smartness.

**chi·ca'no**, n., fem. -**a.** a person of Mexican descent.

**chick'en**, n. hen or rooster.

**chicken pox**, contagious virus disease of children.

**chic'o·ry**, n. plant with leaves used in salad and roots used as a coffee substitute.

**chide**, v.t., v.i. scold; rebuke.

**chief**, n. 1. principal person. —adj. 2. main.

**chief'tain**, n. leader of a tribe or clan.

**child**, n., pl. **children**. 1. human being before puberty. 2. offspring. —**child'birth'',** n. —**child'hood'',** n. —**child'like'',** adj.

**child'ish**, adj. characteristic of children, esp. as regards behavior or judgment.

**chil'i**, n. dish of beef, red pepper, etc. Also, **chili con car'ne**.

**chill**, n. 1. perceptible cold. —adj. 2. chilly. —v.t. 3. cause to be cold.

**chill'y**, adj., -**ier, -iest**. cold.

**chime**, n. 1. bell, esp. in a clock. —v.t., v.i. 2. sound with chimes.

**chim'ney**, n., pl. -**nies**. passage for smoke or heat.

**chim·pan'zee'**, n. medium-sized ape.

**chin**, n. part of the face at the lower jaw.

**chi'na**, n. 1. porcelain. 2. dishes, etc.

**chink**, n. narrow crack.

**chintz**, n. printed cotton, usually glazed.

**chip**, n., v., -**ped, -ping.** n. 1. small cut or broken piece. 2. token used in gambling, etc. 3. (computers) the basic component of miniaturized electronic circuitry. —v.t. 4.

knock chips from. —*v.i.* **5.** break into chips.

**chip'munk''**, *n.* small North American squirrel.

**chirp**, *v.i.* make short, shrill, birdlike noises.

**chis'el**, *n.* **1.** cutting tool driven at one end. —*v.t.* **2.** cut with a chisel.

**chiv'al·ry**, *n.* **1.** medieval institution of knighthood. **2.** courage, gallantry, etc. —**chiv'al·rous,** *adj.*

**chlo·rine** (klō'rēn), *n.* greenish chemical used for disinfection. —**chlo'ri·nate''**, *v.t.*

**chlo'ro·form''**, *n.* volatile liquid anaesthetic.

**chlo'ro·phyll**, *n.* green substance in plants.

**choc'o·late**, *n.* dark-brown substance made from or flavored with cacao seeds.

**choice**, *n.* **1.** act or instance of choosing. **2.** thing chosen.

**choir** (kwīr), *n.* chorus, esp. one singing religious music.

**choke**, *v.t.* **1.** cut off the breath of. —*v.i.* **2.** suffer from the cutting-off of breath.

**choose**, *v.t.* **1.** decide upon as best to take, do, etc. —*v.i.* **2.** make a choice.

**chop**, *v.t.*, *v.i.* **1.** cut with small blows. —*n.* **2.** meat cut from the rib, shoulder, or loin.

**chor·al** (kōr'al), *adj.* pertaining to or for a chorus.

**chord** (kōrd), *n.* combination of musical tones.

**chore**, *n.* routine or hard task.

**chor·e·og·ra·phy** (kōr''ē ahg'rə fē), *n.* art of planning or executing ballets or dances. —**chor''e·o·graph'ic**, *adj.* —**chor''e·og'ra·pher,** *n.*

**chor'tle**, *v.i.*, *v.t.* speak with chuckles.

**cho·rus** (kō'rəs), *n.* **1.** singing group. **2.** repeated part of a song composed in stanzas.

**chow**, *n. Informal.* food.

**chow'der**, *n.* soup of milk, clams, fish, etc.

**chris'ten**, *v.t.* baptize.

**Chris'tian**, *n.* **1.** believer in Christ. —*adj.* **2.** consistent with the teachings of Christ, esp. regarding charity or salvation. —**Chris''ti·an'i·ty,** *n.*

**Christ'mas**, *n.* celebration of the birth of Christ, usually December 25.

**chrome**, *n.* chromium or a chromium alloy.

**chro'mi·um**, *n.* corrosion-resistant metallic element.

**chro'mo·some''**, *n.* gene-bearing body.

**chron'ic**, *adj.* **1.** long-lasting or recurrent. **2.** suffering from a chronic ailment.

**chron'i·cle**, *n.* chronological record.

**chro·nol'o·gy**, *n., pl.* **-gies.** recording of events in order of occurrence. —**chron''o·log'i·cal,** *adj.*

**chro·nom'e·ter**, *n.* highly accurate timepiece.

**chrys·an'the·mum**, *n.* showy late-blooming flower.

**chub'by**, *adj.* **-bier, -biest.** plump.

**chuck'le**, *v.i.* laugh softly.

**chug**, *n.* **1.** sound of an engine exhaust. —*v.i.* **2.** move with chugs.

**chunk**, *n.* thick fragment.

**chunk'y**, *adj.*, **-ier, -iest.** short and thick.

**church**, *n.* **1.** religious organization. **2.** religious building. —**church' go''er,** *n.* —**church'ly,** *adj.* —**church'man,** *n.*

**church'yard''**, *n.* grounds of a church, esp. when used as a cemetery.

**churl**, *n.* surly, ill-mannered person. —**churl'ish,** *adj.*

**churn**, *n.* **1.** device for shaking cream to form butter. —*v.t.*, *v.i.* **2.** stir or shake.

**chute** (shōot), *n.* slide for transferring materials, etc.

**ci'der**, *n.* apple juice.

**ci·gar'**, *n.* roll of tobacco leaves for smoking.

**cig''a·rette'**, *n.* roll of tobacco in paper for smoking.

**cinch**, *n.* **1.** *Informal.* something easy. **2.** strap for securing a saddle.

**cin'der**, *n.* ash.

**cin'e·ma**, *n.* motion picture or pictures.

**cin'na·mon**, *n.* East Indian spice.

**ci'pher**, *n.* **1.** code. **2.** zero.

**cir'ca**, *prep.* around; used in dating.

**cir'cle**, *n.* closed two-dimensional curve with one center.

**cir'cuit**, *n.* **1.** continuous path of movement. **2.** path of an electric current.

**cir·cu'i·tous**, *adj.* roundabout.

**cir'cuit·ry**, *n.* components of an electrical circuit.

**cir·cu·lar**, *adj.* 1. shaped like a circle. —*n.* 2. pamphlet, etc. for general distribution.

**cir'cu·late''**, *v.i.* 1. move in a closed, continuous path. —*v.t.* 2. cause to move in either of these ways. —**cir'cu·la·to''ry**, *adj.*

**cir'cu·la'tion**, *n.* act or instance of circulating.

**cir·cum·cise''**, *v.t.* cut away the foreskin of. —**cir''cum·ci'sion**, *n.*

**cir''cum'fer·ence**, *n.* dimension along the line of a circle.

**cir''cum·lo·cu'tion**, *n.* wordy, evasive speech.

**cir'cum·scribe''**, *v.t.* 1. draw a circle around. 2. confine.

**cir'cum·spect''**, *adj.* cautious.

**cir'cum·stance''**, *n.* 1. accompanying condition. 2. chance. 3. **cir·cumstances**, state of material welfare.

**cir''cum·stan'tial**, *adj.* 1. pertaining to circumstances or circumstance. 2. pertaining to legal evidence implying but not proving something.

**cir''cum·vent''**, *v.t.* prevent or overcome with cunning.

**cir'cus**, *n.* traveling show of animals, acrobats, etc.

**cir'rus**, *n.* feathery cloud formation.

**cis'tern**, *n.* tank for water storage.

**cite''**, *v.t.* 1. mention. 2. summon before a court. —**ci·ta'tion**, *n.*

**cit'i·zen**, *n.* member of a state or other political entity. —**cit'i·zen·ship''**, *n.*

**cit'rus**, *adj.* of or pertaining to lemons, oranges, limes, etc. —**cit'ric**, *adj.*

**cit'y**, *n., pl.* **-ies.** 1. large community. 2. government of such a community.

**civ'ic**, *adj.* pertaining to cities or their citizens.

**civ'ics**, *n., pl.* study of the relation of citizens to political entities.

**civ·il**, *adj.* 1. not military or religious. 2. polite. —**ci·vil'i·ty**, *n.*

**civil engineering**, engineering of public works or the like. —**civil engineer.**

**ci·vil'ian**, *n.* person outside any military or police organization.

**civ''i·li·za'tion**, *n.* lawful, orderly state of society.

**civ'i·lize''**, *v.t.* cause to adopt civilization.

**clad**, *adj.* dressed.

**claim**, *v.t.* 1. designate for oneself. 2. assert as true. 3. require. —*n.* 4. something claimed. —**claim'ant, claim'er**, *n.*

**clair·voy'ance**, *n.* sensitivity to things not usually seen, esp. the supernatural. —**clair·voy'ant**, *adj., n.*

**clam**, *n.* bivalve mollusk.

**clam'my**, *adj.*, **-mier, -miest.** cold and moist.

**clam'or**, *n.* 1. loud outcry. —*v.i.* 2. make such an outcry, as in demanding or complaining.

**clamp**, *n.* 1. mechanical device for holding things together. —*v.t.* 2. fasten with a clamp.

**clan·des'tine**, *adj.* secret; stealthy.

**clang**, *n.* loud ringing noise.

**clap**, *v.i.* strike the palms of the hands together.

**clar'et**, *n.* dry red table wine.

**clar'i·fy''**, *v.t.* make clear.

**clar''i·net'**, *n.* reed woodwind instrument.

**clar'i·ty**, *n.* clearness, esp. to the understanding.

**clash**, *v.i.* strike together violently.

**clasp**, *n.* 1. folding fastener. 2. embrace. 3. grasp, as of the hand. —*v.t.* 4. hold with or in a clasp.

**class**, *n.* 1. category or grade. 2. group of students taught or graduating together.

**clas'sic**, *adj.* 1. excellent of its kind. —*n.* 2. something excellent of its kind.

**clas'si·cal**, *adj.* 1. pertaining to Greco-Roman antiquity or art. 2. traditional.

**clas'si·fy''**, *v.t.* put into meaningful categories. —**clas''si·fi·ca'tion**, *n.*

**clat'ter**, *n.* loud rattling noise.

**clause**, *n.* 1. unit of a sentence. 2. unit of a document.

**claw**, *n.* 1. hooked paw or foot. —*v.t., v.i.* 2. scratch or grasp with or as with a claw.

**clay**, *n.* earth in a readily molded state.

**clean**, *adj.* 1. free of dirt, germs, impurities, etc. —*v.t.* 2. make clean.

**cleanse**, *v.t.* make clean.

**clear**, *adj.* 1. perfectly transparent. 2. lucid. —*v.t.* 3. make clear. 4. pass without colliding with.

**clear'ance,** n. space between two obstructions.

**clear'ing,** n. forest area free of trees.

**cleat,** n. object attached to a surface to improve traction, give reinforcement, etc.

**cleave,** v.t., v.i. split.

**clef,** n. Music. symbol establishing pitch.

**cleft,** n. narrow opening; crack.

**clem'ent,** adj. merciful. —**clem'en·cy,** n.

**clench,** v.t. press or bind firmly together.

**cler'gy,** n., pl. -**gies.** priests, ministers, and other religious leaders. —**cler'gy·man,** n.

**cler'i·cal,** adj. 1. pertaining to clerks. 2. pertaining to clergy.

**clerk,** n. 1. record keeper. 2. retail employee.

**clev'er,** adj. able in understanding, contriving, etc.

**cli·ché,** n. trite metaphor or phrase.

**click,** n. 1. sharp noise from striking, buckling, etc. —v.t., v.i. 2. move with a click.

**cli'ent,** n. person who buys professional services.

**cli''en·tele,** n. clients of a professional man, merchant, etc.

**cliff,** n. abrupt rise of land.

**cli'mate,** n. characteristic weather. —**cli·mat'ic,** adj.

**cli'max,** n. point of greatest interest, emotion, tension, etc.

**climb,** v.t. 1. move upward upon or within. —v.i. 2. climb something.

**clinch,** v.t. 1. establish firmly. —n. 2. act or instance of clinching.

**cling,** v.i. 1. hold firmly. 2. stay close.

**clin'ic,** n. place for treating outpatients.

**clin'i·cal,** adj. 1. pertaining to clinics. 2. impersonally analytical.

**clip,** v.t. 1. cut, as with scissors. 2. fasten. —n. 3. fastener.

**clip'per,** n. 1. fast sailing vessel. 2. **clippers,** device for cutting hair.

**clip'ping,** n. article cut from a periodical.

**clique,** n. exclusive social group. —**cliqu'ish,** adj.

**cloak,** n. long, loose garment worn over the shoulders.

**clob'ber,** v.t. Informal. beat.

**clock,** n. machine for measuring time.

**clod,** n. lump of earth.

**clog,** v.t. 1. stop flow through;

choke. —v.i. 2. become stopped up. —n. 3. thick-soled shoe.

**clois'ter,** n. covered walk in a monastery, etc.

**clone,** n., v. (biology) a genetic duplicate of an organism.

**close,** v.t. (klōz) 1. block or fill, as with a door. 2. deny public access to. —n. 3. conclusion. —adj. (klōs) 4. near; not far. 5. confined.

**clos'et,** n. small storage room.

**close'-up'',** n. photograph at close range.

**clot,** n. 1. lump, esp. of coagulated blood. —v.i. 2. form a clot.

**cloth,** n. material of interwoven fibers.

**clothe,** v.t. put clothes on.

**clothes,** n., pl. things to cover the human body. Also, **cloth'ing.**

**cloud,** n. mass of vapor in the sky. —**cloud'y,** adj.

**clove,** n. tropical spice.

**clo'ver,** n. three-leafed herb.

**clown,** n. entertainer with funny antics.

**cloy'ing,** adj. repulsively sweet, sentimental, etc.

**club,** n. 1. stick, etc. for striking blows. 2. social group. 3. suit of playing cards.

**clue,** n. 1. indication of the solution to a puzzle.

**clump,** n. cluster, as of trees.

**clum'sy,** adj., -**sier,** -**siest.** without skill or care. —**clum'si·ly,** adv. —**clum'si·ness,** n.

**clus'ter,** n. 1. loose group. —v.t., v.i. 2. gather in a group.

**clutch,** v.t., v.i. 1. grasp violently. —n. 2. device for engaging a machine with its mover.

**clut'ter,** v.t. fill with unwanted things.

**coach,** n. 1. enclosed horse-drawn carriage. 2. bus. 3. railroad passenger car. 4. trainer. —v.t. 5. train, rehearse, or prompt.

**co·ag'u·late,** v.i., v.t. turn from a liquid to a semi-solid. —**co·ag''u·la'tion,** n.

**coal,** n. 1. combustible mineral. 2. ember.

**co''a·lesce',** v.i. unite.

**co''a·li'tion,** n. act of uniting for a specific purpose.

**coal oil,** kerosene.

**coarse,** adj. 1. roughly made. 2. unrefined. —**coars'en,** v.t., v.i.

**coast,** n. land by a sea, etc. —**coast'al,** adj.

**coat**, *n.* 1. cold-weather garment. 2. jacket. 3. Also, **coat'ing**, layer of material.

**coat of arms**, *Heraldry.* arms of a person, state, etc.

**coax**, *v.t.*, persuade with flattery or wheedling.

**cob'ble**, *v.t.* 1. repair, as shoes. —*n.* 2. Also, **cob'ble·stone''**, large pebble used for paving.

**cob'web''**, *n.* web of a spider.

**co·caine'**, *n.* narcotic from a tropical plant.

**cock**, *n.* 1. rooster. —*v.t.* 2. make ready for firing, as a gun.

**cock'eyed''**, *adj. Informal.* awry; wrong.

**cock'pit''**, *n.* space for an airplane crew.

**cock'roach''**, *n.* crawling insect found in buildings.

**cock'sure''**, *adj.* foolishly self-assured.

**cock'tail''**, *n.* mixed alcoholic drink.

**cock'y**, *adj.*, **-ier**, **-iest**. *Informal.* showily self-assured.

**co'coa**, *n.* drink made from roasted cacao powder.

**co'co·nut'**, *n.* fruit of a palm tree, whose flesh and juice are consumed.

**co·coon'**, *n.* case of certain insect pupas, made of a thread.

**cod**, *n.*, *pl.* **cod**, **cods**. edible northern saltwater fish. Also, **cod'-fish''**.

**cod'dle**, *v.t.* take excessive care of; pamper.

**code**, *n.* 1. set of laws or principles. 2. formula for secret messages.

**cod'i·fy''**, *v.t.* put into systematic form, esp. in writing.

**co·ed'**, *n. Informal.* woman in a coeducational school. Also, **co'-ed''**.

**co·ed''u·ca'tion**, *n.* enrollment of men and women in the same school.

**co·ef·fi'cient**, *n.* multiplier.

**co·erce'**, *v.t.* compel by force or threats. —**co·er'cion**, *n.*

**co''ex·ist'**, *v.i.* 1. exist together. 2. live together without dispute.

**cof'fee**, *n.* drink made from the roasted seed of a tropical shrub.

**cof'fin**, *n.* burial chest.

**cog**, *n.* gear tooth.

**co'gent**, (kō'jənt) *adj.* forcefully convincing, as an argument.

**cog'i·tate''**, *v.t.*, *v.i.* ponder.

**co·gnac'** (kon'yak), *n.* French brandy.

**cog'nate''**, *adj.* related.

**cog'ni·zance**, *n.* official notice. —**cog'ni·zant**, *adj.*

**cog'wheel''**, *n.* gear wheel, esp. in a clock, toy, etc.

**co·hab'it**, *v.i.* live together, esp. out of wedlock.

**co·here'**, *v.i.* 1. stick together. 2. be rationally connected. —**co·her'ent**, *adj.*

**co·he'sion**, *n.* tendency of particles. to hold together.

**coif·fure'**, *n.* hair style.

**coil**, *n.* 1. spiral or helix. —*v.t.*, *v.i.* 2. wind into a coil.

**coin**, *n.* 1. piece of metal used as money. —*v.t.* 2. stamp as money. —**coin'age**, *n.*

**co''in·cide'**, *v.i.* happen at the same time. —**co·in'ci·dence**, *n.* —**co·in''ci·den'tal**, **co·in'ci·dent**, *adj.*

**col'an·der**, *n.* large strainer.

**cold**, *adj.* 1. having a relatively low temperature. 2. feeling a lack of warmth.

**cold'blood''ed**, *adj.* without emotion, conscience, etc.

**cold war**, prolonged hostile situation without fighting.

**col·lab'o·rate''**, *v.i.* work together, as on a project. —**col·lab''o·ra'tion**, *n.* —**col·lab'o·ra''tor**, *n.* —**col·lab''o·ra'tion·ist**, *n.*

**col·lapse'**, *v.i.* 1. fall because of weakness. —*n.* 2. act or instance of collapsing.

**col'lar**, *n.* band worn around the neck.

**col'lar·bone''**, *n.* bone between the breastbone and shoulder blade; clavicle.

**col·lat'er·al**, *n.* 1. security for a loan. —*adj.* 2. accompanying.

**col'league**, *n.* professional associate.

**col·lect'**, *v.t.*, *v.i.* gather together. —**col·lect'or**, *n.* —**col·lec'tion**, *n.*

**col·lect'ed**, *adj.* with one's emotions under control.

**col·lec'tive**, *adj.* involving cooperation.

**col'lege**, *n.* generalized institution of higher learning. —**col·le'giate**, *adj.*

**col·lide'**, *v.i.* strike against another or each other while moving. —**col·li'sion**, *n.*

**col'lie**, *n.* large, long-haired dog.

**col·lo·qui·al**, *adj.* pertaining to or used in informal conversation only. —**col·lo'qui·al·ism**, *n.*

**col·lu'sion**, *n.* unlawful conspiracy.

**co'lon**, *n.* 1. part of the large intestine. 2. punctuation mark written thus:

**colo·nel** (kar'nəl), *n.* military officer between a lieutenant colonel and a brigadier general. —**colo'nel·cy**, *n.*

**col'o·nize**, *v.t.* establish colonies in.

**col'o·ny**, *n., pl.* **-nies.** 1. region in the possession of a foreign nation. 2. community of settlers. 3. group of social insects, etc. —**co·lon'i·al**, *adj., n.* —**col'on·ist**, *n.*

**col'or**, *n.* 1. property deriving from specific wavelengths of light. —*v.t.* 2. give color to. —**col'or·ful**, *adj.* —**col'or·ing**, *n.*

**col'ored**, *n.* Negro; black.

**col'or·less**, *adj.* not vivid.

**co·los'sal**, *adj.* gigantic; enormous.

**colt**, *n.* young male horse.

**col'umn**, *n.* 1. narrow, upright structural support. 2. stack of printed or written lines read together. 3. file of troops.

**co'ma**, *n.* pathological unconsciousness.

**comb**, *n.* pronged device for arranging the hair or other fibers.

**com·bat**, *n.* (kom'bat) 1. battle. —*v.t.* (kəm bat') 2. fight or oppose. —**com·bat'ant**, *n., adj.*

**com''bi·na'tion**, *n.* act or instance of combining.

**com·bine'**, *v.t., v.i.* join together. —**com·bus'ti·ble**, *adj.*

**com·bus'tion**, *n.* act of burning. —**com·bus'ti·ble**, *adj.*

**come**, *v.i.* 1. move to this place. 2. occur; happen.

**co·me'di·an**, *n.* humorous performer. Also *fem.,* **co·me'di·enne'**.

**com'e·dy**, *n., pl.* **-dies.** 1. drama with a happy ending. 2. amusing situation.

**com'et**, *n.* cloud of fine dust in orbit around the sun.

**com'fort**, *n.* 1. feeling of well-being. —*v.t.* 2. console or reassure.

**com'fort·a·ble**, *adj.* 1. enjoying comfort. 2. promoting comfort.

**com'fort·er**, *n.* quilt.

**com'ic**, *adj.* amusing. Also, **com'i·cal**.

**com'ma**, *n.* a mark, used especially

to separate phrases or clauses in a sentence.

**com·mand'**, *v.t.* 1. order or direct. —*n.* 2. order. 3. authority or control.

**com''man·deer'**, *v.t.* take control of by authority or force.

**commander in chief**, *n., pl.* **commanders in chief.** supreme military commander.

**com·mand'ment**, *n.* order, esp. a standing one from a deity.

**com·mem'o·rate''**, *v.t.* honor or preserve the memory of. —**com·mem''o·ra'tion**, *n.* —**com·mem'o·ra·tive**, *adj.*

**com·mence'**, *v.t., v.i.* begin.

**com·mence'ment**, *n.* 1. beginning. 2. high-school graduation ceremony.

**com·mend'**, *v.t.* 1. praise. 2. recommend. —**com·mend'a·ble**, *adj.* —**com''men·da'tion**, *n.*

**com·men'su·rate**, *adj.* equal or in proportion.

**com'ment**, *n.* 1. remark or remarks on something observed. —*v.i.* 2. make a comment.

**com'men·tar''y**, *n., pl.* **-ries.** set of explanatory notes.

**com'men·ta''tor**, *n.* person who comments on current events.

**com'merce**, *n.* purchasing and sale of merchandise.

**com·mer'cial**, *adj.* pertaining to commerce.

**com·mer'cial·ism**, *n.* emphasis on ready mass saleability rather than on quality, taste, etc.

**com·mer'cial·ize''**, *v.t.* make, sell, etc. for maximum profit.

**com·min'gle**, *v.t., v.i.* blend.

**com·mis'er·ate''**, *v.i.* feel sympathetic sorrow.

**com·mis'sion**, *n.* 1. entrusted task. 2. military officership. 3. committee. 4. salesman's percentage of the amount of a sale. —*v.t.* 5. entrust or authorize.

**com·mis'sion·er**, *n.* head of a municipal department or commission.

**com·mit'**, *v.t.* 1. obligate. 2. state the position of in a controversy. 3. do, esp. a crime. 4. send for confinement. —**com·mit'ment**, *n.*

**com·mit'tee**, *n.* chosen group of persons with specified responsibilities.

**com·mod'i·ty**, *n., pl.* **-ties.** *Commerce.* material or article, as opposed to a service.

**com'mon**, *adj.* 1. pertaining to many or to all. 2. not unusual. 3. vulgar.

**common law**, law based on custom and court decisions.

**com'mon·place''**, *adj.* 1. completely or tritely familiar. —*n.* 2. something commonplace.

**common sense**, ordinary good judgment. —**com'mon-sense''**, **com'mon·sen'si·cal**, *adj.*

**com'mon·wealth''**, *n.* 1. federation of states. 2. state.

**com·mo'tion**, *n.* uproar.

**com·mu'nal**, *adj.* pertaining to or shared by a community or group.

**com·mune'**, *v.i.* (kə myōōn') 1. be in intimate communication or sympathy. —*n.* (kom'yōōn) 2. community sharing goods, responsibilities, etc.

**com·mu'ni·ca·ble**, *adj.* 1. able to be communicated. 2. able to be transferred, as an illness.

**com·mu'ni·cant**, *n.* partaker of the Eucharist.

**com·mu'ni·cate**, *v.t.* 1. make understood to others. 2. exchange messages. 3. be in communion. 4. be connected, as rooms. —**com·mu'ni·ca'tion**, *n.*

**com·mu'ni·ca·tive**, *adj.* talkative or confiding.

**com·mun'ion**, *n.* 1. state of intimacy. 2. *Christianity.* sharing of bread and wine in remembrance of Christ.

**com·mu'ni·qué**, *n.* official message or news release.

**com'mu·nism**, *n.* political theory demanding public ownership of economic resources. —**com'mu·nis'tic**, *adj.* —**com'mu·nist**, *n., adj.*

**com·mu'ni·ty**, *n., pl.* **ties.** 1. town, etc. 2. sharing in common.

**com·mute'**, *v.t.* 1. alter, as a prison sentence. —*v.i.* 2. travel regularly, as between home and work. —**com'mu·ta'tion**, *n.*

**com·pact'**, *adj.* (kəm pakt') 1. occupying a minimal space. —*n.* (kom'pakt) 2. small cosmetic case.

**com·pan'ion**, *n.* person who keeps one company. —**com·pan'ion·ship''**, *n.*

**com·pan'ion·a·ble**, *adj.* willing to keep one company.

**com'pa·ny**, *n., pl.* **nies.** 1. fellowship; companionship. 2. business organization or association.

**com·pa'ra·ble**, *adj.* allowing comparison.

**com·par'a·tive**, *adj.* 1. involving comparison. 2. in comparison to other cases. —**com·par'a·tive·ly**, *adv.*

**com·pare'**, *v.t.* 1. examine for similarities and differences. 2. regard or describe as similar.

**com·par'i·son**, *n.* 1. act or instance of comparing. 2. similarity.

**com·part'ment**, *n.* division of a larger space.

**com'pass**, *n.* 1. instrument for establishing or indicating direction. 2. **compasses**, instrument for drawing circles.

**com·pas'sion**, *n.* sympathy, esp. with suffering or weakness. —**com·pas'sion·ate**, *adj.*

**com·pat'i·ble**, *adj.* 1. content together. 2. logically consistent. —**com·pat''i·bil'i·ty**, *n.*

**com·pa'tri·ot**, *n.* fellow national.

**com·pel'**, *v.t.* force.

**com·pen'sate**, *v.t.* 1. pay, as for work or damage. —*v.i.* 2. serve to offset or make up for something else. —**com'pen·sa'tion**, *n.*

**com·pete'**, *v.i.* act in rivalry. —**com''pe·ti'tion**, *n.* —**com·pet'i·tive**, *adj.* —**com·pet'i·tor**, *n.*

**com·pe'tent**, *adj.* 1. able to work, etc. adequately. 2. legally authorized. —**com'pe·tent·ly**, *adv.* —**com'pe·tence**, **com'pe·ten·cy**, *n.*

**com·pile'**, *v.t.* gather or publish together, as documents.

**com·pla'cen·cy**, *n.* satisfaction, esp. with oneself. —**com·pla'cent**, *adj.*

**com·plain'**, *v.i.* discuss one's grievance with others. —**com·plain'er**, *n.*

**com·plaint'**, *n.* act or instance of complaining.

**com·ple·ment**, *n.* (kom'plə ment) 1. something that completes. 2. wholeness. —*v.t.* (com'plə ment'') 3. complete.

**com·plete'**, *adj.* 1. entire; with nothing missing. 2. finish. —**com·plete'ly**, *adv.* —**com·ple'tion**, *n.*

**com·plex'**, *adj.* (kəm pleks') 1. not readily analyzed or understood. —*n.* (kom'pleks) 2. *Psychology.* **a.** group of impulses controlling behavior. **b.** obsessive attitude. —**com·plex'i·ty**, *n.*

**com·plex'ion**, n. color and texture of the skin.

**com'pli·cate''**, v.t. 1. make difficult to do or understand. 2. make unnecessarily complex. —**com''·pli·ca'tion**, n.

**com·pli·ment**, n. (kom'plə mənt) 1. expression of praise. —v.t. (kom'pləment'') 2. pay a compliment to.

**com''pli·men'ta·ry**, adj. 1. serving as a compliment. 2. granted free of charge.

**com·ply'**, v.i. act as ordered or urged. —**com·pli'ance**, n. —**com·pli'ant**, adj.

**com·po'nent**, n. part of a whole.

**com·pose'**, v.t. 1. create or organize artistically. 2. constitute.

**com·posed'**, adj. apparently calm.

**com·pos'ite**, adj. made of many constituents.

**com''po·si'tion**, n. 1. something composed. 2. method of composing. 3. nature, as of constituents or traits.

**com·po'sure**, n. apparent calm.

**com·pound'**, adj. (kom'pownd) 1. not simple; complex. —n. 2. substance of mixed elements. 3. building enclosure. —v.t. (kəm pownd') 4. mix or make by mixing. 5. permit unlawfully.

**com''pre·hend'**, v.t. 1. have a conception or understanding of. 2. include. —**com''pre·hen'sion**, n. —**com''pre·hen'si·ble**, adj.

**com''pre·hen'sive**, adj. including all or most elements. —**com''·pre·hen'sive·ly**, adv. —**com''·pre·hen'sive·ness**, n.

**com·press'**, v.t. (kəm pres') 1. press to lessen volume. 2. put under pressure. —n. (kahm'pres) 3. pad of cloth applied as an aid to medicine. —**com·pres'sion**, n.

**com·prise'**, v.t. 1. include. 2. consist of.

**com''pro·mise''**, n. 1. expedient but not fully satisfactory agreement. —v.t. 2. make a compromise. —v.i. 3. endanger in reputation, etc.

**com·pul'sion**, n. act or instance of compelling. —**com·pul'sive**, adj. —**com·pul'so·ry**, adj.

**com·punc'tion**, n. uneasy, guilty feeling.

**com·pute'**, v.t. determine by calculation. —**com''pu·ta'tion**, n.

**com'rade''**, n. 1. close friend. 2. associate.

**con·cave'**, adj. curving inward. —**con·cav'i·ty**, n.

**con·ceal'**, v.t. hide or keep secret. —**con·ceal'ment**, n.

**con·cede'**, v.t. 1. admit as true. 2. acknowledge defeat in. 3. grant.

**con·ceit'**, n. 1. excessive pride. 2. fanciful idea or expression.

**con·ceit'ed**, adj. full of conceit.

**con·ceive'**, v.i. 1. form an idea. 2. become pregnant. —v.t. 3. imagine as possible or true. —**con·ceiv'a·ble**, adj. —**con·ceiv'a·bly**, adv.

**con'cen·trate''**, v.t. 1. focus. 2. increase in strength. —v.i. 3. focus attention or effort.

**con'cept**, n. idea of something possible. —**con·cep'tu·al**, adj.

**con·cep'tion**, n. act or instance of conceiving.

**con·cern'**, v.t. 1. be the business of. 2. cause care or anxiety in. —n. 3. business or affair. 4. care or anxiety. 5. business organization.

**con·cern'ing**, prep. on the subject of.

**con'cert**, n. series of musical compositions performed at one time.

**con·cert'ed**, adj. performed in an agreed manner.

**con·ces'sion**, n. 1. act or instance of conceding. 2. something conceded.

**con·cil'i·ate''**, v.t. pacify or appease. —**con·cil'i·a'tor**, n. —**con·cil'i·a·to''ry**, adj. —**con·cil'i·a'tion**, n.

**con·cise'**, adj. confined to essentials, as a piece of writing. —**con·cise'ness**, n.

**con·clude'**, v.t. 1. end. 2. reach an opinion or decision. —**con·clu'sion**, n.

**con·clu'sive**, adj. compelling a certain opinion or decision.

**con·coct'**, v.t. 1. make of varied ingredients. 2. devise. —**con·coc'tion**, n.

**con·com'i·tant**, adj. accompanying. —**con·com'i·tant·ly**, adv.

**con'cord**, n. harmonious agreement.

**con'course**, n. space or hall for accommodating crowds.

**con'crete'**, adj. (kon krēt') 1. real; material. —n. (kon'krēt) 2. material of cement and stone, etc.

**con·cu'bine''**, n. wife of less than full status.

**con·cur'**, *v.i.* agree. —**con·cur'rent**, *adj.* —**con·cur'rence**, *n.*

**con·cus'sion**, *n.* 1. shock, as from a blow. 2. malfunctioning of the mind or body from a blow.

**con·demn'**, *v.t.* 1. disapprove of strongly. 2. reject as unfit. —**con''dem·na'tion**, *n.*

**con·dense'**, *v.t., v.i.* 1. turn from a gas to a liquid. —*v.t.* 2. put in succinct form. —**con''den·sa'tion**, *n.* —**con·dens'er**, *n.*

**con''de·scend'**, *v.i.* 1. show kindness or affability to an inferior. —*v.t.* 2. do with a good grace despite superior status. —**con''de·scen'sion**, *n.*

**con'di·ment**, *n.* flavor or seasoning.

**con·di'tion**, *n.* 1. state of health, repair, etc. 2. something necessary or required. —*v.t.* 3. put in condition. 4. accustom.

**con·di'tion·al**, *adj.* subject to certain conditions.

**con·dole'**, *v.i.* express sorrowful sympathy. —**con·dol'ence**, *n.*

**con''do·min'i·um**, *n.* 1. multiunit group of privately owned dwelling units. 2. territory under a joint rule.

**con·done'**, *v.t.* fail to forbid or disapprove of.

**con·duce'**, *v.i.* tend or lead. —**con·duc'ive**, *adj.*

**con·duct'**, *v.t.* (kən dukt') 1. lead or direct. 2. transmit. 3. behave. —*n.* (kahn'dukt) 4. behavior.

**con·duc'tor**, *n.* 1. leader of a band or orchestra. 2. person in charge of a train, etc. 3. thing that transmits electricity, heat, etc.

**con'duit** (kahn'dit), *n.* channel for wiring or fluids.

**cone**, *n.* 1. solid generated by rotating an isosceles triangle around its centerline. 2. fruit of an evergreen.

**con·fec'tion**, *n.* food made with sugar. —**con·fec'tion·er**, *n.* —**con·fec'tion·er·y**, *n.*

**con·fed'er·a·cy**, *n., pl.* -cies. alliance.

**con·fed'er·ate**, *n.* (kən fed'ər ət) 1. ally or accomplice. —*adj.* 2. allied. —*v.t., v.i.* (kən fed'ər āt') 3. ally. —**con·fed'er·a'tion**, *n.*

**con·fer'**, *v.t.* 1. bestow. —*v.i.* 2. consult or discuss. —**con'fer·ence**, *n.*

**con·fess'**, *v.t.* 1. admit as true. 2.

profess belief in. 3. hear the confession of.

**con·fes'sion**, *n.* 1. act or instance of confessing. 2. admission of sins by a penitent.

**con·fes'sion·al**, *n.* place where a priest hears confessions.

**con·fes'sor**, *n.* priest who hears confessions.

**con'fi·dant'**, *n.* person in whom one confides. Also, *fem.,* **con'fi·dante'**.

**con·fide'**, *v.i.* 1. place trust, esp. by relating secrets. —*v.t.* 2. entrust to someone's care or hearing.

**con'fi·dence**, *n.* 1. trust. 2. self-assurance. —**con'fi·dent**, *adj.* —**con'fi·dent·ly**, *adv.*

**con''fi·den'tial**, *adj.* 1. to be kept as secret. 2. entrusted with secrets. —**con''fi·den'tial·ly**, *adv.*

**con·fine'**, *v.t.* (kən fīn') 1. keep within limits or boundaries. 2. keep as if a prisoner.

**con·firm'**, *v.t.* 1. certify as true. 2. approve formally. 3. admit fully to a church. —**con''fir·ma'tion**, *n.*

**con'fis·cate**, *v.t.* seize by authority. —**con''fis·ca'tion**, *n.*

**con''fla·gra'tion**, *n.* fire causing major damage.

**con·flict'**, *n.* (kahn'flikt) 1. fight. —*v.i.* (kən flikt') 2. be hostile in disagreement.

**con·form'**, *v.i.* 1. form one's appearance, manners, etc. according to prevailing standards. 2. act or be in accordance with a law, rule, etc. 3. be similar. —*v.t.* 4. cause to conform. —**con·form'i·ty**, *n.*

**con·form'ist**, *n.* person who conforms unquestioningly.

**con·found'**, *v.t.* confuse.

**con·front'**, *v.t.* 1. approach or face hostilely. 2. force to face.

**con·fuse'**, *v.t.* 1. hamper in the powers of perception, analysis, decision, etc. 2. mistake for another. —**con·fu'sion**, *n.*

**con·geal'**, *v.t., v.i.* thicken or freeze.

**con·gen'i·al**, *adj.* agreeable.

**con·gen'i·tal**, *adj.* from the time of birth.

**con·gest'**, *v.t.* fill to excess. —**con·ges'tion**, *n.*

**con·glom'er·ate**, *v.t., v.i.* (kən glahm'ə rāt') 1. form into a mass. —*n.* (kən glahm'ə rət) 2. mass of small elements. —**con·glom'er·a'tion**, *n.*

**con·grat'u·late''**, *v.t.* show sympathetic pleasure, as for success or good luck. —**con·grat'u·la'tion**, *n.* —**con·grat'u·la·to'ry**, *adj.*

**con'gre·gate''**, *v.t.*, *v.i.* gather into a group or assembly. —**con'gre·ga'tion**, *n.*

**con'gress**, *n.* **1.** legislative body. **2.** formal gathering. —**con·gres'sion·al**, *adj.*

**Con'gress·man**, *n.* member of the U.S. Congress, esp. the House of Representatives.

**con·gru'ous**, *adj.* **1.** congruent. **2.** appropriate. —**con·gru'i·ty**, *n.*

**con·jec'ture**, *n.*, *v.t.*, *v.i.* guess.

**con·join'**, *v.t.*, *v.i.* join together.

**con'ju·gal**, *adj.* marital.

**con'ju·gate''**, *v.t.* give the inflections of a verb. —**con''ju·ga'tion**, *n.*

**con·junc'tion**, *n.* **1.** union or combination. **2.** coincidence. **3.** word linking others in a sentence. —**con·junc'tive**, *adj.*

**con·junc'ture**, *n.* combination of events.

**con'jure**, *v.t.* cause to appear as by magic. —**con'jur·er**, **con'jur·or**, *n.*

**con·nect'**, *v.t.* **1.** join. —*v.i.* **2.** adjoin. —**con·nec'tor**, **con·nec'ter**, *n.* —**con·nec'tive**, *adj.* —**con·nec'tion**, *n.*

**con·nive'**, *v.i.* **1.** conspire. **2.** permit crime, etc. to occur by ignoring it.

**con''nois·seur'**, *n.* person with refined knowledge.

**con·note'**, *v.t.* imply through wording, etc. —**con''no·ta'tion**, *n.*

**con'quer**, *v.t.* overcome, as in war. —**con'quer·or**, *n.*

**con'quest**, *n.* act or instance of conquering.

**con'science**, *n.* inner prompting to do good or repent evil. —**con''sci·en'tious**, *adj.*

**con'scious**, *adj.* **1.** aware of the surrounding world. **2.** aware of some specific thing. **3.** deliberate. —**con'scious·ness**, *n.*

**con'script**, (kahn'skript), *n.* conscripted person. —**con·scrip'tion**, *n.*

**con'se·crate''**, *v.t.* dedicate, as to deity. —**con''se·cra'tion**, *n.*

**con·sec'u·tive**, *adj.* one after the other.

**con·sen'sus**, *n.* general agreement on a question.

**con·sent'**, *n.* **1.** permission. **2.** agreement. —*v.i.* **3.** give permission.

**con'se·quence''**, *n.* result.

**con'se·quent''**, *adj.* resulting.

**con''se·quen'tial**, *adj.* **1.** important. **2.** consequent.

**con·serv'a·tive**, avoiding excesses, etc. —**con·serv'a·tism**, *n.*

**con·serv'a·to'ry**, *n.*, *pl.* **-ries.** **1.** greenhouse. **2.** art or music school.

**con·serve'**, *v.t.* keep from decaying, being squandered, etc.

**con·sid'er**, *v.t.* think of the importance, implications, etc. of.

**con·sid'er·a·ble**, *adj.* rather important.

**con·sid'er·ate**, *adj.* respectful of the feelings of others.

**con·sid''er·a'tion**, *n.* **1.** state of being considerate. **2.** act of considering.

**con·sign'**, *n.* **1.** deliver. **2.** entrust. —**con·sign'ment**, *n.*

**con·sist'**, *v.i.* **1.** be composed. **2.** have essential nature.

**con·sis'ten·cy**, *n.* **1.** agreement with something already done, stated, or implied. **2.** ability to hold together, as of a liquid. —**con·sis'tent**, *adj.* —**con·sis'tent·ly**, *adv.*

**con·sole'**, *v.t.* soothe or cheer in grief or annoyance. —**con''so·la'tion**, *n.*

**con·sol'i·date''**, *v.t.*, *v.i.* unite into a solid; whole. —**con·sol''i·da'tion**, *n.*

**con''som·mé'**, *n.* soup based on a clear meat broth.

**con'so·nant**, *adj.* **1.** in harmony. —*n.* **2.** speech sound other than a vowel. —**con'so·nance**, *n.*

**con·sort'**, *v.i.* (kən sort') **1.** be in company of association. —*n.* (kahn'sort) **2.** spouse of a sovereign.

**con·sor'ti·um**, *n.*, *pl.* **-tia.** international business alliance.

**con·spic'u·ous**, *adj.* **1.** readily observed. **2.** compelling observation.

**con·spire'**, *v.t.* plan secretly as a group. —**con·spir'a·cy**, *n.*

**con'sta·ble**, *n.* policeman.

**con'stant**, *adj.* **1.** continual. **2.** faithful. —**con'stan·cy**, *n.*

**con''stel·la'tion**, *n.* pattern of stars.

**C**
**D**

**con''ster·na'tion**, *n.* horrified shock.

**con·sti·pate''**, *v.t.* impair the movement of the bowels. —**con''sti·pa'tion**, *n.*

**con·stit'u·ent**, *adj.* **1.** forming an essential part. —*n.* **2.** voter. **3.** constituent thing. —**con·stit'u·en·cy**, *n.*

**con'sti·tute''**, *v.t.* **1.** combine to form. **2.** be tantamount to.

**con''sti·tu'tion**, *n.* **1.** fundamental law. **2.** body, esp. as regards health.

**con''sti·tu'tion·al**, *adj.* pertaining to a constitution.

**con·strain'**, *v.t.* compel.

**con·strict'**, *v.t.* force to be narrow. —**con·stric'tion**, *n.*

**con·struct'**, *v.t.* build. —**con·struc'tor**, *n.* —**con·struc'tion**, *n.*

**con·struc'tive**, *adj.* useful or helpful.

**con·strue'**, *v.t.* interpret.

**con'sul**, *n.* government agent in a foreign city who assists his nationals there. —**con'sul·ar**, *adj.* —**con'sul·ate**, *n.*

**con·sult'**, *v.t.* seek advice or information from. —**con''sul·ta'tion**, *n.*

**con·sul'tant**, *n.* person who is consulted.

**con·sume'**, *v.t.* **1.** use up in the process of living, etc. **2.** destroy, as by fire.

**con·sum'er**, *n.* person who uses goods or services for himself rather than in business.

**con·sum'mate**, *adj.* (kən sum'ət) **1.** perfect. —*v.t.* (kahn'səm ất') **2.** complete, esp. the state of marriage by sexual intercourse. —**con''sum·ma'tion**, *n.*

**con·sump'tion**, *n.* **1.** act or instance of consuming. **2.** tuberculosis of the lungs. —**con·sump'tive**, *adj.*

**con'tact**, *n.* **1.** touch. **2.** communication. **3.** connection.

**con·ta'gious**, *adj.* distributed by personal contact, as disease. —**con·ta'gion**, *n.*

**con·tain'**, *v.t.* enclose; include. —**con·tain'er**, *n.*

**con·tam'in·ate''**, *v.t.* spoil the purity of.

**con'tem·plate''**, *v.t.* **1.** regard or think of intently. **2.** anticipate. —**con''tem·pla'tion**, *n.* —**con'tem·pla''tive**, *adj.*

**con''tem·po·rar''y**, *adj., n., pl.*

-**ries**. *adj.* **1.** Also, **con·tem''·po·ra'ne·ous** of the same time. **2.** modern. —*n.* **3.** person or thing of the same age.

**con·tempt'**, *n.* **1.** disapproval involving a feeling of one's own superiority. **2.** defiance, as of a court order. —**con·tempt'i·ble**, *adj.*

**con·tend'**, *v.t.* **1.** assert forcibly. —*v.i.* **2.** fight or be in opposition.

**con·tent'**, *n.* (kahn'tent) **1.** something contained. (kən tent') **2.** contentment. —*adj.* **3.** satisfied. —**con·tent'ed**, *adj.* —**con·tent'ed·ly**, *adv.* —**con·tent'ed·ness**, *n.*

**con·ten'tion**, *n.* **1.** dispute. **2.** argument or assertion.

**con·ten'tious**, *adj.* quarrelsome.

**con·tent'ment**, *n.* contented state.

**con·test'**, *n.* (kahn'test) **1.** competition or fight. —*v.i.* (kən test') **2.** dispute. **3.** fight to gain or hold. —**con·test'ant**, *n.*

**con'text**, *n.* circumstances giving exact meaning.

**con'ti·nent**, *n.* **1.** major land mass. —*adj.* **2.** sexually abstemious. —**con''ti·nen'tal**, *adj.*

**con·tin'gen·cy**, *n., pl.* -**cies**. chance occurrence.

**con·tin'u·al**, *adj.* **1.** repeated without pause. **2.** continuous. —**con·tin'u·al·ly**, *adv.*

**con·tin'ue**, *v.t., v.i.* **1.** not stop. **2.** recommence. **3.** extend. —*v.i.* **4.** remain. —**con·tin''u·a'tion**, *n.* —**con·tin'u·ance**, *n.*

**con·tin'u·ous**, *adj.* uninterrupted. —**con''tin·u'i·ty**, *n.*

**con·tort'**, *v.t.* twist out of shape. —**con·tor'tion**, *n.*

**con'tour**, *n.* outline of a form.

**con'tra·band'**, *n.* goods unlawful to import or export.

**con·tract'**, *n.* (kahn'trakt) **1.** formal business agreement. —*v.t.* (kən trakt') **2.** undertake or establish by contract. **3.** be afflicted with. —*v.i.* **4.** become smaller.

**con'trac·tor**, *n.* person who undertakes work by contract.

**con''tra·dict'**, *v.t.* **1.** declare to be falsely stated. **2.** declare to have not spoken the truth. —**con''tra·dic'tion**, *n.* —**con''tra·dic'to·ry**, *adj.*

**con·tral'to**, *n., pl.* -**tos**. lowest female singing voice.

**con'tra·ry**, *n., pl.* -**ries**, *adj. n.* (kahn'trer ē) **1.** something opposite. —*adj.* **2.** opposite. **3.** (kəntrer'ē) stubborn; perverse. —**contrar'i·ly,** *adv.*

**con·trast',** *v.i.* (kən trast') **1.** reveal differences from another or others. —*n.* (kahn'trast) **2.** act or instance of contrasting. **3.** something notably different.

**con·trib'ute,** *v.t., v.i.* give toward a desired total. —**con·trib'u·tor,** *n.* —**con''tri·bu'tion,** *n.* —**contrib'u·to''ry,** *adj.*

**con·trite',** *adj.* repentant.

**con·trive',** *v.t.* **1.** devise or invent. **2.** bring about. —**con·triv'ance,** *n.*

**con·trol',** *v.t.* **1.** govern or direct. **2.** restrain. —*n.* **3.** ability to control. **4.** Often, **controls,** means of controlling. —**con·trol'la·ble,** *adj.*

**con·trol'ler,** *n.* financial manager.

**con''tro·ver'sy,** *n., pl.* **-sies.** earnest debate. —**con''tro·ver'sial,** *adj.*

**con·tu'sion,** *n.* bruise.

**con''va·lesce',** *v.i.* become better after illness. —**con''va·les'cent,** *n., adj.* —**con''va·les'cence,** *n.*

**con·vene',** *v.i., v.t.* assemble in a meeting.

**con·ven'ience,** *n.* **1.** ease or handiness. **2.** something promoting this. —**con·ven'ient,** *adj.*

**con'vent,** *n.* community of nuns.

**con·ven'tion,** *n.* **1.** assembly of a political party, professional association, etc. **2.** something customary.

**con·ven'tion·al,** *adj.* **1.** ordinary. **2.** customary.

**con·verge',** *v.t., v.i.* join by oblique movement. —**con·ver'gence,** *n.* —**con·ver'gent,** *adj.*

**con·ver'sant,** *adj.* familiar; skilled.

**con''ver·sa'tion,** *n.* informal talk. —**con''ver·sa'tion·al,** *adj.*

**con·verse',** *v.i.* (kən vərs') **1.** carry on a conversation. —*adj.* (kahn'vərs) **2.** in reverse order or position. —*n.* **3.** something converse.

**con·vert',** *v.t.* (kən vərt') **1.** change from one thing or state to another. **2.** acquire a new religion. —*v.i.* **3.** be converted. —*n.* (kahn'vərt) **4.** person with a new religion. —**con·vert'er, con·vert'or,** *n.* —**con·vert'i·ble,** *adj.*

**con·vex',** *adj.* curving outward.

**con·vey',** *v.t.* transport. —**con·vey'**er, **con·vey'or,** *n.* —**con·vey'ance,** *n.*

**con·vict',** *v.t.* (kən vikt') **1.** find guilty. —*n.* (kahn'vikt) **2.** person found guilty.

**con·vic'tion,** *n.* **1.** act or instance of convicting or being convicted. **2.** strongly held belief.

**con·vince',** *v.t.* cause to believe.

**con·viv'i·al,** *adj.* fond of company.

**con·voke',** *v.t.* call to an assembly. —**con''vo·ca'tion,** *n.*

**con·voy',** *n.* (kahn'voi) **1.** ships, etc. with a protective escort. —*v.t.* (kən voi') **2.** escort protectively.

**con·vulse',** *v.t.* **1.** agitate. **2.** rack with laughter or anger. —**con·vul'sion,** *n.* —**con·vul'sive,** *adj.*

**cook,** *v.t., v.i.* prepare (food) by heating. —*n.* **2.** person who cooks. —**cook'book'',** *n.*

**cook'ie,** *n.* small baked sweet cake.

**cool,** *adj.* **1.** slightly cold; not warm. —*v.t.* **2.** make cool. —*v.i.* **3.** become cool. —**cool'ness,** *n.*

**coop,** *n.* shelter for chickens, etc.

**co·op'er·ate',** *v.i.* act in harmony or together with others. —**co''op'er·a'tion,** *n.*

**co·op'er·a·tive,** *adj.* **1.** willing to cooperate. **2.** jointly owned by the users. —*n.* **3.** cooperative store, etc.

**co·or'di·nate,** *adj.* (ko''or'də nət) **1.** equal in importance. *v.t.* (ko''or'də nāt'') **2.** put in proper interaction.

**co''or·di·na'tion,** *n.* proper interaction, esp. of the limbs or muscles.

**cop,** *Informal. n.* policeman.

**cope,** *v.i.* attack and overcome a problem or emergency.

**co'pi·ous,** *adj.* abundant.

**cop'per,** *n.* reddish metallic element.

**cop'y,** *n., pl.* **ies,** *n.* **1.** imitation of an original. **2.** individual published book. **3.** words to be printed. —*v.t.* **4.** make or be a copy of.

**cop'y·right'',** *n.* exclusive right to publish a book or license its publication.

**cor'al,** *n.* hardened skeletons of a marine animal.

**cord,** *n.* strong string.

**cor'dial,** *adj.* **1.** warmly friendly. —*n.* **2.** liqueur. —**cor''di·al'i·ty,** *n.*

**cor'don,** *n.* **1.** circle of guards. —*v.t.* **2.** put a cordon around.

**cor´du·roy´´**, n. ribbed cotton.

**core**, n. central part or element.

**cork**, n. 1. bark of an oak tree. 2. stopper made of this bark.

**cork´screw´´**, n. augerlike device for pulling corks.

**corn**, n. 1. American plant with kernels on a cob. 2. small hard seed of a cereal plant. 3. painful growth on the foot. —**corn´-starch´´**, n.

**cor·ne·a**, n. outer coating of the eyeball.

**cor´ner**, n. 1. angular junction. —v.t. 2. trap in a corner. 3. get a monopoly on.

**cor·net´**, n. trumpetlike musical instrument.

**cor´nice**, n. major horizontal molding on or at the top of a wall.

**cor´´o·na´tion**, n. installation of a monarch.

**cor´o·ner**, n. official who investigates suspicious deaths.

**cor´´o·net´**, n. crown of a noble.

**cor´po·ral**, adj. 1. bodily. —n. 2. lowest noncommissioned military officer.

**cor´po·rate**, adj. pertaining to organizations.

**cor´´po·ra´tion**, n. 1. business organization existing as an entity apart from its members. 2. municipal government.

**corpse**, n. dead body.

**corps** (kor), n., pl. **corps** (korz). military branch.

**cor´pu·lence**, n. fatness. —**cor´-pu·lent**, adj.

**cor´pus·cle** (kor´pus əl), n. blood or lymph cell.

**cor·rect´**, adj. 1. accurate. 2. according to rules. —v.t. 3. make correct. —**cor·rec´tion**, n. —**cor·rec´tive**, adj.

**cor´re·late´´**, v.t. 1. put into a mutual relationship. —v.i. 2. have a mutual relationship. —**cor´re·la´tion**, n.

**cor´re·spond´´**, v.i. 1. write or exchange letters, news, etc. 2. match. —**cor´re·spond´ence**, n. —**cor´re·spond´ent**, n. n.

**cor´ri·dor´´**, n. narrow passageway.

**cor·rob´o·rate´´**, v.t. support or confirm with evidence, etc. —**cor·rob´o·ra´tion**, n.

**cor·rode´**, v.t., v.i. decay, esp. by chemical action. —**cor·ro´sion**, n.

**cor´ru·gate´´**, v.t., v.i. bend into parallel ridges and furrows.

**cor·rupt´**, adj. 1. impure. —v.t. 2. make corrupt. —**cor·rupt´i·ble**, adj. —**cor·rup´tion**, n.

**cor·sage´** (kor sahz´), n. small bouquet for a party dress.

**cor´set**, n. garment for shaping the torso.

**cor·tege´**, n. ceremonial procession.

**cos·met´ic**, n. 1. preparation applied to the body to improve its appearance. —adj. 2. improving outer appearance.

**cos´mic**, adj. pertaining to the cosmos.

**cos´´mo·pol´i·tan**, adj. belonging to the entire world.

**cos´mos**, n. the entire universe.

**cost**, v.t. 1. require or exact as specified. —n. 2. something given up in exchange.

**cost´ly**, adj., -lier, -liest. costing much.

**cos´tume**, n. dress, esp. of a special or unusual kind.

**cot**, n. narrow folding bed.

**cot´tage**, n. small house.

**cot´ton**, n. fiber from a plant of the mallow family.

**couch**, n. bedlike article of furniture.

**cough**, n. 1. loud expulsion of breath from the lungs, as to clear the throat. —v.i. 2. emit a cough.

**coun´cil**, n. body of legislators, advisors, etc.

**coun´sel**, v.t. 1. advise. 2. legal representative. 3. advice. —**coun´se·lor, coun´sel·lor**, n.

**count**, v.t. 1. note one by one to get a total. —n. 2. act or instance of counting. 3. continental European nobleman equal to an earl.

**coun´te·nance**, n. face, esp. with regard to expression.

**count´er**, n. 1. person or thing that counts. 2. tablelike surface for serving, displaying goods, etc.

**coun´ter**, —adj. 1. opposed. —adv. 2. in opposition. —**coun´-ter·act´**, v.t. —**coun´ter·at-tack´´**, v.t., v.i., n. —**coun´ter·bal´´ance**, v.t., n.

**coun´ter·feit´´**, v.t. 1. imitate closely, esp. money. —adj. 2. having been counterfeited. —n. 3. something counterfeit.

**coun´ter·mand´´**, v.t. cancel with a contrary order.

**coun´ter·part´´**, n. 1. similar person or thing. 2. duplicate.

**count´ess**, n. wife of a count or earl.

C
D

**count'less**, *adj.* innumerable.

**coun'try**, *n.*, *pl.* **-tries. 1.** rural area. **2.** land of which one is a citizen. **3.** region. —**coun'try man**, *n.*

**coun'try·side"**, *n.* rural terrain.

**coun'ty**, *n.* political division of a U.S. state.

**coup de grace** (koō'de grahs'), something putting an end to a miserable existence.

**coupe** (koō pā'), *n.* two-door hardtop car.

**cou'ple**, *n.* **1.** pair. —*v.t.*, *v.i.* **2.** join one to the another. —**coup'ling**, *n.*

**cou'pon**, *n.* valuable certificate to be cut or detached from a bond, advertisement, etc.

**cour'age**, *n.* bravery or fortitude. —**cou·ra'geous**, *adj.*

**cou'ri·er**, *n.* messenger.

**course**, *n.* **1.** path or direction of a moving thing. **2.** natural progress or outcome. **3.** phase of a meal. **4.** program of instruction in one subject.

**court**, *n.* **1.** Also, **court'yard**, area surrounded by buildings. —*v.t.* **2.** woo. —**court'house"**, *n.* —**court'room"**, *n.*

**cour'te·ous**, *adj.* polite.

**cour'te·san**, *n.* prostitute.

**cour'te·sy**, *n.*, *pl.* **-sies.** politeness.

**cour'ti·er**, *n.* member of a royal court.

**court'ly**, *adj.*, **-lier**, **-liest.** worthy of a royal court, esp. in manner.

**court'-mar'tial**, *n.*, *pl.* **courts-martial**, military court or trial.

**court'ship"**, *n.* wooing.

**cous'in**, *n.* offspring of an uncle or aunt.

**cove**, *n.* small inlet or bay.

**cove'nant**, *n.* agreement.

**cov'er**, *v.t.* **1.** put a lid, shelter, etc. over. **2.** conceal. —*n.* **3.** something that covers. —**cov'er·age**, *n.* —**cov'er·ing**, *n.*

**cov'er·let**, *n.* bedspread.

**cov'er-up"**, *n.* plot to conceal guilt or guilty actions.

**cov'et**, *v.t.* desire enviously. —**cov'et·ous**, *adj.*

**cow**, *n.* four-footed milk-giving animal. —**cow'hide"**, *n.*

**cow'ard**, *n.* person without courage. —**cow'ard·ly**, *adj.*, *adv.* —**cow'ard·ice**, *n.*

**cow'boy"**, *n.* ranch worker. Also, **cow'hand"**.

**cow'er**, *v.i.* cringe.

**coy**, *adj.* affectedly shy.

**coy·o'te**, *n.* small North American wolf.

**co'zy**, *adj.*, **-zier**, **-ziest.** snug and comfortable.

**crab**, *n.* four-legged crustacean.

**crab'ap'ple**, *n.* small, sour apple.

**crack**, *v.i.*, *v.t.* **1.** break across abruptly. —*n.* **2.** act or instance of cracking. **3.** narrow break or opening.

**crack'er**, *n.* crisp wafer.

**crack'pot"**, *n. Informal.* person with delusions.

**cra'dle**, *n.* rocking, high-sided bed for a baby.

**craft**, *n.*, *pl.* **crafts** (for 1), **craft** (for 2). **1.** cunning. **2.** vehicle for movement through water or air.

**crafts'man**, *n.* skilled handworker. —**crafts'man·ship"**, *n.*

**craft'y**, *adj.* **-ier**, **-iest.** cunning.

**cram**, *v.t.* **1.** pack tightly or excessively. —*v.i.* **2.** *Informal.* study in a hasty, superficial way.

**cramp**, *n.* painful muscular contraction.

**crane**, *n.* **1.** long-legged, long-billed water bird. **2.** hoisting machine.

**crank**, *n.* **1.** rotating device incorporating a lever. **2.** *Informal.* person with an ill temper or delusion. —*v.t.* **3.** move with a crank.

**crank'y**, *adj.*, **-ier**, **-iest.** ill-tempered.

**cran'ny**, *n.*,

**craps**, *n.* dice game.

**crash**, *n.* **1.** destructive collision, fall, etc. **2.** coarse linen. —*v.i.* **3.** suffer a crash. —*v.t.* **4.** cause to have or produce a crash.

**crate**, *n.* wooden shipping case.

**cra'ter**, *n.* pit in the ground made by volcanic eruption, meteors, bombs, etc.

**crave**, *v.t.* desire or request eagerly. —**crav'ing**, *n.*

**crawl**, *v.i.* **1.** move on several legs with the body horizontal. —*n.* **2.** crawling movement.

**cray'on**, *n.* stick of pigmented material for making lines or tones.

**craze**, *v.t.* make insane.

**cra'zy**, *adj.*, **-zier**, **-ziest.** insane.

**creak**, *v.i.* make a squeak or groan from bending or rubbing.

**cream**, *n.* **1.** richer part of milk. **2.** substance with a creamlike or salvelike consistency. —**cream'y**, *adj.*

**C D**

**cream′er,** n. cream pitcher.

**crease,** n. **1.** ridge made by pressing. —v.t. **2.** make a crease or creases in.

**cre·ate′,** v.t. **1.** bring into existence. **2.** bring about. —**cre·a′tion,** n.

**cre·a′tive,** adj. **1.** pertaining to creation. **2.** of an original mind; inventive.

**cre·a′tor,** n. **1.** person who creates. **2. the Creator,** God.

**cre·den′tials,** n. documentation proving authority, identity, etc.

**cred′i·ble,** adj. able to be believed.

**cred′it,** n. **1.** money paid or owed to one. **2.** praise or good reputation. —v.t. **3.** believe.

**cred′it·a·ble,** adj. deserving of credit.

**cred′i·tor,** n. person to whom a debt is owed.

**cred′u·lous,** adj. too ready to believe things. —**cre·du′li·ty,** n.

**creed,** n. formally stated belief.

**creek,** n. small stream.

**creep,** v.i. crawl.

**cre·mate′,** v.t. burn at a funeral. —**cre·ma′tion,** n. —**cre·ma·to′ry, cre′ma·to′ri·um,** n.

**cres′cent,** n. shape like that of a new moon.

**crest,** n. uppermost edge or feature.

**crest′fal′len,** adj. abashed.

**cre·vasse′,** n. crevice, esp. in a glacier.

**crev′ice,** n. deep, narrow gap.

**crew,** n. labor force, esp. on a ship.

**crib,** n. **1.** small child's bed with high slatted sides. **2.** receptacle for corn, animal fodder, etc.

**crick′et,** n. grasshopperlike insect.

**crime,** n. violation of the law.

**crim′in·al,** adj. **1.** pertaining to or guilty of crime. —n. **2.** committer of crimes.

**crim′son,** n. deep red.

**cringe,** v.i. crouch or draw back from fear.

**crin′kle,** v.t., v.i. **1.** wrinkle. **2.** rustle, as crisp paper.

**crip′ple,** v.t. **1.** deprive of the use of arms or legs. —n. **2.** crippled person.

**cri′sis,** n., pl. **-ses.** point that determines a good or bad outcome.

**crisp,** n. **1.** brittle. **2.** clear; fresh.

**cri·ter′i·on,** n., pl. **-ions, -ia.** basis for judgment.

**crit′ic,** n. person who evaluates good and bad qualities.

**crit′i·cal,** adj. **1.** pertaining to crises. **2.** fault-finding.

**crit′i·cize′,** v.t. **1.** evaluate. **2.** find fault with. —**crit′i·cism,** n.

**croak,** v.i. **1.** make a deep froglike noise. —n. **2.** croaking sound.

**cro·chet** (krō shā′), v.t. make with a hooked needle and thread.

**crock,** n. earthenware vessel. —**crock′er·y,** n.

**croc′o·dile′,** n. large tropical river reptile.

**crook,** n. **1.** hooked staff. **2.** curve. **3.** Informal. thief.

**crook′ed,** adj. **1.** full of bends. **2.** dishonest.

**croon,** v.i., v.t. sing or hum in low, sweet sounds.

**crop,** n. **1.** yield at a harvest. **2.** whip.

**cro·quet** (krō kā′), n. lawn game with balls driven by mallets.

**cro·quette′,** n. deep-fried piece of ground meat, etc.

**cross,** n. **1.** upright with a side-to-side beam as a symbol of Christianity. **2.** mixture of breeds. —v.t. **3.** go across. —adj. **4.** ill-tempered. —**cross′breed′,** v.t., n. —**cross′road′,** n. —**cross′roads′,** n., sing. —**cross′wise′, cross′ways′,** adv. —**cross′ly,** adv.

**crotch,** n. **1.** place where a tree limb branches from a larger one. **2.** place where the legs meet.

**crotch′et,** n. eccentric whim or attitude. —**crotch′et·y,** adj.

**crouch,** v.i., n. stoop or squat.

**croup,** n. inflammation of respiratory passages.

**crow,** v.i. **1.** cry like a rooster. —n. **2.** crowing sound.

**crowd,** n. **1.** large, random group. —v.i. **2.** push one's way.

**crown,** n. **1.** symbol of sovereignty. —v.t. **2.** give a crown to.

**cru′cial,** adj. decisive.

**cru′ci·ble,** n. melting pot.

**cru′ci·fix′,** n. image of the Christian cross.

**cru′ci·fy′,** v.t. nail to a cross as punishment. —**cru′ci·fix′ion,** n.

**crude,** adj. **1.** unrefined or unfinished. **2.** boorish. —**crud′i·ty,** n.

**cru′el,** adj. **1.** causing suffering. **2.** desiring to cause suffering. —**cru′el·ty,** n.

**cru′et,** n. small bottle for oil, vinegar, etc.

**cruise,** v.i. **1.** travel slowly, as for

recreation or inspection. —n. **2.** act or instance of cruising.

**cruis'er**, n. large, lightly armored warship.

**crumb**, n. small fragment, esp. from dough.

**crum'ble**, v.t., v.i. break or drop in pieces.

**crum'ple**, v.i., v.t. collapse into wrinkles.

**crunch**, v.t. crush, chew, grind, etc. with a brittle sound.

**cru·sade'**, n. **1.** Christian campaign to recover the tomb of Christ from the Muslims. —**cru·sad'er**, n.

**crush**, v.t. **1.** break or squeeze with pressure. —n. **2.** crowd. —**crush'er**, n.

**crust**, n. hardened outer surface. —**crust'y**, adj.

**crus·ta'cean**, n. sea animal with jointed feet and a hard outer shell.

**crutch**, n. prop for a lame person.

**crux**, n., pl. **cruxes, cruces.** decisive feature or aspect.

**cry**, v.i., n., pl. **cries.** v.i. **1.** weep loudly. **2.** utter a call. —n. **3.** act or instance of crying.

**cryp'tic**, adj. defying interpretation.

**cryp·tog'ra·phy**, n. encoding and decoding of messages, etc.

**crys'tal**, n. geometrically formed fused mineral, sugar, etc. —**crys'tal·line**, adj. —**crys'tal·lize''**, v.t., v.i.

**cub**, n. young animal.

**cube**, n. solid with six square sides. —**cu'bic**, adj. —**cu'bi·cal**, adj.

**cu'bi·cle**, n. small alcove.

**cuck'oo''**, n. bird with a two-note call.

**cu'cum''ber**, n. long, green fruit used in salads or as pickles.

**cud**, n. food chewed by cows, etc. after regurgitation.

**cud'dle**, v.t. **1.** hold and caress. —v.i. **2.** lie or curl up snugly.

**cudg'el**, n. short club.

**cue**, n. signal for speech or action.

**cuff**, n. feature terminating a sleeve or trouser leg.

**cui·sine''**, n. manner of cooking.

**cu'li·nar''y**, adj. pertaining to cooking.

**cull**, v.t. select.

**cul'mi·nate''**, v.i. reach a final development. —**cul'mi·na'tion**, n.

**cul'pa·ble**, adj. at fault.

**cul'prit**, n. **1.** accused person. **2.** guilty person.

**cult**, n. religious sect. —**cult'ist**, n.

**cul'ti·vate''**, v.t. work on to grow crops.

**cul'ti·va'tion**, n. **1.** development of culture, manners, etc. **2.** act or instance of cultivating.

**cul'ture**, n. society, esp. with regard to its art or technology. —**cul'tur·al**, adj.

**cum'ber·some**, adj. heavy; burdensome.

**cu'mu·la''tive**, adj. increasing from additions.

**cun'ning**, adj. **1.** crafty; sly. **2.** clever; skillful. —n. **3.** craftiness; slyness. **4.** skill.

**cup**, n. small bowllike drinking utensil.

**cup'board**, n. storage cabinet, esp. for dishes or food.

**cu·pid'i·ty**, n. greed; avarice.

**cu·ra'tor**, n. custodian or director of a museum department.

**curb**, n. **1.** Also, **curb'ing,** edge of a sidewalk. **2.** something that restrains. —v.t. **3.** check or restrain.

**cur'dle**, v.t., v.i. form into curds.

**cure**, n. **1.** method of remedial treatment, esp. for disease. **2.** recovery from disease. —v.t. **3.** restore to health; heal. **4.** preserve, as food.

**cur'few**, n. ban on being out late.

**cu·ric'u·lum**, n. pl. **-lums, -la.** program of studies.

**cu·ri·o** (kyŏŏr′ē ō′′), n. small beautiful or rare object.

**cu'ri·ous** (kyŏŏr′ē as), adj. **1.** inquisitive. **2.** odd. —**cu'ri·ous·ly**, adv. —**cu''ri·os'i·ty**, n.

**curl**, v.t., v.i. **1.** form into spiral shapes; coil. —n. **2.** something with a curved or twisted form. —**curl'y**, adj.

**cur'rant**, n. **1.** small seedless raisin. **2.** acid edible berry of a wild shrub.

**cur'ren·cy**, n. money.

**cur'rent**, adj. **1.** happening in the present. —n. **2.** continuous movement of a fluid. —**cur'rent·ly**, adv.

**cur'ry**, n. spicy condiment.

**curse**, n. **1.** prayer, etc. invoking harm to another. —v.t. **2.** make the object of a curse.

**cur'sor**, n. indicator on a computer monitor showing where the next input will appear.

**cur·so'ry**, adj. hasty or superficial.

**curt**, adj. rude; abrupt. —**curt'ly**, adv.

**cur·tail'**, *v.t.* cut short.

**cur'tain**, *n.* cloth hanging before a window, theater stage, etc.

**curt'sy**, *n.* woman's bow in which the knees are bent.

**cur'va·ture**, *n.* curve.

**curve**, *n.* continuous line continually changing direction.

**cush'ion**, *n.* soft pad for support.

**cus'tard**, *n.* sweet milk and egg mixture that sets after cooking.

**cus'to·dy**, *n., pl.* **-dies.** guardianship; care. 2. legal restraint; imprisonment. **—cus·to'di·an,** *n.*

**cus'tom**, *n.* habitual practice or manner of thinking. **—cus'tom·ar''y**, *adj.* **—cus'tom·ar'i·ly**, *adv.*

**cus'to·mer**, *n.* buyer; purchaser.

**cut**, *v.t.* 1. divide or penetrate with something sharp. 2. form with sharp tools. 3. terminate abruptly. **—***n.* 4. act or instance of cutting.

**cute**, *adj.* attractive; pretty.

**cu'ti·cle**, *n.* outer layer of skin.

**cut'ler·y**, *n.* cutting tools, esp. for food.

**cut'let**, *n.* slice or patty of food for frying or broiling.

**cut'ter**, *n.* 1. person or implement for cutting. 2. ship's boat with oars. 3. Coast Guard ship.

**cy'cle**, *n.* 1. repeated series. 2. two-wheeled vehicle. **—***v.i.* 3. ride a cycle. **—cy'clist,** *n.*

**cy'clone**, *n.* storm with rotating winds.

**cyl'in·der**, *n.* 1. solid generated by a rectangle rotated on its centerline. 2. expansion chamber in an engine. **—cy·lin'dri·cal,** *adj.*

**cym·bal** (sim'bal), *n.* one of a pair of concave brass or bronze plates struck together.

**cyn'ic**, *n.* person who sees all actions as selfishly motivated. **—cyn'i·cal**, *adj.* **—cyn·i·cism** (sin'ə siz''əm), *n.*

**cy'press**, *n.* scaly-leaved evergreen tree.

**cyst**, *n.* abnormal sac or growth, usually filled with fluid.

**cza·ri'na**, *n.* wife of a czar.

**czar** (zar), *n.* Slavic emperor. Also *fem.,* **cza·ri'na.**

# D

**D, d**, *n.* fourth letter of the English alphabet.

**dab**, *v.t.* touch or apply lightly.

**dab'ble**, *v.i.* be superficially active.

**daf'fo·dil''**, *n.* plant with yellow flowers and long leaves.

**daft**, *adj.* 1. insane. 2. silly.

**dag'ger**, *n.* short pointed weapon.

**dahl'ia**, *n.* showy perennial flowering plant.

**dai'ly**, *adj., n., pl.* **-lies.** *adj.* 1. happening each day. **—***n.* 2. daily periodical.

**dain'ty**, *adj.,* **-tier, -tiest.** delicate; fine.

**dair'y**, *n., pl.* **-ies.** place where milk and milk products are produced. **—dair'y·man,** *n.*

**da·is** (dā'is), *n., pl.* **-ises.** raised platform.

**dai'sy**, *n., pl.* **-sies.** flower with a yellow diskshaped centre and white petals.

**dale**, *n.* valley.

**dal'ly**, *v.i.* 1. play in a loving way. 2. delay; waste time.

**dam**, *n.* 1. barrier to hold back water. **—***v.t.* 2. obstruct, as with a dam.

**dam'age**, *n.* 1. injury. 2. **damages,** compensation for injury. **—***v.t.* 3. injure; harm.

**dam'ask**, *n.* fabric woven in patterns.

**damn**, *v.t.* condemn. **—dam·na'tion,** *n.*

**damp**, *adj.* moist. **—damp'ness,** *n.*

**damp'en**, *v.t.* 1. make damp. 2. deaden or depress, as the spirits.

**dance**, *v.i.* 1. move one's body and feet in rhythm, esp. to music. **—***n.* 2. social gathering for dancing. **—dancer,** *n.*

**dan·de·li'on**, *n.* weedy plant with yellow flowers.

**dan'druff**, *n.* scales that form on the scalp and fall off.

**dan'dy**, *n., pl.* **-dies,** *adj.,* **-dier, -diest.** *n.* 1. man overly particular about his appearance. —*adj.* 2. *Informal.* very good.

**dan′ger**, *n.* exposure to harm; risk. —**dan′ger·ous**, *adj.*

**dan′gle**, *v.i., v.t.* hang loosely.

**dank**, *adj.* unpleasantly moist.

**dap′per**, *adj.* 1. neat. 2. small and active.

**dare**, *v.i.* have the necessary courage or audacity. —**dar′ing**, *adj., n.*

**dark**, *adj.* 1. having little or no light. —*n.* 2. absence of light. —**dark′en**, *v.t., v.i.* —**dark′ness**, *n.*

**dar′ling**, *n.* 1. person dear to another. —*adj.* 2. very dear; cherished.

**darn**, *v.t.* mend by weaving rows of stitches.

**dart**, *n.* 1. small pointed missile usually thrown by hand. —*v.t., v.i.* 2. move suddenly and swiftly.

**dash**, *v.t.* 1. hurl violently. —*v.i.* 2. rush; sprint. —*n.* 3. short race.

**dash′board″**, *n.* instrument panel.

**dash′ing**, *adj.* 1. lively. 2. showy; stylish.

**da′′ta**, *n. pl.* 1. facts; figures. 2. (computers) information stored in a memory.

**da′′ta·base**, *n.* (computers) a structured file facilitating data access and manipulation.

**date**, *n.* 1. day of the month. 2. appointment. 3. sweet, fleshy fruit of a palm tree. —*v.t.* 4. give a date to.

**daub**, *v.t.* cover or smear with a soft, muddy substance.

**daugh′ter**, *n.* female child. —**daugh′ter·ly**, *adj.*

**daugh′ter-in-law″**, *n., pl.* **daughters-in-law.** son's wife.

**daunt**, *v.t.* frighten; dishearten. —**daunt′less**, *adj.*

**daw′dle**, *v.i.* waste time. —**daw′dler**, *n.*

**dawn**, *v.i.* 1. begin to grow light in the morning. —*n.* 2. break of day.

**day**, *n.* 1. period between sunrise and sunset. 2. period of earth's rotation on its axis.

**day′dream″**, *n.* 1. period of pleasant, dreamy thought. —*v.t.* 2. have daydreams.

**day′light″**, *n.* 1. light of day. 2. openness.

**daze**, *v.t.* 1. stun; bewilder. —*n.* 2. stunned condition.

**daz′zle**, *v.t.* overwhelm with intense light.

**dea′con**, *n.* cleric just below a priest in rank.

**dead**, *adj.* no longer alive.

**dead′line″**, *n.* latest time by which something must be completed.

**dead′lock″**, *n.* 1. frustrated standstill. —*v.t., v.i.* 2. bring or come to a deadlock.

**dead′ly**, *adj.,* **-lier, -liest.** 1. likely to cause death. 2. typical of death. —**dead′li·ness**, *n.*

**deaf**, *adj.* incapable of hearing. —**deaf′ness**, *n.* —**deaf′en**, *v.t.*

**deal**, *v.t.* 1. portion out. 2. administer, as a blow. —*v.i.* 3. do or have business. 4. portion out cards, etc. —*n.* 5. business transaction or agreement. —**deal′er**, *n.*

**dean**, *n.* college official who supervises students or faculty.

**dear**, *adj.* 1. beloved. 2. expensive. —*n.* 3. beloved person. —**dear′ly**, *adv.*

**dearth** (dərth), *n.* scarcity; lack.

**death**, *n.* 1. act of dying. 2. state of being dead. —**death′less**, *adj.* —**death′like″**, *adj.* —**death′ly**, *adj., adv.*

**de·base′**, *v.t.* lower in value.

**de·bate′**, *v.t.* 1. discuss; argue. —*n.* 2. discussion of opposing views. —**de·bat′a·ble**, *adj.*

**de·bauch′**, *v.t.* 1. corrupt; seduce. —*n.* 2. debauchery; seduction. —**de·bil′i·tate′**, *v.t.* weaken. —**de·bil′i·ta′tion**, *n.*

**de·bil′i·ty**, *n., pl.* **-ties.** weakness.

**deb′it**, *n.* recorded debt.

**deb′o·nair′**, *adj.* 1. courteous; pleasantly mannered. 2. carefree.

**de·bris′** (də brē′), *n.* rubbish; remains.

**debt**, *n.* 1. something owed. 2. condition of owing. —**debt′or**, *n.*

**deb′u·tante″**, *n.* girl making a society debut.

**de·but′** (də byōō′), *n.* 1. first public appearance. 2. formal introduction into society.

**dec′ade**, *n.* ten-year period.

**dec′a·dence**, *n.* decay; deterioration. —**dec′a·dent**, *adj., n.*

**de·cant′er**, *n.* ornamental bottle, esp. for wine.

**de·cap′i·tate′**, *v.t.* behead.

**de·cay′**, *v.i., v.t.* 1. deteriorate; rot. —*n.* 2. deterioration.

**de·cease′**, *n.* 1. death. —*v.i.* 2. die. —**de·ceased′**, *adj., n.*

**de·ceit′**, *n.* lying; fraud. —**de·ceit′ful**, *adj.*

**de·ceive′**, *v.t.* mislead.

**de·cent**, *adj.* 1. appropriate. 2. not offensive to modesty. 3. respectable. 4. adequate. —**de′cent·ly**, *adv.* —**de′cen·cy**, *n.*

**de·cen·tral·ize**, *v.t.* free from dependency on a central authority, source, etc. —**de·cen′tral·i·za′tion**, *n.*

**de·cep′tion**, *n.* 1. act or instance of deceiving. 2. fraud. —**de·cep′tive**, *adj.*

**de·cide′**, *v.t.* reach a decision regarding.

**dec′i·mal**, *adj.* 1. based on the number ten. —*n.* 2. decimal fraction.

**de·ci′pher**, *v.t.* determine the meaning of.

**de·ci′sion**, *n.* 1. choice or judgment. 2. emphasis; firmness.

**de·ci′sive**, *adj.* 1. determining an outcome or conclusion. 2. emphatic; firm. —**de·ci′sive·ly**, *adv.* —**de·ci′sive·ness**, *n.*

**deck**, *n.* 1. floor of a ship, bridge, etc. 2. pack of playing cards.

**de·clare′**, *v.t.* 1. make known. 2. say emphatically. —**de·clar′a·tive**, *adj.* —**dec″la·ra′tion**, *n.*

**de·clen′sion**, *n.* 1. grammatical inflection of nouns, pronouns, or adjectives. 2. decline.

**de·cline′**, *v.t.*, *v.i.* 1. bend or slope downward. 2. refuse. —*v.i.* 3. give grammatical inflections. —*n.* 4. deterioration.

**de″com·pose′**, *v.t.*, *v.i.* 1. break up into parts. 2. decay. —**de″com·po·si′tion**, *n.*

**de·cor′**, *n.* style of decoration.

**dec′o·rate′**, *v.t.* adorn. —**dec′o·ra′tive**, *adj.* —**dec′o·ra′tor**, *n.* —**dec″o·ra′tion**, *n.*

**dec′o·rous**, *adj.* proper.

**de·co′rum**, *n.* propriety.

**de·coy′**, *n.* 1. artificial bird used as a lure in hunting. 2. lure. —*v.t.* 3. lure into a trap.

**de·crease′**, *v.t.*, *v.i.* 1. gradually lessen. —*n.* 2. lessening.

**de·cree′**, *n.* 1. edict. —*v.t.* 2. ordain by decree.

**de·crep′it**, *adj.* worn by old age or long use.

**de·cry′**, *v.t.* denounce.

**ded′i·cate′**, *v.t.* 1. set apart; devote. 2. inscribe. —**ded″i·ca′tion**, *n.*

**de·duce′**, *v.t.* infer; derive.

**de·duct′**, *v.t.* subtract; take away.

**de·duc′tion**, *n.* 1. act or result of reasoning from the general to the

specific. 2. amount deducted. —**de·duc′tive**, *adj.*

**deed**, *n.* 1. something that is done; an act. 2. legal conveyance esp. of land.

**deem**, *v.t.*, *v.i.* believe; adjudge.

**deep**, *adj.* extending far downward or inward. —**deep′en**, *v.t.*, *v.i.* —**deep′ly**, *adv.*

**deer**, *n.*, *pl.* **deer**, **deers**. ruminant animal, the males of which have antlers or horns.

**de·face′**, *v.t.* mar; disfigure.

**de·fame′**, *v.t.* attack the reputation of; slander. —**def″am·a′tion**, *n.* —**de·fam′a·to′ry**, *adj.*

**de·fault′**, *n.* 1. failure, esp. to pay a debt. —*v.t.*, *v.i.* 2. fail, esp. to pay, when required.

**de·feat′**, *v.t.* 1. overthrow; conquer. —*n.* 2. act or instance of defeating.

**de·fect′**, *n.* 1. (dē′fekt, dē fekt′) imperfection; fault. —*v.i.* (dē fekt′) 2. desert a cause, esp. to join another. —**de·fec′tive**, *adj.* —**de·fec′tion**, *n.* —**de·fec′tor**, *n.*

**de·fend′**, *v.t.* 1. protect; guard against attack. 2. support with one's words. —**de·fend′er**, *n.*

**de·fend′ant**, *n.* Law. accused person.

**de·fense′**, *n.* 1. protection against attack. 2. justification. 3. Law. reply to a charge. —**de·fense′·less**, *adj.* —**de·fen′si·ble**, *adj.*

**de·fen′sive**, *adj.* 1. pertaining to defense. 2. anxious to justify oneself. —*n.* 3. situation of a defender.

**de·fer′**, *v.t.*, *v.i.* 1. postpone. —*v.i.* 2. yield politely. —**de·fer′ment**, *n.* —**def′er·ence**, *n.* —**de″fer′ra′tion**, *n.*

**de·fi′ance**, *n.* open disregard of or bold resistance to authority. —**de·fi′ant**, *adj.*

**de·fi′cien·cy**, *n.*, *pl.* **-cies**. lack; inadequate amount. —**de·fi′cient**, *adj.*

**def′i·cit**, *n.* deficiency, esp. of assets.

**de·file′**, *v.t.* 1. desecrate. 2. make filthy. —**de·file′ment**, *n.*

**de·fine′**, *v.t.* 1. state the meaning of. 2. determine. —**def′i·ni′tion**, *n.*

**def′i·nite**, *adj.* exact.

**de·fin′i·tive**, *adj.* conclusive.

**de·flate′**, *v.t.*, *v.i.* 1. collapse by releasing air. 2. increase in purchasing power. —de·fla'tion, n. —de·fla'tion·ar'y, adj.

de·flect', v.t., v.i. turn from a course; swerve. —de·flec'tion, n.

de·form', v.t. 1. mar the form of. 2. make ugly. —de·form'i·ty, n.

de·fraud', v.t. cheat; take rights or property of by fraud.

de·fray', v.t. pay, as expenses.

de·frost', v.t., v.i. free or be freed of ice.

deft, adj. skillful.

de·fy', v.t. 1. openly resist. 2. challenge.

de·gen·er·ate, adj. (dē·jen'ər ət) 1. deteriorated. —v.i. (dē·jen'ər āt) 2. deteriorate. —de·gen'er·a'tion, n.

de·grade', v.t. reduce in quality or rank. —de"gra·da'tion, n.

de·gree', n. 1. unit of temperature. 2. 360th of a circle.

de·i·fy', v.t. make a god of.

deign, v.t., v.i. condescend.

de·i·ty, n., pl. -ties. god or goddess.

de·ject', v.t. dishearten. —de·jec'tion, n.

de·lay', v.t. 1. hinder; make late. —v.i. 2. linger; procrastinate.

de·lec'ta·ble, adj. delightful; delicious.

del·e·gate, n. (del'ə gāt) 1. representative. —v.t. (del'ə gāt) 2. send as a representative. —del'e·ga'tion, n.

de·lete', v.t. remove from a text.

de·lib·er·ate, v.t.i., v.i. (dē lib'ər āt) 1. ponder. —adj. (dē·lib'ər ət) 2. intentional. 3. unhurried. —de·lib'er·ate·ly, adv. —de·lib'er·a'tion, n.

del'i·ca·cy, n., pl. -cies. 1. fineness of quality. 2. choice food.

del'i·cate, adj. 1. fine in quality or texture. 2. easily damaged. 3. considerate; tactful. 4. functioning precisely. —del'i·cate·ly, adv.

de·li'cious, adj. 1. pleasing to taste. 2. delectable.

de·light', v.t., v.i. 1. give great pleasure. —n. 2. joy or great pleasure. —de·light'ed, adj. —de·light'ful, adj.

de·lin'e·ate', v.t. trace the outline of. —de·lin"e·a'tion, n.

de·lin'quent, adj. 1. neglectful of duty or law. 2. late, as a debt. —n. 3. delinquent person. —de·lin'quen·cy, n.

de·lir'i·um, n. temporary excited mental disorder. —de·lir'i·ous, adj.

de·liv'er, v.t. 1. set free or save. 2. hand over. 3. assist at the birth of. 4. present to an audience. 5. distribute. —de·liv'er·ance, n. —de·liv'er·y, n.

del'ta, n. deposit of soil formed at a divided river mouth.

de·lude', v.t. mislead.

del·uge (del'yōōj), n., v.t. flood.

de·lu'sion, n. false conception, esp. one persistent and opposed toreason.

delve, v.i. dig.

de·mand', v.t. 1. ask for boldly; claim as a right. 2. require. —n. 3. act or instance of demanding. 4. thing demanded.

de·mean', v.t. debase; humble.

de·mean'or, n. behavior or conduct.

de·mer'it, n. 1. mark against a person for a fault.

de·mo'bi·lize', v.t. free from military service; disband.

de·moc'ra·cy, n. government by the people. —dem'o·crat', n. —dem"o·crat'ic, adj.

Dem'o·crat, n. member of the Democratic party.

de·mol'ish, v.t. destroy. —dem"o·li'tion, n.

de'mon, n. 1. evil spirit; devil. 2. person regarded as evil.

dem'on·strate", v.t. 1. prove in detail. 2. explain by example. 3. reveal. —v.i. 4. call public attention to one's attitude. —dem"on·stra'tion, n. —dem'on·stra'tor, n.

de·mor'al·ize", v.t. lower the morale of.

de·mote', v.t. lower in rank.

de·mur', v.i. object.

de·mure', adj. modest; coy.

den, n. cave of a wild animal.

de·ni'al, n. contradiction.

de·nom"i·na'tion, n. 1. name. 2. religious sect.

de·note', v.t. indicate; mean.

de·nounce', v.t. 1. accuse openly. 2. inform against. —de·nounce'ment, n.

dense, adj. thick. —den'si·ty, n.

dent, n. hollow area made by a blow.

den'tal, adj. pertaining to teeth or dentistry.

den'tist, n. doctor specializing in teeth and gums. —den'tist·ry, n.

den'ture, n. set of false teeth.

**de·nun″ci·a′tion,** *n.* accusation.

**de·ny′,** *v.t.* 1. reject as untrue. 2. refuse to give or allow. 3. refuse something to.

**de·o′dor·ant,** *n.* preparation for destroying odors.

**de·part′,** *v.i.* 1. leave; go away. 2. die. —**de·par′ture,** *n.*

**de·part′ment,** *n.* 1. part or section. 2. field of activity. —**de·part″men′tal,** *adj.*

**de·pend′,** *v.i.* 1. look outside oneself for support, help, etc. 2. be according to conditions. —**de·pend′a·ble,** *adj.* —**de·pend′ent,** *adj.,* —*n.* —**de·pend′ence, de·pend′en·cy,** *n.*

**de·pict′,** *v.t.* 1. portray; delineate. 2. describe. —**de·pic′tion,** *n.*

**de·plete′,** *v.t.* exhaust or reduce in amount. —**de·ple′tion,** *n.*

**de·plore′,** *v.t.* regret strongly. —**de·plor′a·ble,** *adj.*

**de·port′,** *v.t.* expel from a country. —**de″por·ta′tion,** *n.*

**de·port′ment** *n.* conduct or behaviour.

**de·pose′,** *v.t.* 1. remove from office or power. 2. testify. —**dep″o·si′tion,** *n.*

**de·pos′it,** *v.t.* 1. put in a bank, etc. 2. give in partial payment. 3. drop or cause to settle. 4. something deposited. —**de·pos′i·tor,** *n.*

**de·pot** (dē′pō), *n.* 1. bus or railroad station. 2. storage place for military supplies.

**de·prave′,** *v.t.* corrupt. —**de·prav′i·ty,** *n.*

**dep′re·cate″,** *v.t.* 1. express disapproval of. 2. belittle.

**de·pre·ci·ate** (dē prē′shē āt″), *v.t., v.i.* 1. lessen in value or seeming importance. —*v.t.* 2. belittle. —**de·pre″ci·a′tion,** *n.*

**de·press′,** *v.t.* 1. deject; sadden. 2. push down. —**de·pressed′,** *adj.* —**de·press′ant,** *n.*

**de·pres′sion,** *n.* 1. act of depressing or being depressed. 2. depressed state. 3. period when business and employment decline.

**de·prive′,** *v.t.* withhold from. —**de″pri·va′tion,** *n.*

**depth,** *n.* quality of being deep.

**dep′u·ty,** *n., pl.* **-ties.** person appointed to act as a substitute for another.

**de·rail′,** *v.t., v.i.* run off the rails.

**de·range′,** *v.t.* 1. disturb the arrangement of. 2. make insane.

**der′e·lict″,** *adj.* 1. abandoned by its owner. —*n.* 2. something abandoned, esp. a ship.

**de·ride′,** *v.t.* mock. —**de·ri′sion,** *n.* —**de·ri′sive,** *adj.*

**de·rive′,** *v.t.* obtain from a source. —**der″i·va′tion,** *n.* —**de·riv′a·tive,** *adj., n.*

**der′rick,** *n.* 1. crane for lifting and moving heavy objects. 2. tall framework over an oil well.

**de·scend** (di send′) *v.t.* 1. move down, along or through. 2. be derived from specified ancestors. —**des·cent′,** *n.* —**de·scen′dant,** *n.*

**de·scribe′,** *v.t.* 1. give a conception or account of. 2. trace by movement. —**de·scrib′a·ble,** *adj.* —**de·scrip′tion,** *n.* —**de·scrip′tive,** *adj.*

**des′e·crate″,** *v.t.* profane.

**de·seg′re·gate″,** *v.t., v.i.* eliminate racial segregation in. —**de·seg″re·ga′tion,** *n.*

**de·sert′,** *v.t.* (de zart′) 1. abandon. —*n.* 2. Often, **deserts,** something deserved. 3. (dez′ərt) wasteland, esp. a sandy one. —**de·sert′er,** *n.* —**de·ser′tion,** *n.*

**de·serve′,** *v.t.* have as a rightful outcome or reward. —**de·serv′ing,** *adj., n.*

**de·sign′,** *v.t.* 1. plan the form and making of. 2. contrive. —*n.* 3. plan or pattern. 4. scheme or intention. —**de·sign′er,** *n.*

**des′ig·nate″,** *v.t.* 1. specify; indicate. 2. name. —**des″ig·na′tion,** *n.*

**de·sign′er,** *n.* 1. one who designs. —*adj.* 2. of or pertaining to clothing, etc. styled by a designer, as *designer jeans.*

**de·sire′,** *v.t.* 1. long for. 2. request. —*v.i.* 3. have a desire. —*n.* 4. craving. 5. request. 6. lust. 7. thing desired. —**de·sir′a·ble,** *adj.* —**de·sir″a·bil′i·ty,** *n.* —**de·sir′ous,** *adj.*

**desk,** *n.* table with drawers used for writing.

**des′o·late,** *adj.* (des′ə lit) 1. barren. —*v.t.* (des′ə lāt″) 2. make barren. —**des″o·la′tion,** *n.*

**de·spair′,** *v.i.* 1. lose hope. —*n.* 2. hopelessness.

**des′per·ate,** *adj.* reckless due to despair. —**des″per·a′tion,** *n.*

**des′pi·ca·ble,** *adj.* contemptible.

**de·spise′,** *v.t.* scorn; loathe.

**de·spite′,** *prep.* in spite of.

**de·spond'**, *v.i.* lose hope or courage. —**de·spond'ent**, *adj.*

**des'pot**, *n.* tyrant or absolute ruler. —**des·pot'ic**, *adj.* —**des'pot·ism**, *n.*

**des·sert'**, *n.* sweet course ending a meal.

**des''ti·na'tion**, *n.* place to be reached.

**des'tine**, *v.t.* 1. intend. 2. predetermine.

**des'tin·y**, *n.*, *pl.* **-nies.** 1. predetermined course of events. 2. rate.

**des'ti·tute''**, *adj.* 1. deprived. 2. without means of existence. —**des''ti·tu'tion**, *n.*

**de·stroy'**, *v.t.* 1. damage so as to eliminate. 2. kill.

**de·stroy'er**, *n.* light, fast warship.

**de·struc'tion**, *n.* 1. act or instance of destroying. 2. agency by which one is destroyed. —**de·struct'i·ble**, *adj.* —**de·struc'tive**, *adj.*

**des'ul·to''ry**, *adj.* 1. random. 2. disconnected.

**de·tach'**, *v.t.* separate; disconnect.

**de·tach'ment**, *n.* 1. state of being detached. 2. military unit on a special mission.

**de·tail'**, *n.* subordinate part or feature.

**de·tain'**, *v.t.* 1. keep from going on; delay. 2. keep in custody. —**de·ten'tion**, *n.*

**de·tect'**, *v.t.* discover. —**de·tec'tion**, *n.*

**de·tec'tive**, *n.* investigator seeking private or hidden information.

**de·ter'**, *v.t.* discourage or prevent. —**de·ter'ment**, *n.* —**de·ter'rent**, *n.*

**de·ter'gent**, *adj.* 1. cleansing. —*n.* 2. preparation used for cleaning.

**de·te'ri·o·rate''**, *v.t.*, *v.i.* worsen. —**de·te'ri·o·ra'tion**, *n.*

**de·ter''mi·na'tion**, *n.* 1. act or instance of determining. 2. firmness of resolve.

**de·ter'mine**, *v.t.* 1. settle. 2. ascertain.

**de·ter'mined**, *adj.* showing determination.

**de·test'**, *v.t.* hate.

**det'o·nate''**, *v.t.*, *v.i.* explode. —**det''o·na'tion**, *n.*

**de·tour'**, *n.* roundabout course.

**de·tract'**, *v.t.* 1. take away. —*v.i.* 2. take a desirable quality.

**det'ri·ment**, *n.* 1. injury or loss.

2. something that causes injury or loss. —**det''ri·men'tal**, *adj.*

**de·val'u·ate''**, *v.t.* lessen in value.

**dev·as'tate''**, *v.t.* destroy everywhere. —**dev''as·ta'tion**, *n.*

**de·vel'op**, *v.t.* 1. bring to maturity or completeness. 2. elaborate. 3. fall ill with. 4. *Photography.* bring out the picture on. —*v.i.* 5. be developed. —**de·vel'op·ment**, *n.*

**de'vi·ate''**, *v.i.* turn aside; digress. —**de''vi·a'tion**, *n.*

**de·vice'**, *n.* tool, etc.

**dev'il**, *n.* 1. fiend of hell. 2. **the Devil**, Satan. 3. malicious or formidable person. —**dev'il·ish**, *adj.* —**dev'il·ry, dev'il·try**, *n.*

**de'vi·ous**, *adj.* 1. indirect; circuitous. 2. shifty; not straightforward. —**de'vi·ous·ly**, *adv.*

**de·vise'**, *v.t.* 1. contrive. 2. bequeath.

**de·void'**, *adj.* empty of something specified.

**de·vote'**, *v.t.* dedicate. —**de·vot'ed**, *adj.*

**de''vo·tee'**, *n.* admirer or enthusiast.

**de·vo'tion**, *n.* 1. dedication. 2. devout act, esp. a prayer.

**de·vour'**, *v.t.* eat hungrily.

**de·vout'**, *adj.* pious; very religious.

**dew**, *n.* moisture condensed at ground level. —**dew'y**, *adj.*

**dex'ter·ous**, *adj.* skillful; cunning. Also, **dex'trous**. —**dex·ter'i·ty**, *n.*

**di''a·be'tes**, *n.* disease characterized by the body's inability to use sugar properly. —**di''a·be'tic**, *adj.*, *n.*

**di''a·bol'ic**, *adj.* devilish. Also, **di''a·bol'i·cal**.

**di'ag·nose''**, *v.t.* 1. make a diagnosis of. 2. establish by diagnosis.

**di''ag·no'sis**, *n.*, *pl.* **-ses.** determination of the nature of an illness or situation. —**di''ag·nos'tic**, *adj.*

**di·ag'o·nal**, *adj.* 1. connecting two nonadjacent angles. 2. oblique. —*n.* 3. something that is diagonal.

**di'a·gram''**, *n.* chart or plan that explains something simply.

**di'al**, *n.* 1. disk or strip with a calibrated edge, as on a clock or gauge. 2. disk turned to get radio frequencies, make telephone calls, etc. —*v.t.* 3. obtain or reach by turning a dial.

**di·a·lect**, n. variety of a language peculiar to a region or class.

**di·a·logue**, n. conversation between two or more people. Also, **di·a·log**.''

**di·am·e·ter**, n. 1. straight line passing through the centre of a circle. 2. length of such a line. —**di·a·met'ri·cal**, adj.

**di·a·mond**, n. 1. hard, transparent crystallization of carbon. 2. **diamonds**, suit of playing cards.

**dia·per**, n. piece of absorbent material that forms a baby's undercloth.

**di·a·phragm** (dī'ə fram''), n. muscular wall, esp. between the chest and abdomen.

**di''ar·rhe'a**, n. intestinal disorder characterized by too frequent and too loose bowel movements.

**di'a·ry**, n. daily record of experiences.

**di'a·tribe''**, n. bitter denunciation.

**dice**, n. pl., sing. **die**, small cubes marked on each side with one to six spots, used in games.

**di·chot'o·my**, n. division into two parts.

**dic'tate''**, v.t., v.i. speak for preservation in writing. —**dic·ta'tion**, n.

**dic·ta'tor**, n. de facto absolute ruler. —**dic'ta·tor·ship''**, n.

**dic'tion**, n. 1. choice of words. 2. enunciation.

**dic''tion·ar'y**, n., pl. -ies. book explaining the meanings, etc. of alphabetically listed words.

**di·dac'tic**, adj. intended for instruction.

**die**, v.i. 1. cease to live. —n. 2. shaping device.

**di'et**, n. 1. food normally eaten. 2. legislature. —**di·e'tar'y**, adj. —**di''e·ti'tian, di''e·ti'cian**, n. —**di''e·tet'ic**, adj.

**dif'fer**, v.i. 1. be different. 2. disagree.

**dif'fer·ence**, n. 1. unlikeness. —**dif'fer·ent**, adj.

**dif''fer·en'tial**, adj. pertaining to difference.

**dif''fer·en'ti·ate''**, v.t. 1. make unlike. —v.i. 2. make a distinction.

**dif'fi·cult**, adj. 1. hard to do or understand. 2. hard to deal with or satisfy. —**dif'fi·cul'ty**, n.

**dif'fi·dent**, adj. shy; self-conscious. —**dif'fi·dence**, n.

**dif·fuse'**, v.t., v.i. 1. (dif fyooz') spread; disseminate; spread. —adj. (dif fyoos') 2. not concentrated. —**dif·fu'sion**, n.

**dig**, v.t. 1. cut into or turn over. 2. form by digging. —v.i. 3. break up earth, etc. by digging. —n. 4. act or instance of digging. 5. taunting remark.

**di·gest'**, v.t. transform food in the body so it is absorbable. —**di·gest'i·ble** adj. —**di·ges'tion**, n. —**di·ges'tive**, adj.

**dig'it**, n. 1. finger or toe. 2. any Arabic figure: 0 to 9.

**dig'i·tal**, adj. represented by numerals.

**dig'ni·fied''**, adj. showing dignity; stately.

**dig'ni·fy''**, v.t. honor; give dignity to.

**dig''ni·tar'y**, n., pl. -ies. eminent person, esp. because of rank.

**di·gress'**, v.i. wander away from the main subject or purpose. —**di·gres'sion**, n.

**dike**, n. dam built to prevent flooding.

**di·lap'i·dat''ed**, adj. ruined; broken down.

**di·late'**, v.t., v.i. widen; expand. —**di·la'tion, dil''a·ta'tion**, n.

**dil'a·to''ry**, adj. delaying.

**di·lem'ma**, n. predicament requiring a puzzling choice between two alternatives.

**dil''et·tante'**, n., pl. -tantes, -tanti. amateur, superficial artist, thinker, etc.

**dil'i·gent**, adj. hard-working. —**dil'i·gence**, n.

**dill**, n. plant with aromatic leaves and seeds used for flavoring.

**di·lute'**, v.t. water down; thin out. —**di·lu'tion**, n.

**dim**, adj. dimmer, dimmest, v. adj. 1. not bright; indistinct. 2. not clearly seeing or understanding. —v.t., v.i. 3. make or grow dim. —**dim'ly**, adv.

**dime**, n. ten-cent coin.

**di·men'sion**, n. length, breadth, or height. —**di·men'sion·al**, adj.

**di·min'ish**, v.t., v.i. lessen in size or importance. —**dim''i·nu'tion**, n.

**di·min'u·tive**, adj. 1. very small. —n. 2. suffix or variant modifying a word to indicate smallness.

**dim'ple**, n. small, natural hollow, esp. on the cheek or chin.

**din**, n. confused or continuous noise.

**dine**, v.i. eat dinner.

**di′ner**, *n.* **1.** person eating. **2.** railroad dining car. **3.** restaurant resembling such a car.

**din·gy** (din′jē), *adj.*, **-gier, -giest.** dark; grimy.

**din′ner**, *n.* main meal of the day.

**di′no·saur′′**, *n.* large reptile of prehistoric times.

**di·o·cese** (dī′ə sēs′′), *n.* district under a bishop.

**dip**, *v.t.* **1.** lower briefly and raise. **2.** remove with a scoop. —*v.i.* **3.** plunge abruptly. —*n.* **4.** short swim or bath. **5.** abrupt plunge or slope.

**di·plo′ma**, *n.* certificate conferring a degree.

**di·plo′mat′**, *n.* official representing a state. —**di·plo′ma·cy**, *n.* —**dip′′lo·mat′ic**, *adj.*

**dire**, *adj.*, **direr, direst.** dreadful. Also, **dire′ful.**

**di·rect′**, *adj.* **1.** straight. —*v.t.* **2.** guide. **3.** supervise or command. —**di·rect′ly**, *adv.* —**di·rect′ness**, *n.* —**di·rec′tor**, *n.*

**di·rec′tion**, *n.* **1.** line toward a place, point of the compass, etc. **2.** instruction. **3.** act, instance, or responsibility of directing. —**di·rec′tion·al**, *adj.*

**di·rec′tive**, *n.* general order.

**di·rec′to·ry**, *n.*, *pl.* **-ries.** book with names, addresses, etc.

**dir′i·gi·ble**, *n.* maneuverable airship.

**dirt**, *n.* **1.** any unclean substance; filth. **2.** soil.

**dirt′y**, *adj.*, **-ier, -iest. 1.** not clean; soiled. **2.** indecent.

**dis·a′ble**, *v.t.* make incapable or unfit. —**dis′′a·bil′i·ty**, *n.*

**dis′′ad·van′tage**, *n.* unfavorable circumstance.

**dis′′a·gree′**, *v.i.* **1.** fail to agree. **2.** quarrel. —**dis′′a·gree′ment**, *n.*

**dis′′a·gree′a·ble**, *adj.* not agreeable; unpleasant. —**dis′′a·gree′a·bly**, *adv.*

**dis′′ap·pear′**, *v.i.* **1.** vanish. **2.** cease to exist. —**dis′′ap·pear′ance**, *n.*

**dis′′ap·point′**, *v.t.* thwart the expectations or hopes of. —**dis′′ap·point′ment**, *n.*

**dis′′ap·prove′**, *v.t.*, *v.i.* not to approve. —**dis′′ap·prov′al**, *n.*

**dis·arm′**, *v.t.* **1.** take away or deprive of weapons. **2.** make friendly. —*v.i.* **3.** reduce armed forces. —**dis·ar′ma·ment**, *n.*

**dis′′ar·ray′**, *v.t.* **1.** throw into disorder. —*n.* **2.** disorder; confusion.

**dis·as′ter**, *n.* cause of much damage. —**dis·as′trous**, *adj.*

**dis′′a·vow′**, *v.t.* disclaim knowledge of or responsibility for.

**dis·band′**, *v.t.*, *v.i.* break up, as an organisation.

**dis′′be·lieve′**, *v.t.*, *v.i.* refuse to believe. —**dis′′be·lief′**, *n.*

**dis·card′**, *v.t.* (dis kärd′) throw away.

**dis·cern′** (di sûrn′), *v.t.* perceive; recognize. distinguish. —**dis·cern′ment**, *n.* —**dis·cern′ing**, *adj.*

**dis·charge′** (dis chärg′) **1.** emit. **2.** shoot or fire. **3.** release or dismiss from service. —*n.* (dis′charj) **4.** act, instance, or means of discharging. **5.** something discharged.

**dis·ci′ple**, *n.* follower of a teacher or teaching.

**dis′ci·pline**, *n.* **1.** training that develops self-control. **2.** punishment. —*v.t.* **3.** train. **4.** punish. —**dis′ci·pli·na′′ry**, *adj.*

**dis·claim′**, *v.t.* disown.

**dis·close′**, *v.t.* reveal or uncover. —**dis·clo′sure**, *n.*

**dis′co**, *n.* **1.** discotheque; a club featuring dancing to rock music. **2.** a style of dance music with a pronounced beat.

**dis·com′fort**, *n.* lack of comfort.

**dis′′con·cert′**, *v.t.* upset; disarrange; perturb.

**dis′′con·nect′**, *v.t.* finish the connection of; separate.

**dis′′con·tent′**, *adj.* Also, **dis′′con·tent′ed**, dissatisfied with something; not content. —*n.* **2.** dissatisfaction; lack of content.

**dis′′con·tin′ue**, *v.t.*, *v.i.* stop. —**dis′′con·tin′u·ance, dis′′con·tin′u·a′′tion**, *n.*

**dis·cord′**, *n.* **1.** lack of harmony. **2.** disagreement.

**dis′count′**, *n.* **1.** reduction in price. —*v.t.* **2.** deduct from a bill. **3.** advance with deduction or interest. **4.** sell at less than the regular price. **5.** disregard. —**dis·count′a·ble**, *adj.*

**dis·cour′age**, *v.t.* hamper or stop with predictions of failure, disapproval, etc. —**dis·cour′age·ment**, *n.*

**dis·course′**, *n.* (dis′kors) **1.** conversation. **2.** essay or lecture. —*v.i.* (dis kors′) **3.** converse.

**dis·cour′te·sy**, *n.*, *pl.* **-sies.** lack

of courtesy; rudeness. —**dis·cour'-te·ous**, adj.

**dis·cov'er**, v.t. perceive for the first time. —**dis·cov'er·er**, n. —**dis·cov'er·y**, n.

**dis·cred'it**, v.t. 1. cast doubt on. 2. injure the reputation of. —n. 4. state of being discredited.

**dis·creet'**, adj. prudent.

**dis·crep'an·cy**, n. inconsistency.

**dis·cre'tion**, n. 1. prudence. 2. freedom of choice in actions.

**dis·crim'i·nate**, v.i. 1. make careful distinctions. 2. show unjust favor or disfavor. —**dis·crim'i·na'tion**, n.

**dis·cur'sive**, adj. rambling; wandering from topic to topic.

**dis·cuss'**, v.t. talk or write about. —**dis·cus'sion**, n.

**dis·dain'**, v.t. scorn; despise. —**dis·dain'ful**, adj.

**dis·ease'**, n. ailment; sickness.

**dis''em·bark'**, v.i. leave a ship or aircraft. —**dis''em·bar·ka'tion**, n.

**dis''en·chant'**, v.t. destroy the enthusiasm of. —**dis''en·chant'·ment**, n.

**dis''en·gage'**, v.t., v.i. disconnect.

**dis·fa'vor**, n. disapproval.

**dis·fig'ure**, v.t. mar.

**dis·grace'**, n. 1. state or cause of shame. —v.t. 2. bring shame upon. —**dis·grace'ful**, adj.

**dis·grun'tle**, v.t. make discontent or sulky.

**dis·guise'**, v.t. 1. render temporarily unrecognizable. —n. 2. something that disguises.

**dis·gust'**, v.t. 1. offend the good taste or senses of. —n. 2. sickening dislike.

**dish**, n. 1. shallow container for food. 2. food that is served.

**dis·heart'en**, v.t. discourage.

**dis·hon'est**, adj. not honest. —**dis·hon'est·ly**, adv. —**dis·hon'es·ty**, n.

**dis·hon'or**, n. 1. lack of respect; disgrace. —v.t. 2. disgrace. —**dis·hon'or·a·ble**, adj.

**dis''il·lu'sion**, v.t. free from illusion. —**dis''il·lu'sion·ment**, n.

**dis''in·cline'**, v.t. make unwilling or averse. —**dis''in·cli'na'tion**, n.

**dis''in·fect'**, v.t. rid of infection. —**dis''in·fect'ant**, n., adj.

**dis''in·her'it**, v.t. deprive of inheritance.

**dis·in'te·grate''**, v.t., v.i. separate into elements.

**dis·in'ter·est·ed**, adj. impartial.

**dis·joint'ed**, adj. incoherent.

**disk**, n. thin, flat, round object.

**disk·ette'**, n. (computers) a 5-1/4- or a 3-1/2-inch flexible disk used for data storage.

**dis·like'**, v.t. 1. regard with aversion or distaste. —n. 2. aversion; distaste.

**dis·lo'cate'**, v.t. put out of the proper or customary place. —**dis'·lo·ca'tion**, n.

**dis·lodge'**, v.t. force from a place.

**dis·loy'al**, adj. not loyal; unfaithful. —**dis·loy'al·ty**, n.

**dis·mal'**, adj. 1. gloomy; dreary. 2. causing dreariness or misery.

**dis·man'tle**, v.t. 1. deprive of strip of equipment. 2. take apart.

**dis·may'**, v.t. 1. dishearten. —n. 2. disheartenment.

**dis·mem'ber**, v.t. deprive of limbs.

**dis·miss'**, v.t. direct or allow to leave. —**dis·mis'sal**, n.

**dis·mount'**, v.i. alight from a horse, bicycle, etc.

**dis''o·be'di·ent**, adj. not obedient. —**dis''o·be'di·ence**, n. —**dis''o·bey'**, v.i.

**dis·or'der**, n. confusion. —**dis·or'der·ly**, adj.

**dis·or'gan·ize''**, v.t. throw into confusion.

**dis·own'**, v.t. repudiate.

**dis·par'age**, v.t. belittle.

**dis'pa·rate**, adj. distinct in kind. —**dis·par'i·ty**, n.

**dis·pas'sion·ate**, adj. impartial.

**dis·patch'**, v.t. 1. send off. —n. 2. sending-off.

**dis·pel'**, v.t. scatter; drive off.

**dis·pen'sa·ry**, n., pl. **-ries**. place where medical aid is given.

**dis''pen·sa'tion**, n. act or instance of dispensing.

**dis·pense'**, v.t. 1. distribute. —v.i. 2. dispense with, a. forgo. b. get rid of.

**dis·perse'**, v.t., v.i. scatter.

**dis·place'**, v.t. put out of place.

**dis·play'**, v.t., n. exhibit.

**dis·please'**, v.t. offend. —**dis·pleas'ure**, n.

**dis·pose'**, v.t. 1. arrange. —v.i. 2. rid oneself. —**dis·pos'a·ble**, adj. —**dis·pos'al**, n.

**dis''po·si'tion**, n. 1. temperament. 2. disposal.

dis''pos·sess', *v.t.* deprive of possession.

dis''pro·por'tion, *n.* lack of proportion. —dis''pro·por'tion·ate, *adj.*

dis·prove', *v.t.* prove false.

dis·pute', *v.i., v.t.* 1. argue. —*n.* 2. act or instance of disputing.

dis·qual'i·fy', *v.t.* make or declare unqualified. —dis·qual'i·fi·ca'tion, *n.*

dis''re·gard', *v.t.* 1. ignore. —*n.* 2. neglect.

dis''re·pair', *n.* impaired condition.

dis''re·pute', *n.* bad reputation. —dis·rep'u·ta·ble, *adj.*

dis''re·spect', *n.* lack of respect. —dis''re·spect'ful, *adj.*

dis·robe', *v.t., v.i.* undress.

dis·rupt', *v.t., v.i.* break up.

dis·sat'is·fy', *v.t.* fail to satisfy; displease. —dis·sat'is·fac'tion, *n.*

dis·sect', *v.t.* 1. cut apart. 2. examine closely. —dis·sec'tion, *n.*

dis·sem'ble, *v.t., v.i.* disguise.

dis·sem'i·nate'', *v.t.* distribute widely.

dis·sen'sion, *n.* disagreement or quarreling.

dis·sent', *v.i.* 1. disagree. —*n.* 2. disagreement.

dis''ser·ta'tion, *n.* formal essay; thesis.

dis·sim'i·lar, *adj.* not similar.

dis·si'pate, *v.t.* 1. scatter. 2. squander. —*v.i.* 3. live in extravagance or vice. —dis''si·pa'tion, *n.*

dis'si·pat''ed, *adj.* living in extravagance or vice.

dis·so'ci·ate', *v.t.* break the connection between.

dis''so·lute', *adj.* dissipated.

dis·solve', *v.t., v.i.* melt; combine with a liquid.

dis'so·nance, *n.* musical discord. —dis'so·nant, *adj.*

dis·suade', *v.t.* deter by persuasion.

dis'tance, *n.* 1. interval of space or time. 2. remoteness. —dis'tant, *adj.*

dis'taste', *n.* dislike. —dis·taste'ful, *adj.*

dis·tend', *v.t., v.i.* expand.

dis·till', *v.t.* make or purify by evaporation and condensation. —*v.i.* 2. become distilled. —dis·till'er, *n.* —dis·till'er·y, *n.* —dis''til·la'tion, *n.*

dis·tinct', *adj.* 1. individual. 2. clearly noticeable or understandable.

dis·tinc'tion, *n.* 1. act or instance of distinguishing. 2. difference. 3. eminence. 4. something that gives or betokens eminence.

dis·tinc'tive, *adj.* characteristic.

dis·tin'guish, *v.t.* 1. characterize as individual. 2. make eminent or excellent. —dis·tin'guished, *adj.*

dis·tort', *v.t.* alter from a normal shape.

dis·tract', *v.t.* 1. prevent from concentrating. 2. bewilder. —dis·trac'tion, *n.*

dis·tract'ed, *adj.* frantic. Also, dis·traught'.

dis·tress', *n.* 1. pain or need. —*v.t.* 2. cause distress in.

dis·trib'ute, *v.t.* 1. give out in portions. 2. disperse. —dis''tri·bu'tion, *n.* —dis·trib'u·tor, *n.*

dis'trict, *n.* distinct geographical area.

dis·trust', *n.* 1. lack of trust. —*v.t.* 2. place no trust in. —dis·trust'ful, *adj.*

dis·turb', *v.t.* end the quiet state of. —dis·turb'ance, *n.*

ditch, *n.* channel dug in the ground.

dit'to, *n., pl.* -tos. the same as before.

di·van', *n.* long, low couch.

dive, *v.i.* 1. fall intentionally. —*n.* 2. act, instance, or form of diving. —div'er, *n.*

di·verge', *v.i.* part in two or more directions. —di·ver'gent, *adj.* —di·ver'gence, *n.*

di·verse', *adj.* 1. different. 2. various. —di·ver'si·ty, *n.*

di·vert', *v.t.* 1. turn aside from a path or course. 2. entertain; amuse. —di·ver'sion, *n.*

di·vest', *v.t.* 1. deprive or strip. 2. rid.

di·vide', *v.t.* 1. separate into parts or classes. —*v.i.* 2. separate.

div'i·dend', *n.* number to be divided.

di·vine', *adj.* godly or godlike. 2. religious.

di·vin'i·ty, *n., pl.* -ties. 1. deity. 2. theology.

di·vis'i·ble, *adj.* able to be divided, esp. evenly.

di·vi'sion, *n.* 1. act or instance of dividing. 2. military unit.

di·vi'sive, *adj.* causing disunity.

di·vorce', *n.* 1. legal dissolution of a marriage. —*v.t.* 2. separate oneself from by a divorce. **3.** separate by a divorce. —di·**vorce'ment**, *n.*

**di·vor'cee'**, *n.* divorced woman.

**di·vulge'**, *v.t.* reveal.

**diz'zy**, *adj.* unsteady.

**do**, *v.t.*, **did, done, doing.** be at work upon or occupied with.

**doc'ile**, *adj.* readily disciplined.

**dock**, *n.* **1.** place for ships between voyages. **2.** pier or wharf.

**dock'et**, *n.* list of agenda, esp. of a court.

**doc'tor**, *n.* **1.** person who practices medicine. **2.** person with a high academic degree. —**doc'tor·ate**, *n.*

**doc'trine**, *n.* body of teaching, esp, in religion or politics.

**doc'u·ment**, *n.* **1.** writing, etc. used as a proof. —*v.t.* **2.** prove or support with documents. —**doc'u·men·ta'tion**, *n.*

**doc'u·men'ta·ry**, *adj.* pertaining to documents.

**dodge**, *v.t.* avoid by moving quickly.

**doe**, *n.* female of certain animals, as deer or rabbits.

**dog**, *n.* four-legged domestic animal.

**dog'ged**, *adj.* stubborn in difficulty.

**dog'ma**, *n.* doctrine, esp. in religion, regarded as unquestionable.

**dog·mat'ic**, *adj.* **1.** pertaining to or published as dogma. **2.** offering personal opinions as dogma. —**dog'ma·tism**, *n.*

**dole**, *n.* **1.** money, food, etc. given to the unemployed. —*v.t.* **2.** portion out sparingly.

**dole'ful**, *adj.* sad.

**doll**, *n.* toy shaped like a baby or other human being.

**dol'lar**, *n.* currency unit of the U.S., Canada, etc.

**do'lor·ous**, *adj.* sorrowful or painful.

**do·main'**, *n.* **1.** territory of a ruler. **2.** area of influence or power.

**dome**, *n.* structure like an upcurved segment of a sphere.

**do·mes'tic**, *adj.* **1.** pertaining to the home. **2.** belonging to or originating in one's own country.

**do·mes'ti·cate''**, *v.t.* adapt to domesticconditions.

**dom·i·cile''**, *n.* **1.** residence. —*v.t.* **2.** house.

**dom'i·nant**, *adj.* prevailing. —**dom'i·nance**, *n.*

**dom'i·nate''**, *v.t.* master. —**dom''i·na'tion**, *n.*

**dom'i·neer''**, *v.t.*, *v.i.* tyrannize.

**do·min'ion**, *n.* territory reigned over or ruled by a sovereign.

**dom'i·no''**, *n.*, *pl.* **-noes.** small plaque marked with spots.

**don**, *v.t. Archaic.* put on, as clothes.

**do'nate'**, *v.t.*, *v.i.* give, resp. in charity or friendship. —**do·na'tion**, *n.* —**do'nor**, *n.*

**don'key**, *n.*, *pl.* **-keys.** domesticated ass.

**doom**, *n.* death or annihilation.

**door**, *n.* **1.** movable partition for barring access. **2.** Also, **door'way''**, entrance.

**dope**, *n. Informal.* **1.** habit-forming drug. **2.** fool.

**dor'mant**, *adj.* **1.** asleep or at rest. **2.** not active.

**dor'mi·to''ry**, *n.*, *pl.* **-ries.** place for residents of an institution to sleep.

**dose**, *n.* amount of medicine taken at one time. —**dos'age**, *n.*

**dos·si·er** (dos''sē a'), *n.* file of documents on one subject.

**dot**, *n.* tiny round mark.

**dou'ble**, *adj.* **1.** twice as many or large as usual. —*adv.* **2.** twice. —*n.* **3.** duplicate. —*v.t.* **4.** fold over. **5.** make twice as much or as many of. —*v.i.* **6.** fold in two. —**doub'ly**, *adv.*

**dou'ble·cross''**, *v.t. Informal.* cheat or betray.

**doubt**, *v.t.* **1.** be unsure or skeptical of. —*n.* **2.** uncertainty or distrust. —**doubt'ful**, *adj.* —**doubt'less**, *adv.*

**dough**, *n.* pastry mixture of flour and water for baking. —**dough'y**, *adj.*

**douse**, *v.t.* plunge into or drench with liquid.

**dove**, *n.* cooing pigeonlike bird.

**dow'dy**, *adj.*, **-dier, -diest.** plainly or untidily dressed, made up, etc.

**down**, *adv.*, *adj.* **1.** to or at a lower place. **2.** to or in a lower condition, amount, etc. —*adj.* **3.** soft feathers or hair. —*v.t.* **4.** put down. —**down'stairs''**, *adv.*, *adj.*, *n.* —**down'ward**, **down'wards**, *adv.* —**down'y**, *adj.*

**down'fall''**, *n.* fall, as from power or eminence.

**down'grade''**, *v.t.* **1.** demote. —*adv.*, *adj.* **2.** downward.

**down'heart'ed**, *adj.* discouraged.

**down'hill''**, *adv.*, *adj.* downward.

**down'stairs"**, *adv.* to or at a lower level.

**down'town"**, *adv., adj.* toward or in the business district of a town.

**down'trod"den**, *adj.* oppressed.

**dow'ry**, *n., pl.* **-ries.** property bestowed on a bride by her family.

**doze**, *v.i.* sleep lightly.

**doz'en**, *n., pl.* **-ens** or (after a number) **-en.** group of twelve.

**drab**, *n, adj.,* **drabber, drabbest.** *n.* 1. yellow-brown. —*adj.* 2. dreary. —**drab'ly**, *adv.* —**drab'ness,** *n.*

**draft**, *n.* 1. act or amount of drawing. 2. current of air. 3. order to pay. 4. selection for conscription. —*v.t.* 5. make a draft of. 6. conscript. —**draft'ee**, *n.* —**draft'y,** *adj.*

**drafts'man**, *n.* person who makes working drawings or sketches.

**drag**, *v.t.* 1. pull with effort. —*v.t.* 2. move slowly or with effort.

**drag'on**, *n.* mythical large reptile.

**drain**, *n.* 1. channel for carrying away liquids. —*v.t.* 2. remove through a channel. —**drain'age,** *n.*

**dram**, *n.* eighth part of an apothecary's ounce or fluid ounce.

**dra'ma**, *n.* 1. play. 2. theater as an art. —**dram'a·tist**, *n.* —**dram'a·tize"**, *v.t.* —**dra·mat'ic**, *adj.*

**drape**, *n.* 1. cloth hanging or curtain. —*v.t., v.i.* 2. hang loosely or in folds. —**drap'er·y,** *n.*

**dras'tic**, *adj.* severe or extreme.

**draught**, *n., v.t., adj.* draft.

**draw**, *v.t.* 1. pull, attract, or take in 2. elicit or provoke. 3. receive. 4. sketch with a pencil, pen, etc. 5. *Nautical.* need a depth of. —*v.i.* 6. exert a pulling force. 7. move. 8. pass smoke, etc. readily. 9. make demands. 10. lessen in size. —*n.* 11. act or instance of drawing. 12. even final score. —**draw'ing,** *n.*

**draw'back"**, *n.* lessening of advantage.

**draw'bridge"**, *n.* bridge that can be lifted or pulled.

**draw·er** (drôr), *n.* sliding compartment in a piece of furniture.

**drawl**, *n.* 1. slow speech. —*v.t., v.i.* 2. speak in a drawl.

**drawn**, *adj.* haggard.

**dread**, *n.* 1. fearful anticipation. —*v.t.* 2. anticipate fearfully.

**dread'ful**, *adj.* 1. very bad. 2. inspiring dread.

**dream**, *n.* 1. succession of images appearing in sleep or reverie. —*v.i.* 2. imagine in a dream. —*v.i.* 3. have a dream. —**dream'y,** *adj.*

**drear'y**, *adj.,* **-ier, -iest.** causing sadness or boredom.

**dredge**, *v.t.* 1. dig, esp. under water. —*n.* 2. digging device.

**dregs**, *n., pl.* sediment, as of wine.

**drench**, *v.t.* soak with falling liquid.

**dress**, *n.* 1. put clothing on. —*v.i.* 2. put on clothing. —*n.* 3. clothing. 4. skirt. —**dress'mak"er,** *n.*

**dres'ser**, *n.* 1. person who dresses. 2. chest of drawers with a mirror.

**dres'sing**, *n.* 1. material applied to wounds, bruises, etc. 2. sauce for salad.

**drib'ble**, *v.t.* 1. let drip untidily. —*n.* 2. act or instance of dribbling.

**dri'er**, *n.* thing or substance for drying.

**drift**, *v.i.* 1. be carried by a current. —*n.* 2. drifting motion. 3. pile of wind-driven snow.

**drill**, *n.* 1. boring tool. 2. system of exercises. —*v.t.* 3. bore with a drill. 4. train or exercise with a drill.

**drink**, *n.* 1. liquid for swallowing. —*v.t.* 2. swallow as a drink. —*v.i.* 3. swallow liquid. —**drink'er,** *n.*

**drip**, *v.i.* fall in drops.

**drive**, *v.t.* 1. force along. 2. compel 3. control, as a vehicle. —*v.i.* 4. operate a road vehicle. —*n.* 5. energy. —**driv'er**, *n.* —**drive'way,** *n.*

**driz'zle**, *n.* 1. fine rain. —*v.i., v.t.* 2. rain in fine drops.

**droll**, *adj.* oddly amusing. —**drol'ly**, *adv.* —**droll'ness, drol'ler·y,** *n.*

**drone**, *n.* 1. low hum. 2. nonworking male bee. —*v.i.* 3. emit a drone.

**droop**, *v.i.* hang loosely. —**droop'y,** *adj.*

**drop**, *v.t.* 1. allow to fall. —*v.i.* 2. fall. —*n.* 3. globule of liquid that falls or is about to fall.

**drought**, *n.* long dry spell. Also, **drouth.**

**drown**, *v.i., v.t.* 1. suffocate in water. —*v.t.* 2. flood.

**drowse**, *v.i.* be close to sleep. —**drows'y,** *adj.*

**drudge**, *v.i.* do dull, hard work. —**drudg'er·y,** *n.*

**drug**, *n.* 1. medicinal substance. 2.

narcotic, hallucinogen, etc.
—**drug'gist,** n. —**drug'store'',** n.

**drum,** n. percussion musical instrument. —**drum'mer,** n. —**drum'stick'',** n.

**drunk,** adj. overcome by alcohol.

**drunk'ard,** n. alcoholic.

**drunk'en,** adj. drunk.

**dry,** adj., **drier, driest.** adj. 1. free of moisture. 2. thirsty. —v.t. 3. free of moisture. —v.i. 4. become dry. —**dry'ly,** adv. —**dry'ness,** n.

**dry'-clean'',** v.t. clean with chemicals rather than water. —**dry cleaner.**

**du'al,** adj. 1. pertaining to two. 2. twofold.

**du'bi·ous,** adj. doubtful.

**duch'ess,** n. woman equal in rank to a duke.

**duch'y,** n., pl. -ies. area ruled by a duke or duchess.

**duck,** n. 1. flat-billed waterfowl. —v.i. 2. stoop or crouch to avoid a blow.

**duct,** n. passage for fluids.

**due,** adj. 1. owed. 2. expected to arrive.

**du'el,** n. formal mortal combat between two persons.

**du·et',** n. musical composition for two.

**duke,** n. nobleman next in rank to a prince.

**dull,** adj. 1. not interesting. 2. not sharp. —**dull'ness, dul'ness,** n.

**du'ly,** adv. in a due manner.

**dumb,** adj. 1. unable to speak or make sound. 2. Informal. stupid.

**dumb''wait'er,** n. hoist for food.

**dum'my,** n., pl. -ies, adj. 1. lifesized object in human form. 2. imitation or mockup.

**dump,** v.t. 1. throw or pour down and abandon. —n. 2. place for refuse.

**dump'ling,** n. rounded piece of baked dough, sometimes with a fruit filling.

**dump''ster,** n. a large, metal bin for holding garbage until pick-up.

**dun,** n. 1. dull gray-brown. —v.t. 2. attempt to recover a debt from.

**dunce,** n. poor learner.

**dune,** n. mound of wind-driven sand.

**dung,** n. manure.

**dun'ga·rees',** n., pl. blue cotton work pants or overalls.

**dun'geon,** n. dark prison, as in a castle.

**dunk,** v.t. dip into a drink.

**dupe,** v.t. 1. cheat. —n. 2. person who is cheated. —**dup'er,** n.

**du'pli·cate'',** v.t. imitate exactly. —**du''pli·ca'tion,** n.

**du·plic'i·ty,** n., pl. **ties.** deceit.

**du'ra·ble,** adj. long-lasting; sturdy. —**dura·bil'i·ty,** n.

**du·ra'tion,** n. period of existence.

**du·ress',** n. coercion.

**dur'ing,** prep. in or throughout the period of.

**dusk,** n. 1. darker part of twilight. 2. gloom.

**dust,** n. 1. powder, esp. of earth. —v.t. 2. remove dust from. —**dust'y,** adj.

**du'ti·ful,** adj. faithful to duty.

**du'ty,** n., pl. -ties. 1. moral requirement. 2. requirement by authority. 3. action, conduct, etc. required by morality or authority. 4. tax on an import.

**dwarf,** n., pl. **dwarfs, dwarves.** abnormally small living thing.

**dwell,** v.i. have one's habitation. —**dwell'er,** n. —**dwel'ling,** n.

**dwin'dle,** v.i. diminish.

**dye,** n. 1. stain for cloth, etc. —v.t. 2. stain with dye. —**dy'er,** n. —**dye'stuff,** n.

**dy·nam'ic,** adj. 1. pertaining to motion. 2. vigorous, as a person. —**dy·nam'i·cal·ly,** adv. —**dy'na·mism,** n.

**dy'na·mo'',** n., pl. -mos. electrical generator.

**dy'nas·ty,** n., pl. -ties. succession of rulers in one family.

**dys'en·ter''y,** n. intestinal inflammation.

**dys·pep'si·a,** n. indigestion.

# E

**E, e,** n. fifth letter of the English alphabet.

**each,** adj. 1. every one individually. 2. apiece.

**ea'ger,** adj. full of desire. —**ea'ger·ly,** adv.

**ear,** n. 1. part of the body for hearing. 2. grain-bearing part of a plant.

**E**
**F**

**ear'ly**, *adj.*, *adv.*, **-lier**, **-liest**. before the expected time. 2. toward the beginning.

**earn**, *v.t.* work or deserve to acquire.

**ear'nest**, *adj.* sincere; serious. —**ear'nest·ly**, *adv.*

**earth**, *n.* 1. this planet. 2. soil. —**earth·en**, *adj.* —**earth'ly**, *adj.*

**earth'y**, *adj.* matter-of-fact.

**ease**, *n.* 1. freedom from toil, pain, etc. —*v.t.* 2. make easy.

**east**, *n.* 1. direction to the right of north. 2. eastern area. —*adj.*, *adv.* 3. toward, in, or from the east. —**east'ern**, *adj.*

**eas'y**, *adj.*, **-ier**, **-iest**. 1. not difficult. 2. free of pain, etc. —**eas'i·ly**, *adv.* —**eas'i·ness**, *n.*

**eat**, *v.t.*, **ate**, **eaten**, **eating**. 1. consume as food. 2. dissolve, erode, etc.

**eaves'drop''**, *v.i.* overhear conversation, esp. intentionally.

**ebb**, *n.* 1. going-out of a tide. —*v.i.* 2. go out, as the tide.

**e·bul'lient**, *adj.* exuberant.

**ec·cen'tric**, *adj.* 1. peculiar in manner. 2. off center. —*n.* 3. eccentric person. —**ec''cen·tric'i·ty**, *n.*

**ec·cle''si·as'tic**, *adj.* pertaining to churches. Also, **ec·cle''si·as'ti·cal**.

**ech'o**, *n.*, *pl.* **-oes**, *n.* 1. reflected sound. —*v.t.* 2. reflect as an echo.

**e·col'o·gy**, *n.*, *pl.* **-gies**. 1. study of the relation of living things to their environment. 2. system permitting living things to exist. —**e'co·log'i·cal**, *adj.* —**e·col'o·gist**, *n.*

**e''co·nom'i·cal**, *adj.* thrifty.

**e''co·nom'ics**, *n.* 1. *sing.* study of wealth. 2. *pl.* resources and demands on wealth. —**e''co·nom'ic**, *adj.* —**e·con'o·mist**, *n.*

**e·con'o·my**, *n.*, *pl.* **-mies**. 1. thrift. 2. system of producing and dividing wealth. —**e·con'o·mize''**, *v.t.*

**ec·sta'sy**, *n.*, *pl.* **-sies**. state of overwhelming emotion. —**ec·stat'ic**, *adj.*, *n.*

**ec'ze·ma**, *n.* scaly skin disease.

**ed'dy**, *n.*, *pl.* **dies**, *n.* 1. turbulence of water or wind. —*v.i.* 2. move in an eddy.

**edge**, *n.* 1. outer limit. 2. sharp intersection. —*v.t.* 3. border. —*v.i.* 4. sidle. —**edge'wise''**, **edge'ways''**, *adv.*

**ed'i·ble**, *adj.* suitable for eating.

**e'dict**, *n.* decree.

**ed'i·fice**, *n.* building.

**ed'i·fy''**, *v.t.* educate or improve the mind of.

**ed'it**, *v.t.* prepare for publication or presentation. —**ed'i·tor**, *n.* —**ed''i·tor'ial**, *n.*, *adj.*

**e·di'tion**, *n.* printing of a book.

**ed'u·cate''**, *v.t.* develop the mind, knowledge or skill of. —**ed''u·ca'tion**, *n.* —**ed''u·ca'tion·al**, *adj.* —**ed'u·ca''tor**, *n.*

**eel**, *n.* long, snakelike fish.

**ef·face'**, *v.t.* eliminate all trace of.

**ef·fect'**, *n.* 1. result. 2. influence. 3. effects, personal property. —*v.t.* 4. cause. —**ef·fec'tive**, *adj.* —**ef·fec'tu·al**, *adj.*

**ef·fem'i·nate**, *adj.* unmanly.

**ef''fer·vesce'**, *v.i.* bubble. —**ef''fer·ves'cent**, *adj.* —**ef''fer·ves'cence**, *n.*

**ef·fete'**, *adj.* decadent.

**ef''fi·ca'cious**, *adj.* producing the desired result. —**ef'fi·ca·cy**, *n.*

**ef·fi'cient**, *adj.* efficacious without waste. —**ef·fi'cien·cy**, *n.*

**ef·fi'gy**, *n.*, *pl.* **-gies**. copy or image, esp. in three dimensions.

**ef'fort**, *n.* 1. expenditure of strength, thought, etc. 2. attempt. —**ef'fort·less**, *adj.*

**ef·fron'ter·y**, *n.* impudence.

**ef·fu'sion**, *n.* outpouring of enthusiasm. —**ef·fu'sive**, *adj.*

**e·gal'i·tar''i·an**, *adj.* believing that all people should be equal.

**e'go**, *n.* self. —**e'go·cen'tric**, *adj.*, *n.*

**e'go·tism**, *n.* self-conceit; vanity. —**e'go·tist''**, *n.* —**e''go·tis'tic**, *adj.*

**e·gre'gious**, *adj.* conspicuous in a bad way.

**eight**, *n.* seven plus one. —**eighth**, *adj.*

**eight·een'**, *n.* seventeen plus one.

**eight'y**, *n.* eight times ten. —**eight'i·eth**, *adj.*

**ei·ther** (ē' th ər, ī' th ər), *adj.* 1. one or the other but not both. 2. each. —*pron.* 3. one or the other. —*conj.* 4. (used to emphasize choice). —*adj.* 5. as well.

**e·jac'u·late''**, *v.t.*, *v.i.* exclaim. —**e·jac''u·la'tion**, *n.*

**e·ject'**, *v.t.* hurl or force out.

**e·lab'o·rate**, (ē lab'ə rət) 1. having many parts or aspects. —*v.t.* (ē lab'ə rāt') 2. plan in detail. —**e·lab''o·ra'tion**, *n.*

**e·lapse'**, *v.i.* pass, as time.

**e·las'tic**, *adj.* able to recover from stretching or bending. —*n.* elastic material or object. —**e·las'tic'i·ty,** *n.*

**e·late'**, *v.t.* raise in spirits.

**el'bow**, *n.* joint halfway up the arm. —*v.t., v.i.* push with the elbows.

**el'der**, *adj.* 1. senior. —*n.* 2. senior. 3. shrub with red or purple berries. —**eld'est**, *adj.* —**eld'er·ly,** *adj.*

**e·lect'**, *v.t.* 1. choose, esp. by a vote. —*adj.* 2. chosen. 3. elected to but not yet in public office. —**e·lec'tion**, *n.* —**e·lec'tor**, *n.* —**e·lec'tor·al**, *adj.* —**e·lec'tor·ate**, *n.* —**e·lec'tive**, *adj.*

**e·lec'tric'i·ty**, *n.* 1. property of motion in certain particles composing matter. 2. current created by such motion. —**e·lec'tric**, *adj.* —**e·lec'tri·cal**, *adj.*

**e·lec'tro·cute'**, *v.t.* injure or kill with electricity.

**e·lec'trode**, *n.* object conducting electricity into or out of a battery, etc.

**e·lec'tron**, *n.* negatively charged particle of an atom.

**e·lec·tron'ics**, *n., sing.* study of the action of electrons and its application to technology. —**e·lec'tron'ic**, *adj.*

**el'e·gant**, *adj.* tasteful and dignified. —**el'e·gance,** *n.*

**el'e·gy**, *n., pl.* **-gies.** poem of lament, esp. for the dead. —**el''e·gi'ac, el''e·gi'a·cal,** *adj.*

**el'e·ment**, *n.* 1. basic or basic component. 2. natural environment. 3. **elements**, natural forces, esp. of weather. —**el''e·men'tal,** *adj.*

**el''e·men'ta·ry**, *n.* fundamental; rudimentary.

**el'e·phant**, *n.* large four-legged animal with a long prehensile nose.

**el'e·vate''**, *v.t.* 1. raise to a greater height. 2. raise in rank, spirits, etc.

**el''e·va'tion**, *n.* height.

**el'e·va''tor**, *n.* 1. cabinet or platform for raising or lowering persons or goods. 2. storage place for grain.

**e·lev'en**, *n.* ten plus one.

**elf**, *n., pl.* **elves.** small fairy.

**el·ic'it**, *v.t.* draw forth.

**el'i·gi·ble**, *adj.* suitable for choice.

**e·lim'i·nate''**, *v.t.* get rid of. —**e·lim''i·na'tion,** *n.*

**e·lite'** (i lēt'), *n.* choice element. —**e·lit'ism,** *n.*

**e·lix'ir**, *n.* medicine in a solution of alcohol.

**elm**, *n.* tall deciduous tree.

**el''o·cu'tion**, *n.* public speaking.

**e·lon'gate**, *v.t., v.i.* lengthen.

**e·lope'**, *v.i.* flee, esp. in order to marry.

**e·lo'quent**, *adj.* convincing in speech. —**e·lo'quence,** *n.*

**else**, *adj.* 1. other. 2. more. —*adv.* 3. otherwise.

**else'where''**, *adv.* somewhere else.

**e·lu'ci·date''**, *v.t.* clarify; explain.

**e·lude'**, *v.t.* escape or evade. —**e·lu'sive,** *adj.*

**e·ma'ci·ate''**, *v.t.* make abnormally thin.

**em'a·nate''**, *v.i.* come forth; issue.

**e·man'ci·pate''**, *v.t.* free, as from bondage. —**e·man''ci·pa''tor,** *n.*

**e·mas'cu·late''**, *v.t.* castrate.

**em·balm'**, *v.t.* preserve against decay after death.

**em·bank'**, *v.t.* support, strengthen, etc. with piled earth, etc. —**em·bank'ment,** *n.*

**em·bar'go**, *n., pl.* **-goes.** *n.* ban on shipping or commerce.

**em·bark'**, *v.i.* 1. set forth, esp. on a ship. —*v.t., v.i.* 2. board, esp. a ship. —**em''bar·ka'tion,** *n.*

**em·bar'rass**, *v.t.* 1. make ashamed or self-conscious. 2. put at a loss for money.

**em'bas·sy**, *n.* mission to a foreign government.

**em·bed'**, *v.t.* sink and fix firmly.

**em·bel'lish**, *v.t.* decorate.

**em'ber**, *n.* red-hot piece of fuel.

**em·bez'zle**, *v.t.* steal from an employer, client, etc. —**em·bez'zler,** *n.* —**em·bez'zle·ment,** *n.*

**em·bit'ter**, *v.t.* make bitter.

**em'blem**, *n.* symbolic design. —**em''blem·at'ic,** *adj.*

**em·bod'y**, *v.t.* 1. realize in bodily form. 2. incorporate. —**em·bod'i·ment,** *n.*

**em·boss'**, *v.t.* mark with raised designs or lettering.

**em·brace'**, *v.t.* 1. put the arms around. 2. accept readily. —*v.i.* 3. embrace each other. —*n.* 4. act or instance of embracing.

**em·broi'der**, *v.t.* decorate with

applied colored yarns. —em·broi'-
der·y, n.

em'bry·o", n., pl. -oes. animal or
plant in the first stage of development. —em"bry·on'ic, adj.

e·mend', v.t. correct; edit.

em'er·ald, n. vivid green gem.

e·merge', v.i. appear into notice.
—e·mer'gence, n.

e·mer'gen·cy, n. mishap demanding prompt action.

e·met'ic, adj. 1. causing vomiting.
—n. 2. emetic substance.

em'i·grate", v.i. leave one's country to settle elsewhere. —em'i·-
grant, n., adj.

em'i·nent, adj. high in standing or
rank. —em'i·nence, n.

em·is·sar'y, n., pl. -ies. person
sent on a mission.

e·mit', v.t. send out or forth; discharge. —e·mis'sion, n.

e·mo'tion, n. 1. natural feelings
and reactions. 2. specific feeling
or reaction.

em'per·or, n. ruler of an empire.

em'pha·sis, n., pl. -ses. force or
stress. —em·phat'ic, adj. —em'-
pha·size", v.t.

em'pire, n. number of countries or
regions under one monarch.

em·pir'i·cal, adj. derived from
experience.

em·ploy', v.t. 1. hire or use. —n.
2. hire. —em·ploy'er, n. —em·-
ploy'ee, n. —em·ploy'ment, n.

em·po'ri·um, n., pl. -ums, -a.
store with varied merchandise.

em'press, n. woman married to or
with the rank of an emperor.

emp'ty, adj., -tier, -tiest, adj. 1.
lacking contents. —v.t. 2. make
empty. —v.i. 3. become empty.
—emp'ti·ness, n.

e·mu'late", v.t. imitate, esp. in excellence. —em'u·lous, adj.

e·mul'sion, n. mixture of two liquids made possible by addition of
a third. —e·mul'si·fy", v.t.

en·act', v.t. 1. make into law. 2.
represent in a play. —en·act'-
ment, n.

en·am'el, n. 1. glassy, fused coating. 2. hard, glossy paint. 3. exterior material of teeth. —v.t. 4.
cover with enamel.

en·am'ored, adj. full of love.

en·camp', v.i., v.t. camp. —en·-
camp'ment, n.

en·case', v.t. enclose.

en·chant', v.t. 1. charm. 2. put a
magic spell on.

en·cir'cle, v.t. surround.

en·close', v.t. 1. surround. 2. put
into a container, envelope, etc.
—en·clo'sure, n.

en·com'pass, v.t. 1. surround. 2.
include.

en·core (ahn'kōr), interj. 1.
again: request to a musician. —n.
2. repetition of a musical performance.

en·coun'ter, v.t. 1. happen to
meet. 2. meet in combat. —n. 3.
act or instance of encountering.

en·cour'age, v.t. give courage or
resolution to.

en·croach', v.i. trespass. —en·-
croach'ment, n.

en·cum'ber, v.t. burden or hinder. —en·cum'brance, n.

en·cy"clo·pe'di·a, n. reference
work dealing at length with all
areas of knowledge. Also, en·cy"-
clo·pae'di·a.

end, n. 1. far or final part. 2. result. 3. purpose. —v.t. 4. put an
end to. —v.i. 5. come to an end.
—end'less, adj.

en·dan'ger, v.t. put in danger.

en·deav'or, v.t., n. attempt.

en·dorse', v.t. 1. write on the back
of, esp. a signature. 2. approve.

en·dow', v.t. 1. provide with personal resources or qualities. 2.
give money for.

en·dure', v.t. 1. tolerate. 2. suffer.
—v.i. 3. survive. —en·dur'ance,
n.

en'e·my, n., pl. -mies. 1. person
who wishes one harm. 2. hostile
nation or military force.

en'er·gy, n., pl. -gies. 1. force
able to produce motion, heat,
light, etc. 2. vigor.

en'er·vate", v.t. deprive of vitality.

en·force', v.t. administer forcefully, as a law. —en·force'ment, n.

en·gage', v.t. 1. commit. 2. commit to marriage. 3. hire. 4. hold
or connect with. 5. meet and
fight.

en·gag'ing, adj. charming.

en·gen'der, v.t. bring into being.

en'gine, n. 1. machine producing
mechanical force, esp. by means of
heat energy. 2. locomotive.

en"gi·neer', n. 1. person who designs systems or structures applying static or dynamic forces or various sources of energy. 2. skilled
operator of machines, etc. —en"-
gi·neer'ing, n.

**en·grave′**, v.t. form designs or letters with shallow cuts on wood, steel, etc. —**en·grav′er**, n.

**en·gross′**, v.t. capture the attention of.

**en·gulf′**, v.t. swallow up; submerge.

**en·hance′**, v.t. increase or improve.

**e·nig·ma**, n., pl. **-mas**. puzzle. —**e′nig·mat′ic**, adj.

**en·join′**, v.t. forbid.

**en·joy′**, v.t. 1. get pleasure from. 2. have the benefit of.

**en·large′**, v.t. 1. make larger. —v.i. 2. become larger.

**en·light′en**, v.t. free of ignorance or wrong attitudes.

**en·list′**, v.t., v.i. enroll. —**en·list′ment**, n.

**en·mi·ty**, n., pl. **-ties**. hostility.

**e·nor′mi·ty**, n., pl. **-ties**. 1. wickedness. 2. outrage.

**e·nor′mous**, adj. beyond normal size or extent. —**e·nor′mous·ly**, adv.

**e·nough′**, n., adj., adv. n. 1. as much as is wanted; sufficiency. —adj. 2. adequate; sufficient. —adv. 3. sufficiently.

**en·quire′**, v.t., v.i. inquire. —**en·quir′y**, n.

**en·rage′**, v.t. put in a rage.

**en·rich′**, v.t. make rich or richer. —**en·rich′ment**, n.

**en·roll′**, v.t. name on a list or record. —**en·roll′ment**, n.

**en route**, on the way.

**en·sconce′**, v.t. put in a snug or secure place.

**en·sem′ble**, n. related group.

**en·sign′**, n. 1. flag, as on a ship. 2. lowest commissioned naval officer.

**en·slave′**, v.t. make a slave of.

**en·sue′**, v.i. follow, esp. as a consequence.

**en·sure′**, v.t. make sure.

**en·tail′**, v.t. necessitate.

**en·tan·gle**, v.t. trap or impede.

**en·ter**, v.t. 1. go into. 2. have enrolled in or admitted to something. 3. list or record.

**en′ter·prise′**, n. 1. project with some risk. 2. willingness to undertake such projects.

**en′ter·tain′**, v.t. 1. have as a guest. 2. amuse. 3. consider. —**en′ter·tain′ment**, n.

**en·thu′si·asm**, n. intense approval, or favor. —**en·thu′si·ast**, n. —**en·thu′si·as′tic**, adj.

**en·tice′**, v.t. tempt, esp. deceitfully.

**en·tire′**, adj. complete. —**en·tire′ly**, adv. —**en·tire′ty**, n.

**en·ti·tle**, v.t. give a right or claim.

**en·ti·ty**, n., pl. **-ties**. one that exists.

**en″to·mol′o·gy**, n. study of insects. —**en″to·mol′o·gist**, n.

**en·tou·rage** (ahn″tŏŏ rahzh′), n. followers of an important person.

**en′trails**, n., pl. internal organs, esp. viscera.

**en·trance**, n. (in′trans) 1. way of entering. 2. right to enter. 3. act of entering. —v.t. (en trans′) 4. fill with wonder.

**en·trap′**, v.t. catch, as if in a trap.

**en·treat′**, v.t., v.i. ask earnestly. —**en·treat′y**, n.

**en·try**, n., pl. **-tries**. 1. entrance. 2. something noted. 3. competitor.

**e·nu′mer·ate″**, v.t. cite one by one. 2. count.

**e·nun′ci·ate″**, v.t., v.i. speak distinctly. —**e·nun′ci·a″tion**, n.

**en·vel′op**, v.i. wrap up.

**en′ve·lope″**, n. 1. paper cover for letters, papers, etc. 2. outer covering.

**en·vi′ron·ment**, n. 1. surroundings. 2. conditions. —**en·vi′ron·men′tal**, adj.

**en·vis′age**, v.t. visualize; contemplate.

**en·vi′sion**, v.t. contemplate as likely.

**en′voy**, n. diplomatic representative.

**en′vy**, n. 1. resentment over another's good luck. —v.t. 2. feel envy toward. —**en′vi·a·ble**, adj. —**en′vi·ous**, adj.

**e′on**, n. very long period.

**ep′ic**, adj. 1. heroic. —n. 2. poem about heroism.

**ep′i·cure″**, n. person with refined tastes, esp. for food and drink. —**ep′i·cu·re′an**, adj., n.

**ep′i·dem′ic**, adj. 1. spreading through a community. —n. 2. epidemic disease.

**ep′i·gram″**, n. witty observation. —**ep′i·gram·mat′ic**, adj.

**ep′i·logue″**, n. final statement of a play, etc.

**e·pis′co·pal**, adj. pertaining to or governed by a bishop.

**ep′i·sode″**, n. occurrence. —**ep″·i·sod′ic**, adj.

**e·pis′tle**, n. letter; written message.

**ep′i·taph″**, n. inscription on a tomb.

**ep′i·thet″**, n. characterizing name.

**E**
**F**

**e·pit'o·me''**, *n.*, *pl.* **-mes. 1.** summary. **2.** typical example. —**e·pit'o·mize''**, *v.t.*

**ep'och**, *n.* distinct historical or geological period. —**ep'och·al**, *adj.*

**eq'ua·ble**, *adj.* emotionally steady.

**e'qual**, *adj.* **1.** of the same amount, rank, etc. **2.** competent; adequate. —*n.* **3.** equal person or thing. —*v.t.* **4.** be equal to. —**e·qual'i·ty**, *n.* —**e'qual·ize''**, *v.t.*

**e·quate'**, *v.t.* regard as equal. —**e·qua'tion**, *n.*

**e·qua'tor**, *n.* imaginary line bisecting the earth. —**e''qua·to'ri·al**, *adj.*

**e''qui·lat'er·al**, *adj.* with equal sides.

**e''qui·lib'ri·um**, *n.* balance.

**e'qui·nox''**, *n.* time of equal day and night periods, marking the beginning of spring or autumn.

**e·quip'**, *v.t.* furnish with what is necessary. —**e·quip'ment**, *n.*

**e'qui·ta·ble**, *adj.* just; fair.

**e'qui·ty**, *n.* **1.** fairness. **2.** value of something in excess of money owed for it.

**e·quiv'a·lent**, *adj.*, *n.* equal. —**e·quiv'a·lence**, *n.*

**e·quiv'o·cal**, *adj.* of doubtful meaning or nature.

**er'a**, *n.* distinctive historical period.

**e·rad'i·cate''**, *v.t.* eliminate by destroying.

**e·rase'**, *v.t.* obliterate. —**e·ra'sure**, *n.*

**e·rect'**, *adj.* **1.** upright. —*v.t.* **2.** build. —**e·rec'tion**, *n.*

**er'mine**, *n.* weasel with white winter fur.

**e'ro**, *n.*, *pl.* **-roes. 1.** person of courage and accomplishment. **2.** protagonist. Also, *fem.*, **he'ro·ine**. —**he·ro'ic**, *adj.* —**he'ro·ism**, *n.*

**e·rode'**, *v.t.*, *v.i.* wash away or out. —**e·ro'sion**, *n.*

**e·rot'ic**, *adj.* pertaining to or arousing sexual desire. —**e·rot'i·cism**, *n.*

**err**, *v.i.* be in error.

**er'rand**, *n.* journey for some purpose.

**er'rant**, *adj.* wandering.

**er·rat'ic**, *adj.* unreliable.

**er·ra'tum**, *n.*, *pl.* **-a.** printing or writing error.

**er·ro'ne·ous**, *adj.* in error.

**er'ror**, *n.* mistaken belief or action.

**er'u·dite''**, *adj.* informed; scholarly.

**e·rupt'**, *v.i.* break forth.

**es'ca·late''**, *v.i.* **1.** rise on an escalator. **2.** increase rapidly.

**es'ca·la''tor**, *n.* endless moving stair.

**es'ca·pade''**, *n.* reckless adventure.

**es·cape'**, *v.t.*, *v.i.* **1.** flee. —*v.t.* **2.** evade the notice of. —*n.* **3.** act or instance of escaping.

**es·cap'ism**, *n.* tendency to attempt to escape reality.

**es·chew'**, *v.t.* shun; do without.

**es·cort'**, *v.t.* (i skort') **1.** take charge of and accompany. —*n.* (es'kort) **2.** person or thing that escorts.

**es'crow**, *n. Law.* state of property that is temporarily held in trust for another.

**es''o·ter'ic**, *adj.* reserved for an understanding few.

**es'pi·o·nage''**, *n.* practice of spying.

**es·pouse'**, *v.t.* **1.** marry. **2.** devote oneself to. —**es·pous'al**, *n.*

**es·say'**, *n.* (es'sā) **1.** writing on some theme. —*v.t.* (es sā') **2.** attempt. —**es'say·ist**, *n.*

**es'sence**, *n.* **1.** basic nature. **2.** concentrated substance.

**es·sen'tial**, *adj.* **1.** indispensable. —*n.* **2.** something indispensable.

**es·tab'lish**, *v.t.* **1.** bring into being. **2.** prove.

**es·tate'**, *n.* **1.** personal property. **2.** grounds belonging to a house.

**es·teem'**, *n.* **1.** evaluation. —*v.t.* **2.** deem.

**es·ti·mate**, *n.* (es'tə mət) **1.** rough calculation or appraisal. —*v.t.* (es'tə māt'') **2.** make an estimate of.

**es·trange'**, *v.t.* lose the affection of.

**es'tu·ary**, *n.*, *pl.* **-ies.** tidal river mouth.

**et cetera**, and other persons or things. Abbreviated **etc.**

**e·ter'nal**, *adj.* lasting or valid forever.

**e'ther**, *n.* **1.** upper part of the atmosphere. **2.** volatile, flammable anaesthetic or solvent.

**e·the're·al**, *adj.* **1.** delicate. **2.** unearthly.

**eth'ics**, *n.* **1.** study of right and wrong in actions. **2.** *pl.* **a.** Also, **eth'ic**, personal standards of right and wrong action. **b.** standards of conduct adopted by professionals. —**eth'i·cal**, *adj.*

**eth'nic**, *adj*. 1. pertaining to distinct nations or tribes. —*n*. 2. member of a minority national group. —**eth·nic'i·ty**, *n*.

**et'i·quette**, *n*. code of acceptable conduct.

**e''ty·mol'o·gy**, *n*. study of word origins.

**eu'lo·gy**, *n*., *pl.* -gies. praise in speech or writing. —**eu'lo·gize**, *v.t*.

**eu'phe·mism**, *n*. expression substituted for a less agreeable one. —**euphe·mis'tic**, *adj*.

**eu·pho'ri·a**, *n*. sensation of wellbeing. —**eu·phor'ic**, *adj*.

**eu''tha·na'si·a**, *n*. killing to prevent or end suffering.

**e·vac'u·ate**, *v.t*. 1. empty. 2. send to a place of security.

**e·vade'**, *v.t*. avoid or escape from. —**e·va'sion**, *n*. —**e·va'sive**, *adj*.

**e·val'u·ate''**, *v.t*. estimate the worth of.

**e''van·gel'i·cal**, *adj*. 1. pertaining to the New Testament. 2. emphasizing salvation through Jesus.

**e·van'gel·ist**, *n*. 1. author of a Gospel. 2. itinerant preacher. —**e·van'gel·ism**, *n*.

**e·vap'o·rate''**, *v.t.*, *v.i*. turn into vapor.

**eve**, *n*. time just before.

**e'ven**, *adj*. 1. level or smooth. 2. unvarying. 3. equal. 4. divisible by two. 5. with nothing owed. —*adv*. 6. although improbable. 7. yet; still. —*v.t*. 8. make even. —**e'ven·ness**, *n*.

**eve'ning**, *n*. time between afternoon and night.

**e·vent'**, *n*. something that happens. —**e·vent'ful**, *adj*.

**e·ven'tu·al**, *adj*. at some future time. —**e·ven'tu·al·ly**, *adv*.

**e·ven''tu·al'i·ty**, *n*., *pl.* -ties. possible occurrence.

**ev'er**, *adv*. at any time.

**ev'er·green'**, *adj*. 1. with green leaves all the year round. —*n*. 2. evergreen tree or plant.

**ev'er·y**, *adj*. 1. each individual. 2. any possible.

**ev'er·y·where''**, *adv*. at or to every place.

**e·vict'**, *v.t*. drive out, as from rented lodgings.

**ev'i·dence**, *n*. 1. matter supporting an argument. —*v.t*. 2. make evident.

**ev'i·dent**, *adj*. obvious.

**e'vil**, *adj*. 1. wrong or wicked. 2. injurious. —**e'vil·ly**, *adv*.

**e·vince'**, *v.t*. make obvious.

**e·voke'**, *v.t*. call forth. —**e·voc'a·tive**, *adj*. —**ev''o·ca'tion**, *n*.

**e·volve'**, *v.t.*, *v.i*. develop gradually. —**ev''o·lu'tion**, *n*.

**ex·ac'er·bate''** (eks as'ər bāt), *v.t*. aggravate.

**ex·act'**, *adj*. 1. accurate. 2. precise. —*v.t*. 3. extort or demand. —**ex·act'ing**, *adj*. —**ex·ac'tion**, *n*.

**ex·ag'ger·ate''**, *v.t*. overstate the importance of.

**ex·alt'**, *v.t*. 1. raise in status. 2. praise. —**ex''al·ta'tion**, *n*.

**ex·am'ine**, *v.t*. 1. inspect. 2. test for knowledge.

**ex·am'ple**, *n*. 1. sample. 2. illustrative instance.

**ex·as'per·ate''**, *v.t*. anger or annoy seriously.

**ex'ca·vate''**, *v.t*. dig, as in or from earth.

**ex·ceed'**, *v.t*. 1. be in excess of. 2. surpass.

**ex·cel'**, *v.t.*, *v.i*. surpass.

**ex'cel·lent**, *adj*. among the finest of its kind.

**ex·cept'**, *prep*. 1. Also, **ex·cept'ing**, aside from. —*v.t*. 2. exclude or disregard. —**ex·cep'tion**, *n*.

**ex·cep'tion·al**, *adj*. highly unusual.

**ex'cerpt**, *n*. quotation, esp. printed.

**ex·cess'**, *n*. (ik ses', ek'ses'') 1. lack of self-restraint or moderation. 2. surplus. —*adj*. (ek'ses'') 3. surplus. —**ex·ces'sive**, *adj*.

**ex·change'**, *v.t*. 1. give in return for something else. —*n*. 2. act or instance of exchanging.

**ex·cise'**, *n*. 1. (ek'sīz) tax on merchandise. —*v.t*. (ik sīz') 2. cut out. —**ex·ci'sion**, *n*.

**ex·cite'**, *v.t*. 1. stimulate. 2. rouse emotionally.

**ex·claim'**, *v.i.*, *v.t*. shout or speak loudly and emotionally. —**ex''cla·ma'tion**, *n*.

**ex·clude'**, *v.t*. leave or keep out. —**ex·clu'sion**, *n*. —**ex·clu'sive**, *adj*.

**ex'cre·ment**, *n*. excreted matter.

**ex·crete'**, *v.t*. eliminate as waste from the body. —**ex·cre'tion**, *n*. —**ex'cre·to''ry**, *adj*.

**ex·cur'sion**, *n*. short pleasure journey.

**ex·cuse'**, *v.t*. (iks kyōōz') 1. remove or mitigate the blame of or for. 2. forgive. 3. permit to leave. —*n.* (eks kyōōs') 4. something that excuses. —ex·cus'a·ble, *adj.* —ex·cus'a·bly, *adv.*

ex'e·cute', *v.t.* 1. perform. 2. kill after condemnation. —ex''e·cu'tion, *n.* —ex''e·cu'tion·er, *n.*

ex·ec'u·tive, *adj.* 1. concerned with administration of laws, policies, etc. —*n.* 2. person in an executive capacity.

ex·ec'u·tor, *n.* person who administers a will. Also, *fem.*, ex·ec'u·trix.

ex·em'pla·ry, *adj.* serving as a good example.

ex·em'pli·fy', *v.t.* be an example of.

ex·empt', *v.t., adj.* free from an obligation.

ex'er·cise'', *n.* 1. activity developing skill, knowledge, strength, etc. 2. performance. 3. exercises, ceremony. —*v.t.* 4. cause to do exercises. 5. put into effect.

ex·ert', *v.t.* put into action. —ex·er'tion, *n.*

ex·hale', *v.t., v.i.* breathe out. —ex''ha·la'tion, *n.*

ex·haust', *v.t.* 1. empty; deplete. 2. tire thoroughly. —*n.* 3. waste gas, etc. from machinery. —ex·haus'tion, *n.*

ex·haus'tive, *adj.* omitting nothing.

ex·hib'it, *v.t., n.* display. —ex''hi·bi'tion, *n.* —ex·hib'i·tor, *n.*

ex''hi·bi'tion·ism, *n.* ostentation; self-display.

ex·hil'a·rate'', *v.t.* 1. fill with delight. 2. stimulate.

ex·hort', *v.t.* urge strongly. —ex''hor·ta'tion, *n.*

ex·hume', *v.t.* dig up after burial.

ex·i'gen·cy, *n., pl.* -cies. urgency. exigent, *adj.*

ex'ile, *v.t.* 1. banish from a country. —*n.* 2. state of banishment. 3. exiled person.

ex·ist', *v.i.* 1. have being. 2. be alive. —ex·ist'ence, *n.* —ex·ist'ent, *adj.*

ex'it, *n.* 1. departure. 2. means of departure.

ex·on'er·ate'', *v.t.* declare guiltless.

ex·or'bi·tant, *adj.* beyond reason or moderation. —ex·or'bi·tance, *n.*

ex'or·cize'', *v.t.* expel with incantations. —ex'or·cism, *n.*

ex·ot'ic, *adj.* markedly foreign.

ex·pand', *v.t., v.i.* widen. —ex·pan'sion, *n.* —ex·pan'sive, *adj.*

ex·panse', *n.* broad, unbroken area.

ex·pa'ti·ate'', *v.i.* talk or write at length.

ex·pa'tri·ate, *n.* person living outside his country.

ex·pect', *v.t.* 1. regard as going to happen. 2. regard as obligatory.

ex·pec'to·rate'', *v.t., v.i.* spit.

ex·pe'di·ent, *adj.* 1. useful on a given occasion. 2. determined by self-interest alone. —*n.* 3. something expedient. —ex·pe'di·en·cy, *n.*

ex'pe·dite'', *v.t.* 1. make faster or easier. 2. do quickly.

ex''pe·di'tion, *n.* journey for exploration or invasion. —ex''pe·di'tion·ar''y, *adj.*

ex''pe·di'tious, *adj.* prompt.

ex·pel', *v.t.* 1. oust. 2. emit.

ex·pend', *v.t.* 1. spend. 2. use up. —ex·pend'i·ture, *n.*

ex·pend'a·ble, *adj.* able or intended to be sacrificed.

ex·pense', *n.* 1. act or instance of spending. 2. cost.

ex·pen'sive, *adj.* high in price.

ex·pe'ri·ence, *n.* 1. something lived through. 2. knowledge from life, work, etc. —*v.t.* 3. have experience of.

ex·per'i·ment, *n.* 1. test establishing facts. —*v.i.* 2. engage in experiments.

expert, *n.* person with specialized knowledge or skill. —ex'pert·ly, *adv.* —ex''per·tise', ex'pert·ness, *n.*

ex·pire', *v.i.* 1. die. 2. cease to be in effect. 3. breathe out. —ex''pi·ra'tion, *n.*

ex·plain', *v.t.* 1. make understandable or meaningful. 2. account for. —ex''pla·na'tion, *n.* —ex·plan'a·to''ry, *adj.*

ex'ple·tive, *n.* exclamation.

ex'pli·ca·ble, *adj.* able to be explained.

ex·plic'it, *adj.* 1. clear. 2. outspoken.

ex·plode', *v.t., v.i.* burst from internal pressure. —ex·plo'sive, *adj., n.* —ex·plo'sion, *n.*

ex·ploit', *n.* (eks'ploit') 1. daring deed. —*v.t.* (iks ploit') 2. take advantage of. —ex''ploi·ta'tion, *n.* —ex·ploit'a·tive, *adj.*

ex·plore', *v.t., v.i.* investigate thor-

**E**
**F**

ough·ly. —ex·plor'er, *n.* —ex"·plo·ra'tion, *n.* —ex·plor'a·to'·ry, *adj.*

ex·po'nent, *n.* 1. expounder of a principle. 2. *Math.* number indicating how many times a quantity is to be multiplied by itself.

ex·port', *v.t.* (ik sport', eks'port) 1. ship out of the country. —*n.* (eks'port) 2. something exported.

ex·pose', *v.t.* 1. reveal. 2. make vulnerable. —ex·pos'ure, *n.*

ex·pos'tu·late", *v.i.* argue in objection.

ex·pound', *v.t.* state or explain.

ex·press', *v.t.* 1. communicate adequately. 2. squeeze. 3. precise; definite. —*n.* 4. vehicle on a fast, direct schedule. 5. agency for sending things. —ex·press'ive, *adj.*

ex·pres'sion, *n.* 1. means of expressing. 2. facial attitude. 3. revelation of feeling.

ex·pro'pri·ate", *v.t.* seize for public use.

ex·pul'sion, *n.* act or instance of being expelled.

ex·punge', *v.t.* erase.

ex'pur·gate", *v.t.* censor.

ex'qui·site, *adj.* of extreme refinement.

ex'tant, *adj.* alive; present.

ex·tend', *v.t.* 1. stretch or expand. 2. offer. —*v.i.* 3. be extended. —ex·ten'sion, *n.*

ex·ten'sive, *adj.* large in extent or scope.

ex·tent', *n.* amount or degree of extending.

ex·ten'u·ate", *v.t.* prompt leniency for.

ex·te'ri·or, *adj.* 1. outer or outward. —*n.* 2. outside.

ex·ter'mi·nate", *v.t.* destroy wholly.

ex·ter'nal, *adj.* exterior; outward.

ex·tinct', *adj.* no longer in existence.

ex·tinc'tion, *n.* dying-out or destruction.

ex·tin'guish", *v.t.* put out of existence, as a flame.

ex·tol', *v.t.* praise highly.

ex·tort', *v.t.* obtain by threats or force. —ex·tor'tion, *n.* —ex·tor'tion·ist, *n.* —ex·tor'tion·ate", *adj.*

ex'tra, *adj.* additional.

ex·tract', *v.t.* (ik strakt') 1. draw out. —*n.* (ek'strakt) 2. something extracted. —ex·trac'tion, *n.*

ex'tra·dite", *v.t.* surrender for prosecution to a foreign country.

ex·tra'ne·ous, *adj.* 1. from outside. 2. irrelevant.

ex·traor'di·nar'y, *adj.* 1. remarkable. 2. out of the ordinary.

ex·trav'a·gant, *adj.* beyond economy, reason, etc. —ex·trav'a·gance, *n.*

ex·treme', *adj.* 1. farthest. 2. ultimate. 3. immoderate. 4. farthest point, position, etc.

ex·trem'i·ty, *n., pl.* -ties. *n.* 1. something extreme. 2. end. 3. extremities, hands and feet.

ex'tri·cate", *v.t.* free.

ex'tro·vert", *n.* person oriented toward the outside world. —ex"·tro·ver'sion, *n.*

ex·u'ber·ant, *adj.* full of health and spirits. —ex·u'ber·ance, *n.*

ex·ude', *v.t.*, *v.i.* 1. pass through the pores. 2. seem to radiate. —exu·da'tion, *n.*

ex·ult', *v.i.* rejoice.

eye, *n.* 1. organ of sight. 2. eyelike opening. 3. visual sensitivity. —eye'ball", *n.* —eye'brow", *n.* —eye'lid", *n.* —eye'sight", *n.*

eye'lash", *n.* row of stiff hairs over the eye.

eye'sore", *n.* unpleasant sight.

# F

F, f., *n.* 1. sixth letter of the English alphabet. 2. sixth-best grade.

fa'ble, *n.* 1. moralizing story. 2. legend.

fab'ric, *n.* cloth.

fab'ri·cate", *v.t.* 1. assemble. 2. invent for deception.

fab'u·lous, *adj.* wonderful.

fa·cade', (fa sahd'), *n.* decorative building front.

face, *n.* 1. front of the human head. 2. main surface. 3. outer appearance. —*v.t.* 4. confront. —*v.i.* 5. look or be turned toward. —fa'cial, *adj.*

fac'et, *n.* 1. plane surface of a gem, etc. 2. aspect.

**fa·ce′tious**, *adj.* joking; impish; frivolous.

**fac′ile**, *adj.* revealing no effort.

**fa·cil′i·tate′′**, *v.t.* make easy.

**fa·cil′i·ty**, *n., pl.* -ties. 1. ease. 2. skill. 3. **facilities**, equipment, staff, etc.

**fac·sim′i·le**, *n.* copy; reproduction.

**fact**, *n.* objective truth. —**fac′tu·al**, *adj.*

**fac′tion**, *n.* group promoting its own interests.

**fac′tor**, *n.* 1. influential thing. 2. quantity multiplied by another.

**fac′to·ry**, *n., pl.* -ries. place of manufacture.

**fac′ul·ty**, *n., pl.* -ties. 1. aptitude or ability. 2. teaching staff.

**fad**, *n.* brief fashion or whim.

**fade**, *v.i.* 1. lose color or freshness. 2. disappear slowly.

**Fahr′en·heit′′**, *adj.* pertaining to a temperature scale with the freezing point of water at 32 degrees and the boiling point at 212 degrees.

**fail**, *v.t.* 1. attempt without success. 2. not to do. 3. disappoint. —*v.i.* 4. have no success. 5. die away. —**fail′ure**, *n.*

**faint**, *adj.* 1. weak. —*n.* 2. temporary loss of consciousness. —*v.i.* 3. go into a faint. —**faint′ly**, *adv.*

**fair**, *adj.* 1. honest; just. 2. beautiful or handsome. 3. light. 4. mediocre. 5. sunny. 6. gathering for sales or display. —**fair′ly**, *adv.*

**fair′y**, *n., pl.* -ies. creature with magic powers.

**faith**, *n.* 1. belief; confidence. 2. loyalty. 3. religion.

**fake**, *adj.* 1. false. —*n.* 2. something false. —*v.t.* 3. give a false appearance of. —**fak′er**, *n.*

**fall**, *v.i.* 1. descend without support. —*n.* 2. act or instance of falling. 3. autumn.

**fal′la·cy**, *n., pl.* -cies. instance of false reasoning. —**fal·la′cious**, *adj.*

**fal′li·ble**, *adj.* capable of mistakes. —**fal′li·bil′i·ty**, *n.*

**fal′low**, *adj.* unplanted.

**false**, *adj., faiser, falsest.* 1. not true. 2. untruthful or unfaithful. —**false′ly**, *adv.* —**false′hood′′**, *n.* —**fal′si·fy′′**, *v.t.* —**fal′si·ty**, *n.*

**fal′ter**, *v.i.* act, speak, etc. hesitantly or unsteadily.

**fame**, *n.* widespread reputation. —**fa′mous, famed**, *adj.*

**fa·mil′iar**, *adj.* 1. well known. 2. well acquainted. —**fa·mil′i·ar′i·ty**, *n.* —**fa·mil′iar·ize′′**, *v.t.*

**fam′i·ly**, *n., pl.* -lies. 1. group of relatives. 2. group of related things. —**fa·mil′ial**, *adj.*

**fam′ine**, *n.* severe food shortage.

**fam′ish**, *v.t.* starve.

**fan**, *n.* 1. device for moving air. 2. *Informal.* devotee. —*v.t.* 3. cool or move with a fan.

**fa·nat′ic**, *n.* irrational enthusiast or hater.

**fan′cy**, *adj.,* -cier, -ciest, *n., v.t. adj.* 1. elaborate. —*n.* 2. imagination. 3. liking. —*v.t.* 6. take a liking to. —**fan′ci·ful**, *adj.* —**fan′ci·ly**, *adv.*

**fan′fare′**, *n.* 1. introductory call of trumpets, etc. 2. publicity.

**fang**, *n.* long, pointed tooth.

**fan·tas′tic**, *adj.* odd and extravagant.

**fan′ta·sy**, *n., pl.* -sies. 1. imagination. 2. something imagined.

**far**, *adj., adv., farther, farthest.* at or to a great distance.

**farce**, *n.* ridiculous comedy. —**far′ci·cal**, *adj.*

**fare**, *n.* 1. money paid to travel. 2. food. —*v.i.* 3. prosper or succeed.

**fare′well′**, *interj., n., adj.* goodbye.

**far′-fetched′**, *adj.* implausible.

**farm**, *n.* 1. place for raising plants or animals. —*v.t.* 2. cultivate.

**far′sight′′ed**, *adj.* 1. provident. 2. seeing distant objects better than close ones.

**fas′ci·nate′′**, *v.t.* hold the entire attention of.

**fash′ion**, *n.* 1. manner of acting. 2. prevailing style. —*v.t.* 2. make.

**fast**, *adj.* 1. speedy. 2. firm; fixed. —*adv.* 3. firmly. —*v.i.* 4. abstain from food or drink. —*n.* 5. act or instance of fasting.

**fast′en**, *v.t.* attach; make secure. —**fas′ten·er**, *n.* —**fast′en·ing**, *n.*

**fas·tid′i·ous**, *adj.* not readily pleased.

**fat**, *adj., fatter, fattest, n. adj.* 1. having much fat. —*n.* 2. greasy material.

**fa′tal**, *adj.* causing death or destruction. —**fa′tal·ly**, *adv.*

**fate**, *n.* 1. power determining events. 2. death.

**fa´ther,** n. 1. male parent. 2. founder or originator. 3. Christian priest. —**fa´ther·hood´,** n.

**fa´ther-in-law´,** n., pl. **fathers-in-law.** father of a spouse.

**fath´om,** n. 1. Nautical. unit of 6 linear feet. —v.t. 2. probe to understand.

**fa·tigue´,** n. 1. weariness. 2. fatigues, military work clothes. —v.t. 3. tire thoroughly.

**fat´ten,** v.t. 1. make fat. —v.i. 2. become fat.

**fat´ty,** adj. containing fat.

**fat´u·ous,** adj. foolishly self-satisfied. —**fa·tu´i·ty,** n.

**fau´cet,** n. valve for running water; tap.

**fault,** n. defect.

**fa´vor,** n. 1. act of kindness. 2. approval. —v.t. 3. do a favor for. 4. treat as a favorite. 5. advocate or support. —**fa´vor·ite,** adj., n.

**fawn,** v.i. 1. show servility. —n. 2. young deer.

**faze,** v.t. daunt.

**fear,** n. 1. desire to escape danger. 2. awe. —v.t. 3. have fear of. 4. believe with regret.

**fea´si·ble,** adj. able to be done; practical.

**feast,** n. 1. religious festival. 2. lavish meal. —v.i. 3. have a feast.

**feat,** n. act of skill or daring.

**feath´er,** n. part of a bird's covering.

**fea´ture,** n. 1. distinct aspect. 2. features, face. —v.t. 4. present as a feature.

**fe´ces,** n., pl. solid excrement. —**fe´cal,** adj.

**feck´less,** adj. 1. ineffectual. 2. irresponsible.

**fe´cund,** adj. fertile. —**fe·cun´di·ty,** n.

**fed´er·al,** adj. 1. composed of federated states. 2. pertaining to a federation.

**fed´er·a´tion,** n. union of states or federations under a central government or authority.

**fee,** n. charge for services.

**fee´ble,** adj., **-bler, -blest.** without energy or force.

**feed,** v.t. 1. nourish with food. —v.i. 2. eat. —n. 3. animal food.

**feed´´back´,** n. 1. noise caused by a microphone picking up its own amplified signal. 2. reactions to an idea or course of action.

**feel,** v.t. 1. sense by touch. 2. be aware of. 3. believe. —v.i. 4. be

sensed as specified. —n. 5. feeling; sensation.

**feign,** v.t. pretend.

**feint,** n. 1. false attack made as a diversion. —v.i. 2. make a feint.

**fe·lic´i·tate´,** v.t. congratulate.

**fe·lic´i·ty,** n., pl. **-ties.** happiness.

**fe´line,** adj. pertaining to the cat family.

**fell,** v.t. cause to fall.

**fel´low,** n. man.

**felt,** n. fabric of compacted wool, etc.

**fe´male,** adj. 1. pertaining to the sex bearing offspring. —n. 2. someone or something female.

**fem´i·nine,** adj. characteristic of girls and women. —**fem´i·nin´i·ty,** n.

**fence,** n. 1. light barrier. —v.i. 2. fight with thrusting swords.

**fend,** v.t. drive or ward.

**fend´er,** n. cover for a wheel on a vehicle.

**fer·ment´,** v.t. (fər ment´) 1. break down, as through bacterial action. —v.i. 2. be broken down, as an organic substance. —n. (fûr´ment) 3. anticipatory excitement. —**fer´men·ta´tion,** n.

**fern,** n. fronded plant reproduced by spores.

**fe·ro´cious,** adj. savage. —**fe·roc´i·ty,** n.

**fer´ret,** n. 1. weasellike animal. —v.i. 2. hunt; search.

**fer´ry,** n., pl. **-ries,** v.t. n. 1. Also, **fer´ry·boat´.** boat on a shuttle service. 2. service running such a boat. —v.t. 3. transport by or as by a ferry.

**fer´tile,** adj. yielding offspring, crops, etc. —**fer·til´i·ty,** n. —**fer´til·ize´,** v.t.

**fer´vent,** adj. passionate. Also, **fer´vid.** —**fer´ven·cy, fer´vor,** n.

**fes´ti·val,** n. occasion of celebration or merrymaking. —**fes´tive,** adj. —**fes·tiv´i·ty,** n.

**fetch,** v.t. 1. get. 2. summon.

**fete** (fāt), n. 1. festive entertainment. —v.t. 2. honor with a fete. Also, **fête.**

**fet´id,** adj. evil-smelling.

**fet´ish,** n. subject of obsessive concern.

**fet´ter,** n., v.t. shackle or chain.

**fe´tus,** n., pl. **-tuses.** unborn young in its later state. —**fe´tal,** adj.

**feud,** n. murderous rivalry between families.

**feu'dal·ism,** *n.* system of serfs and overlords.

**fe'ver,** *n.* excess of body temperature.

**fe'ver blis'ter,** *n.* a cold sore.

**few,** *adj., pron., n.* some but not many.

**fi·an·cé** (fē''ahn sā'), *n.* man engaged to be married. Also, *fem.,* **fi''an·cée'.**

**fi·as'co,** *n.* failure.

**fib,** *n.* 1. minor lie. —*v.i.* 2. tell a fib.

**fi'ber,** *n.* long, thin piece of material. Also, **fi'bre.**

**fick'le,** *adj.* capricious.

**fic'tion,** *n.* 1. not factually true. 2. novels, etc.

**fic·ti'tious,** *adj.* not factually true.

**fid'dle,** *n.* 1. violin. —*v.i.* 2. play a fiddle. 3. fumble.

**fi·del'i·ty,** *n.* faithfulness.

**fid'get,** *v.i.* move or fumble nervously.

**field,** *n.* 1. area of open land. 2. area of work or knowledge.

**fiend,** *n.* 1. evil spirit. 2. vicious person. —**fiend'ish,** *adj.*

**fierce,** *adj.,* fiercer, fiercest. 1. savage. 2. violent.

**fier'y,** *adj.,* -ier, -iest. 1. covered or filled with fire. 2. passionate.

**fife,** *n.* small flute.

**fif'teen',** *n.* ten plus five. —**fif'-teenth',** *adj.*

**fifth,** *adj.* 1. following the fourth. —*n.* 2. fifth thing, person, or part.

**fif'ty,** *n., adj.* five times ten. —**fif'-ti·eth,** *adj.*

**fig,** *n.* small, sweet tree fruit.

**fight,** *n.* 1. dispute or competition with violence. 2. angry argument. —*v.t.* 3. make a fight against. —*v.i.* 4. engage in a fight.

**fig'ment,** *n.* something merely imaginary.

**fig'u·ra·tive,** *adj.* using or forming a figure of speech.

**fig'ure,** *n.* 1. shape. 2. numeral. 3. sum. —*v.t., v.t.* 4. calculate.

**fil'a·ment,** *n.* narrow thread or wire.

**file,** *n.* 1. group of documents. 2. tool for rubbing. 3. front-to-rear row. —*v.t.* 4. preserve in a file. 5. rub with a file.

**fil'i·al,** *adj.* pertaining to or appropriate in a son or daughter.

**fil'i·bus''ter,** *n.* speech hindering legislation.

**fil'i·gree'',** *n.* lace-like gold or silver wirework.

**fill,** *v.t.* 1. cause to be completely occupied. 2. satisfy the requirements of. —*v.i.* 3. become full. —*n.* 4. enough to fill.

**fil·let** (fil'ā), *n.* boneless lean cut of meat or fish.

**film,** *n.* 1. thin coating. 2. strip or sheet for registering photographic images. —*v.t.* 3. make a motion picture or photograph of.

**fil'ter,** *n.* 1. something screening out unwanted things. —*v.t.* 2. pass through a filter. —*v.i.* 3. exclude with a filter.

**filth,** *n.* foul matter.

**fin,** *n.* bladelike extension.

**fi'nal,** *adj.* at the end. —**fi·nal'i·ty,** *n.*

**fi·na·le** (fi nä'lē), *n.* concluding feature.

**fi'nal·ist,** *n.* competitor in a final contest.

**fi·nance** (fi nans', fi'nans), *n.* 1. management of money. 2. **finances,** resources of money. —*v.t.* 3. lend or obtain money for. —**fi·nan'cial,** *adj.* —**fi''nan·cier',** *n.*

**find,** *v.t.* 1. come upon by chance. 2. succeed in a search for. —*n.* 3. valuable discovery. —**find'ing,** *n.*

**fine,** *adj.,* finer, finest, *n., v.t. adj.* 1. in tiny pieces. 2. excellent. —*n.* 3. money penalty. —*v.t.* 4. impose a fine on.

**fi·nesse'** *n.* skill, esp. in human relations.

**fine''-tune'',** *v.* to make minor adjustments.

**fin'ger,** *n.* extension of the hand.

**fin'ish,** *v.t.* 1. bring to an end. 2. give a desired surface to. —*v.i.* 3. end an activity.

**fi·nite** (fīnīt), *adj.* not endless.

**fir,** *n.* cone-bearing evergreen tree.

**fire,** *n.* 1. burning. 2. deep feeling. 3. discharge of guns. —*v.t.* 4. set fire to. 5. discharge, as of a gun. —**fire'proof'',** *adj.*

**fire'arm'',** *n.* weapon operated by explosives.

**fire'works'',** *n., pl.* explosive and burning devices used in celebrations.

**firm,** *adj.* 1. unyielding. 2. steady. —*n.* 3. business organization.

**fir'ma·ment,** *n.* heavens.

**first,** *adj., adv.* 1. at the very front or beginning. 2. before all others. —*n.* 3. first person or thing.

**first'-hand'**, *adj.*, *adv.* without intermediaries.

**fis'cal**, *adj.* pertaining to income and expense; financial.

**fish**, *n.*, *pl.* **fish**, *v.i.* **1.** cold-blooded water animal, breathing with gills. —*v.i.* **2.** attempt to catch fish. —**fish'er·man**, *n.*

**fis'sion**, *n.* splitting; cleaving.

**fis'sure**, *n.* crack.

**fist**, *n.* ball of the hand and fingers for striking.

**fit**, *v.*, *adj.*, **fitter, fittest**, *n.* *v.i.* **1.** be suitable, esp. in size. —*v.i.* **2.** be suitable for. **3.** cause to be suitable. —*adj.* **4.** suitable. **5.** healthy. —*n.* **6.** manner of fitting. **7.** bodily seizure.

**fit'ful**, *adj.* intermittent; spasmodic.

**fit'ting**, *adj.* suitable.

**five**, *adj.*, *n.* four plus one.

**fix**, *v.t.* **1.** repair or adjust. **2.** prepare. **3.** establish firmly. —**fix'i·ty**, *n.*

**fix·a'tion**, *n.* psychological obsession.

**fix'ture**, *n.* attached piece of equipment.

**fizz**, *v.i.* emit a buzzing bubbling sound.

**fiz'zle**, *v.i.* **1.** fail. —*n.* **2.** failure.

**flab'by**, *adj.* fat, soft, and weak.

**flac·cid** (flak'sid) *adj.* flabby.

**flag**, *n.* **1.** emblem-bearing cloth. **2.** Also, **flag'stone''**, flat paving stone. —*v.t.* **3.** signal with a flag.

**fla'grant**, *adj.* outrageously evident. —**fla'gran·cy**, *n.*

**flail**, *n.* **1.** hand-held threshing device. —*v.t.* **2.** beat or move in a flaillike manner.

**flair**, *n.* shrewd perceptiveness or talent.

**flake**, *n.* **1.** thin piece. —*v.i.* **2.** fall off in flakes.

**flam·boy'ant**, *adj.* brashly ostentatious.

**flame**, *n.* burning gas. —*v.i.* **2.** be burned with flames.

**flam'ma·ble**, *adj.* burnable.

**flange**, *n.* perpendicular edge.

**flank**, *n.* **1.** side. —*v.t.* **2.** be beside. **3.** attack or get around the flank of.

**flan'nel**, *n.* loosely woven wool or cotton.

**flap**, *n.* **1.** hinged panel. **2.** sound of flapping. —*v.t.*, *v.i.* **3.** move to and fro.

**flare**, *v.i.* **1.** blaze. **2.** curve outward. —*n.* **3.** torchlike signal.

**flash**, *n.* **1.** momentary bright light. **2.** moment. —*v.i.* **3.** emit a flash. —*v.t.* **4.** cause to flash.

**flash'light''**, *n.* hand-held battery-operated light.

**flask**, *n.* bottle, often flat.

**flat**, *adj.*, **flatter, flattest**, *n.* *adj.* **1.** without rises or hollows. **2.** absolute. **3.** featureless. **4.** *Music.* slightly low in pitch. —*n.* **5.** apartment. **6.** something flat. —**flat'ten**, *v.t.*, *v.i.*

**flat'ter**, *v.t.* compliment, as in order to wheedle.

**flaunt**, *v.t.* display proudly.

**fla'vor**, *n.* **1.** taste. **2.** Also, **fla'vor·ing**, something giving a certain taste. —*v.t.* **3.** add a flavor to.

**flaw**, *n.* shortcoming; fault.

**flax**, *n.* threadlike plant fiber for linen.

**flay**, *v.t.* skin.

**flea**, *n.* bloodsucking, wingless jumping insect.

**fledg'ling**, *n.* beginner at a profession, etc.

**flee**, *v.t.*, *v.i.* escape; run.

**fleece**, *n.* **1.** covering of a sheep, etc. —*v.t.* **2.** cheat. —**fleec'y**, *adj.*

**fleet**, *n.* **1.** ships under one command. —*adj.* **2.** swift.

**fleet'ing**, *adj.* passing quickly.

**flesh**, *n.* **1.** muscle tissue. **2.** soft part of a plant. **3.** animal meat.

**flesh'ly**, *adj.* bodily; sensual.

**flex**, *n.*, *v.t.*, *v.i.* bend. —**flex'i·ble**, *adj.*

**flex'time, flex''i·time**, *n.* system in which work hours are flexible.

**flick**, *n.* **1.** quick, light motion. —*v.t.* **2.** throw, etc. with such a motion.

**flick'er**, *v.i.* have a wavering light or appearance.

**flight**, *n.* **1.** act or instance of flying or fleeing. **2.** stair between floors.

**flight'y**, *adj.*, **-ier, -iest.** overly emotional or whimsical.

**flim'sy**, *adj.*, **-ier, -iest.** readily torn or broken.

**flinch**, *v.i.* hold back or retreat, as from a blow.

**fling**, *v.t.* **1.** hurl. —*n.* **2.** act or instance of flinging. **3.** brief indulgence.

**flint**, *n.* spark-producing gray siliceous rock. —**flint'y**, *adj.*

**flip**, *v.t.* **1.** toss jerkily. —*n.* **2.** act or instance of flipping.

**E F**

**flip'pant,** adj. cheerfully disrespectful.

**flip'per,** n. flat limb for paddling.

**flirt,** v.i. 1. make mild erotic advances. 2. consider something unseriously.

**flit,** v.i. move quickly and lightly.

**float,** v.i. 1. be carried on water, etc. —n. 2. something that floats.

**flock,** n. 1. group of sheep, etc. —v.i. 2. join in a flock.

**flog,** v.t. whip.

**flood,** n. 1. overflow, as of a river. —v.t., v.i. 2. fill to excess.

**floor,** n. 1. supporting interior surface. 2. bottom surface. 3. right to speak. —v.t. 4. supply with a floor. —floor'ing, n.

**floor ex'er·cise'',** n. tumbling maneuvers performed on a mat in a competitive gymnastics event.

**flop,** v.t., v.i. 1. overturn heavily. —v.i. 2. move clumsily. 3. Informal. fail. —n. 4. act or instance of flopping.

**flo'ral,** adj. pertaining to flowers.

**flor'id,** adj. 1. ruddy. 2. gaudy.

**flo'rist,** n. flower merchant.

**floss,** n. soft down or twisted thread.

**flo·til'la,** n. small fleet.

**flounce,** v.i. 1. move quickly and jerkily. —n. 2. act or instance of flouncing.

**floun'der,** n. 1. edible flat fish. —v.i. 2. struggle.

**flour,** n. powdered grain, etc.

**flour'ish,** v.i. 1. thrive. —v.t. 2. wave.

**flout,** v.t. show scorn for.

**flow,** v.i. 1. move steadily, as a liquid. —n. 2. act or instance of flowing.

**flow'er,** n. 1. petaled seed-producing part of a plant; blossom. —v.i. 2. produce blossoms.

**flu,** n. influenza.

**fluc'tu·ate'',** v.i. change rate or quantity irregularly.

**flue,** n. passage for smoke, etc.

**flu'ent,** adj. speaking or writing readily.

**flu'id,** n. 1. flowing. —n. 2. liquid or gas.

**fluke,** n. 1. barb. 2. stroke of luck.

**flunk,** v.t., v.i. Informal. fail at school.

**flur'ry,** n., pl. -ries. brief spells of activity, weather, etc.

**flush,** v.t. 1. wash out. 2. frighten from cover. —v.i. 3. be flushed. 4. blush. —n. 5. act or instance of flushing. —adj. 6. even. 7. wealthy.

**flus'ter,** v.t. confuse.

**flute,** n. 1. high-pitched wind instrument. 2. Also, **flut'ing,** longitudinal concavity. —**flut'ist,** n.

**flut'ter,** v.t., v.i. 1. oscillate rapidly. —n. 2. excited state.

**flux,** n. 1. fluid state. 2. substance aiding metal fusion.

**fly,** v., **flew, flown, flying,** n., pl. **flies.** v.i. 1. move in the air. 2. go quickly. —v.t. 3. cause to move in the air. 4. flee from. —n. 5. two-winged insect.

**foam,** n. 1. fine bubbles. —v.i. 2. emit or break into foam.

**fo'cus,** n., pl. **-cuses, -ci,** v., **-cused, -cusing.** n. 1. point of concentration. 2. state of sharpness or clarity. —v.t. 3. bring into focus.

**fod'der,** n. food for horses, cows, etc.

**foe,** n. enemy.

**fog,** n. 1. water vapor obscuring vision. —v.t., v.i. 2. obscure with fog.

**foi'ble,** n. weakness.

**foil,** v.t. 1. frustrate. —n. 2. thin metal sheeting. 3. pointed sword. 4. contrasting feature.

**fold,** v.t., v.i. 1. double over. 2. wrap. —n. 3. folded place.

**fol'i·age,** n. leaves.

**folk,** n. 1. folks. a. people. b. relatives. —adj. 2. pertaining to ethnic groups.

**fol'low,** v.t. 1. go after or along. 2. happen after. 3. conform to. 4. learn from or understand. —v.i. 5. go or happen after. 6. be logically deducible.

**fol'ly,** n., pl. **-lies.** mad or foolish thing or disposition.

**fo·ment',** v.t. incite, as trouble.

**fond,** adj. full of affection.

**fon'dle,** v.t. handle fondly.

**font,** n. baptismal basin.

**food,** n. material that nourishes.

**fool,** n. 1. person of bad judgment. —v.t. 2. deceive. —v.i. 3. act like a fool.

**fool'hard''y,** adj., **-dier, -diest** unwisely audacious.

**foot,** n. 1. extremity of a leg. 2. lowermost feature; bottom; pedestal. 3. unit of 12 inches. —**foot'-hold'',** n.

**foot'ball'',** n. 1. game with a kicked ball. 2. ball used.

**foot'ing,** n. 1. support for a foot. 2. basis.

**foot''print,** n. 1. mark left by a

foot. 2. area required for an office machine.

**for**, prep. 1. in favor of. 2. in place of. 3. in order to reach, etc. 4. to be used, etc. by. 5. during. 6. obtaining in exchange. 7. considering the nature of. —conj. 8. because.

**for'age**, v.i., n. search, as for food.

**for'ay**, n. plundering expedition.

**for·bear'**, v., -bore, -borne, -bearing. v.t. 1. refrain. —v.i. 2. control oneself.

**for·bid'**, v.t., -bade or -bidden, -bidding. 1. give an order against. 2. prevent.

**force**, n. 1. agency influencing events. 2. power. 3. compulsion. 4. organization or group. —v.t. 5. compel.

**ford**, n. 1. wadeable part of a stream. —v.t. 2. wade across.

**fore**, adj., adv. 1. forward. —n. 2. front.

**fore'bear''**, n. ancestor.

**fore·bod'ing**, n. premonition.

**fore·cast''**, v.t. 1. predict. —n. 2. prediction.

**fore·close'**, v.t. deprive a mortgagor of the right of redeeming.

**fore'fath''er**, n. ancestor.

**fore'fin''ger**, n. finger nearest the thumb.

**fore·go'ing**, adj. preceding.

**fore·gone'**, adj. 1. determined in advance. 2. previous.

**fore'ground''**, n. area nearest the viewer.

**fore'head**, n. front of the head between the eyebrows and hair.

**for'eign**, adj. 1. belonging to an area outside the country. 2. not belonging where found.

**fore'man**, n. supervising worker.

**fo·ren'sic**, adj. pertaining to public debate.

**fore·run'ner**, n. predecessor.

**fore·see'**, v.t. anticipate. —fore'sight'', n.

**fore·shad'ow**, v.t. hint at in advance.

**for'est**, n. area of trees. —for''es·ta''tion, n. —for'es·try, n.

**fore·stall''**, v.t. prevent by early action.

**fore·tell'**, v.t. predict.

**fore'thought''**, n. planning, etc. in advance.

**for·ev'er**, adv. eternally.

**fore'word''**, n. book introduction.

**for'feit**, v.t. 1. have taken away because of a misdeed, etc. —n. 2. something forfeited. —adj. 3. forfeited. —for'fei·ture, n.

**forge**, n. 1. place for hammering hot metal. —v.t. 2. shape or assemble by hammering. 3. counterfeit. —v.i. 4. move against obstacles. —forg'er·y, n.

**for·get'**, v.t., -got, -gotten, -getting. 1. lose the memory of. 2. ignore. —for·get'ful, adj.

**for·give'**, v.t., -gave, -given, -giving. regard without ill despite an offense. —for·giv'a·ble, adj.

**for·go'**, v.t., -went, -gone, -going. do without.

**fork**, n. 1. pronged lifting instrument. 2. division into two branches from one. —v.i. 3. divide into two branches.

**for·lorn'**, adj. forsaken. —for·lorn'ly, adv.

**form**, n. 1. outline or contour. 2. basic organizing principle. 3. information blank. —v.t. 4. give form to. 5. develop.

**for'mal**, adj. 1. emphasizing rules or customs. 2. explicit. 3. correct in manner. —for'mal·ly, adv.

**for'mat**, n. basic design or plan.

**for'mer**, adj. 1. past. 2. being the first of two mentioned. —for'mer·ly, adv.

**for'mi·da·ble**, adj. 1. awe-inspiring. 2. difficult.

**for'mu·la**, n., pl. -las, -lae. 1. rule to be followed. 2. words to be uttered. 3. ingredients to be used. —for'mu·late'', v.t.

**for'ni·cate''**, v.i. have illicit sexual intercourse.

**for·sake'**, v.t., -sook, -saken, -saking. give up.

**fort**, n. 1. strongly fortified place. 2. army post.

**forte** (fort), n. special ability.

**forth**, adv. 1. forward. 2. outward.

**forth'com''ing**, adj. soon to appear.

**forth'right''**, adj. frank.

**forth'with''**, adv. without delay.

**for'ti·fy''**, v.t. 1. make resistant to attack. 2. strengthen.

**for'ti·tude''**, n. persistent courage.

**fort'night''**, n. two-week period.

**for'tress**, n. large fort.

**for·tu'i·tous**, adj. happening by chance.

**for'tu·nate**, adj. lucky.

**for'tune**, n. 1. luck. 2. riches.

E
F

**for'ty,** *adj., n.* four times ten. —**for'ti·eth,** *adj.*

**fo'rum,** *n.* place for or occasion of public discussion.

**for'ward,** *adv.* 1. Also, **for'wards,** to the front. —*adj.* 2. at the front. 3. presumptuous.

**fos'sil,** *n.* hardened or petrified plant or animal.

**fos'ter,** *v.t.* 1. raise, as young. 2. promote. —*adj.* 3. in a family relationship of adoption rather than blood.

**foul,** *adj.* 1. dirty. 2. disgusting. 3. unethical. —*v.t.* 4. make foul. 5. obstruct or tangle. —*n.* 6. illicit act. —**foul'ly,** *adv.*

**found,** *v.t.* establish.

**found'er,** *v.i.* 1. sink. 2. break down. —*n.* 3. person who founds.

**found'ling,** *n.* child abandoned by unknown parents.

**foun'dry,** *n., pl.* **-dries.** place for casting metal.

**foun'tain,** *n.* source of flowing water.

**four,** *adj., n.* three plus one. —**fourth,** *adj., n.*

**four'teen',** *adj., n.* ten plus four.

**fowl,** *n., pl.* **fowl.** 1. any bird. 2. domestic bird eaten as food.

**fox,** *n.* 1. small canine predatory animal. —*v.t.* 2. cheat; trick.

**foy'er,** *n.* lobby, esp. of a theater.

**fra'cas,** *n.* brawl.

**frac'tion,** *n.* portion.

**frac'tious,** *adj.* rebellious.

**frac'ture,** *n., v.t., v.i.* break.

**frag'ile,** *adj.* readily broken.

**frag'ment,** *n.* 1. broken or tornaway piece. —*v.t., v.i.* 2. break into pieces.

**fra'grant,** *adj.* sweet-smelling. —**fra'grance,** *n.*

**frail,** *adj.* 1. fragile. 2. weak, physically or morally. —**frail'ty,** *n.*

**frame,** *n., v.t.,* **framed, framing.** *n.* 1. open structure. 2. border. —*v.t.* 3. make a frame for. 4. put into words or concepts.

**fran'chise,** *n.* 1. right to vote. 2. right to do business.

**frank,** *adj.* 1. not deceitful or evasive. —*n.* 2. right to mail without postage.

**frank'furt·er,** *n.* wiener.

**fran'tic,** *adj.* wild with emotion. —**fran'ti·cal·ly,** *adv.*

**fra·ter'nal,** *adj.* brotherly.

**fra·ter'ni·ty,** *n., pl.* **-ties.** male social organization.

**frat'er·nize'',** *v.i.* be in friendly association.

**fraud,** *n.* 1. deceit for gain. 2. impostor. —**fraud'u·lent,** *adj.*

**fraught,** *adj.* filled, as with some quality.

**fray,** *v.t., v.i.* 1. wear thin. —*n.* 2. fight.

**freak,** *n.* oddity, esp. of nature.

**freck'le,** *n.* brownish skin spot.

**free,** *adj.,* **freer, freest,** *v.t., adj.* 1. not bound or controlled. 2. without charge. 3. without obstructions. —*adv.* 4. without charge. —*v.t.* 5. make free. —**free'dom,** *n.*

**free'hand'',** *adj., adv.* without rulers, compasses, etc.

**free'lance'',** *n.* 1. person paid by the assignment. —*v.i.* 2. work as a freelance.

**freeze,** *v.t., v.i.* 1. harden from cold. —*v.i.* 2. suspend all visible motion. —*n.* 3. suspension of change.

**freight,** *n.* 1. merchandise, etc. in transit. —*v.t.* 2. load with freight.

**fre·net'ic,** *adj.* frantic.

**fren'zy,** *n., pl.* **-zies.** wild excitement.

**fre'quen·cy,** *n., pl.* **-cies.** number of occurrences in a given period.

**fre'quent,** *adj.* (frē'kwənt) 1. occurring often. —*v.t.* (frē kwənt') 2. be often present at.

**fresh,** *adj.* 1. in good, new condition. 2. rested and energetic. 3. inexperienced. —**fresh'en,** *v.t., v.i.*

**fresh'man,** *n.* person in his first year, esp. in school or Congress.

**fret,** *v.i.* 1. be anxious. —*v.t.* 2. fray or gnaw. —*n.* 3. state of anxiety. 4. repeated geometrical design. —**fret'work'',** *n.*

**fri'a·ble,** *adj.* readily crumbled.

**fri'ar,** *n.* monk.

**fric'as·see'',** *n.* 1. cut and stewed meat. —*v.t.* 2. make a fricassee of.

**fric'tion,** *n.* 1. rubbing. 2. resistance to sliding. 3. conflict; antagonism.

**Fri'day,** *n.* sixth day.

**friend,** *n.* 1. person who likes or is helpful to one. 2. supporter or sympathizer. —**friend'ly,** *adj.*

**frieze,** *n.* horizontal decorative band.

**frig'ate,** *n.* 1. sailing warship with one gun deck. 2. medium-sized modern warship.

**fright**, n. sudden fear. —**fright′en**, v.t.

**frig′id**, adj. 1. cold. 2. sexually unresponsive.

**frill**, n. 1. minor ornament. 2. something unnecessary.

**fringe**, n. 1. border. 2. edging or parallel loose strands. —v.t. 3. supply or constitute a fringe for.

**frisk**, v.i. 1. gambol; frolic. —**frisk′y**, adj.

**frit′ter**, v.t. 1. waste gradually. —n. 2. fried cake.

**friv′o·lous**, adj. without proper seriousness. —**fri·vol′i·ty**, n.

**fro**, adv. **to and fro**, away and back again.

**frock**, n. robe; dress.

**frog**, n. leaping amphibian.

**frol′ic**, v.i. 1. romp. 2. make merry. —n. 3. occasion of frolicking.

**from**, prep. 1. beginning or originating at. 2. with no opportunity or use of. 3. as unlike. 4. because of.

**frond**, n. branchlike leaf.

**front**, n. 1. foremost part or surface. 2. vertical side. 3. pretense; mask. 4. forward battle area. —v.i. 5. face. —**front′age**, n. —**front′al**, adj.

**fron·tier′**, n. outer limit. —**fron′tiers·man**, n.

**fron′tis·piece″**, n. illustration beginning a book.

**frost**, n. 1. frozen vapor. 2. freezing temperature. —v.t. 3. cover with frost. 4. cover with frosting.

**frost′bite″**, n. injury to the body from freezing.

**frost′ing**, n. sweetened coating for a cake; icing.

**froth**, n., v.i. foam. —**froth′y**, adj.

**frown**, v.i. 1. expression of displeasure. —v.i. 2. assume such an expression. 3. look with disapproval.

**fru′gal**, adj. 1. thrifty. 2. meager. —**fru′gal·ly**, adv.

**fruit**, n. 1. juicy, seedbearing growth. 2. reward of endeavor. —**fruit′ful**, adj. —**fru·i′tion**, n. —**fruit′less**, adj.

**frump**, n. dowdy woman.

**frus′trate″**, v.t. prevent from succeeding.

**fry**, v.t. cook in a grease, over direct heat.

**fudge**, n. 1. soft candy made of butter, milk, sugar and flavouring. —v.i. 2. cheat.

**fu′el**, n. 1. substance for burning.

—v.t. 2. supply with fuel. —v.i. 3. take on fuel.

**fu′gi·tive**, n. 1. person who flees. —adj. 2. fleeing. 3. transitory.

**ful′crum**, n. support for a lever.

**ful·fill′**, v.t. 1. satisfy. 2. accomplish.

**full**, adj. 1. completely occupied. 2. complete. 3. broad or ample. —adv. 4. completely. 5. directly. —**ful′ly**, adv. —**full′ness**, **ful′ness**, n.

**ful′some**, adj. annoyingly excessive.

**fum′ble**, v.i. 1. grope. —v.t. 2. handle clumsily. —n. 3. act or instance of fumbling.

**fume**, n. 1. odor, smoke, etc. —v.t. 2. treat with fumes. —v.i. 3. show petulance. 4. give off fumes.

**fum′i·gate″**, v.t. expose to fumes, as to kill vermin.

**fun**, n. 1. enjoyment. 2. source of enjoyment.

**func′tion**, n. 1. purpose. 2. ceremony. —v.i. 3. operate; work.

**func′tion·ar″y**, n., pl. -ries. official.

**fund**, n. 1. money for a purpose. 2. funds, ready money.

**fun′da·men′tal**, adj. 1. basic; essential. —n. 2. something fundamental.

**fun′da·men′tal·ism**, n. literal belief in a sacred text. Also, **Fun″da·men′tal·ism**.

**fu′ner·al**, n. ceremony of farewell to the dead.

**fu·ne′re·al**, adj. mournful; solemn.

**fun′gus**, n., pl. -gi or -guses. spore-reproduced plant without chlorophyll. —**fun′gous**, adj.

**fun′nel**, n. 1. tapered channel used to help pouring. 2. smokestack.

**fun′ny**, adj., -nier, -niest. 1. comical. 2. peculiar.

**fur**, n. thick animal hair with its hide. —**fur′ry**, adj.

**fu′ri·ous**, adj. 1. wildly angry. 2. wild.

**furl**, v.t. bundle up.

**fur′long**, n. eighth of a mile.

**fur′lough**, n. military leave of absence. —v.t. 2. grant a furlough to.

**fur′nace**, n. heating chamber.

**fur′nish**, v.t. 1. supply. 2. put furniture in.

**fur′nish·ings″**, n. pl. furniture and decorative objects.

**fur′ni·ture**, n. tables, chairs, etc.

**E**

**F**

**fu'ror**, *n.* frenzied excitement.

**fur'ri·er**, *n.* dealer in furs.

**fur'row**, *n.* 1. groove or wrinkle.
—*v.t.* 2. make furrows in.

**fur'ther**, *adv.* 1. to a greater distance or extent. 2. in addition.
—*adj.* 3. additional. 4. farther.
—*v.t.* 5. promote. —**fur'ther·ance**, *n.*

**fur'ther·more''**, *adv.* in addition.

**fur'thest**, *adj.* 1. most distant.
—*adv.* 2. to the greatest distance or extent.

**fur'tive**, *adj.* sneaking.

**fu'ry**, *n., pl.* -ries. extreme rage.

**fuse**, *n.* 1. Also, **fuze**, detonating device. 2. device of fusible metal for preventing electrical overloads.
—*v.t., v.i.* 3. melt. —**fu'si·ble**, *adj.* —**fu'sion**, *n.*

**fu'sil·lade''**, *n.* discharge of massed guns.

**fuss**, *n.* 1. unreasonable show of concern. —*v.i.* 2. make a fuss.

**fu'tile**, *adj.* vain; useless. —**fu·til'i·ty**, *n.*

**fu'ture**, *n.* 1. time to come. 2. what will happen. 3. promise of success.

**fuzz**, *n.* fine hair or fibres.

# G

**G, g**, *N.* seventh letter of the English alphabet.

**ga'ble**, *n.* wall area perpendicular to a roof ridge.

**gadg'et**, *n.* mechanical contrivance.
—**gadg'et·ry**, *n.*

**gag**, *n.* 1. device to prevent speech by stopping the mouth. 2. joke.
—*v.t.* 3. silence with a gag. —*v.i.* 4. retch.

**gai'e·ty**, *n., pl.* -ties. 1. quality of being gay. 2. merrymaking.

**gai'ly**, *adv.* in a gay manner.

**gain**, *v.t.* 1. acquire. 2. reach.
—*v.i.* 3. profit. —*n.* 4. profit.

**gain''say''**, *v.t.* 1. deny. 2. contradict.

**gait**, *n.* manner of walking or running.

**ga'la**, *adj.* 1. festive. —*n.* 2. celebration.

**ga·lax·y**, *n., pl.* -ies. vast cluster of stars. —**ga·lac'tic**, *adj.*

**gale**, *n.* high wind.

**gall**, *n.* 1. liquid secreted by the liver. 2. *Informal.* impudence.

**gal'lant**, *adj.* 1. brave; high-spirited. 2. polite to women. —**gal'lan·try**, *n.*

**gal'ler·y**, *n., pl.* -ies. 1. covered passage. 2. uppermost theater balcony. 3. place for the display of art.

**gal'ley**, *n., pl.* -leys, 1. rowed ship. 2. ship's kitchen.

**gal'lon**, *n.* liquid measure of 4 quarts or 128 fluid ounces.

**gal'lop**, *n.* fastest gait of a horse.

**gal'lows**, *n., pl.* -lowses, -lows. frame for hanging condemned persons.

**gall'stone''**, *n.* stony mass in the gall bladder.

**ga·losh'**, *n.* rubber or rubberized boot.

**gal·van'ic**, *adj.* pertaining to electric currents, esp. from batteries.

**gal'va·nize''**, *v.t.* 1. apply electricity to. 2. plate with zinc.

**gam'bit**, *n.* opening in chess involving a sacrifice.

**gam'ble**, *v.i.* 1. stake money on the outcome of a game, race, etc.
—*v.t.* 2. stake by gambling. —*n.* 3. risky undertaking.

**gam'bol**, *v.i. n.* romp.

**game**, *n.* 1. contest decided by skill or chance. 2. hunted animals or birds. —*adj.* 3. *Informal.* willing to meet a challenge.

**gam'ut**, *n.* complete range.

**gan'der**, *n.* male goose.

**gang**, *n.* group of workers, criminals, etc. acting or associating together.

**gan'gling**, *adj.* awkwardly tall. Also, **gan'gly**.

**gan'gli·on**, *n., pl.* -a, -ons. mass of nerve cells.

**gan'grene**, *n.* decay of body tissue deprived of blood.

**gang'ster**, *n.* member of a criminal gang.

**gang'way''**, *n.* 1. entrance to a ship. —*interj.* 2. clear the way!

**gap**, *n.* opening; hiatus.

**gape**, *v.i.* 1. open wide. 2. stare with stupefied astonishment.

**ga·rage'**, *n.* place for keeping automobiles.

**garb**, *n.* clothing.

**gar'bage**, *n.* food refuse.

**gar'ble**, *v.t.* confuse.

**genuine**

**gar′den**, *n.* 1. area for growing plants. —*v.i.* 2. work in a garden.

**gar·gan′tu·an**, *adj.* gigantic.

**gar′goyle**, *n.* fantastic waterspout.

**gar′ish**, *adj.* vulgarly showy.

**gar′land**, *n.* wreath.

**gar′lic**, *n.* strong-flavored material from a plant bulb.

**gar′ment**, *n.* article of clothing.

**gar′net**, *n.* deep-red gemstone.

**gar′nish**, *v.t.* 1. decorate. —*n.* 2. decoration.

**gar′ret**, *n.* attic.

**gar′ri·son**, *n.* resident body of troops.

**gar·rote′**, *n.* 1. device for strangling. —*v.t.* 2. kill with a garrote.

**gar·ru′lous**, *adj.* talkative. —**gar·ru′li·ty,** *n.*

**gar′ter**, *n.* band for holding up a stocking.

**gas**, *n.* 1. expansive fluid. 2. gasoline. —*v.t.* 3. injure or kill with a gas. —**gas′e·ous**, *adj.* —**gas′sy**, *adj.*

**gash**, *n.* long, deep cut.

**gas′ket**, *n.* seal against leakage.

**gas′o·hol**, *n.* a mixture of gasoline and alcohol.

**gas′o·line′**, *n.* engine fuel derived from petroleum.

**gasp**, *v.i.* 1. sudden, short breath. —*n.* 2. act or instance of gasping.

**gas′tric**, *adj.* pertaining to the stomach.

**gas·tron′o·my**, *n.* cooking as an art.

**gate**, *n.* 1. open-air door. 2. Also **gate′way″,** structure holding such a door.

**gath′er**, *v.t.* 1. bring together. 2. infer. —*v.i.* 1. come together. 3. increase. —**gath′er·ing,** *n.*

**gauche** (gōsh), *adj.* socially awkward.

**gaud′y**, *adj.,* **-ier, -iest.** bright and showy.

**gauge** (gāj), *n.* 1. measuring instrument. 2. standard measure. —*v.t.* 3. measure. 4. estimate the amount of. Also, **gage.**

**gaunt**, *adj.* lean; bony.

**gaunt′let**, *n.* 1. glove with a flaring cuff. 2. hazardous route.

**gauze**, *n.* loosely woven cloth.

**gav′el**, *n.* hammerlike noisemaker.

**gawk**, *v.i.* stare stupidly.

**gawk′y**, *adj.,* **-ier, -iest.** ungainly.

**gay**, *adj.* 1. cheerful. 2. homosexual. ——**gay″e·ty**, **gai′·e·ty**, *n.* —**gay′ly**, *adv.*

**gaze**, *v.i.* look steadily.

**ga·zette′**, *n.* published official record.

**gaz′et·teer′**, *n.* geographical reference work.

**gear**, *n.* 1. Also, **gear′wheel″,** toothed machine wheel. 2. mechanical assembly. 3. equipment.

**gel′a·tin**, *n.* jellylike substance from bones or various vegetable substances.

**geld**, *v.t.* castrate.

**gel′id**, *adj.* icy.

**gem**, *n.* jewel.

**gen′der**, *n.* Grammar. classification into masculine, feminine, and neuter.

**gene**, *n.* entity by which hereditary characteristics are transmitted.

**ge′ne·al′o·gy**, *n.*, *pl.* **-gies.** study of ancestry.

**gen′er·al**, *adj.* 1. pertaining to a whole group. 2. unspecific. 3. common. —*n.* 4. military officer ranking above a colonel.

**gen″er·al′i·ty**, *n.*, *pl.* **-ties.** statement supposed to be generally true.

**gen′er·al·ize″**, *v.i.* infer or speak in generalities.

**gen′er·ate″**, *v.t.* bring into being.

**gen″er·a′tion**, *n.* 1. group of persons of about the same age. 2. period of about 30 years. 3. production, esp. of electricity.

**gen′er·a″tor**, *n.* machine for producing electricity.

**ge·ner′ic**, *adj.* pertaining to a group.

**gen′er·ous**, *adj.* 1. giving freely. 2. ample. —**gen′er·os′i·ty**, *n.*

**ge·net′ics**, *n.* study of heredity.

**ge′ni·al**, *adj.* warmly outgoing.

**gen′i·tals**, *n.*, *pl.* sexual organs. Also, **gen″i·ta′li·a.** —**gen′i·tal**, *adj.*

**gen′ius**, *n.* 1. presiding spirit. 2. great mental power. 3. person with such powers.

**gen·teel′**, *adj.* overrefined. —**gen·til′i·ty**, *n.*

**gen′tile**, *n.* 1. non-Jew. —*adj.* 2. non-Jewish.

**gen′tle**, *adj.* mild in manner or effect.

**gen′tle·man**, *n.* 1. man of the upper class. 2. well-mannered man.

**gen′try**, *n.* persons of the upper class.

**gen′u·flect″**, *v.i.* bend the knee in homage.

**gen′u·ine**, *adj.* 1. true; real. 2. sincere.

**G
H**

**ge·nus,** *n., pl.* **genera, genuses.** 1. type. 2. *Biology.* distinctive group of plant or animal species.

**ge·og·ra·phy,** *n., pl.* **-phies.** 1. study of the earth or its features. 2. terrain.

**ge·ol·o·gy,** *n.* study of the earth's crust. —**ge″o·log′ic, ge″o·log′i·cal,** *adj.*

**ge·om·e·try,** *n., pl.* **-tries.** study of points, lines, planes, and solids. —**ge″o·met′ric, ge″o·met′ri·cal,** *adj.*

**ge″o·phys′ics,** *n.* study of the effects of climate, etc. on the earth.

**ger′i·at′rics,** *n.* medicine dealing with old age.

**germ,** *n.* 1. disease-causing organism. 2. origin.

**ger·mane′,** *adj.* relevant.

**ger′mi·nate′,** *v.i., v.t.* sprout. —**ger′mi·na′tion** *n.*

**ger′ry·man′der,** *v.t.* manipulate election districts so as to favor one side.

**ges·tate′,** *v.t.* bear in the uterus.

**ges·tic′u·late′,** *v.i.* make gestures.

**ges′ture,** *n.* 1. move the hands, arms, etc. as a signal. —*n.* 2. act or instance of gesturing. 3. act intended to impress others.

**get,** *v.* got, gotten, getting. *v.t.* 1. take or receive. 2. cause to be or do. —*v.i.* 3. become. 4. go or arrive.

**gey′ser,** *n.* natural eruption of water or steam.

**ghast′ly,** *adj.,* **-lier, -liest.** horrible ghostlike.

**gher′kin,** *n.* small pickle.

**ghet′to,** *n., pl.* **-toes.** neighborhood populated by particular minority ethnic group.

**ghost,** *n.* spirit from the dead.

**ghoul,** *n.* 1. robber of the dead. 2. person morbidly fascinated by disasters. —**ghoul′ish,** *adj.*

**gi′ant,** *n.* 1. greatly oversized creature or thing. —*adj.* 2. gigantic.

**gib′ber** (jib′ər), *v.i.* make incoherent utterances. —**gib′ber·ish,** *n.*

**gibe** (jib), *v.i., n.* jeer.

**gib′let** (jib′lit), *n.* internal organ of fowl.

**gid′dy,** *adj.,* **-dier, -diest.** 1. dizzy. 2. frivolous.

**gift,** *n.* 1. something given. 2. natural ability.

**gi·gan′tic,** *adj.* huge.

**gig′gle,** *v.i.* 1. laugh in a quick, high-pitched way. —*n.* 2. act or instance of giggling.

**gild,** *v.t.* cover with gold leaf.

**gill,** *n.* 1. (jil) quarter of a pint; 4. fluid ounces. 2. (gill) breathing apparatus of a fish, etc.

**gim′let,** *n.* small boring tool.

**gim′mick,** *n.* gadget.

**gin,** *n.* 1. distilled grain liquor. 2. cotton seed remover. —*v.t.* 3. process with a cotton gin.

**gin′ger,** *n.* tropical spice.

**gin′ger·ly,** *adj.* 1. cautious. —*adv.* 2. cautiously.

**ging′ham,** *n.* checked or striped cotton.

**gi·raffe′,** *n.* long-necked, long-legged African animal.

**gird,** *v.t.* girded or girt, girding. surround, as with a belt.

**gird′er,** *n.* major structural beam.

**gir′dle,** *n.* 1. woman's undergarment. 2. belt. —*v.t.* 3. encircle.

**girl,** *n.* young female.

**girth,** *n.* circumference.

**gist** (jist), *n.* basic meaning or content.

**give,** *v.,* gave, given, giving, *n., v.t.* 1. transfer. 2. make a present of. 3. concede. —*v.i.* 5. yield, as to force. —*n.* 6. compressibility.

**gla′cial,** *adj.* icy.

**gla′cier,** *n.* broad, moving mass of ice.

**glad,** *adj.,* gladder, gladdest. 1. happy. 2. quite willing. —**glad′den,** *v.t., v.i.*

**glade,** *n.* open space in a forest.

**glad′i·a′tor,** *n.* swordsman in ancient Roman contests.

**glad′i·o′lus,** *n., pl.* **-luses, -li.** flower with spikes of funnel-shaped blossoms. Also, **glad′i·o′la.**

**glam′or,** *n.* mysterious charm. Also, **glam′our.**

**glance,** *v.i.* 1. look briefly. 2. ricochet. —*n.* 3. act or instance of glancing.

**gland,** *n.* bodily organ that extracts and processes elements in the blood. —**glan′du·lar,** *adj.*

**glare,** *n.* 1. dazzling brightness. 2. furious look. —*v.i.* 3. cast a glare.

**glar′ing,** *adj.* 1. dazzlingly bright. 2. flagrant.

**glass,** *n.* 1. substance of fused silicates. 2. object of this substance. 3. object with a lens or lenses. 4. **glasses,** lenses in a frame, used to aid vision. —**glas′sy,** *adj.*

**glaze,** *v.t.* 1. fill with glass, as a window. 2. put a glassy coating

on. —*v.i.* 3. become glassy. —*n.*
4. glassy coating.

**gla'zier,** *n.* person who glazes windows.

**gleam,** *n.* 1. beam of light. —*v.i.* 2. emit a gleam.

**glean,** *v.t., v.i.* gather.

**glee,** *n.* joy.

**glen,** *n.* small valley.

**glib,** *adj.,* **glibber, glibbest.** unconvincingly ready with explanations.

**glide,** *v.i., v.t.* 1. slide. —*n.* 2. act or instance of gliding.

**glid'er,** *n.* unpowered aircraft.

**glim'mer,** *n., v.i.* gleam.

**glimpse,** *v.t.* 1. see briefly or in part. —*n.* 2. act or instance of glimpsing.

**glint,** *v.i., n.* gleam or glitter.

**glis'ten,** *v.i.* reflect with a dull shine.

**glitch,** *n.* (computers) a problem or error in a program.

**glit'ter,** *v.i.* 1. shine or reflect brightly. —*n.* 2. act or instance of glittering.

**gloat,** *v.i.* experience proud or malicious pleasure.

**globe,** *n.* 1. the earth. 2. model of the earth. 3. spherical object. —**glob'al,** *adj.*

**glob'ule,** *n.* tiny ball or drop.

**gloom,** *n.* 1. darkness. 2. sadness or dreariness.

**glo'ri·fy,** *v.t.* 1. give glory to. 2. exaggerate the importance or worth of.

**glo'ry,** *n., pl.* **-ries.** *v.i.* 1. high honor. 2. splendor or splendid feature. —*v.i.* 3. take pride.

**gloss,** *n.* 1. sheen. 2. explanation.

**glos'sa·ry,** *n., pl.* **-ries.** list of terms with definitions.

**glove,** *n.* garment for the hand.

**glow,** *v.i.* 1. give off soft light or color. —*n.* 2. act or instance of glowing.

**glow'er,** *v.i.* stare threateningly.

**glu'cose,** *n.* sugar in fruit and honey.

**glue,** *n.* 1. adhesive substance. —*v.t.* 2. fasten with glue.

**glum,** *adj.,* **glummer, glummest.** gloomy; moody.

**glut,** *v.i.* 1. eat to excess. —*v.t.* 2. satiate. 3. oversupply. —*n.* 4. act or instance of glutting.

**glut'ton,** *n.* person who overeats.

**glyc'er·in,** *n.* liquid derived from fats and oils. Also, **glyc'er·ine.**

**gnarled,** *adj.* twisted or knotted, like a tree trunk.

**gnash,** *v.t.* grind in anger or frustration.

**gnat,** *n.* small, stinging insect.

**gnaw,** *v.t., v.i.* bite away gradually.

**gnome,** *n.* dwarf who guards treasure.

**go,** *v.i.* went, going, *n., pl.* goes. *v.i.* 1. leave. 2. operate. 3. belong. 4. become.

**goad,** *n., v.t.* prod.

**goal,** *n.* 1. object to be reached or attained. 2. *Sports.* area to be defended.

**goat,** *n.* horned, cud-chewing mammal.

**goat·ee',** *n.* small, pointed beard.

**gob'ble,** *v.t.* 1. eat greedily. —*v.i.* 2. make turkeylike sounds. —*n.* 3. sound of a turkey.

**go'-be·tween',** *n.* arranger of bargains between others.

**gob'let,** *n.* stemmed, deep-bowled drinking vessel.

**gob'lin,** *n.* evil supernatural being.

**god,** *n.* 1. one of the supreme beings. 2. **God,** the Supreme Being.

**god'child'',** *n.* child sponsored in religion by a godparent.

**god'ly,** *adj.,* **-lier, -liest.** devout.

**god'par'ent,** *n.* sponsor of a godchild. Also, *masc.,* **god'fa''ther,** *fem.,* **god'mother.**

**god'send',** *n.* piece of good luck.

**gog'gle,** *v.i.* stare with eyes bulging. —*n.* 2. **goggles,** protective glasses.

**go'ing,** *adj.* 1. current. 2. operative. —*n.* 3. departure. 4. conditions.

**gold,** *n.* soft, yellow, precious metallic element. —**gold'en,** *adj.*

**gold'fish'',** *n.* small yellow-orange fish.

**golf,** *n.* outdoor game played with balls knocked from ground level with clubs.

**gon'do·la,** *n.* 1. one-oared Venetian boat. 2. low-sided railroad freight car. 3. airship cabin. —**gon''do·lier',** *n.*

**gong,** *n.* thin brass disk beaten to produce sound.

**gon'or·rhe'a,** *n.* a venereal disease.

**good,** *adj.,* **better, best,** *n., adj.* 1. right; proper. 2. kind. 3. beneficial. —*n.* 5. good purpose or result. 6. **goods,** valuable objects or material.

**good''bye',** *interj.* 1. (departing salutation). —*n.* 2. saying of goodbye. Also, **good''by'.**

**G**
**H**

**good·ly**, adj., **-lier**, **-liest**. considerable in amount.

**goose**, n., pl. **geese**. web-footed ducklike bird.

**go'pher**, n. 1. burrowing rodent. 2. prairie squirrel.

**gore**, n. 1. blood. 2. triangular segment. —v.t. 3. pierce, as with a horn.

**gorge**, n. 1. narrow canyon. 2. gullet. —v.t. 3. glut. —v.i. 4. eat greedily.

**gor'geous**, adj. dazzlingly attractive.

**go·ril'la**, n. powerful manlike African ape.

**Gos'pel**, n. teachings of Jesus and the Apostles.

**gos'sa·mer**, adj. 1. light and frail. —n. 2. cobweb.

**gos'sip**, n. 1. rumors and conjectures about others. 2. person who originates or spreads these. —v.i. 3. engage in gossip. —**gos'sip·y**, adj.

**gouge**, n. 1. chisel for cutting grooves. —v.t. 2. cut out with a scooping motion.

**gourd**, n. decorative fruit of the squash or melon family.

**gour'mand** (gŏŏr'mand), n. heavy eater and drinker.

**gour'met** (gŏŏr mā') n. connoisseur of food and drink.

**gout**, n. illness causing pain in the joints.

**gov'ern**, vb. 1. have authority over. 2. guide. 3. determine.

**gov'ern·ment**, n. 1. system for running a country. 2. group in political control.

**gov'er·nor**, n. 1. supreme local official. 2. device for controlling machinery speed.

**gown**, n. long outer garment.

**grab**, v.t., v.i., n. snatch.

**grace**, n. 1. beauty of form, movement or manner. 2. kindness or favor. 3. prayer before a meal. —v.t. 4. add grace to, as by being present.

**gra'cious**, adj. 1. charming in manner or style. 2. kind.

**gra·da'tion**, n. succession of increasing or decreasing amounts, etc.

**grade**, n. 1. step in a progressive series. 2. Also, **gra'di·ent**. —v.t. 3. assign a grade to. 4. give a level to, as a road.

**grad'u·al**, adj. in small amounts. —**grad'u·al·ly**, adv.

**grad·u·ate**, v.t. (grad'yŏŏ āt'') 1. leave after satisfying academic requirements. 2. certify as having satisfied requirements. 3. divide into grades. —n. (grad'yŏŏ ət) 4. person who has graduated. —adj. 5. postbaccalaureate.

**graf·fi'to** (grafe'tŏ), n., pl. **-ti**. writing or drawing by a passer-by.

**graft**, n. 1. transplant of organic material. 2. dishonest use of public funds. —v.t. 3. transplant. 4. obtain by graft.

**grain**, n. 1. hard seed as of wheat. 2. hard particle. 3. pattern of fiber, as in wood.

**gram**, n. metric unit of weight, about 1/28 of an ounce. Also, **gramme**.

**gram'mar**, n. forms and arrangement of words. —**gram·mat'i·cal**, adj.

**gran'a·ry**, n., pl. **-ries**. place for storing grain.

**grand**, adj. 1. impressive. 2. illustrious. —**gran'deur**, n.

**grand'child''**, n. child of a son or daughter.

**gran·di·ose'**, adj. 1. full of grandeur. 2. pompous.

**grand'par''ent**, n. parent of a parent.

**grand'stand''**, n. stand for spectators at sporting events.

**gran'ite**, n. grainy igneous rock.

**grant**, v.t. 1. give. 2. admit. —n. 3. something granted.

**gran'u·late''**, v.t. form as or in granules.

**gran'ule**, n. small particle —**gran'u·lar**, adj.

**grape**, n. small juicy fruit.

**grape'fruit''**, n. large, sharp-tasting citrus fruit.

**graph**, n. two-dimensional visual representation of interrelated data.

**graph'ic**, adj. 1. pertaining to two-dimensional visual art. 2. vividly realistic.

**grap'ple**, v.i. 1. wrestle; struggle. —v.t. 2. grasp and hold.

**grasp**, v.t. 1. take hold of with the hand; clutch. 2. comprehend. —v.i. 3. make clutching motions. —n. 4. act or instance of grasping. 5. ability to grasp.

**grass**, n. narrow-leafed green plant with seedlike fruit.

**grass'hop''per**, n. jumping, plant-eating insect.

**grate**, n. 1. scrape into particles. 2. grind. —v.i. 3. grind or rasp. 4.

be irritating. —*n.* **5.** Also, **grat'-ing**, framework of metal, etc. bars.

**grate'ful**, *adj.* **1.** appreciative of favors. **2.** welcome.

**grat'i·fy''**, *v.t.* be pleasing to.

**grat'i·tude''**, *n.* appreciation for favors.

**gra·tu'i·tous**, *adj.* **1.** gratis. **2.** uncalled-for.

**gra·tu'i·ty**, *n., pl.* **-ties.** gift, esp. a tip.

**grave**, *adj.* **1.** solemn. **2.** important; serious. —*n.* **3.** place of burial.

**grav'el**, *n.* mixture of stone fragments. —**grav'el·ly**, *adj.*

**grav'i·tate''**, *v.i.* **1.** move by gravity. **2.** move or tend naturally.

**grav'i·ty**, *n.* **1.** seriousness. **2.** pull toward the center of the earth.

**gra'vy**, *n., pl.* **-ies.** meat juice, or a sauce from this.

**gray**, *adj.* **1.** mixed black and white. **2.** dreary.

**graze**, *v.t.*, *v.i.* **1.** scrape in passing. **2.** feed on grasses.

**grease**, *n.* (grēs) **1.** thick, fatty or oily substance. —*v.t.* (grēz) **2.** coat or lubricate with grease. —**greas'y**, *adj.*

**great**, *adj.* **1.** large. **2.** eminent.

**greed**, *n.* excessive passion for money, food, etc.

**green**, *n.* **1.** color of leaves and plants. **2. greens**, leafy vegetables. —*adj.* **3.** of the color green. **4.** unripened or unprocessed.

**greet**, *v.t.* **1.** acknowledge meeting. **2.** receive in a specified way.

**gre·gar'i·ous**, *adj.* associating with others of one's kind.

**gre·nade'**, *n.* small hand bomb.

**grey'hound''**, *n.* fast, slender hound.

**grid**, *n.* system of crisscrossed elements.

**grid'dle**, *n.* pan for cooking pancakes, etc.

**grid'iron''**, *n.* **1.** broiling frame. **2.** football field.

**grid'lock''**, *n.* severe, urban traffic jam.

**grief**, *n.* **1.** great unhappiness. **2.** ruin; failure.

**griev'ance**, *n.* **1.** cause for complaint. **2.** complaint.

**grieve**, *v.i.* **1.** suffer grief. —*v.t.* **2.** cause grief to.

**griev'ous**, *adj.* seriously injurious.

**grill**, *n.* **1.** gridiron. **2.** broiled dish. —*v.t.* **3.** broil.

**grim**, *adj.*, **grimmer**, **grimmest**. **1.** harsh. **2.** menacing.

**gri'mace**, *n.* **1.** smirk, esp. of displeasure. —*v.i.* **2.** give such a smirk.

**grime**, *n.* clinging dirt. —**grim'y** *adj.*

**grin**, *n.* **1.** broad, toothy smile. —*v.i.* **2.** give such a smile.

**grind**, *v.t.* **1.** wear down with pressure or friction. **2.** turn the crank of.

**grip**, *v.t.* **1.** grasp firmly. —*n.* **2.** firm grasp. **3.** handle.

**gripe**, *v.t.* **1.** produce pain in the bowels. —*v.i.* **2.** complain. —*n.* **3.** pain in the bowels. **4.** complaint.

**gris'ly**, *adj.*, **-lier, -liest.** horrible.

**grist**, *n.* grain for grinding. —**grist'-mill''**, *n.*

**gris'tle**, *n.* cartilage. —**gris'tly**, *adv.*

**grit**, *n.* **1.** rough, hard particles. **2.** fortitude. —*v.t.* **3.** grind together, as the teeth. —**grit'ty**, *adj.*

**griz'zled**, *adj.* with gray hair.

**griz'zly**, *adj.*, **-zlier, -zliest**, *n.*, *adj.* **1.** grayish. —*n.* **2.** Also, **grizzly bear**, large, ferocious American bear.

**groan**, *n.* **1.** deep utterance, as of pain. —*v.i.* **2.** give such an utterance.

**gro'cer**, *n.* food merchant. —**gro'cer·y**, *n.*

**grog'gy**, *adj.*, **-gier, -giest**. befuddled.

**groin**, *n.* junction of the abdomen and thighs.

**groom**, *n.* **1.** man at his wedding. **2.** tender of horses. —*v.t.* **3.** comb, etc. to make tidy.

**groove**, *n.* **1.** long, shallow depression. —*v.t.* **2.** make a groove in.

**grope**, *v.i.* feel for something blindly.

**gross**, *adj.* **1.** coarse. **2.** flagrant. **3.** before deductions. —*n.* **4.** *pl.* **gross**, quantity of 144.

**gro·tesque'**, *adj.* fantastically distorted.

**grouch**, *v.i.* **1.** sulk. —*n.* **2.** sulky mood. **3.** person who sulks.

**ground**, *n.* **1.** solid surface of the earth. **2.** earth. **3. grounds**, **a.** basis. **b.** land of an estate or institution. **c.** dregs of coffee, etc.

**ground'hog''**, *n.* woodchuck.

**group**, *n.* **1.** number of persons or things considered together. *v.t.*, *v.i.* **2.** form into a group or groups.

**G**
**H**

**grouse**, n., pl. **grouse**, n. 1. plump game bird. —v.i. 2. complain.

**grove**, n. cluster of trees.

**grov'el**, v.i. 1. crouch low or crawl. 2. behave servilely.

**grow**, v., **grew, grown, growing**. v.i. 1. become. 2. develop. —v.t. 3. cause to live, as plants. —**growth**, n.

**growl**, n. 1. low, rumbling vocal noise. —v.i. 2. make such a noise.

**grub**, v.i., v.t. 1. dig. —n. 2. beetle larva. 3. drudge.

**grub'by**, adj., **-bier, -biest**. nastily dirty.

**grudge**, n. 1. long-held resentment. —v.t. 2. begrudge.

**grue'some**, adj. horrifying or loathsome.

**gruff**, adj. curt.

**grum'ble**, v.i. complain in a suppressed manner.

**grum'py**, adj., **-pier, -piest**. surly.

**grunt**, n. 1. throaty sound caused by exertion, etc. —v.i. 2. utter such a sound.

**guar''an·tee'**, n. 1. firm assurance. 2. promise to make good if necessary. —v.t. 3. assure with a guarantee. Also, **guar'an·ty**. —**guar'an·tor'**.

**guard**, v.t., v.i. 1. watch, esp. in order to protect or confine. —n. 2. person or group that guards. 3. protection. 4. protective device.

**guard'i·an**, n. 1. person who guards. 2. person responsible for a minor or incompetent.

**guer·ril'la**, n. irregular soldier using surprise tactics.

**guess**, v.t. 1. form an opinion about without knowing. —n. 2. act or instance of guessing.

**guest**, n. 1. enjoyer of hospitality. 2. customer of a hotel, etc.

**guf·faw'**, n. 1. raucous laugh. —v.i. 2. emit such a laugh.

**guide**, v.t. 1. tell how to proceed. —n. 2. person or thing that guides.

**guile**, n. unscrupulous cunning.

**guilt**, n. 1. responsibility for a wrong action. 2. shame.

**guise**, n. semblance.

**gui·tar'**, n. six-stringed plucked instrument.

**gulch**, n. deep narrow ravine.

**gulf**, n. 1. ocean area partly surrounded by land. 2. wide deep void.

**gul'let**, n. throat.

**gul'li·ble**, adj. credulous.

**gul'ly**, n., pl. **-lies**. narrow ravine.

**gulp**, v.t., v.i. 1. swallow hastily. —n. 2. act or instance of gulping.

**gum**, n. 1. sticky, semisolid substance. 2. area of flesh surrounding teeth. —v.t. 3. stick with gum.

**gun**, n. 1. weapon shooting a missile by means of an explosive charge. —v.t., v.i. 2. hunt with a gun. —**gun'ner·y**, n.

**gun·pow'der**, n. explosive used in guns.

**gun·wale** (gun'l), n. upper edge of a ship's side.

**gu'ru**, n. Hindu spiritual teacher.

**gush**, v.i. 1. flow out abundantly. 2. express oneself effusively. —n. 3. act or instance of gushing.

**gust**, n. 1. strong puff of air. 2. sudden outburst.

**gus'to**, n. great enjoyment or vigor.

**gut**, n. 1. intestine. 2. guts, _Informal._ courage. —v.t. 3. destroy the inside of.

**gut'ter**, n. 1. channel for rain water. 2. realm of sordidness. —v.t. 3. splutter before being extinguished, as a candle.

**gut'tur·al**, adj. pertaining to or produced in the throat.

**guy**, n. 1. _Informal._ male person. 2. wire used to steady wire.

**guz'zle**, v.i., v.t. drink greedily.

**gym·na'si·um**, n., pl. **-ums, -a.** place for physical exercise.

**gym·nas'tics**, n. pl. physical exercises.

**gy''ne·col'o·gy**, n. branch of medicine concerned with women's diseases. —**gy''ne·col'o·gist,** n.

**gyp**, n., v.t. _Informal._ swindle.

**gy·rate'**, v.i. whirl.

**gy'ro·scope'**, n. object maintaining its position by the inertia of a rapidly turned wheel.

# H

**H, h,** n. eighth letter of the English alphabet.

**hab'it**, n. 1. custom, esp. one hard to depart from. 2. distinctive costume. —**ha·bit'u·al,** adj. —**ha·bit'u·ate'',** v.t.

**hab'i·tat''**, *n.* usual area of habitation.

**hab''i·ta'tion**, *n.* home.

**hack'er**, *n.* a computer enthusiast.

**hag**, *n.* ugly old woman.

**hag'gard**, *adj.* weary-looking.

**hag'gle**, *v.i.* dispute over a price.

**hail**, *v.t.* 1. greet loudly. 2. shout to. 3. welcome as desirable. —*n.* 4. frozen rain in small balls. —**hail'stone''**, *n.*

**hair**, *n.* 1. slender growth from the skin. 2. these growths collectively.

**hale**, *adj.* 1. full of health and vigor. —*v.t.* 2. summon forcibly.

**half**, *n., pl.* **halves**, *adj., adv., n.* 1. one of two equal divisions. —*adj.* 2. being a half. —*adv.* 3. as far as a half.

**hal''i·to'sis**, *n.* bad breath.

**hall**, *n.* 1. large room, as for meetings. 2. Also, **hall'way''**, corridor or vestibule.

**hal·lu''ci·na'tion**, *n.* deluded perceptions of a nonexistent sight, sound, etc.

**ha'lo**, *n., pl.* **-los, -loes.** ring of light, as around the portrayed head of a holy person.

**halt**, *v.t., v.i., n.* stop.

**hal'ter**, *n.* line for securing an animal.

**halve**, *v.t.* 1. divide into halves. 2. reduce by half.

**ham**, *n.* upper part of a hog's hind leg.

**ham'bur''ger**, *n.* sandwich of ground beef in a bun. Also, **ham'burg.**

**ham'let**, *n.* small village.

**ham'mer**, *n.* device for beating or driving with blows.

**ham'mock**, *n.* flexible bed suspended at the ends.

**ham'per**, *v.t.* 1. encumber. —*n.* 2. covered basket.

**hand**, *n.* 1. extremity of the arm. 2. active part. 3. hired worker. 4. handwriting. 5. side or direction. —*v.t.* 6. give with the hand. —**hand'ful**, *n.*

**hand'i·cap''**, *n.* 1. hindrance. —*v.t.* 2. hinder.

**hand'i·work''**, *n.* work done by hand.

**hand'ker·chief''**, *n.* small wiping cloth.

**han'dle**, *n.* 1. something to be grasped. —*v.t.* 2. grasp, as in order to wield. 3. manage or dominate. 4. sell.

**hand'some''**, *adj.* 1. good-looking. 2. generous.

**hands''-on'**, *adj.* practical; making actual use of, as *hands-on training.*

**hand'writ''ing**, *n.* freehand writing.

**hand'y**, *adj.,* **-ier, -iest.** convenient. —**hand'i·ly**, *adv.* —**hand'i·ness**, *n.*

**hand'y·man'**, *n.* man who does odd jobs.

**hang**, *v.,* **hung** or (for 2) **hanged**, **hanged**, *v.t.* 1. hold up from above. 2. kill by suspending from a rope around the neck. —*v.i.* 3. be hung or suspended.

**hang'ar**, *n.* aircraft shelter.

**han'ker**, *v.i.* yearn.

**hap'haz''ard**, *adj.* 1. random. 2. by chance.

**hap'pen**, *v.i.* come about by chance. —**hap'pen·ing**, *n.*

**hap'py**, *adj.,* **-pier, -piest.** 1. feeling pleased. 2. fortunate.

**ha·rangue'**, *n.* 1. long vehement speech. —*v.t.* 2. deliver a harangue to.

**ha·rass'**, *v.t.* trouble persistently.

**har'bin·ger**, *n.* forerunner.

**har'bor**, *n.* 1. sheltered place for shipping. —*v.t.* 2. shelter.

**hard**, *adj.* 1. unyielding. 2. difficult. —*adv.* 3. energetically. —**hard'en**, *v.t., v.i.*

**hard'ly**, *adv.* barely; scarcely.

**hard'ware''**, *n.* 1. tools, fasteners, etc. 2. (computers) equipment, as microchips, disk drives, printers, etc.

**har'dy**, *adj.,* **-dier, -diest.** *n.* 1. of much endurance. 2. vigorous. —**har'di·ly**, *adv.*

**hare**, *n.* rabbitlike mammal.

**ha'rem**, *n.* 1. women's quarters of a Muslim house. 2. its inhabitants.

**hark**, *v.i.* listen.

**hark'en**, *v.i.* hearken.

**har'lot**, *n.* prostitute.

**harm**, *n.* 1. injury. —*v.t.* 2. injure.

**har·mon'i·ca**, *n.* mouth organ.

**har'mo·ny**, *n.* 1. pleasant combination. 2. agreement; accord.

**har'ness**, *n.* straps, etc. on an animal that pulls or carries.

**harp**, *n.* 1. large plucked stringed instrument. —*v.i.* 2. speak tediously.

**har·poon'**, *n.* spear for whales, etc.

**har'row**, *n.* 1. device for breaking and leveling plowed ground. —*v.t.*

G
H

**har'ry**, v.t. harass.

**harsh**, adj. unpleasantly rough.

**har'vest**, n. 1. occasion of gathering crops. 2. crop gathered. —v.t. 3. gather as a harvest.

**hash**, n. chopped mixture of meat and vegetables.

**has'sle**, n., v.i. squabble.

**has'sock**, n. cushionlike seat.

**haste**, n. speed, esp. when excessive.

**has'ten**, v.t., v.i. hurry.

**hat**, n. head garment, esp. a formal one.

**hatch**, v.t. 1. bring forth from eggs. —v.i. 2. open to release young. —n. 3. Also, **hatch'way''**, opening serving as a door or window.

**hatch'et**, n. short-handled chopping tool.

**hate**, v.t. 1. dislike violently. n. 2. Also, **hat'red**, feeling of hating.

**haugh'ty**, adj., **-tier, -tiest.** arrogant.

**haul**, v.t., v.i. 1. pull. —n. 2. act or instance of hauling.

**haunch**, n. area from upper thigh to buttock.

**haunt**, v.t. 1. be often present at. —n. 2. favorite place or resort.

**have**, v.t., **had, having.** 1. own or possess. 2. acquire. 3. experience or engage in. 4. cause. 5. be obliged.

**ha'ven**, n. place of shelter.

**hav'oc**, n. vast destruction.

**hawk**, n. bird of prey.

**haw'ser**, n. mooring or towing rope.

**hay**, n. grass, etc. dried as fodder.

**haz'ard**, n., v.t. risk.

**haze**, n. 1. light mist or vapor. —v.t. 2. harass or humiliate.

**ha'zel**, n. tree of the birch family. —**ha'zel-nut''**, n.

**he**, pron., pl. **they**, n., pl. **he's** pron. male person or animal mentioned.

**head**, n. 1. part of the body for thinking, eating, seeing, etc. 2. director. 3. uppermost or working feature. —v.t. 4. direct. —v.i. 5. direct oneself.

**head'line''**, n. title of a newspaper article.

**head'-on''**, adj., adv. with the front end or ends foremost.

**head'quar''ters**, n., pl. main center of command.

**head'strong''**, adj. willful and impulsive.

**head'way''**, n. forward motion.

**heal**, v.t. 1. return to health. 2. make whole again.

**health**, n. 1. well-being. 2. condition of the body or mind.

**heap**, n. 1. loose pile. —v.t. 2. pile up.

**hear**, v.t. 1. perceive through the ears. 2. understand from others. 3. listen to.

**heark'en**, v.i. listen carefully.

**hear'say''**, n. rumor.

**hearse**, n. funeral car.

**heart**, n. 1. organ that pumps b l o o d . 2. c o m p a s s i o n orsensitivity. 3. courage. 4. enthusiasm. 5. center. 6. essence. —**heart'less**, adj.

**heart'break''**, n. great sorrow.

**heart'en**, v.t. encourage.

**hearth**, n. floor of a fireplace, furnace.

**heart'y**, adj., **-ier, -iest.** enthusiastic.

**heat**, n. 1. warmth. 2. strong feeling. —v.t., v.i. 3. warm.

**hea'then**, n., pl. **-thens, -then,** adj., n. 1. person not Christian, Jewish, or Muslim. —adj. 2. pertaining to such persons.

**heave**, v., **heaved** or **hove, heaving.** v.t. 1. lift, or lift and throw, with effort. —v.i. 2. rise and fall in rhythm.

**heav'en**, n. 1. **heavens,** sky. 2. **Heaven,** dwelling of God, the angels, and the blessed.

**heav'y**, adj., **-ier, -iest.** 1. with much weight. 2. with much difficulty. —v.t., v.i. 3. warm.

**heck'le**, v.t. harass verbally.

**hec'tare**, n. area of 10,000 square meters.

**hec'tic**, adj. 1. feverish. 2. hasty and confused.

**hedge**, n. 1. barrier of close-growing shrubs. —v.t. 2. partition off with a hedge.

**heed**, v.t. 1. pay attention to. —n. 2. attention.

**heel**, n. 1. rear of the foot. 2. something similar in form or location. —v.i., v.t. 3. lean; list.

**heft'y**, adj., **-ier, -iest.** heavy; large.

**heif'er**, n. young cow.

**height**, n. 1. dimension from bottom to top. 2. raised area. 3. highest point.

**height'en**, v.t. make higher.

**hei'nous**, adj. outrageously wicked.

**heir**, *n.* a person who inherits. Also, *fem.*, **heir'ess.**

**heir'loom''**, *n.* family possession.

**hel'i·cop''ter**, *n.* aircraft flying by means of a propellerlike rotor.

**he'li·um**, *n.* light gaseous chemical element.

**he'lix**, *n.*, *pl.* **-lixes, -lices.** rising curve. —**hel'i·cal,** *adj.*

**hell**, *n.* Also **Hell**, place of confinement for those not redeemed. —**hel'lish,** *adj.*

**hel·lo'**, *interj.* (exclamation of greeting).

**helm**, *n.* means of steering a ship.

**hel'met**, *n.* protective head covering.

**help**, *v.t.* 1. assist. 2. rescue. 3. prevent or mitigate. —*v.i.* 4. be useful. —*n.* 5. assistance. 6. rescue.

**help'mate''**, *n.* helpful companion. Also, **help'meet''.**

**hem**, *n.* 1. edge formed on a cloth. —*v.t.* 2. make a hem on.

**hem'i·sphere''**, *n.* 1. half a sphere. 2. half of the earth.

**hem'lock''**, *n.* 1. pinelike evergreen. 2. poisonous plant related to parsley.

**hem'or·rhage**, *n.* massive loss of blood.

**hemp**, *n.* Asiatic plant used for rope and hashish.

**hen**, *n.* female bird, esp. a chicken.

**hence**, *adv.* 1. away. 2. from this time. 3. therefore.

**hence'forth'**, *adv.* from now on.

**hench'man**, *n.* assistant villain.

**her**, *pron.* 1. objective of *she.* —*adj.* 2. pertaining to a female previously mentioned.

**her'ald**, *n.* signifier of what is to come.

**her'ald·ry**, *n.* study of coats of arms, etc. —**he·ral'dic,** *adj.*

**herb** (*arb*), *n.* annual seed plant used in cookery or medicine. —**herb'al,** *adj.*

**herd**, *n.* 1. group of cows, sheep, etc. 2. person who tends such a group. —*v.i.*, *v.t.* 3. gather or move as a herd.

**here**, *adv.* 1. in or to this place. 2. now.

**here·af'ter**, *adv.* 1. after this. —*n.* 2. next world.

**here'by'**, *adv.* by this means.

**he·red'i·tar''y**, *adj.* so by inheritance or heredity.

**here·in'**, *adv.* in this.

**her'e·sy**, *n.*, *pl.* **-sies.** contradiction of a dogma.

**her'it·age**, *n.* traditions, etc. from predecessors.

**her·met'ic**, *adj.* airtight.

**her'mit**, *n.* person willingly living alone. —**her'mit·age**, *n.*

**her'ni·a**, *n.* abdominal rupture.

**he'ro·in**, *n.* morphine-based narcotic.

**her'on**, *n.* wading bird.

**her'pes**, *n.* a viral infection causing sores.

**her'ring**, *n.* North Atlantic fish.

**hers**, *pron.* something belonging or pertaining to her.

**her·self'**, *pron.* intensive and reflexive of *she.*

**hertz**, *n.* Physics. one cycle per second.

**hes'i·tate**, *v.i.* 1. be unresolved. 2. pause briefly. 3. be reluctant. —**hes'i·tant,** *adj.*

**het''er·o·ge'ne·ous**, *adj.* 1. dissimilar. 2. of dissimilar components.

**het''er·o·sex'u·al**, *adj.* 1. attracted solely to the opposite sex. —*n.* 2. heterosexual person.

**hew**, *v.t.*, **hewed, hewed** or **hewn, hewing.** chop.

**hex**, *v.t.* 1. put an evil spell on. —*n.* 2. evil spell.

**hex'a·gon''**, *n.* six-sided plane figure.

**hi·a'tus**, *n.*, *pl.* **-tuses, -tus.** interruption.

**hi'ber·nate''**, *v.i.* be dormant through winter.

**hic'cup**, *n.* 1. sharp sound due to involuntary contraction of the diaphragm. —*v.i.* 2. emit such a sound. Also, **hic'cough.**

**hide**, *v.*, **hid, hidden, hiding,** *n.*, *v.t.* 1. keep from being seen. —*v.i.* 2. conceal oneself. —*n.* 3. animal skin.

**hid'e·ous**, *adj.* horribly ugly.

**hi'er·ar''chy**, *n.*, *pl.* **-ies.** organization of higher officials.

**hi''er·o·glyph'ic**, *n.* picture representing a word or sound.

**high**, *adj.* 1. being or reaching far up. 2. of a specified height. 3. superior. 4. mighty large in amount. —*adv.* 5. in or to a high place or situation.

**high'light''**, *n.* 1. brilliant reflection. 2. salient fact. —*v.t.* 3. emphasize.

**high'way''**, *n.* major road.

**hi'jack''**, *v.t. Informal.* take in transit by robbery.

**G**
**H**

**hike**, *v.i.* 1. go for a long walk. —*n.* 2. long walk.

**hi·lar'i·ous**, *adj.* very funny.

**hill**, *n.* distinctive area of rising ground.

**hil'lock**, *n.* small hill.

**hilt**, *n.* handle of a sword, etc.

**him**, *pron.* objective of he.

**him·self'**, *pron.* 1. intensive or reflexive of him. 2. his true self.

**hind**, *adj.*, **hinder, hindmost** or **hindermost.** behind.

**hin'der**, *v.t.* stop or slow down. —*adj.* 2. rear. —**hin'drance,** *n.*

**hind'sight'**, *n.* belated perception.

**hinge**, *n.* 1. support allowing the supported part to turn. —*v.i.* 2. depend.

**hint**, *n.* 1. something that allows an inference to be made. —*v.t.* 2. imply. —*v.i.* 3. make a hint.

**hip**, *n.* area around the upper leg joints.

**hip''po·pot'a·mus**, *n.*, *pl.* **-muses, -mi.** large river-loving African mammal.

**hire**, *v.t.* employ or use for wages or a fee.

**hire'ling**, *n.* unscrupulous mercenary.

**hir'sute**, *adj.* hairy.

**his**, *pron.* 1. something belonging or pertaining to him. —*adj.* 2. pertaining to him.

**hiss**, *n.* 1. prolonged s- like sound. —*v.i.* 2. emit a hiss.

**his'to·ry**, *n.*, *pl.* **-ries.** 1. study of the past. 2. account of the past. 3. known or recorded past. 4. determining forces as inferred from past events. —**his·tor'i·an,** *n.* —**his·tor'ic, his·tor'i·cal,** *adj.*

**hit**, *v.t.* 1. come against or send something against with force. —*v.i.* 2. come by chance. 3. strike a blow. —*n.* 4. accurate discharge of a missile. 5. successful song, etc.

**hitch**, *v.t.* 1. tie or harness. —*n.* 2. simple knot. 3. obstacle or drawback.

**hitch'hike''**, *v.i.* solicit a free automobile ride.

**hith'er**, *adv.* 1. to this place. —*adj.* 2. nearer.

**hith'er·to''**, *adv.* until now.

**hive**, *n.* 1. beehive. 2. **hives**, itchy skin condition.

**hoard**, *n.* precious hidden accumulation.

**hoarse**, *adj.* having a harsh sound.

**hoar'y**, *adj.*, **-ier, -iest.** gray-haired from age.

**hoax**, *n.* fraud.

**hob'ble**, *v.i.* 1. limp. —*v.t.* 2. hamper.

**hob'by**, *n.*, *pl.* **-bies.** spare-time activity.

**hob'nob''**, *v.i.* be on social terms.

**ho'bo**, *n.*, *pl.* **-bos, -boes.** migrant worker.

**hock'ey**, *n.* game played with long, clublike sticks and a puck.

**ho·cus-po'cus**, *n.* trickery.

**hod**, *n.* 1. trough for bricks or mortar. 2. coal scuttle.

**hodge'podge''**, *n.* random mixture.

**hoe**, *n.* long-handled tool for loosening earth.

**hog**, *n.* pig raised for meat.

**hoist**, *v.t.* 1. lift, as by a crane. —*n.* 2. hoisting device.

**hold**, *v.t.* 1. have in the hand. 2. keep from moving or changing. 3. embrace. 4. contain. 5. possess. 6. carry on. 7. consider. —*v.i.* 8. remain firm or fixed. —*n.* 9. act or instance of holding. 10. means of holding. 11. cargo space.

**hole**, *n.* opening, esp. a deep one.

**hol'i·day''**, *n.* 1. day specially celebrated. 2. day of no work.

**hol'i·ness**, *n.* 1. quality of being holy. 2. **Holiness**, title of respect for a pope.

**hol'low**, *adj.* 1. empty inside. 2. worthless; vain. 3. booming.

**hol'ly**, *n.*, *pl.* **-lies.** evergreen shrub with red berries.

**hol'lo·caust''**, *n.* widely destructive fire.

**hol'ster**, *n.* pistol holder.

**ho'ly**, *adj.*, **-lier, -liest.** 1. dedicated to religion. 2. spiritually pure.

**hom'age**, *n.* reverent respect.

**home**, *n.* 1. place of residence. 2. one's own place. —*adv.* 3. to one's home. 4. into the proper place.

**home'ly**, *adj.*, **-lier, -liest.** 1. commonplace. 2. not handsome or beautiful.

**home'y**, *adj.*, **-ier, -iest.** cozy.

**hom'i·cide''**, *n.* killing of one person by another.

**hom'i·ly**, *n.*, *pl.* **-lies.** sermon or moral lecture.

**ho''mo·ge'ne·ous**, *adj.* of uniform composition or content. —**ho''mo·ge·ne'i·ty,** *n.*

**ho·mog'e·nize''**, *v.t.* make homogeneous.

ho''mo·sex'u·al, *adj.* sexually attracted to one's own sex.

hone, *v.t.* bring to a fine, sharp edge.

hon'est, *adj.* 1. without desire to steal, lie, etc. 2. genuine. —hon'es·ty, *n.*

hon'ey, *n., pl.* -neys. syrup made by bees from flowers.

hon'ey·comb'', *n.* structure with hexagonal cells made by bees to store honey.

hon'ey·moon'', *n.* vacation of newlyweds.

hon'ey·suck''le, *n.* climbing plant with sweet blossoms.

hon'or, *n.* 1. high respect. 2. good reputation. 3. integrity. 4. chastity. 5. conferred distinction. —v.t. 6. hold in honor. 7. confer distinction or praise on. 8. accept as valid.

hon''or·if'ic, *adj.* conferring honor.

hood, *n.* 1. cloth covering for the head and nape. 2. engine cover of an automobile, etc.

hood'lum, *n.* violent criminal.

hoof, *n., pl.* hoofs, hooves. hard foot covering of a horse, etc.

hook, *n.* 1. curved object for hanging or attaching things. —v.t. 2. attach with a hook. —v.i. 3. curve as a hook does.

hoop, *n.* circular band.

hoot, *n.* loud, shrill sound.

hop, *v.i.* 1. jump on one foot or with both feet together. —n. 2. act or instance of hopping.

hope, *v.i.* 1. belief that something good may happen. 2. source or cause of such a belief. —v.t., v.i. 3. entertain hopes.

hop'per, *n.* funnel-like chute.

horde, *n.* 1. swarm; multitude. —v.i. 2. gather in a horde.

ho·ri'zon, *n.* apparent edge of a scene.

ho''ri·zon'tal, *adj.* running across, like a featureless horizon.

hor'mone'', *n.* substance influencing one part of the body but made in another.

horn, *n.* 1. hard, pointed protuberance from an animal head. 2. substance of this. 3. pointed projection. 4. wind instrument.

hor'net, *n.* yellow and black wasp.

hor'o·scope'', *n.* chart of zodiacal signs.

hor·ren'dous, *adj.* horrible.

hor'ri·ble, *adj.* causing horror.

hor'rid, *adj.* causing horror.

hor'ri·fy'', *v.t.* fill with horror.

hor'ror, *n.* strong fear and disgust.

hors d'oeuvre (or derv'), *n., pl.* hors d'oeuvres. appetizer.

horse, *n.* 1. four-footed grass eating animal. 2. supporting frame. —horse'back'', *adv., n.*

horse'laugh'', *n.* loud, open laugh.

horse'play'', *n.* rough play.

horse'pow''er, *n.* unit of power equalling 33,000 foot-pounds/minute or 746 watts.

horse'shoe'', *n.* iron reinforcement for a hoof in the form of an open loop.

hor'ti·cul'ture, *n.* gardening.

hose, *n., pl.* (for 1) hoses, (for 2) hose. 1. flexible tube for water, etc. 2. long stocking.

ho'sier·y, *n.* stockings.

hos'pice, *n.* facility for terminally ill persons.

hos'pi·ta·ble, *adj.* readily offering hospitality.

hos'pi·tal, *n.* place for healing.

hos''pi·tal'i·ty, *n.* generosity to visitors.

host, *n.* 1. Also, *fem.,* hos'tess. person who entertains guests. 2. organism supporting parasites. 3. multitude. 4. wafer eaten in Holy Communion.

hos'tage, *n.* prisoner kept to enforce demands.

hos'tile, *adj.* in a state of enmity.

hot, *adj.,* hotter, hottest. 1. very warm. 2. very spicy. 3. intense, as in emotion.

ho'tel', *n.* place renting rooms and often serving food.

hound, *n.* 1. hunting dog. —v.t. 2. persecute.

hour, *n.* twenty-fourth of a day.

house, *n., pl.* houses, (n. (hows)) 1. building to live in. 2. family. 3. business firm. 4. legislative body. —v.t. (howz) 5. provide lodgings or shelter for.

house'hold'', *n.* inhabitants of a house.

house'hold''er, *n.* 1. head of a household. 2. owner of a house.

house'keep''er, *n.* person responsible for keeping a house in order.

house'wife'', *n.* wife who runs a home.

hous·ing (howz'ing), *n.* 1. complex of dwellings. 2. provision of dwellings.

G
H

**hov′er,** *v.i.* 1. remain poised in the air. 2. linger near by.

**how,** *adv.* 1. in what way. 2. in what state. 3. for what reason. 4. to what extent.

**how·ev′er,** *adv.* 1. regardless of how. —*conj.* 2. nevertheless.

**howl,** *v.i.* 1. raise a loud, animal-like cry. 2. laugh uproariously.

**hub,** *n.* center of a wheel.

**hub′bub,** *n.* confusion; disorder.

**huck′ster,** *n.* peddler.

**hud′dle,** *n.* 1. close, irregular group. —*v.i.* 2. gather in a huddle.

**hue,** *n.* 1. color. 2. tint.

**huff,** *n.* mood of silent resentment.

**hug,** *v.t., v.i.* 1. embrace. —*v.t.* 2. keep close to. —*n.* 3. embrace.

**huge,** *adj.* very large.

**hulk,** *n.* hull of a ship deprived of masts, etc.

**hull,** *n.* 1. shell of a seed, etc. 2. body of a ship.

**hum,** *v.i.* 1. make an inarticulate sound between closed lips. —*v.t.* 2. render by humming. —*n.* 3. low, continuous murmur.

**hu′man,** *adj.* 1. being a man, woman, or child. 2. characteristic of man.

**hu·mane′,** *adj.* 1. merciful. 2. civilizing.

**hu′man·ism,** *n.* intellectual movement centered around man.

**hu·man′i·tar′i·an,** *n.* 1. philanthropist. —*adj.* 2. philanthropic.

**hu·man′i·ty,** *n.* 1. human beings collectively. 2. quality of being humane.

**hum′ble,** *adj.* -bler, -blest, *adj.* 1. unpretentious; unconceited. 2. low in rank. —*v.t.* 3. make humble. —**hum′bly,** *adv.*

**hum′drum″,** *adj.* drearily ordinary.

**hu′mid,** *adj.* moist. —**hu·mid′i·fy″,** *v.t.* —**hu·mid′i·ty,** *n.*

**hu·mil′i·ate′,** *v.t.* cause to feel shame.

**hu·mil′i·ty,** *n.* humble quality.

**hu′mor,** *n.* 1. mood. 2. comical quality. 3. bodily fluid. —**hu′mor·ist,** *n.* —**hu′mor·ous,** *adj.*

**hump,** *n.* high lump on a back of a camel.

**hu′mus,** *n.* soil with decayed leaf matter, etc.

**hunch,** *n.* intuitive feeling.

**hun′dred,** *adj., n.* ten times ten. —**hun′dredth,** *adj.*

**hun′dred·weight″,** *n.* U.S. 100 pounds.

**hun′ger,** *n.* 1. desire to eat. 2. deprivation of food. 3. strong desire. —*v.i.* 4. be hungry. —**hun′gry,** *adj.*

**hunt,** *v.t.* 1. pursue to kill or harass. —*v.i.* 2. hunt game. 3. search. —*n.* 4. act or instance of hunting. —**hunt′er, hunts′man,** *fem.,* **hunt′ress,** *n.*

**hur′dle,** *n.* 1. barrier to be leapt. —*v.t.* 2. leap over.

**hurl,** *n.* throw with force.

**hur·rah′,** *interj., n.* (shout of approval). Also, **hur·ray′.**

**hur′ri·cane″,** *n.* tropical cyclone.

**hur′ry,** *v.i.* 1. move or act quickly. —*v.t.* 2. cause to hurry. —*n.* 3. reason for hurrying. 4. eagerness to hurry.

**hurt,** *v.t.* 1. damage; injure. 2. pain the feelings of. —*v.i.* 3. cause pain. 4. do harm. —*n.* 5. damage; injury. —**hurt′ful,** *adj.*

**hur′tle,** *v.i.* move at high speed.

**hus′band,** *n.* woman's spouse.

**hus′band·ry,** *n.* 1. farming. 2. management.

**hush,** *n., v.t.* silence.

**husk,** *n.* 1. outer covering. —*v.t.* 2. remove the husk from.

**hus′ky,** *adj.* 1. hoarse. 2. robust.

**hus′tle,** *v.t.* 1. jostle. 2. force roughly. —*v.i.* 3. move or act energetically. —*n.* 4. act or instance of hustling.

**hut,** *n.* small, crude dwelling.

**hutch,** *n.* 1. cupboard. 2. coop for rabbits, etc.

**hy′a·cinth″,** *n.* bell-shaped flower of the lily family.

**hy′brid,** *n.* 1. offspring or product of mixed species or varieties.

**hy′drant,** *n.* valved pipe from a water main.

**hy·drau′lic,** *adj.* 1. operated by liquid pressure. —*n.* 2. **hydraulics,** study of the mechanical properties of liquids.

**hy′dro·car′bon,** *n.* compound of hydrogen and carbon.

**hy′dro·gen,** *n.* flammable gaseous element.

**hy″dro·pho′bi·a,** *n.* rabies.

**hy·e′na,** *n.* wolflike African or Asian animal.

**hy′giene,** *n.* 1. system of health preservation. 2. cleanliness. —**hy″gien′ic,** *adj.*

**hymn,** *n.* poem or song of praise, as to God.

**hype,** *n.* exaggerated publicity.

**hy·per·bo·le'',** *n.* exaggeration for rhetorical effect.

**hy''per·sen'si·tive,** *adj.* too sensitive.

**hy''per·ten'sion,** *n.* excessive blood pressure.

**hy'phen,** *n.* dash, -, used to join words or syllables. —**hy'phen·ate'',** *v.t.*

**hyp·no'sis,** *n., pl.* **-ses.** sleeplike, obedient condition induced by suggestion from another.

**hy''po·chon'dri·a,** *n.* fear of imaginary illness.

**hy·poc'ri·sy,** *n., pl.* **-sies.** false pretension to virtue, affection, etc. —**hy'po·crite,** *n.* —**hy''po·crit'i·cal,** *adj.*

**hy''po·der'mic,** *adj.* 1. under the skin. —*n.* 2. hypodermic injection or injecting device.

**hy·poth'e·sis,** *n., pl.* **-ses.** unproved theory. —**hy''po·thet'i·cal,** *adj.*

**hys·te'ri·a,** *n.* pathologically excitable condition. —**hys·ter'i·cal,** *adj.*

# I

**I, i,** *n.* 1. ninth letter of the English alphabet. —*pron.* 2. **I,** (first person singular as a subject).

**ice,** *n.* 1. water frozen solid. 2. frozen dessert. —*v.t.* 3. put ice over or around. 4. put icing over. —*v.i.* 5. freeze or form ice. —**ice'box'',** *n.* —**ice'skate'',** *n.* —**ic'y,** *adj.*

**i·de'a,** *n.* image in the mind; conception.

**i·de'al,** *adj.* 1. perfect. 2. imaginary. —*n.* 3. something perfect.

**i·den'ti·cal,** *adj.* exactly alike or the same.

**i·den'ti·fy'',** *v.t.* 1. establish the identity of. 2. associate with another person or thing.

**i·den'ti·ty,** *n., pl.* **-ties.** 1. state of being identical. 2. individuality.

**i''de·ol'o·gy,** *n., pl.* **-gies.** political or social doctrine. —**i''de·o·log'i·cal,** *adj.*

**id'i·om,** *n.* 1. dialect. 2. combination of words with a nonliteral meaning.

**id''i·o·syn'cra·sy,** *n., pl.* **-sies.** personal trait.

**id'i·ot,** *n.* feeble-minded person. —**id'i·o·cy,** *n.*

**i'dle,** *adj.,* **idler, idlest.** 1. not at work or in use. 2. lazy. 3. frivolous. —**id'ly,** *adv.*

**i'dol,** *n.* 1. statue of a god. 2. idealized person. —**i'dol·ize'',** *v.t.*

**i·dol'a·try,** *n., pl.* **-tries.** worship of idols. —**i'dol·a·ter,** *n.* —**i·dol'a·trous,** *adj.*

**i'dyll,** *n.* 1. poem of pastoral life. 2. beautiful episode. Also, **i'dyl.** —**i·dyl'lic,** *adj.*

**if,** *conj.* 1. on condition that. 2. supposing that. 3. whether.

**ig'loo,** *n., pl.* **-loos.** domed Eskimo snow house.

**ig·nite',** *v.t., v.i.* set on or catch fire. —**ig·ni'tion,** *n.*

**ig·no'ble,** *adj.* base; mean.

**ig·no·min'y,** *n.* shame. —**ig''no·min'i·ous,** *adj.*

**ig''no·ra'mus,** *n., pl.* **-muses.** ignorant person.

**ig'no·rant,** *adj.* 1. uneducated. 2. unaware. —**ig'no·rance,** *n.* —**ig'no·rant·ly,** *adv.*

**ig·nore',** *v.t.* take no heed of.

**ill,** *adj.,* **worse,** (for 1) **worst,** *adv.,* **worse, worst,** *n.,* *adj.* 1. bad. 2. sick. —*adv.* 3. badly. 4. scarcely.

**il·le'gal,** *adj.* unlawful.

**il·leg'i·ble,** *adj.* unable to be read.

**il''le·git'i·mate,** *adj.* 1. not legitimate. 2. born out of wedlock.

**il·lic'it,** *adj.* not allowed.

**il·lit'er·ate,** *adj.* 1. unable to read. —*n.* 2. illiterate person.

**ill'ness,** *n.* sickness.

**il·log'i·cal,** *adj.* opposed to logic.

**il·lu'mi·nate'',** *v.t.* 1. Also, **il·lu'mine,** light up. 2. elucidate. 3. decorate with gold and colour.

**il·lu'sion,** *n.* 1. deceptive impression. 2. false conception. —**il·lu'sive,** —**il·lu'so·ry,** *adj.*

**il·lus'trate'',** *v.t.* 1. explain with examples. 2. add pictures to, as a narrative.

**il·lus'tri·ous,** *adj.* distinguished; famous.

**im'age,** *n.* 1. picture. 2. popular conception. —**im'age·ry,** *n.*

**i·mag'ine,** *v.t.* 1. create in the mind. 2. suppose to exist. 3. believe wrongly to exist. —**i·mag'in·a·ble,** *adj.* —**i·mag'in·a''ry,**

**I**

**K**

*adj.* —i·**mag'i·na'tion,** *n.* —i·**mag'i·na·tive,** *adj.*

im·**bal'ance,** *n.* lack of balance.

im·**be·cile,** *n.* idiot. —im'be·cil'i·ty, *n.*

im·**bibe',** *v.t., v.i.* drink.

im·**bue',** *v.t.* permeate.

im'i·**tate',** *v.t.* have the same characteristics as. —im'i·ta'tion, *n.* —im'i·ta'tor, *n.* —im'i·ta'tive, *adj.*

im·**mac'u·late,** *adj.* without dirt or sin.

im·**ma'nent,** *adj.* inherent.

im''ma·**te'ri·al,** *adj.* 1. irrelevant. 2. not composed of matter.

im''ma·**ture,** *n.* with an undeveloped character.

im·**meas'ur·a·ble,** *adj.* not to be measured.

im·**me'di·ate,** *adj.* 1. unseparated by anything else. 2. direct. —im·me'di·a·cy, *n.*

im''me·**mo'ri·al,** *adj.* from before memory.

im·**mense',** *adj.* huge. —im·men'si·ty, *n.* —im·mense'ly, *adv.*

im·**merse',** *v.t.* bury completely, as in a liquid.

im'mi·**grate',** *v.i.* enter a country to settle. —im'mi·grant, *n., adj.* —im'mi·gra'tion, *n.*

im·**mi'nent,** *adj.* soon to happen.

im·**mo'bile,** *adj.* fixed in place. —im'mo·bil'i·ty, *n.* —im·mo'bi·lize', *v.t.*

im·**mod'er·ate,** *adj.* lacking moderation.

im·**mod'est,** *adj.* lacking modesty. —im·mod'es·ty, *n.*

im·**mo'late',** *v.t.* kill as a sacrifice.

im·**mor'al,** *adj.* not moral.

im·**mor'tal,** *adj.* 1. never to die. 2. never to be forgotten. —*n.* 3. immortal being.

im·**mov'a·ble,** *adj.* fixed in place.

im·**mune',** *adj.* proof against disease, etc.

im·**mu'ta·ble,** *adj.* unchangeable.

imp, *n.* small demon. —imp'ish, *adj.*

im·**pact',** *n.* (im'pakt) 1. violent shock. —*v.t.* (im pakt') 2. force against something else.

im·**pair',** *v.t.* put out of order.

im·**pale',** *v.t.* pierce and support with a sharpened pole, etc.

im·**pan'el,** *v.t.* enroll in for as a jury.

im·**part',** *v.t.* reveal, as news.

im·**par'tial,** *adj.* unbiased.

im·**pas'sa·ble,** *adj.* impossible to pass along or over.

im·**passe',** *n.* deadlock.

im·**pas'sioned,** *adj.* passionate.

im·**pas'sive,** *adj.* revealing no emotion.

im·**pa'tient,** *adj.* without patience.

im·**peach',** *n.* try for wrongdoing in office.

im·**pec'ca·ble,** *adj.* flawless.

im''pe·**cu'ni·ous,** *adj.* penniless.

im·**pede',** *v.t.* hinder.

im·**ped'i·men'ta,** *n., pl.* things to be carried along.

im·**pel',** *v.t.* 1. drive forward. 2. urge.

im·**pend',** *v.i.* be about to happen.

im·**pen'e·tra·ble,** *adj.* impossible to penetrate.

im·**per'a·tive,** *adj.* vitally necessary.

im·**per·cep'ti·ble,** *adj.* impossible or difficult to perceive.

im·**per'fect,** *adj.* 1. flawed; deficient. 2. pertaining to uncompleted or continuing action. —im·per'fect·ly, *adv.* —im''per·fec'tion, *n.*

im·**pe'ri·al,** *adj.* pertaining to empires or emperors.

im·**per'il,** *v.t.* endanger.

im·**pe'ri·ous,** *adj.* imposing one's will on others.

im·**per'ish·a·ble,** *adj.* not perishable.

im·**per'ma·nent,** *adj.* not permanent.

im·**per'son·ate'',** *v.t.* pretend to be, as in acting.

im·**per'ti·nent,** *adj.* insolent.

im·**per'vi·ous,** *adj.* impenetrable, esp. by moisture.

im·**pet'u·ous,** *adj.* hasty; rash.

im·**pe'tus,** *n.* force in motion.

im·**pinge',** *v.i.* encroach.

im·**plac'a·ble,** *adj.* impossible to appease.

im·**ple'ment,** *n.* 1. piece of equipment. —*v.t.* 2. put in effect.

im'pli·**cate',** *v.t.* reveal as party to a crime.

im''pli·**ca'tion,** *n.* act of implying or implicating.

im·**plic'it,** *adj.* 1. implied. 2. absolute, as trust.

im·**plore',** *v.t.* plead earnestly.

im·**ply',** *v.t.* suggest as existing or being so.

im''po·**lite',** *adj.* rude.

im·**pon'der·a·ble,** *adj.* 1. immeasurable. —*n.* 2. something imponderable.

**im·port'**, v.t. (im port') 1. bring into a country, esp. for sale. 2. signify. —n. (im'port) 3. something imported. 4. significance.

**im·por'tant**, adj. 1. of great significance. 2. of great power.

**im·pose'**, v.t. 1. force to accept. —v.i. 2. take advantage. —**im·po·si'tion**, n.

**im·pos'si·ble**, adj. 1. not possible. 2. totally unsuitable or disagreeable.

**im·pos'tor**, n. person pretending to an identity, competence, etc. he does not have. —**im·pos'ture**, n.

**im'po·tent**, adj. 1. helpless. 2. incapable of sexual intercourse. —**im'po·tence, im'po·ten·cy**, n.

**im·pound'**, v.t. seize and hold legally.

**im·preg'na·ble**, adj. proof against attack.

**im·preg'nate''**, v.t. 1. saturate. 2. make pregnant.

**im·press'**, v.t. 1. command respectful attention. 2. print.

**im·pres'sion**, n. 1. mental effect. 2. vague idea.

**im·pris'on**, v.t. confine in prison.

**im·prob'a·ble**, adj. unlikely.

**im·promp'tu**, adj., adv. without preparation.

**im·prove'**, v.t., v.i. make or become better.

**im·pro·vise''**, v.t. 1. create at short notice or with what is available. —v.i. 2. perform extemporaneously.

**im·pugn'**, v.t. oppose as false.

**im'pulse**, n. 1. surge of force. 2. sudden decision to act.

**im·pure'**, adj. 1. adulterated. 2. immoral. —**im·pur'i·ty**, n.

**im·pute'**, v.t. attribute.

**in**, prep. 1. surrounded or contained by. 2. during. 3. into. 4. subjected to. —adv. 5. to the inside.

**in-**, prefix meaning "not" or "lack of."

**in''ad·vert'ent**, adj. due to unawareness or oversight.

**in·al'ien·a·ble**, adj. not to be taken away.

**in·ane'**, adj. pointless; silly. —**in·an'i·ty**, n.

**in·au'gu·rate''**, v.t. begin a term.

**in'breed'**, v.t., v.i. breed from closely related stocks.

**in''can·des'cent**, adj. glowing from heat.

**in''can·ta'tion**, n. formula producing a magic spell.

**in''ca·pac'i·tate''**, v.t. make unable or incompetent.

**in·car'cer·ate''**, v.t. imprison.

**in·car'nate**, adj. (in kahr'nət) 1. in fleshly, mortal form. —v.t. (in kahr'nāt) 2. create in incarnate form.

**in·cen'di·ar''y**, adj., n., pl. **-ies**. adj. 1. causing fires. —n. 2. incendiary bomb. 3. deliberate setter of fires.

**in·cense'**, n. (in'sens) 1. gum or resin giving off perfumed smoke. —v.t. (in sens') 2. enrage.

**in·cen'tive**, n. motive.

**in·cep'tion**, n. beginning.

**in·ces'sant**, adj. never ceasing.

**in'cest**, n. sexual relations between very close relatives.

**inch**, n. 1. twelfth part of a foot, as a linear measure. —v.i., v.t. 2. move very slowly.

**in'ci·dence**, n. frequency of occurrence.

**in'ci·dent**, n. 1. something that happens. 2. minor fight, etc.

**in''ci·den'tal**, adj. 1. happening in connection with something important. —n. 2. something incidental. 3. miscellaneous item.

**in·cin'er·ate''**, v.t., v.i. burn to ashes. —**in·cin'er·at''or**, n.

**in·cip'i·ent**, adj. beginning to develop.

**in·cise'**, v.t. cut into. —**in·ci'sion**, n.

**in·ci'sive**, adj. penetrating in perception.

**in·ci'sor**, n. human front tooth.

**in·cite'**, v.t. urge to act.

**in·cline'**, v.i. (in klīn') 1. slope or slant. 2. have a tendency or bias. —v.t. 3. cause to incline. —n. (in' klīn) 4. slope. —**in·cli·na'tion**, n.

**in·close'**, v.t. enclose.

**in·clude'**, v.t. have or consider among other things. —**in·clu'sion**, n.

**in·clu'sive**, adj. 1. including the limiting items mentioned. 2. considering everything.

**in·cog'ni'to**, adj. under an assumed name.

**in'come'**, n. money received.

**in''com·mu'ni·ca'do**, adj. without being allowed to communicate.

**in·cor'po·rate''**, v.t., v.i. 1. form into a corporation. —v.t. 2. embody.

**I K**

**in·cor'ri·gi·ble**, *adj.* incapable of correction.

**in·crease'**, *v.t.* 1. add to. —*v.i.* 2. become larger or more numerous.

**in'crease'**, *n.* increase.

**in·crim'i·nate'**, *v.t.* 1. accuse of crime. 2. subject to such accusation.

**in'cu·bate'**, *v.t.* 1. hatch. 2. encourage the development of.

**in·cum'bent**, *adj.* 1. obligatory. 2. in office. —*n.* 3. present office holder.

**in·cur'sion**, *n.* invasion.

**in·debt'ed**, *adj.* owing a debt of money or gratitude.

**in·deed'**, *adv.* 1. truly. —*interj.* 2. (exclamation of surprise).

**in·del'i·ble**, *adj.* impossible to erase.

**in·dem'ni·fy''**, *v.t.* compensate for.

**in·dent'**, *v.t.* 1. notch. 2. begin to the right of the normal margin.

**in·den'ture**, *n.* 1. contract, esp. for work. —*v.t.* 2. bind with an indenture.

**in''de·pen'dent**, *adj.* free of or needing no outside control.

**in'dex**, *n., pl.* **-dexes, -dices,** *n.* 1. orderly list of subjects. 2. something that indicates. 3. forefinger. —*v.t.* 4. make an index for.

**in'di·cate'**, *v.t.* 1. call attention to. 2. imply.

**in·dict'** (in dīt'), *v.t.* charge with crime.

**in'di·gent**, *adj.* needy.

**in·di·ges'tion**, *n.* difficulty in digesting food; discomfort caused by this.

**in·dig'nant**, *adj.* righteously angry.

**in·dig'ni·ty**, *n., pl.* **-ties.** offense to dignity.

**in'di·go'**, *n.* deep blue dye.

**in''di·vid'u·al**, *adj.* 1. separate or distinct. 2. pertaining to one person or thing.

**in·doc'tri·nate''**, *v.t.* instill doctrine into.

**in'do·lent**, *adj.* making little effort.

**in'doors'**, *adv.* within a building

**in·du'bi·ta·ble**, *adj.* impossible to doubt.

**in·duce'**, *v.t.* 1. persuade. 2. cause. 3. infer.

**in·duc'tion**, *n.* 1. act or instance of inducing or inducting. 2. reasoning from the particular to the general.

**in·dulge'**, *v.t.* satisfy.

**in·dul'gence**, *n.* 1. act or instance of indulging. 2. indulgent manner.

**in·dul'gent**, *adj.* leniently kind.

**in·dus'try**, *n., pl.* **-tries.** 1. manufacture and commerce. 2. type of manufacture or commerce. 3. diligent work.

**in·ept'**, *adj.* 1. unsuitable. 2. foolish or awkward.

**in·ert'**, *adj.* 1. powerless to move. 2. without active properties. —*in·er'tia*, *n.* —*in·er'tial*, *adj.*

**in·ev'i·ta·ble**, *adj.* impossible to avoid.

**in·fa'mous**, *adj.* of evil reputation.

**in'fa·my**, *n., pl.* **-mies.** infamous state or act.

**in'fant**, *n.* very young child.

**in'fan·try**, *n., pl.* **-tries.** corps of foot soldiers.

**in·fat'u·ate''**, *v.t.* make foolish with love.

**in·fect'**, *v.t.* afflict with germs or a virus.

**in·fer'**, *v.t.* conclude from evidence. —*in'fer·ence*, *n.* —*in''fer·en'tial*, *adj.*

**in·fe'ri·or**, *adj.* 1. of lesser worth. 2. inadequate. 3. of lesser rank.

**in·fest'**, *v.t.* penetrate harmfully in large numbers.

**in'fil·trate''**, *v.t.* penetrate in many places.

**in'fi·nite**, *adj.* without bounds or end.

**in''fin·i·tes'i·mal**, *adj.* extremely small.

**in·fin'i·tive**, *n.* form of a verb without person, number, or tense.

**in·firm'**, *adj.* not in good health.

**in·fir'ma·ry**, *n., pl.* **-ries.** place for treating the sick.

**in·flame'**, *v.t.* 1. cause to become red, sore, swollen, etc. 2. rouse to anger, etc. —*in''flam·ma'tion*, *n.* —*in·flam''ma·to'ry*, *adj.*

**in·flam'ma·ble**, *adj.* 1. readily burned. 2. readily aroused to anger, etc.

**in·flate'**, *v.t.* 1. cause inflation in or to. —*v.i.* 2. be filled with air or gas. —*in·flat'a·ble*, *adv.*

**in·fla'tion**, *n.* 1. filling with air or gas. 2. fall in the value of money.

**in·flect'**, *v.t.* vary in tone, form, etc.

**in·flict'**, *v.t.* punish someone with.

**in·flu'ence**, *n.* 1. ability to determine events or decisions. 2. per-

**in·flu·en'tial,** *adj.* having much influence.

**in''flu·en'za,** *n.* contagious virus infection.

**in·form',** *v.t.* give knowledge to.

**in·frac'tion,** *n.* violation, as of a law.

**in·fringe',** *v.t.* 1. violate. —*v.i.* 2. encroach.

**in·fu'ri·ate'',** *v.t.* make furious.

**in·fuse',** *v.t.* 1. instill. 2. steep.

**in·gen'ious,** *adj.* clever. —**in''gen·u'i·ty,** *n.*

**in·gest',** *v.t.* eat.

**in'grate,** *n.* ungrateful person.

**in·gre'di·ent,** *n.* component.

**in·hab'it,** *v.t.* live in.

**in·hale',** *v.t., v.i.* breathe in.

**in·her'it,** *v.t.* be an heir to. —**in·her'i·tance,** *n.*

**in·hib'it,** *v.t.* check; restrain.

**in·iq'ui·ty,** *n., pl.* **-ties.** wickedness or wicked act.

**in·i'tial,** *adj.* 1. beginning. —*n.* 2. beginning letter of a word. —*v.t.* 3. mark with initials.

**in·i'ti·ate',** *v.t.* 1. begin. 2. acquaint with basics. 3. accept as a member with ceremony.

**in·i'ti·a·tive,** *n.* readiness to initiate actions.

**in·ject',** *v.t.* force beneath the skin.

**in·jure,** *v.t.* harm. —**in·ju·ry,** *n.*

**ink,** *n.* pigmented liquid for printing, writing, or drawing.

**in'law'',** *n.* relative by marriage.

**in·lay'',** *v.t.,* **-laid, -laying,** *n., v.t.* 1. set into another piece. —*n.* 2. something inlaid.

**in'mate'',** *n.* person under confinement.

**inn,** *n.* small hotel or restaurant.

**in·nate'',** *adj.* present from birth.

**in'ner,** *adj.* farther inside.

**in'no·cent,** *adj.* 1. free of guilt. 2. unsophisticated. —*n.* 3. innocent person.

**in'no·va'tion,** *n.* new discovery or development.

**in·oc'u·late'',** *v.t.* immunize with an injection.

**in·or'di·nate,** *adj.* excessive.

**in''put,** *n.* 1. something supplied. 2. (computers) data entered into a computer.

**in'quest'',** *n.* coroner's investigation.

**in·quire',** *v.i.* 1. ask. 2. investigate. —**in·quir'y,** *n.*

**in·quis'i·tive,** *adj.* desiring to know many things.

**in·scribe',** *v.t.* write or letter. —**in·scrip'tion,** *n.*

**in·scru'ta·ble,** *adj.* hard to understand.

**in'sect,** *n.* six-legged invertebrate.

**in·sen'sate,** *adj.* insensitive.

**in·sen'si·ble,** *adj.* 1. unconscious. 2. impossible to sense.

**in·sert',** *v.t.* (in surt') 1. place into something. (in'sərt) 2. something inserted. —**in·ser'tion,** *n.*

**in·side',** *adv., prep.* 1. within. —*adj.* 2. inner. —*n.* 3. inner part. —**in·sid'er,** *n.*

**in·sid'i·ous,** *adj.* slyly dangerous.

**in·sight',** *n.* deep understanding.

**in·sig'ni·a,** *n., pl.* distinguishing badges, etc.

**in·sin'u·ate'',** *v.t.* 1. imply slyly. 2. introduce imperceptibly.

**in·sip'id,** *adj.* flavorless; dull.

**in·sist',** *v.t.* make repeated demands or assertions.

**in'so·lent,** *adj.* disrespectful. —**in'so·lence,** *n.*

**in·som'ni·a,** *n.* inability to sleep.

**in·spect',** *v.t.* examine carefully.

**in·spire',** *v.t., v.i.* 1. breathe in. —*v.t.* 2. stimulate to mental activity. 3. arouse in someone.

**in·stall',** *v.t.* put in place.

**in·stall'ment,** *n.* item in a series.

**in'stance,** *n.* 1. example. 2. occasion.

**in'stant,** *n.* 1. moment. —*adj.* 2. happening or ready quickly. 3. imminent. —**in''stan·ta'ne·ous,** *adj.*

**in·stead',** *adv.* in the place.

**in'sti·gate'',** *v.t.* urge, as to action.

**in·still',** *v.t.* implant. Also, **in·stil'.**

**in'stinct,** *n.* inborn prompting or reaction. —**in·stinc'tive,** *adj.* —**in·stinc'tu·al,** *adj.*

**in'sti·tute'',** *n.* 1. professional organization or school. —*v.t.* 2. establish.

**in''sti·tu'tion,** *n.* 1. act or instance of instituting. 2. institute. 3. established law or custom.

**in·struct',** *v.t.,* 1. inform or advise. 2. command. —**in·struc'tor,** *n.*

**in'stru·ment,** *n.* 1. tool, etc. 2. means. 3. measuring device. 4. musical device. 5. legal document.

**in'su·late'',** *v.t.* isolate, esp. from heat, sound, or electricity.

**I**
**K**

**in·su·lin,** *n.* hormone secreted by the pancreas.

**in·sult',** *v.t.* (in sult') 1. treat so as to hurt the feelings. —*n.* (in'sult) 2. epithet, etc. that insults.

**in·sure',** *v.t.* 1. guarantee against loss with money. 2. make sure. —**in·sur'ance,** *n.*

**in·sur'gent,** *n., adj.* revolutionary. —**in·sur'gence,** *n.*

**in''sur·rec'tion,** *n.* revolution.

**in·tact',** *adj.* undamaged.

**in·tan'gi·ble,** *adj.* indefinable.

**in'te·gral,** *adj.* forming an essential part.

**in'te·grate,** *v.t.* 1. make complete. 2. bring together into a whole. 3. end racial segregation in or among.

**in·teg'ri·ty,** *n.* 1. intactness. 2. firmnessof character, honesty, etc.

**in'tel·lect,** *n.* ability to comprehend or reason. —**in''tel·lec'tu·al,** *adj., n.*

**in·tel'li·gence,** *n.* 1. ability to comprehend, reason, and think creatively. 2. news. —**in·tel'li·gent,** *adj.*

**in·tel'li·gi·ble,** *adj.* able to be understood.

**in·tend',** *v.t.* have as a purpose.

**in·tense',** *adj.* 1. very strong. 2. with much emotion. —**in·ten'si·fy,** *v.t., v.i.*

**in·ten'sive,** *adj.* thorough.

**in·tent',** *adj.* 1. earnest. 2. firmly intending. —*n.* 3. purpose.

**in·ten'tion,** *n.* purpose.

**in·ter',** *v.t.* bury.

**in''ter·cede',** *v.i.* mediate. —**in''ter·ces'sion,** *n.*

**in''ter·cept',** *v.t.* halt or attack along the way.

**in''ter·change',** *v.i., v.t.* (in''tar chānj'), 1. exchange. 2. alternate. —*n.* (in'tar chānj') 3. access to an express highway. —**in''ter·change'a·ble,** *adj.*

**in'ter·course',** *n.* 1. communication. 2. copulation.

**in''ter·de·pen'dent,** *adj.* dependent on one another. —**in''ter·de·pen'dence,** *n.*

**in''ter·dict',** *v.t.* (in''tar dikt') 1. prohibit. —*n.* (in'tar dikt'') 2. prohibition. —**in''ter·dic'tion,** *n.*

**in'ter·est,** *n.* 1. willing attention. 2. share in a business. 3. profit on a loan. —*v.t.* 4. obtain willing attention from.

**in''ter·fere',** *v.i.* 1. meddle. 2. intervene. —**in''ter·fer'ence,** *n.*

**in·te'ri·or,** *n.* 1. inside. 2. room. —*adj.* 3. inside.

**in'ter·lop''er,** *n.* person who interferes.

**in'ter·lude'',** *n.* episode, musical piece, etc. between major events.

**in''ter·mar'ry,** *v.i.* 1. become associated by marriage. 2. marry a close relation.

**in''ter·me'di·ar''y,** *adj., n., pl.* -ies. *adj.* 1. coming between. —*n.* 2. go-between.

**in''ter·me'di·ate,** *adj.* coming between.

**in·ter'ment,** *n.* burial.

**in·ter'mi·na·ble,** *adj.* seemingly endless.

**in''ter·mis'sion,** *n.* pause, as between acts of a play.

**in''ter·mit'tent,** *adj.* occurring at intervals.

**in·tern,** *n.* (in'tarn) 1. Also, **in'terne,** assistant resident doctor. —*v.t.* (in tarn') 2. detain and confine.

**in·ter'nal,** *adj.* 1. interior. 2. non-foreign.

**in''ter·na'tion·al,** *adj.* 1. among nations. 2. regardless of nation.

**in·ter'po·late'',** *v.t.* alter with new material.

**in·ter'pret,** *v.t.,* 1. clarify. 2. understand. 3. translate.

**in'ter·ra'cial,** *adj.* among races.

**in''ter·re·late'',** *v.t.* relate one to the other.

**in·ter'ro·gate'',** *v.t.* question. —**in·ter'ro·ga''tor,** *n.* —**inter'rog·a'tive, in''ter·rog'a·to·ry,** *adv.*

**in''ter·rupt'',** *v.t.,* 1. halt with an action, remark etc. 2. break the uniformity of.

**in''ter·sect'',** *v.t., v.i.* cross.

**in'ter·sperse'',** *v.t.* scatter.

**in'ter·state'',** *adj., adv.* from state to state.

**in·ter'stice,** *n.* gap.

**in'ter·val,** *n.* intervening period or space.

**in''ter·vene'',** *v.i.* 1. come or occur between. 2. mediate. —**in''ter·ven'tion,** *n.*

**in'ter·view'',** *n.* 1. person-to-person meeting. —*v.t.* 2. question at an interview.

**in·tes'tine,** *n.* either of two organs for converting food. Also, **in·tes'tines.**

**in·ti·mate**, *adj.* (in'tə mət) 1. emotionally close. 2. personal. 3. thorough. 4. intimate friend. —*v.t.* (in'tə māt') 5. hint. —**in'ti·ma·cy**, *n.* —**in'ti·ma'tion**, *n.*

**in·tim'i·date'**, *v.t.* command through fear.

**in'to**, *prep.* 1. to the interior or depths of. 2. up against. 3. to some material, number of parts, etc.

**in·tox'i·cate'**, *v.t.* make drunk.

**in''tra·mu'ral**, *adj.* within an institution.

**in''tra·si·gent**, *adj.* uncompromising.

**in''tra·ve'nous**, *adj.* into a vein from outside the body.

**in·trep'id**, *adj.* fearless.

**in'tri·cate**, *adj.* complicated; complex. —**in'tri·ca·cy**, *n.*

**in·trigue'**, *v.i.* 1. plot in stealth. —*v.t.* 2. make curious. —*n.* 3. stealthy plot or plotting.

**in·trin'sic**, *adj.* essential; inherent.

**in''tro·duce'**, *v.t.* 1. present for the first time. 2. bring into use. 3. insert. —**in''tro·duc'tion**, *n.* —**in''tro·duc'to·ry**, *adj.*

**in''tro·vert'**, *n.* withdrawn person.

**in·trude'**, *v.i.* 1. come as an interruption or surprise. —*v.t.* 2. force upon others. —**in·tru'sion**, *n.* —**in·tru'sive**, *adj.*

**in''tu·i'tion**, *n.* non-logical insight.

**in'un·date'**, *v.t.* flood.

**in·vade'**, *v.t.* enter with force. —**in·va'sion**, *n.*

**in·val'id**, *n.* (in'və lid) 1. sick person. —*adj.* (in val'id) 2. not valid. —**in·val'i·date'**, *v.t.*

**in·val'u·a·ble**, *adj.* valuable beyond reckoning.

**in·vec'tive**, *n.* verbal attack.

**in·vei'gle**, *v.t.* trick into an action.

**in·vent'**, *v.t.* discover as a product or process. —**in·ven'tion**, *n.* —**in·ven'tive**, *adj.* —**in·ven'tor**, *n.*

**in'ven·to''ry**, *n., pl.* **-ries**, *n.* 1. precise list. 2. stock of goods. —*v.t.* 3. make an inventory of.

**in·vert'**, *v.t.* 1. turn upside down. 2. reverse in order or position. —**in·ver'sion**, *n.*

**in·ver'te·brate**, *adj.* 1. having no backbone. —*n.* 2. invertebrate animal.

**in·vest'**, *v.t.* 1. put into something in the hope of profit. 2. give authority or office to. —*v.i.* 3. invest money. —**in·vest'or**, *n.* —**in·vest'ment**, *n.* —**in·vest'i·ture'**, *n.*

**in·ves'ti·gate'**, *v.t.* examine or explore. —**in·ves'ti·ga'tor**, *n.*

**in·vig'or·ate'**, *v.t.* make vigorous. —**in·vig'or·a'tion**, *n.*

**in·vi'o·la·ble**, *adj.* not to be violated.

**in·vite'**, *v.t.* 1. ask to be present. 2. give a pretext for. —**in''vi·ta'tion**, *n.*

**in''vo·ca'tion**, *n.* prayerlike speech.

**in·voice'**, *n.* list of goods supplied.

**in·voke'**, *v.t.* 1. call upon, as a god. 2. cite as a justification.

**in·volve'**, *v.t.* 1. include as relevant. 2. affect or trouble. 3. occupy. 4. complicate.

**in'ward**, *adj.* 1. inside. 2. toward the inside. 3. mental. —*adv.* 4. Also, **in'wards**, towards the inside. —**in·ward'ly**, *adv.*

**i'on**, *n.* electrically charged atom or group of these.

**i·o'ta**, *n.* minute quantity.

**IQ**, intelligence quotient (measure of intelligence). Also, **I.Q.**

**ir-**, prefix meaning "not" or "lack of".

**ire**, *n.* wrath. —**i·rate'**, *adj.*

**ir''i·des'cent**, *adj.* with a play of rainbow-like colors.

**i'ris**, *n., pl.* **irises**. *n.* 1. pigmented part surrounding the eye pupil. 2. plant with sword-shaped leaves.

**irk**, *v.t.* annoy. —**irk'some**, *adj.*

**i'ron**, *n.* 1. metallic element attracting magnets. 2. device made of iron. 3. **irons**, shackles. —*v.t.* 4. smooth with an iron.

**i'ro·ny**, *n., pl.* **-nies**. figure of speech conveying meaning through words of opposite meaning. —**i·ron'i·cal**, **i·ron'ic**, *adj.*

**ir''re·sist'i·ble**, *adj.* impossible to resist.

**ir'ri·gate'**, *v.t.* introduce water to.

**ir'ri·ta·ble**, *adj.* readily irritated.

**ir'ri·tate'**, *v.t.* 1. annoy. 2. make sore. —**ir'ri·tant**, *adj.*, *n.*

**ir·rupt'**, *v.i.* 1. burst forth; expand.

**i'sin·glass'**, *n.* 1. gelatin from fish bladders. 2. mica.

**is·land** (I'lənd) *n.* 1. body of land surrounded by water. 2. isolated platform, etc.

**is·let** (I'lət), *n.* small island.

**i'so·late'**, *v.t.* keep apart.

**K**

**i·sos'cel·es''**, *adj.* pertaining to triangles with two equal sides.

**i'so·tope''**, *n.* form of an element coinciding in atomic number but not in atomic weight with another.

**is'sue**, *v.t.* 1. give out. 2. publish. —*v.i.* 3. emerge. —*n.* 4. something that issues. 5. periodical of one date. 6. thing in dispute. 7. offspring. 8. result. —**is'su·ance**, *n.*

**isth'mus**, *n.*, *pl.* **-muses.** narrow neck of connecting land between bodies of water.

**it**, *pron.*, *pl.* **they** 1. thing referred to. 2. (subject of various impersonal verbs).

**i·tal'ic**, *adj.* 1. pertaining to letters printed thus: *Italics.* —*n.* 2. italics, italic letters. —**i·tal'i·cize''**, *v.t.*

**itch**, *v.i.* 1. feel a mild irritation tempting one to scratch. 2. desire restlessly. —*n.* 3. act or sense of itching. —**itch'y**, *adj.*

**i'tem**, *n.* 1. listed thing. 2. piece of news. —**i'tem·ize''**, *v.t.*

**it'er·ate''**, *v.t.* repeat.

**i·tin'er·ant**, *adj.* traveling; migratory.

**i·tin'er·ar''y**, *n.*, *pl.* **-ties.** plan of travel.

**its**, *pron.* belonging or pertaining to it.

**it's**, *pron.* contraction of *it is.*

**it·self'**, *pron.* 1. (intensive or reflexive of *it* ). 2. its true self.

**i'vo·ry**, *n.* creamy-white substance of tusks.

**i'vy**, *n.*, *pl.* **ivies.** climbing evergreen vine. —**i'vied**, *adj.*

# J

**J, j,** *n.* tenth letter of the English alphabet.

**jab**, *v.t.*, *v.i.*, *n.* poke.

**jack**, *n.* 1. lifting machine. 2. playing card; knave. 3. flag at a ship's stern. 4. point of connection; place where something is plugged in. —*v.t.* 5. to raise something with a jack.

**jack'al**, *n.* wild African and Asian dog.

**jack'ass''**, *n.* 1. male donkey. 2. fool.

**jack'et**, *n.* 1. short coat. 2. covering.

**jack'knife''**, *n.* 1. folding knife. —*v.i.* 2. fold accidentally at a joint.

**jack'pot''**, *n.* stakes won.

**jack'rab''bit**, *n.* large North American hare.

**jade**, *n.* ornamental stone, usually green.

**jag'ged**, *adj.* with a rough, sharp edge or surface.

**jail**, *n.* 1. prison for short confinements. —*v.t.* 2. put in jail. —**jail'er, jail'or,** *n.*

**jam**, *v.t.*, *v.i.* 1. crowd. 2. stick tight. —*n.* 3. act or instance of jamming. 4. fruit boiled with sugar. 5. *Informal.* adverse situation.

**jamb**, *n.* upright of a doorway or window.

**jan'gle**, *v.i.* jingle harshly.

**jan'i·tor**, *n.* person who takes care of a building.

**jar**, *n.* 1. cylindrical container. 2. jolt. —*v.t.* 3. jolt. —*v.i.* 4. clash. 5. have an irritating effect.

**jar'gon**, *n.* abstruse technical language.

**jaun'dice**, *n.* disease characterized by yellowing due to bile in the blood.

**jaunt**, *n.* pleasure excursion.

**jaun'ty**, *adj.*, **-tier, -tiest.** cheerful.

**jave'lin**, *n.* throwing spear.

**jaw**, *n.* 1. bony framing member of the mouth. 2. gripping part of a vise, etc.

**jay'walk''**, *v.i.* cross a street heedlessly.

**jazz**, *n.* syncopated, rythmic modern music.

**jeal'ous**, *adj.* 1. feeling jealousy. 2. watchful.

**jeans**, *n.*, *pl.* trousers of strong cloth.

**jeep**, *n.* rugged, military-style car.

**jeer**, *v.i.* make scornful utterances.

**Je·ho'vah**, *n.* God.

**jel'ly**, *n.* gelatinous food.

**jeo'pard·ize''**, *v.t.* put in danger. —**jeo'pard·y**, *n.*

**jerk**, *n.* 1. sharp pull. —*v.t.* 2. pull sharply.

**jest**, *n.* joke.

**jet**, *n.* 1. forced stream. 2. jet-propelled airplane.

**jet'sam,** *n.* material thrown overboard.

**jet'ti·son,** *v.t.* throw away or overboard.

**jet'ty,** *n., pl.* **-ties.** pier or wall into the water.

**jew'el,** *n.* precious stone.

**jig,** *n.* **1.** fast dance. **2.** tool guide. —*v.i.* **3.** dance a jig.

**jig'gle,** *v.i., v.t.* move in rapid jerks.

**jig'saw",** *n.* narrow-bladed saw.

**jilt,** *v.t.* reject.

**jin'gle,** *v.i., v.t.* ring lightly and rapidly.

**jinx,** *n.* **1.** bringer of ill-luck. —*v.t.* **2.** bring ill-luck to.

**job,** *n.* **1.** task. **2.** occupation. **3.** duty.

**jock'ey,** *n., pl.* **-keys.** *n.* **1.** rider of race horses. —*v.i.* **2.** maneuver for advantage.

**joc'u·lar,** *adj.* joking; playful.

**jog,** *v.t.* **1.** nudge. —*v.i.* **2.** run steadily.

**join,** *v.t.* **1.** put together. **2.** become a member of. —*v.i.* **3.** come or act together.

**join'er,** *n.* **1.** woodworker. **2.** person who likes to join groups.

**joint,** *n.* **1.** connection. —*adj.* **2.** shared. **3.** sharing with others. —*v.t.* **4.** assemble with joints. —**joint'ly,** *adv.*

**joist,** *n.* floor beam.

**joke,** *n.* **1.** laugh-provoking story or remark. **2.** playful act. —*v.i.* **3.** make a joke.

**jol'ly,** *adj.* **-lier, -liest.** full of high spirits. —**jol'li·ly,** *adv.* —**jol'lity,** *n.*

**jolt,** *v.t.* **1.** shake or bump. —*v.i.* **2.** move bumpily. —*n.* **3.** act or instance of jolting.

**jos'tle,** *v.t., v.i.* shove, as in a crowd.

**jot,** *v.t.* make a note of.

**jounce,** *v.i.* jolt and bounce.

**jour'nal,** *n.* **1.** periodical. **2.** diary.

**jour'nal·ism,** *n.* work for a periodical.

**jour'ney,** *n., pl.* **-neys,** *n.* **1.** long trip. —*v.i.* **2.** go on a journey.

**jo'vi·al,** *adj.* merry.

**jowl,** *n.* lower cheek.

**joy,** *n.* **1.** intense happiness. **2.** source of this.

**joy''stick",** *n.* (computers) grippable device for data manipulation, used mostly for graphics and games.

**ju'bi·lant,** *adj.* rejoicing.

**ju'bi·lee",** *n.* **1.** major anniversary. **2.** time of rejoicing.

**Ju'da·ism,** *n.* Jewish religion. —**Ju·da'ic,** *adj.*

**judge,** *n.* **1.** presider over a trial, contest, etc. **2.** qualified evaluator. —*v.t.* **3.** evaluate. —**judg'ment, judge'ment,** *n.*

**ju·di'cial,** *adj.* pertaining to judges or courts.

**ju·di'ci·ar"y,** *adj., n., pl.* **-ies.** *adj.* **1.** judicial. —*n.* **2.** judges.

**ju·di'cious,** *adj.* with sound judgment.

**ju'do,** *n.* Japanese system of wrestling.

**jug,** *n.* broad vessel with a narrow neck.

**jug'gle,** *v.t.* toss, balance with skill.

**jug'u·lar,** *n.* neck vein.

**juice,** *n.* liquid from a fruit, etc. —**juic'y,** *adj.*

**juke'box",** *n.* coin-operated record player.

**jum'ble,** *v.t.* **1.** mix in disorder. —*n.* **2.** disorderly mixture.

**jump,** *v.i.* **1.** leave the ground with a muscular effort. **2.** move abruptly. **3.** jump over. —*n.* **4.** act or instance of jumping.

**jum'py,** *adj.* **-pier, -piest.** very nervous.

**junc'tion,** *n.* place of joining.

**junc'ture,** *n.* **1.** junction. **2.** moment.

**jun'gle,** *n.* densely grown tropical area.

**jun'ior,** *adj.* **1.** being the son of a father with the same name. **2.** lesser in rank, etc. —*n.* **3.** junior person. **4.** third-year student.

**junk,** *n.* **1.** rejected or worthless material. **2.** Chinese sailing boat.

**junk'et,** *n.* **1.** curdled milk dish. **2.** excursion.

**jun·ta** (hŏŏn tä), *n.* military in power after a coup d'etat.

**ju'ris·dic'tion,** *n.* **1.** administration of justice. **2.** area of authority.

**ju'rist,** *n.* expert in law.

**ju'ry,** *n.* group deciding the outcome of a trial. —**ju'ror,** *n.*

**just,** *adj.* **1.** fair. **2.** righteous. **3.** accurate. —*adv.* **4.** exactly. **5.** only. —**just'ness,** *n.*

**jus'tice,** *n.* **1.** fairness. **2.** righteousness. **3.** administration of law. **4.** judge.

**jus'ti·fy",** *v.t.* give valid reasons for.

**I**

**K**

**jut**, *v.i.* project.

**ju·ven·ile**, *adj.* 1. pertaining to children. —*n.* 2. child.

# K

**K, k**, *n.* eleventh letter of the English alphabet.

**ka·lei'do·scope''**, *n.* device creating symmetrical patterns.

**kan'ga·roo''**, *n.* leaping Australian marsupial.

**kar'at**, *n.* twenty-fourth part pure gold.

**ka·ra'te**, *n.* Japanese technique of fighting.

**kay'ak**, *n.* Eskimo canoe.

**keel**, *n.* central structural member of a ship.

**keen**, *adj.* 1. sharp. 2. eager. 3. shrewd.

**keep**, *v.t.* 1. retain. 2. look after. 3. protect or support. 4. be observant of. —*v.i.* 5. be preserved. 6. abstain. 7. remain or continue. —*n.* 8. support; custody.

**keep'sake''**, *n.* souvenir.

**keg**, *n.* small barrel.

**ken'nel**, *n.* doghouse.

**ker'nel**, *n.* 1. seed. 2. inner nut.

**ker'o·sene''**, *n.* petroleum derivative.

**ketch'up**, *n.* sauce, often made with tomatoes.

**ket'tle**, *n.* pot for boiling water.

**key**, *n.* 1. metal instrument operating a lock. 2. device on a piano, etc. pressed in operating it. 3. thing that explains. 4. system of musical tones. —*adj.* 5. decisive.

**key'board**, *n.* (computers) 1. device resembling a typewriter keyboard used for data input. —*v.* 2. to input data with a keyboard.

**kha'ki**, *n., pl.* -kis. 1. dull yellowish brown. 2. khakis, clothing made of cloth this color.

**kick**, *v.t., v.i.* 1. strike with the foot. —*v.i.* 2. recoil. 3. *Informal.* complain. —*n.* 4. act or instance of kicking. 5. *Informal.* a. grievance. b. thrill.

**kid**, *n.* 1. young goat. 2. *Informal.* child. —*v.t.* 3. *Informal.* tease. —*v.i.* 4. *Informal.* joke.

**kid'nap''**, *v.t.* abduct and hold prisoner. —**kid'nap''er**, *n.*

**kid'ney**, *n.* organ that forms urine.

**kill**, *v.t.* 1. cause to die. 2. end abruptly. —*n.* 3. act or instance of killing.

**kiln** (kil, kiln), *n.* furnace for processing materials.

**ki'lo**, *n., pl.* -los. 1. kilogram. 2. kilometer.

**ki'lo·gram''**, *n.* one thousand grams or 2.2046 pounds.

**ki'lo·hertz''**, *n.* one thousand hertz. Also, **ki'lo·cy''cle.**

**ki'lo·me''ter**, *n.* one thousand meters or 3,281 feet.

**kil'o·watt''**, *n.* one thousand watts.

**kilt**, *n.* Scottish skirt for men.

**ki·mo'no**, *n., pl.* -nos. *n.* full-length Japanese dress.

**kin**, *n.* relatives.

**kind**, *n.* 1. sort. —*adj.* 2. benevolent; compassionate.

**kin'der·gar''ten**, *n.* pre-elementary school.

**kin'dle**, *v.t.* 1. set on fire. 2. arouse.

**kind'ly**, *adj.* 1. kind. —*adv.* 2. in a kind way. 3. graciously; favorably. —**kind'li·ness,** *n.*

**kin'folk''**, *n., pl.* relatives.

**king**, *n.* male national ruler.

**king'dom**, *n.* state ruled by a king.

**kink**, *n.* short loop or coil.

**kin'ship''**, *n.* family relationship.

**kiss**, *n.* 1. touching with the lips as a sign of affection, etc. —*v.t.* 2. give a kiss to. —*v.i.* 3. exchange kisses.

**kit**, *n.* set of equipment.

**kitch'en**, *n.* place for preparing meals.

**kite**, *n.* flying toy on a string.

**kit'ten**, *n.* young cat.

**ki'wi**, *n.* 1. any flightless bird of genus Apteryx. 2. fuzzy fruit of Asian Climbinb plant, the Chinese gooseberry.

**klep''to·ma'ni·a**, *n.* compulsion to steal. —**klep''to·ma'ni·ac**, *n.*

**knack**, *n.* talent.

**knap'sack''**, *n.* sack worn on the back.

**knead**, *v.t.* press and work with the fingers.

**knee**, *n.* joint of the leg.

**kneel**, *v.i.* be upright on the knees.

**knife**, *n., pl.* **knives**, *n.* 1. small cutting tool. —*v.t.* 2. stab with a knife.

**knight**, *n.* 1. possessor of an honorable rank, formerly military. 2. chesspiece.

**knit**, *v.t.* 1. assemble from yarn with two needles. 2. draw together in wrinkles, as the brows. —*v.i.* 3. join again after a fracture.

**knob**, *n.* rounded projection or handle. —**knob′by**, *adj.*

**knock**, *v.t.* 1. hit, as with the fist. 2. *Informal.* disparage. —*v.i.* 3. strike blows. —*n.* 4. act or instance of knocking. 5. adverse happening.

**knoll**, *n.* small, round hill.

**knot**, *n.* 1. fastening of intertwined cord. 2. small cluster. 3. hard lump in wood. 4. one nautical mile per hour. —*v.t.* 5. make into a knot. —**knot′ty**, *adj.*

**know**, *v.t.*, **knew**, **known**, **knowing**. 1. have full evidence. 2. be fully informed or skilled.

**knowl′edge**, *n.* 1. state of knowing. 2. what is known.

**knowl′edge·a·ble**, *adj.* well-informed.

**knuck′le**, *n.* central finger joint.

# L

**L, l**, *n.* twelfth letter of the English alphabet.

**la′bel**, *n.* 1. attached paper with information. —*v.t.* 2. designate with a label.

**la′bor**, *n.* 1. hard work. 2. workers collectively. 3. process of giving birth. —*v.i.* 4. work hard.

**lab′o·ra·to′ry**, *n.*, *pl.* **-ries.** place for scientific research.

**la·bo′ri·ous**, *adj.* difficult; tedious.

**lab′y·rinth″**, *n.* maze.

**lace**, *n.* 1. binding string, as on a shoe. 2. openwork cloth.

**lac′er·ate″**, *v.t.* tear jaggedly.

**lack**, *n.* 1. shortage. —*v.t.* 2. be without.

**la·con′ic**, *adj.* short-spoken; terse.

**lac′quer**, *n.* transparent varnish-like coating.

**lac′y**, *adj.*, **-ier**, **-iest.** open and intricate.

**lad**, *n.* boy.

**lad′der**, *n.* steep set of steps.

**la′dle**, *n.* 1. long-handled bowl for dipping. 2. dip with a ladle.

**la′dy**, *n.*, *pl.* **dies.** 1. respectable woman. 2. title of certain British women.

**lag**, *v.i.* 1. fall behind. —*n.* 2. act or instance of lagging. —**lag′gard**, *n.*, *adj.*

**laid″back″**, *adj.* relaxed; serene.

**lair**, *n.* den, as of an animal.

**lake**, *n.* inland body of water.

**lamb**, *n.* young sheep.

**lame**, *adj.* 1. unable to walk properly. 2. ineffectual.

**la·ment′**, *v.t.*, *v.i.* 1. mourn. —*n.* 2. speech, poem, or song of mourning.

**lamp**, *n.* device for emitting rays of light, etc. —**lamp′post″**, *n.*

**lance**, *n.* 1. spear carried by a horseman. —*v.t.* 2. prick, as to discharge pus.

**land**, *n.* 1. earth's surface above water. 2. nation; country. 3. real estate. —*v.t.* 4. bring to shore or earth. 5. secure; obtain. —*v.i.* 6. come to shore or earth. 7. fall.

**land′ing**, *n.* 1. act of coming to shore or earth. 2. place to land. 3. unstepped area on a stair.

**land′locked″**, *adj.* with little or no access to the sea.

**land′lord″**, *n.* man from whom one rents.

**land′lub′ber**, *n.* *Informal.* nonsailor.

**land′mark″**, *n.* visible aid to finding one's way.

**land′scape″**, *n.* 1. large visible area of land. —*v.t.* 2. create a landscape from.

**land′slide″**, *n.* fall of earth down a slope.

**lane**, *n.* 1. path or narrow road. 2. path of highway travel.

**lan′guage**, *n.* system of communication.

**lank′y**, *adj.*, **-ier**, **-iest.** awkwardly tall and lean.

**lan′o·lin**, *n.* oil from wool used in ointments and cosmetics.

**lan′tern**, *n.* 1. transparent lamp casing.

**lap**, *n.* 1. area between waist and knees when seated. 2. overlap. 3. once around a racetrack. —*v.t.* 4. wrap. 5. overlap. —*v.i.* 6. drink by licking. 7. splash gently.

**la·pel′**, *n.* continuation of a coat collar folded back.

**lapse**, *v.i.* 1. go passively. 2. elapse.

**L**
**M**

3. become void. —*n.* 4. act or instance of lapsing. 5. minor error.

**lar'ce·ny,** *n.* theft.

**lard,** *n.* clarified hog fat.

**lard'er,** *n.* place for storing food.

**large,** *adj., adv.,* **larger, largest,** *adj.* 1. big. 2. large-scale. —*adv.* 3. in a large way.

**lark,** *n.* 1. songbird. 2. frolic. —*v.i.* 3. frolic. animal.

**lar'yn·gi'tis,** *n.* inflammation of the larynx.

**lar'ynx,** *n., pl.* **-ynxes, -ynges.** container of the vocal cords.

**las·civ'i·ous,** *adj.* lustful.

**lash,** *v.t.* 1. tie. 2. whip. —*v.i.* 3. strike. —*n.* 4. whip.

**las'so,** *n., pl.* **-sos, -soes,** *n.* 1. rope for capturing cattle, etc. —*v.t.* 2. capture with a lasso.

**last,** *adj., adv.* 1. after all others. —*n.* 2. last one. —*v.i.* 3. remain. —*v.t.* 4. be enough for.

**latch,** *n.* 1. device to hold a door, etc. shut. —*v.t.* 2. fasten with a latch.

**late,** *adj., adv.,* **later** or (for adj.) **latter latest,** or **last.** *adj., adv.* 1. after the right time. 2. near the end. 3. in recent times. —*adj.* 4. recently alive.

**late'ly,** *adv.* recently.

**la'tent,** *n.* unmanifested or undeveloped.

**la'ter·al,** *adj.* pertaining to a side.

**lathe,** *n.* machine for cutting a rotating object.

**lath'er,** *n.* foam.

**lat'i·tude'',** *n.* 1. north-south measurement. 2. scope.

**la·trine',** *n.* military bathroom.

**lat'ter,** *adj.* 1. more recently mentioned. 2. more recent. —**lat'ter·ly,** *adv.*

**lat'tice,** *n.* screen of crisscrossed strips.

**laud,** *v.t.* praise.

**laugh,** *n.* 1. rhythmic sound indicating amusement, scorn, etc. —*v.i.* 2. make such a sound. —**laugh'a·ble,** *adj.* —**laugh'ter,** *n.*

**launch,** *v.t.* 1. send from land. 2. put into effect, use, etc. —*n.* 3. open boat.

**laun'der,** *v.t.* wash, as clothes.

**laun'dry,** *n., pl.* **-dries.** place for laundering.

**lau'rel,** *n.* 1. shrub with glossy leaves. 2. laurels, honors.

**la'va,** *n.* molten volcanic rock.

**lav'a·to''ry,** *n., pl.* **-ries.** washing place.

**lav'en·der,** *n.* pale purple.

**lav'ish,** *adj.* 1. very ample.

**law,** *n.* 1. rule established by government. 2. legal profession. 3. police. 4. rule of natural phenomena. —**law'ful,** *adj.*

**lawn,** *n.* 1. expanse of grass. 2. sheer cotton or linen.

**law'yer,** *n.* professional legal adviser and representative.

**lax,** *adj.* negligent. —**lax'i·ty,** *n.*

**lax'a·tive,** *adj.* easing constipation.

**lay,** *v.t.,* **laid, laying,** *n., adj., v.t.* 1. set down gently. 2. set in place. 3. place, as emphasis or a claim. —*n.* 4. situation. 5. ballad. —*adj.* 6. not professional or clerical. —**lay'man,** *n.*

**lay'er,** *n.* level or thickness of material.

**la'zy,** *adj.,* **-zier, -ziest.** unwilling to work.

**lead** (lēd for 1 to 6; led for 7) *v.t.* 1. direct or guide. 2. be ahead of. 3. conduct. —*v.i.* 4. tend or result. —*n.* 5. leading role or place. 6. guidance. 7. heavy metallic chemical element. —**lead·er** (lē'dər), *n.* —**lead·en** (led'n), *adj.*

**leaf,** *n., pl.* **leaves,** *n.* 1. flat thin termination of a plant stem. 2. thin sheet. —*v.i.* 3. turn over pages. —**leaf'y,** *adj.*

**league,** *n.* 1. alliance. 2. unit of about 3 miles.

**leak,** *n.* 1. accidental release or admission. —*v.i.* 2. have or pass through a leak. —*v.t.* 3. pass through a leak.

**lean,** *v.t., v.i.* 1. stand against something supporting the upper end. —*v.i.* 2. bend; incline. 3. be disposed. 4. rely. —*adj.* 5. with little fat.

**leap,** *v.t., v.i., n.* jump.

**leap year,** year with 29 days in February.

**learn,** *v.t.* 1. know how. —*v.i.* 2. get information. —**learn'ed,** *adj.*

**lease,** *n.* rental contract.

**leash,** *n.* tether, as for a dog.

**least,** *adj.* 1. smallest in size, importance, etc. —*adv.* 2. to the smallest extent.

**leath'er,** *n.* tanned hide.

**leave,** *v.i.* 1. go away. —*v.t.* 2. go away from. 3. bequeath. —*n.* 4. departure. 5. permission.

**leav'en** (lev'n), *n.* 1. substance making dough rise. —*v.t.* 2. cause to rise.

**lech'er,** n. lustful person.

**lec'ture,** n. 1. informative speech. —v.t. 2. give a lecture to. —v.i. 3. give a lecture.

**ledge,** n. narrow shelf or platform.

**led'ger,** n. accountant's book.

**lee,** adj. away from the wind.

**leech,** n. blood-sucking worm.

**leer,** n. sly, malicious or lustful look.

**lee'way'',** n. scope for action.

**left,** n. 1. west when facing north. 2. liberal or socialistic position. —adv. 3. toward the left.

**leg,** n. 1. supporting and walking limb. 2. vertical support.

**leg'a·cy,** n., pl. -cies. something left to posterity.

**le'gal,** adj. 1. permitted by law. 2. pertaining to law.

**le·ga'tion,** n. office of a diplomat.

**leg'end,** n. 1. folk tale. 2. inscription.

**leg'i·ble,** adj. possible to read. —leg''i·bil'i·ty, n.

**le'gion,** n. large band, esp. of soldiers. —le'gion·ar''y, adj., n. —le''gion·naire', n.

**leg'is·late'',** v.t. 1. determine by law. —v.i. 2. enact laws. —leg''is·la'tion, n. —leg'is·la''tive, adj. —leg'is·la''tor, n.

**leg·is·la'ture,** n. lawmaking body.

**le·git'i·mate,** adj. 1. right; proper. 2. of married parents. —le·git'i·ma·cy, n. —le·git'i·mize'', v.t.

**lei'sure,** n. time for rest or recreation.

**lem'on,** n. yellow citrus fruit.

**lend,** v.t. 1. give for later return. 2. impart.

**length,** n. 1. end-to-end extent. 2. piece measured by length.

**le'ni·ent,** adj. not strict or harsh.

**lens,** n., pl. lenses. transparent object concentrating or dispersing rays of light.

**Lent,** n. Christian time of penance from Ash Wednesday to Easter. —Lent'en, adj.

**leop'ard,** n. spotted cat of the panther family.

**lep'er,** n. person with leprosy.

**lep'ro·sy,** n. deforming chronic disease. —lep'rous, adj.

**les'bi·an,** n. homosexual woman.

**le'sion,** n. bodily injury.

**less,** adj. 1. smaller or fewer. —adv. 2. to a smaller extent. —prep. 3. minus. —les'sen, v.t., v.i.

**les'ser,** adj. smaller; less important.

**les'son,** n. something learned at one time.

**lest,** conj. for fear that.

**let,** v.t. 1. allow. 2. rent. 3. allow to issue.

**let'down'',** n. disappointment.

**le'thal,** adj. deadly.

**leth'ar·gy,** n., pl. -gies. sluggishness. —le·thar'gic, adj.

**let'ter,** n. 1. alphabetic character. 2. message in an envelope. 3. literal meaning.

**let'tuce,** n. green, leafy vegetable.

**leu·ke'mi·a,** n. blood disease.

**lev'ee,** n. embankment against rising water.

**lev'el,** n. 1. point or plane between top and bottom. 2. device for finding horizontals or verticals. 3. point on a scale of values. —adj. 4. flat. 5. horizontal. 6. even. —v.t. 7. make level.

**lev'er,** n. pivoted raising device lifted at one end. —lev'er·age, n.

**lev'i·ty,** n. mirth.

**lev·y** (lev'ē), v.t., n., pl. -ies. v.t. 1. impose for payment. 2. enlist. —n. 3. something levied.

**lewd,** adj. obscene.

**lex'i·con,** n. dictionary.

**li''a·bil'i·ty,** n., pl. -ties. state of being liable.

**li'a·ble,** adj. 1. responsible. 2. subject to something. 3. likely.

**li'ai·son'',** n. 1. connection, as for communication. 2. love affair.

**li'ar,** n. teller of lies.

**li'bel,** n. 1. defamation in writing or print. —v.t. 2. defame by this means. —li'bel·ous, li'bel·lous, adj.

**lib'er·al,** adj. 1. generous. 2. not literal. 3. favoring more civil liberty. —n. 4. person favoring more civil liberty. —lib''er·al'i·ty, n. —lib'er·al·ism, n. —lib'er·al·ize'', v.t.

**lib'er·ate'',** v.t. free. —lib'er·a''tor, n.

**lib'er·tine'',** n. licentious person.

**lib'er·ty,** n., pl. -ties. 1. freedom. 2. privilege.

**li'brar'y,** n., pl. -ies. 1. collection of books. 2. place for books. —li·brar'i·an, n.

**li·bret'to,** n., pl. -tos, -ti. text of an opera, etc. —li·bret'tist, n.

**li'cense,** n. 1. privilege of doing. 2. abuse of liberty. —v.t. 3. grant a license to. —li''cen·see', n. —li·cen'tious, adj.

**lick,** v.t. 1. rub with the tongue. 2.

**L M**

*Informal.* **a.** defeat. **b.** beat. —*v.i.* **3.** lap. —*n.* **4.** act or instance of licking.

**lid,** *n.* cover.

**lie,** *v.i.,* **lay** (for 1, 2) or **lied** (for 3), **lain** (for 1, 2), **lying**. *v.i.* **1.** rest on something horizontal. **2.** be situated. **3.** make statements intended ded to deceive. —*n.* **4.** situation. **5.** lying statement.

**lieu·ten·ant,** *n.* officer below a captain or lieutenant commander.

**life,** *n., pl.* **lives. 1.** period of existence. **2.** living things collectively. **3.** human experience. **4.** way of living.

**life'guard",** *n.* one employed to protect bathers, esp. from drowning, etc.

**lift,** *v.t.* **1.** raise. —*v.i.* **2.** attempt to raise something. **3.** rise. —*n.* **4.** act or instance of lifting. **5.** hoist.

**lig·a·ment,** *n.* body connective tissue.

**light,** *n., adj., v.,* **lighted** or **lit, lighting.** *n.* **1.** visible radiant energy. **2.** lamp. **3.** flame. **4.** truth. —*adj.* **5.** not dark or serious. —*v.t.* **6.** set fire to. **7.** cause to give off light. **8.** show in light.

**light'house",** *n.* tower with a navigational beacon.

**light'ning,** *n.* flash of electricity in the sky.

**like,** *prep.* **1.** similar or similarly to. **2.** characteristic or suggestive of. **3.** inclined to. —*adj.* **4.** similar. —*n.* **5.** similar person or thing. **6.** preference. —*v.t.* **7.** be pleased with. **8.** wish.

**like'ly,** *adj.,* **-lier, -liest,** *adv., adj.* **1.** probable. **2.** suitable. —*adv.* **3.** probably.

**lik'en,** *v.t.* compare.

**like'wise",** *adv.* similarly, also.

**lilt,** *n.* light, bouncy rhythm.

**lil'y,** *n., pl.* **-ies.** flower with trumpet-shaped blossoms.

**limb,** *n.* **1.** large tree branch. **2.** arm or leg.

**lim'ber,** *adj.* flexible.

**lim'bo,** *n.* **1.** abode of the unbaptized, innocent dead. **2.** oblivion.

**lime,** *n.* **1.** calcium oxide. **2.** tart green citrus fruit.

**lime'light",** *n.* state of much publicity.

**lim'er·ick,** *n.* amusing five-lined verse.

**lime'stone",** *n.* stone containing much calcium carbonate.

**lim'it,** *n.* **1.** edge or boundary. **2.**

permissible extent. —*v.t.* **3.** set a limit to.

**lim'ou·sine",** *n.* long, chauffeured automobile.

**limp,** *v.i.* **1.** walk lamely. —*n.* **2.** lame gait. —*adj.* **3.** not rigid or firm.

**lim'pid,** *adj.* clear.

**line,** *n.* **1.** long, narrow mark. **2.** row. **3.** boundary. **4.** course. **5.** transit system. **6.** rope, pipe, etc. **7.** occupation. —*v.t.* **8.** put a lining in. **9.** mark with lines. —*v.i.* **10.** assemble in a line.

**lin'e·age,** *n.* ancestry.

**lin'e·al,** *adj.* **1.** pertaining to direct ancestry. **2.** linear.

**lin'e·ar,** *adj.* pertaining to lines or length.

**lin'en,** *n.* cloth of flax.

**lin'er,** *n.* ship or airplane on scheduled service.

**lin'ger,** *v.i.* remain; stay.

**lin·ge·rie** (lan"ʒə rā'), *n.* women's underwear.

**lin'guist,** *n.* **1.** speaker of many languages. **2.** student of languages.

**lin'i·ment,** *n.* soothing liquid for external use.

**lin'ing,** *n.* material applied to an interior.

**link,** *n.* **1.** unit of a chain or series. **2.** connection. —*v.t., v.i.* **3.** connect. —**link'age,** *n.*

**li·no'le·um,** *n.* smooth sheeting for floors.

**lin'tel,** *n.* beam over a doorway, etc.

**li'on,** *n.* large cat of Africa.

**lip,** *n.* **1.** feature at top and bottom of the mouth. **2.** surface for pouring.

**lip'stick",** *n.* coloring for the lips.

**liq'uor,** *n.* alcoholic liquid.

**liq'ue·fy",** *v.t., v.i.* change to liquid. —**liq"ue·fac'tion,** *n.*

**liq'uid,** *n.* **1.** fluid incapable of indefinite expansion. —*adj.* **2.** in the form of a liquid.

**liq'ui·date",** *v.t.* **1.** terminate, as a business. **2.** kill.

**lisp,** *n.* **1.** mispronunciation of *s* and *z.* —*v.i.* **2.** make such mispronunciations.

**list,** *n.* **1.** series of related items. **2.** tilt, as of a ship. —*v.t.* **3.** put on a list. —*v.i.* **4.** tilt.

**lis'ten,** *v.i.* **1.** hear attentively. **2.** pay heed.

**list'less,** *adj.* indifferent from fatigue, etc.

**lit'a·ny**, *n., pl.* **-nies.** uttered prayer with responses.

**li'ter**, *n.* metric unit equal to 1.0567 liquid quarts or 0.908 dry quart. Also, **li'tre.**

**lit'er·al**, *adj.* according to the exact wording.

**lit'er·ar'y**, *adj.* pertaining to literature.

**lit'er·ate**, *adj.* 1. able to read. 2. well-read. —**lit'er·a·cy**, *n.*

**lit'er·a·ture**, *n.* fiction, poetry, etc. of lasting value.

**lithe**, *adj.* supple.

**lith'o·graph'**, *n.* print from a flat surface with special ink.

**lit'i·gate'**, *v.t., v.i.* contest in a lawsuit. —**lit'i·gant, lit'i·ga'tor**, *n.*

**lit'ter**, *n.* 1. trash. 2. newly-born animals. 3. animal bedding. 4. frame for carrying a person. —*v.t.* 5. scatter carelessly.

**lit'tle**, *adj.* **littler** or **less** or **lesser**, **littlest** or **least**, *adv.*, **less, least**, *n. adj.* 1. small. 2. petty. —*adv.* 3. not much. —*n.* 4. short while. 5. small amount.

**lit'ur·gy**, *n., pl.* **-gies.** ritual of worship.

**liv'a·ble**, *adj.* pleasant to inhabit. Also, **live'a·ble.**

**live'li·hood'**, *n.* means of sustenance.

**live** (liv for 1-5; līv for 6-8). *v.i.* 1. be alive. 2. dwell. 3. spend one's life. 4. depend for existence. —*v.t.* 5. experience or spend. —*adj.* 6. alive. 7. vital. 8. electrically charged.

**live'ly**, *adj.*, **-lier, -liest.** full of vitality.

**liv'en**, *v.t.* 1. make lively. —*v.i.* 2. become lively.

**liv'er**, *n.* organ secreting bile.

**live'stock'**, *n.* cattle, sheep, etc.

**liv'id**, *adj.* 1. discolored. 2. enraged.

**liv'ing**, *adj.* 1. alive. 2. pertaining to being alive. —*n.* 3. livelihood.

**liz'ard**, *n.* scaly, four-legged reptile.

**load**, *n.* 1. something carried. —*v.t.* 2. put a load on or in. 3. supply in large amounts. 4. make ready for firing. —*v.i.* 5. take on a load.

**loaf**, *n., pl.* **loaves.** *n.* 1. regularly shaped piece of bread. —*v.i.* 2. be idle.

**loam**, *n.* rich soil.

**loan**, *n.* 1. act or instance of lending. 2. something lent. —*v.t., v.i.* 3. lend.

**loath**, *adj.* reluctant.

**loathe**, *v.t.* dislike intensely.

**lob'by**, *n., pl.* **-bies.** *n.* 1. entrance room. 2. group seeking favorable legislation.

**lobe**, *n.* rounded projection. *adj.*

**lob'ster**, *n.* sea crustacean with pincers.

**lo'cal**, *adj.* 1. pertaining or limited to a place. 2. making most or all stops. —**lo'cal·ly**, *adv.*

**lo·cal'i·ty**, *n., pl.* **-ties.** 1. location. 2. district.

**lo'cal·ize'**, *v.t.* trace or confine to one place.

**lo'cate**, *v.t.* establish the place of. —**lo·ca'tion**, *n.*

**lock**, *n.* 1. device for securing doors, etc. 2. canal chamber between levels. 3. firing mechanism. 4. curl of hair. —*v.t.* 5. fasten with a lock. 6. shut in or out. —*v.i.* 7. be jammed. —**lock'smith'**, *n.*

**lock'er**, *n.* compartment that can be locked.

**lock'et**, *n.* round case worn as a pendant to a necklace.

**lo''co·mo'tion**, *n.* movement from place to place.

**lo''co·mo'tive**, *n.* 1. railroad traction engine. —*adj.* 2. pertaining to locomotion.

**lo'cust**, *n.* 1. crop-eating insect. 2. flowering tree.

**lodge**, *n.* 1. forest house. 2. fraternity chapter. —*v.t.* 3. house. 4. push into a fixed position. —*v.i.* 5. become fixed. 6. dwell.

**loft**, *n.* open upper floor.

**loft'y**, *adj.*, **-ier, -iest.** very high.

**log**, *n.* 1. cut tree trunk or limb. 2. record of events. —*v.t.* 3. take logs from. 4. record in a log.

**log'a·rithm**, *n.* *Math.* power of one number if multiplied to equal another. —**log''a·rith'mic**, *adj.*

**log'ic**, *n.* 1. correct reasoning. 2. predictable sequence.

**lo·gis'tics**, *n.* science of military housing, supply, etc.

**lo'go**, *n.* symbol or trademark of an enterprise.

**loin**, *n.* 1. Also, **loins**, lower human back. 2. front hindquarter as a cut of meat.

**loi'ter**, *v.i.* linger in one place.

**loll**, *v.i.* remain idle.

**lol'li·pop'**, *n.* candy on a stick for sucking.

L
M

**lone,** *adj.* single; solitary.

**lone'ly,** *adj.,* **-lier, -liest. 1.** sad because alone. **2.** isolated. Also, **lone'some.**

**long,** *adj., adv.,* **longer, longest,** *v.i.* *adj.* **1.** of great distance between ends. **2.** in length. **3.** occupying much time. —*adv.* **4.** for a long time. **5.** from start to finish. **6.** at a long time. **7.** wish passionately. —**long'ing,** *n., adj.*

**lon·gev'i·ty,** *n.* long life.

**lon'gi·tude,** *n.* east-west measurement.

**lon'gi·tu·di·nal,** *adj.* pertaining to length or longitude.

**long'shore''man,** *n.* loader and unloader of ships.

**look,** *v.i.* **1.** direct one's gaze. **2.** search. **3.** appear to be. —*v.t.* **4.** stare at. —*n.* **5.** act or instance of looking. **6.** appearance.

**loom,** *n.* **1.** weaving frame. —*v.i.* **2.** appear indistinctly as huge.

**loon'y,** *adj.,* **-ier, -iest.** *Informal.* crazy.

**loop,** *n.* **1.** closed curve of rope, etc. —*v.t.* **2.** make into a loop. —*v.i.* **3.** form a loop.

**loose,** *adj.,* **looser, loosest,** *adj.* **1.** not tight. **2.** not confined. **3.** not strict or precise. **4.** immoral. —*v.t.* **5.** make loose.

**loot,** *n.* things stolen.

**lop,** *v.t.* chop.

**lop'sid''ed,** *adj.* out of balance.

**lo·qua'cious,** *adj.* talkative.

**lord,** *n.* **1.** landed noble. **2.** the Lord, **a.** god. **b.** Christ.

**lore,** *n.* traditional learning.

**lose,** *v.t.* **1.** fail to keep. **2.** misplace. **3.** fail to win. —*v.i.* **4.** have a loss.

**loss,** *n.* **1.** act or instance of losing. **2.** something lost.

**lot,** *n.* **1.** chance. **2.** personal fate. **3.** area of ground.

**lo'tion,** *n.* skin preparation.

**lot'ter·y,** *n., pl.* **-ies.** choice by chance, esp. of a winner.

**loud,** *adj.* with much noise.

**lounge,** *v.i.* **1.** be idle or relaxed. —*n.* **2.** couch. **3.** place for lounging.

**louse,** *n., pl.* **lice.** parasitic insect.

**lous'y,** *adj.,* **-ier, -iest.** *Informal.* bad.

**lout,** *n.* stupid, offensive person.

**love,** *n.* **1.** powerful attraction to another. **2.** warm concern. **3.** loved person. —*v.t.* **4.** feel love for.

**low,** *adj.* **1.** of less than average height. **2.** of less than average quantity, etc. **3.** depressed. **4.** vulgar. **5.** meanly wicked. —*adv.* **6.** in a low way. —*n.* **7.** something low. —*v.i.* **8.** moo.

**low'brow'',** *adj.* non-intellectual.

**low·er,** *adj.* (lō'ər) **1.** more low. —*v.t.* **2.** cause to be low or lower. —*v.i.* **3.** become low or lower. **4.** (lou'ər) frown.

**low'ly,** *adj.,* **-lier, -liest.** humble.

**loy'al,** *adj.* faithful.

**loz'enge,** *n.* cough drop, etc.

**lu'bri·cate'',** *v.t.* **1.** make slippery. **2.** cause the wearing parts of to slide easily. —**lu'bri·cant,** *n.*

**lu'cid,** *adj.* clear, as to understand.

**luck,** *n.* chance.

**luck'y,** *adj.,* **-ier, -iest.** having or marked by good luck. —**luck'i·ly,** *adv.*

**luc'ra·tive,** *adj.* profitable.

**lu'di·crous,** *adj.* laughable.

**lug,** *v.t.* **1.** haul with effort. —*n.* **2.** projection for lifting, etc.

**lug'gage,** *n.* baggage.

**luke'warm'',** *adj.* **1.** slightly warm. **2.** unenthusiastic.

**lull,** *v.t., v.i., n.* calm.

**lull'a·by'',** *n., pl.* **-bies.** soothing song for children.

**lum'ber,** *n.* **1.** building wood. —*v.i.* **2.** move ponderously.

**lu'mi·nar''y,** *n., pl.* **-ies. 1.** light source. **2.** brilliant person.

**lu''mi·nes'cence,** *n.* light without heat.

**lu'mi·nous,** *adj.* light-giving.

**lump,** *n.* **1.** shapeless mass. **2.** swelling. —*adj.* **3.** collective. —*v.t.* **4.** assemble or treat in a lump. **5.** tolerate despite oneself. —*v.i.* **6.** form in lumps. —**lump'y,** *adj.*

**lu'nar,** *adj.* pertaining to the moon.

**lu'na·tic,** *n.* **1.** insane person. —*adj.* **2.** insane. —**lu'na·cy,** *n.*

**lunch,** *n.* midday meal.

**lunch'eon,** *n.* formal lunch.

**lung,** *n.* breathing organ.

**lunge,** *n.* **1.** sudden move forward. —*v.t., v.i.* **2.** move with a lunge.

**lurch,** *n.* sudden sideways movement.

**lure,** *v.t.* **1.** entice. —*n.* **2.** enticement; bait.

**lu'rid,** *adj.* **1.** glowing through haze. **2.** violently sensational.

**lurk,** *v.i.* be in hiding.

**lus'cious**, *adj.* appealing to the senses.

**lush**, *adj.* rich; abundant.

**lust**, *n.* 1. strong appetite. 2. strong sexual appetite. —*v.i.* 3. feel lust.

**lus'ter**, *n.* 1. sheen. 2. brightness. —**lus'trous**, *adj.*

**lust'y**, *adj.*, **-ier, -iest.** vigorous.

**lux·u'ri·ant**, *adj.* lavishly growing. —**lux·u'ri·ance**, *n.*

**lux'u·ry**, *n.*, *pl.* **-ries.** 1. great comfort or pleasure. 2. something superfluous. —**lux·u'ri·ous**, *adj.*

**lye**, *n.* strong alkaline substance.

**lymph**, *n.* clear, watery body liquid. —**lym·phat'ic**, *adj.*

**lynch**, *v.t.* kill as a mob.

**lyr'ic**, *adj.* 1. pertaining to emotion expressed in poetry. —*n.* 2. lyric poem. 3. Usually, **lyrics**, words to music. —**lyr'i·cal**, *adj.* —**lyr'i·cist**, *n.*

# M

**M, m**, *n.* thirteenth letter of the English alphabet.

**mace**, *n.* 1. war club. 2. symbolic rod of office. 3. spice from nutmeg husks.

**ma·chine'**, *n.* 1. device for doing work. 2. political organization. —*v.t.* 3. shape by machine. —**ma·chin'er·y**, *n.*

**ma·chin'ist**, *n.* worker with machine-operated tools.

**mack'er·el**, *n.*, *pl.* **-el, -els.** North Atlantic fish.

**mac'ra·mé''**, *n.* lace or string tied in patterns.

**mad**, *adj.*, **madder, maddest.** 1. insane. 2. infatuated. 3. angry. —**mad'den**, *v.t.* —**mad'house''**, *n.* —**mad'man''**, **mad'wom''an**, *n.*

**mad'am**, *n.* 1. polite form of address to a woman. 2. woman running a brothel.

**mag'a·zine**, *n.* 1. periodical with covers. 2. storage chamber.

**mag'got**, *n.* wormlike larva. —**mag'got·y**, *adj.*

**mag'ic**, *n.* 1. use of supernatural methods. 2. illusions using sleight of hand. —**mag'i·cal**, *adj.* —**ma·gi'cian**, *n.*

**mag'is·trate**, *n.* minor judge.

**mag·nan'i·mous**, *adj.* above pettiness.

**mag'nate**, *n.* man of wealth or power.

**mag·ne'sium**, *n.* light metallic element.

**mag'net**, *n.* object attracting ferrous metal. —**mag·net'ic**, *adj.*

**mag·nif'i·cent**, *adj.* splendid in form, accomplishments, etc.

**mag'ni·fy''**, *v.t.* increase the apparent or real size of.

**mag'ni·tude''**, *n.* size.

**ma·hog'a·ny**, *n.* reddish-brown tropical wood.

**maid**, *n.* 1. woman servant. 2. young woman.

**maid'en**, *n.* 1. young woman. —*adj.* 2. very first.

**mail**, *n.* 1. material shipped by post offices. 2. flexible armor. —*v.t.* 3. give to a post office for shipping.

**ma'il·gram**, *n.* message teletyped between post offices and finally delivered by mail.

**maim**, *v.t.* mutilate.

**main**, *adj.* 1. principal. —*n.* 2. major utility line. 3. *Archaic.* sea.

**main'frame**, *n.*, *adj.* (computers) large-scale, high-speed computing system.

**main'land''**, *n.* continental land.

**main·tain'**, *v.t.* 1. keep in good order. 2. house, feed, etc. 3. assert persistently. —**main'ten·ance**, *n.*

**maj'es·ty**, *n.* 1. **Majesty**, title of respect for a sovereign. 2. grandeur.

**ma'jor**, *adj.* 1. greater. 2. *Music.* in a scale a half tone above the minor. —*v.i.* 3. *Education.* specialize. —*n.* 4. army officer. 5. specialty in school.

**ma·jor'i·ty**, *n.* greater number.

**make**, *v.t.*, **made, making.** 1. cause to be or occur. 2. force. 3. constitute. 4. earn. 5. interpret.

**make'-be·lieve''**, *n.* imaginary.

**make'shift''**, *adj.* improvised; temporary.

**make'up''**, *n.* 1. constitution; contents. 2. cosmetics, etc.

**mal''a·droit'**, *adj.* clumsy.

**mal'a·dy**, *n.*, *pl.* **-dies.**

**mal'a·prop·ism''**, *n.* ludicrous misuse of a word.

**ma·lar'i·a**, *n.* mosquito-transmitted disease.

**L**
**M**

**male**, *adj.* 1. of the sex that inseminates. —*n.* 2. male being.

**ma·lev'o·lent**, *adj.* wishing harm.

**mal'ice**, *n.* ill will.

**ma·lign'**, *adj.* 1. intending or doing harm. —*v.t.* 2. slander.

**ma·lig'nant**, *adj.* harmful or dangerous.

**mall**, *n.* 1. tree-lined walk or lawn. 2. shopping area.

**mal'let**, *n.* short, heavy hammer.

**mal'nu·tri'tion**, *n.* inadequate nutrition.

**mal·prac'tice**, *n.* improper professional practice.

**malt**, *n.* soaked and dried grain.

**mal'treat'**, *v.t.* treat badly.

**mam'bo**, *n.* dance of Latin American origin.

**mam'mal**, *n.* animal giving milk.

**mam'ma·ry**, *adj.* pertaining to breasts.

**man**, *n.*, *pl.* **men**. 1. human being. 2. adult male human. 3. humanity.

**man'age**, *v.t.* 1. supervise. 2. control. —*v.i.* 4. contrive to succeed. —**man'age·a·ble**, *adj.*

**man'date**, *n.* command.

**man'da·to'ry**, *adj.* required.

**man'di·ble**, *n.* lower jaw bone.

**mane**, *n.* long hair on an animal's neck.

**ma·neu'ver**, *n.* 1. military exercise. 2. controlled movement. —*v.t.*, *v.i.* 3. move under control.

**man'ga·nese'**, *n.* grayish chemical element.

**man'ger**, *n.* feeding trough.

**man'gle**, *v.t.* crush out of shape.

**man'hole'**, *n.* small access hole.

**man'hood'**, *n.* 1. virility. 2. majority.

**ma·ni'a**, *n.* 1. violent insanity. 2. excitement.

**ma·ni'ac'**, *n.* violently insane person.

**man'ic**, *adj.* displaying unstable, frenzied behavior.

**man'i·cure**, *n.* care of the hands.

**man'i·fest'**, *v.t.* 1. make apparent. —*adj.* 2. obvious. —*n.* 3. list of cargo or passengers.

**man'i·fes'to**, *n.*, *pl.* **-toes**. public declaration.

**man'i·fold'**, *adj.* in many forms.

**man·il'la**, *n.* a strong, light brown paper.

**ma·nip'u·late'**, *v.t.* handle cunningly. —**ma·nip'u·la'tor**, *n.*

**man'kind'**, *n.* humankind.

**man'ly**, *adj.*, **-lier**, **-liest**. virile; brave.

**man'ner**, *n.* 1. way of doing. 2. sort. 3. **manners**, personal conduct.

**man'ner·ism**, *n.* personal peculiarity.

**man'nish**, *adj.* man-like.

**man'-of-war'**, *n.* warship.

**man'pow'er**, *n.* available labor force.

**man'sion**, *n.* impressive house.

**man'slaugh'ter**, *n.* unintentional homicide.

**man'tel**, *n.* fireplace surround.

**man'tle**, *n.*, *v.t.* cloak.

**man·u'al**, *adj.* 1. pertaining to or operated by hands. —*n.* 2. handbook. —**man·u'al·ly**, *adv.*

**man''u·fac'ture**, *v.t.* 1. make industrially. —*n.* 2. act or instance of manufacturing. —**man''u·fac'tur·er**, *n.*

**ma·nure'**, *n.* animal feces.

**man'u·script**, *n.* 1. unprinted writing. —*adj.* 2. written or typed.

**man'y**, *adj.*, **more**, **most**. in a large number.

**map**, *n.* 1. measured representation of an area of land, etc. —*v.t.* 2. measure for a map. 3. plan.

**ma'ple**, *n.* broad-leafed deciduous tree.

**mar**, *v.t.* make imperfect.

**ma·raud'er**, *n.* raider and plunderer.

**mar'ble**, *n.* hard, fine-grained limestone.

**march**, *v.i.* 1. walk with measured steps to a cadence. —*v.t.* 2. cause to march. —*n.* 3. marching walk or journey. 4. piece of music accompanying such a walk.

**mare**, *n.* female horse.

**mar'ga·rine**, *n.* butter-like vegetable oil compound.

**mar'gin**, *n.* border or border area.

**ma'ri·jua'na**, *n.* dried hemp leaves and blossoms, sometimes smoked. Also, **ma''ri·hua'na**.

**ma·rine'**, *adj.* 1. pertaining to the sea. —*n.* 2. soldier performing sea duty.

**mar'i·ner**, *n.* sailor.

**mar'i·tal**, *adj.* pertaining to marriage.

**mar'i·time'**, *adj.* pertaining to shipping.

**mark**, *n.* 1. something visible on a surface. 2. target. —*v.t.* 3. make a mark on. 4. indicate. 5. note. 6. review and grade.

**mar'ket**, *n.* 1. place for selling. —*v.t.* 2. offer for sale. —*v.i.* 3. shop.

**mar'ma·lade''**, *n.* fruit preserve.

**ma·roon'**, *v.t.* 1. abandon on a deserted island. —*n.* 2. dark brownish red.

**mar·quee'**, *n.* open projecting shelter.

**mar'row**, *n.* inner bone tissue.

**mar'ry**, *v.t.* 1. take as spouse. 2. unite as spouses. —*v.i.* 3. be married. —**mar'riage**, *n.*

**marsh**, *n.* swamp.

**mar'shal**, *n.* 1. sheriff-like U.S. officer. —*v.t.* 2. put in order. 3. guide; escort.

**mar·su'pi·al**, *n.* animal carrying its young in a pouch.

**mart**, *n.* salesplace.

**mar'tial**, *adj.* pertaining to war or the military.

**mar''ti·net'**, *n.* rigid disciplinarian.

**mar'tyr**, *n.* 1. person who dies or suffers for beliefs. —*v.t.* 2. kill as a martyr.

**mar'vel**, *n., v.i.* wonder. —**mar'vel·ous**, *adj.*

**mas'cot**, *n.* thing kept for luck.

**mas'cu·line**, *adv.* pertaining to or characteristic of males.

**mash**, *v.t.* 1. crush to pulp. —*n.* 2. pulped and watered grain.

**mask**, *n.* 1. face covering. 2. concealment. —*v.t.* 3. cover with a mask.

**mas'och·ism**, *n.* abnormal pleasure obtained from suffering pain.

**ma'son**, *n.* builder with stones, bricks, etc. —**ma'son·ry**, *n.*

**mas'quer·ade''**, *n.* 1. ball of masked and costumed persons. 2. something falsified. —*v.i.* 3. appear falsely.

**mass**, *n.* 1. large, shapeless quantity. 2. *Physics.* matter as related to inertia. 3. Often **Mass**, Eucharistic service. —*v.t., v.i.* 4. gather in a mass.

**mas'sa·cre**, *n.* 1. killing of many. —*v.t.* 2. kill in a massacre.

**mas·sage** (mə sahzh′), *n.* 1. manipulation of muscles, as to stimulate circulation. —*v.t.* 2. give a massage to. —**mas·seur'**, *fem.*, **mas·seuse'**, *n.*

**mas'sive**, *adj.* in a large mass.

**mast**, *n.* tall spar used as a support.

**mas'ter**, *n.* 1. person in control. 2.

accomplished craftsman. —*adj.* 3. principal; controlling. —*v.t.* 4. make submissive. 5. become expert in. —**mas'ter·y**, *n.*

**mas'ter·piece''**, *n.* greatest accomplishment.

**mat**, *n.* 1. thick, flat, flexible object. 2. tangled mass. —*v.t.* 3. cover with mats.

**match**, *n.* 1. fire-making friction device. 2. equal or counterpart. 3. marriage. 4. game. —*v.t.* 5. compare. 6. equal.

**mate**, *n.* 1. spouse. 2. companion. 3. co-worker. 4. one of a pair. 5. ship's officer. —*v.t., v.i.* 6. join as mates.

**ma·te'ri·al**, *n.* 1. that which an object is made of. —*adj.* 2. composed of material. 3. non-spiritual. 4. relevant.

**ma·ter'nal**, *adj.* mother-like. —**ma·ter'ni·ty**, *n.*

**math''e·mat'ics**, *n.* study of the relations of quantities or forms. Also, *Informal,* **math**.

**mat''i·nee'**, *n.* afternoon performance.

**ma'tri·arch''**, *n.* woman acting as master or ruler.

**ma·tric'u·late''**, *v.i., v.t.* enroll as a student.

**mat''ri·mo'ny**, *n., pl.* **-nies**. marriage.

**ma'tron**, *n.* mature woman.

**mat'ter**, *n.* 1. solid, liquid, or gas. 2. affair. 3. importance. —*v.i.* 4. be important.

**mat'tress**, *n.* pad for a bed.

**ma·ture'**, *adj.* 1. fully ripe or grown. 2. due for payment. —*v.t.* 3. make mature. —*v.i.* 4. become mature.

**maud'lin**, *adj.* foolishly sentimental.

**maul**, *v.t.* handle or beat severely.

**mau''so·le'um**, *n., pl.* **-leums, -lea**. large and magnificent tomb.

**max'im**, *n.* rule of conduct.

**max'i·mum**, *n., pl.* **-mums, -ma**, *adj. n.* 1. greatest amount. —*adj.* 2. Also, **max'i·mal**, greatest.

**may**, *v.t.* 1. am, are, or is permitted to. 2. will possibly. 3. can.

**may'be**, *adv.* possibly.

**may'day**, *n.* distress call used by aircraft and ships.

**may'hem''**, *n.* criminal maiming.

**may''on·naise''**, *n.* salad dressing made with egg yolks.

**may'or**, *n.* chief city official.

**L**
**M**

**maze,** *n.* intricate system of corridors, lines, etc.

**mead′ow,** *n.* area of grassy land.

**mea′ger,** *adj.* scanty; inadequate.

**meal,** *n.* **1.** food at one sitting. **2.** coarsely ground grain.

**mean,** *v.t.* **1.** intend. **2.** wish to say. **3.** signify. —*adj.* **4.** ill-tempered. **5.** shabby. **6.** average. —*n.* **7.** part between extremes. **8.** means, a. something serving a purpose. b. personal personal resources. —**mean′ly,** *adv.* —**mean′ness,** *n.*

**mean′ing,** *n.* intended message.

**mean′time′′,** *n.* **1.** time in between. —*adv.* **2.** during the meantime. **3.** at the same time. Also, **mean′while′′.**

**mea′sles,** *n.* virus disease producing a rash.

**meas′ure,** *v.t.* **1.** find the size or amount of. —*v.i.* **2.** amount to. —*n.* **3.** measurement. **4.** means of measuring. **5.** course of action.

**meat,** *n.* **1.** animal flesh. **2.** edible part of a nut. **3.** essential part.

**me·chan′ic,** *n.* **1.** worker with machinery. **2. mechanics,** study of the action of forces.

**me·chan′i·cal,** *adj.* **1.** working by machinery. **2.** unthinkingly automatic.

**mech′a·nism,** *n.* piece of machinery.

**mech′a·nize′′,** *v.t.* equip with machinery.

**med′al,** *n.* metal disk indicating distinction, religious affiliation, etc.

**med′dle,** *v.i.* interfere mischievously.

**me′di·an,** *n.* **1.** *Math.* central in a series of numbers. **2.** *Math.* pertaining to a median. **3.** middle.

**me′di·ate′′,** *v.t.* resolve as an intermediary.

**med′i·cal,** *adj.* pertaining to medicine.

**med′i·cate′′,** *v.t.* treat with medicine. —**med′i·ca′tion,** *n.*

**med′i·cine,** *n.* **1.** science of healing. **2.** healing substance.

**me″di·e′val,** *adj.* pertaining to the Middle Ages.

**me″di·o′cre,** *adj.* of indifferent value.

**med′i·tate′′,** *v.i.* think deeply.

**me′di·um,** *n.,* *pl.* **-ums,** **-a,** *adj.* *n.* **1.** something in the middle. **2.** means. **3.** *pl.* **-media,** means of communication. **4.** *pl.* **mediums,**

communicator with the dead. —*adj.* **5.** intermediate.

**meek,** *adj.* mild; submissive.

**meet,** *v.t.* **1.** come into contact with. **2.** be introduced to. —*v.i.* **3.** be mutually met. —*n.* **4.** sports meeting.

**meg′a·hertz′′,** *n.,* *pl.* **-hertz.** one million hertz.

**meg″a·lo·ma′ni·a,** *n.* delusions of grandeur.

**mel′an·chol′′y,** *n.* **1.** sadness. —*adj.* **2.** sad.

**mel′low,** *adj.* **1.** rich-flavored. **2.** gentle. —*v.t.* **3.** make mellow. —*v.i.* **4.** become mellow.

**mel′o·dra′′ma,** *n.* drama of suspense and emotion.

**mel′o·dy,** *n.,* *pl.* **-dies.** tune.

**mel′on,** *n.* large, juicy fruit.

**melt,** *v.,* **melted, melted** or **molten, melting.** *v.t.,* *v.i.* liquefy by applying heat.

**mem′ber,** *n.* **1.** person in an organization. **2.** component part.

**mem′brane,** *n.* thin organic tissue.

**me·men′to,** *n.,* *pl.* **-tos,** **-toes.** souvenir.

**mem′oirs,** *n.,* *pl.* written personal recollections.

**mem′o·ra·ble,** *adj.* compelling remembrance.

**mem″o·ran′dum,** *n.,* *pl.* **-dums, -da.** note of something to be remembered.

**me·mo′ri·al,** *adj.* **1.** in remembrance. —*n.* **2.** something made or done in remembrance.

**mem′o·rize′′,** *v.t.* act so as to remember.

**mem″o·ry,** *n.,* *pl.* **-ries. 1.** ability to recall past experience. **2.** something remembered. **3.** thing of the past. **4.** (computers) electronic data storage through circuitry or a recording medium.

**men′ace,** *n.* **1.** visible threat. —*v.t.* **2.** threaten.

**me·nag′er·ie,** *n.* collection of captive wild animals.

**mend,** *v.t.* **1.** repair. —*v.i.* **2.** improve in condition. —*n.* **3.** mended place.

**men·da′cious,** *adj.* lying.

**me′ni·al,** *adj.* **1.** servile. —*n.* **2.** menial person.

**men′o·pause′′,** *n.* permanent end of menstruation.

**men′stru·ate′′,** *v.i.* experience menses.

**men′tal,** *adj.* pertaining to the mind.

**migraine**

**men·tal'i·ty**, *n., pl.* **-ties.** mental power.

**men'tion**, *n.* 1. brief allusion. —*v.t.* 2. make a mention of.

**men'tor**, *n.* teacher or advisor.

**men'u**, *n.* list of dishes offered.

**mer'can·tile**, *adj.* pertaining to trade.

**mer'ce·nar'y**, *adj., n., pl.* ies. *adj.* 1. devoted to money-making. 2. done for pay. —*n.* 3. hired soldier.

**mer·chan·dise**, *n.* (mər'chən dīs'') 1. goods for sale. —*v.t.* (mər'chən dīz'') 2. Also, **mer'-chan·dize'**, promote the sale of.

**mer'chant**, *n.* seller of goods.

**mer·cu'ri·al**, *adj.* quick to change.

**mer'cu·ry**, *n.* heavy metallic chemical element.

**mer'cy**, *n., pl.* cies. 1. kindness toward the helpless. 2. lucky thing.

**mere**, *adj.* no more than.

**merge**, *v.t., v.i.* combine.

**merg'er**, *n.* unification of business organizations.

**me·ringue'**, *n.* stiff-beaten egg white.

**mer'it**, *n.* 1. worth. 2. merits, aspects right or wrong. —*v.t.* 3. deserve.

**mer'maid''**, *n.* legendary sea creature, half-woman, half-fish.

**mer'ry**, *adj.,* rier, riest. cheerful.

**mer'ry-go-round''**, *n.* rotating structure giving a pleasure ride.

**mesh**, *n.* 1. open space in a net. 2. net-like material. 3. engagement of gears. —*v.t., v.i.* 4. entangle. —*v.i.* 5. become engaged.

**mess**, *n.* 1. disorder or disorderly scene. 2. difficult situation. 3. military meal. —*v.t.* 4. make untidy. 5. do badly. —*v.i.* 6. eat mess.

**mes'sage**, *n.* 1. communication. 2. idea, etc. to communicate.

**mes'sen·ger**, *n.* carrier of messages.

**me·tab'o·lism**, *n.* breakdown of an organism's nourishment into protoplasm, energy, and waste.

**met'al**, *n.* iron, gold, brass, etc. —**me·tal'lic**, *adj.*

**met''a·mor'pho·sis**, *n.* transformation.

**met'a·phor'**, *n.* use of an analogous idea.

**met''a·phys'ics**, *n.* study of the nature of reality.

**me''te·or·ol'o·gy**, *n.* study of climate and weather.

**me'ter**, *n.* 1. unit of 100 centimeters or 39.37 inches. 2. rhythmic pattern. 3. measuring device for fluids, etc. —*v.t.* 4. measure with a meter.

**meth'od**, *n.* process or system of doing.

**me·thod'i·cal**, *adj.* orderly; deliberate.

**me·tic'u·lous**, *adj.* attentive to details.

**met'ric**, *adj.* 1. pertaining to the metric system. 2. metrical.

**met'ri·cal**, *adj.* 1. pertaining to poetic meter. 2. pertaining to measurement.

**metric system**, decimal system of measurement based on the meter, gram, and liter.

**me·trop'o·lis**, *n.* principal or major city.

**mez'za·nine''**, *n.* balcony-like floor.

**mi'crobe**, *n.* microorganism, esp. harmful.

**mi'cro·chip**, *n.* small wafer of silicon, etc., containing electronic circuits.

**mic''ro·com·pu'ter**, *n.* a complete computing system of compact size, sometimes portable.

**mi'cro·cosm**, *n.* little world.

**mi'cro·film''**, *n.* film with images at greatly reduced size.

**mi''cro·or'gan·ism**, *n.* organism visible only through a microscope.

**mi'cro·phone''**, *n.* instrument transforming sound into electrical impulses.

**mi'cro·scope''**, *n.* instrument for very high magnification.

**mic''ro·wave''**, *n.* electromagnetic radiation of extremely high frequency.

**mid'day''**, *n.* noon.

**mid'dle**, *n.* 1. place with ends equally far away. —*adj.* 2. intermediate.

**mid'dle-aged'**, *adj.* neither young nor old.

**mid'night''**, *n.* twelve o'clock at night.

**midst**, *n.* middle part.

**mid'wife''**, *n.* deliverer of babies. —**mid'wife''ry,** *n.*

**mien**, *n.* manner; bearing.

**might**, *n.* 1. strength. —*v.* 2. (past tense of *may*) 3. will possibly.

**mi'graine**, *n.* intense headache.

L
M

**mi'grate**, v.i. move in a group. —**mi'grant**, adj.

**mild**, adj. not severe or harsh.

**mil'dew''**, n. fungus of damp cloth, etc.

**mile**, n. unit equal to 5,280 feet on land, 6,076 feet on water.

**mile'age**, n. 1. rate per mile. 2. number of miles per unit.

**mil'i·tant**, adj. 1. fighting for a cause. —n. 2. militant person.

**mil'i·tar''y**, adj. 1. pertaining to armed forces. —n. 2. the military, armed forces.

**mi·li'tia**, n. emergency citizen army.

**milk**, n. 1. white fluid secreted by female mammals for nourishing their young. —v.t. 2. get milk from.

**mill**, n. 1. place for processing or manufacturing; factory. 2. tenth of a cent. —v.t. 3. process in a mill. —v.i. 4. move about confusedly. —**mill'er**, n.

**mil'li·gram''**, n. thousandth of a gram.

**mil'li·me''ter**, n. thousandth of a meter.

**mil'lion**, n. a thousand thousand. —**mil'lionth**, adj.

**mil'lion·aire'**, n. owner of at least a million dollars.

**mim'ic**, n., v.t., -icked, -icking. n. 1. person who imitates mannerisms of others. —v.t. 2. imitate as a mimic. —**mim'ic·ry**, n.

**mince**, v.t. 1. chop finely. 2. mitigate the meaning of. —v.i. 3. be affectedly dainty.

**mind**, n. 1. that which thinks. 2. personality. 3. sanity. —v.t. 4. heed. 5. be troubled or annoyed by.

**mine**, pron. 1. my own. —n. 2. excavation for coal or minerals. 3. buried or floated bomb. —v.t. 4. dig from a mine. 5. put mines in. —v.i. 6. work a mine.

**min'er·al**, n. 1. something neither vegetable nor animal. 2. inorganic earth material.

**min'gle**, v.t., v.i. mix together.

**min'i·a·ture''**, n. 1. small copy. 2. small painting. —adj. 3. smaller than standard.

**mi''ni·com·pu'ter**, n. a computing system that is larger than a microcomputer but smaller than a mainframe computer.

**min'i·mize''**, v.t. 1. reduce to a minimum. 2. treat as of minimum importance.

**min'i·mum**, n., pl. -mums, -ma, adj. n. 1. least amount. —adj. 2. Also, **min'i·mal**, least.

**min·is'ter**, n. 1. clergyman. 2. diplomat. 3. cabinet member. —v.i. 4. give help.

**min'is·try**, n., pl. -tries. 1. profession of a minister. 2. government department. 3. act of ministering.

**mi'nor**, adj. 1. lesser in size or importance. 2. —n. person not of age.

**mi·nor'i·ty**, n., pl. -ties. 1. lesser part. 2. social group too small to have control. 3. state of being a minor.

**min'strel**, n. 1. medieval strolling singer. 2. blackface singer.

**mint**, n. 1. place for coining money. 2. plant with aromatic leaves. —adj. 3. absolutely fresh. —v.t. 4. coin.

**min·u·end''**, n. Math. number subtracted from.

**mi'nus**, prep. 1. from which is subtracted. 2. without.

**min·ute**, n. (min'at) 1. one sixtieth of an hour. 2. one sixtieth of a degree of arc. 3. minutes, record of a meeting. —adj. (mi nyoot') 4. tiny. 5. precise.

**mir'a·cle**, n. supernatural event.

**mi·rage'**, n. optical illusion caused by the atmosphere.

**mire**, n. 1. sticky mud. —v.t. 2. stick fast, as with mud.

**mir'ror**, n. 1. reflecting object. —v.t. 2. reflect.

**mirth**, n. gaiety.

**mis''ap·pro'pri·ate''**, v.t. take and use wrongly.

**mis·car'ry**, v.i. 1. give birth to a fetus that cannot live. 2. go wrong. —**mis·car'riage**, n.

**mis''cel·la'ne·ous**, adj. various. —**mis·cel·la·ny**, n.

**mis'chief**, n. 1. damage. 2. malice. 3. gentle malice. —**mis'chie·vous**, adj.

**mis''de·mea'nor**, n. offence less serious than a felony.

**mi'ser**, n. morbid saver of money. —**mi'ser·ly**, adj.

**mis'er·a·ble**, adj. 1. very unhappy. 2. causing misery. 3. contemptibly meager or poor.

**mis'er·y**, n., pl. -ies. suffering.

**mis'fit'**, n. person unhappy in society.

**mis·for'tune**, *n.* 1. bad luck. 2. piece of bad luck.

**mis·giv'ing**, *n.* apprehension; doubt.

**mis'hap'**, *n.* unfortunate incident.

**mis·lay'**, *v.t.* put somewhere later forgotten.

**mis·lead'**, *v.t.* 1. advise or urge wrongly. 2. deceive.

**mis·no'mer**, *n.* wrong name.

**mis·place'**, *v.t.* 1. mislay. 2. put in a wrong place.

**miss**, *v.t., v.i., n., pl.* **misses**. *v.t.* 1. fail to hit, seize, meet, etc. 2. be lonely without. —*n.* 3. act or instance of missing. 4. **Miss**, title for an unmarried woman.

**mis'sile**, *n.* something thrown or shot to hit a target.

**mis'sion**, *n.* 1. commanded or requested journey. 2. group of missionaries. 3. group sent to a place. 4. duty or purpose.

**mis'sion·ar'y**, *n., pl.* **-ies.** person sent to make religious conversions.

**mist**, *n.* 1. thin fog. —*v.t.* 2. fog. —*v.i.* 3. become misty.

**mis·take'**, *n.* 1. wrong act or opinion. —*v.t.* 2. understand wrongly. —**mis·tak'a·ble,** *adj.*

**mis'tress**, *n.* 1. female master. 2. unmarried female sexual partner.

**mis·trust'**, *v.t.* 1. have no trust in. —*n.* 2. lack of trust.

**mis·use'**, *v.t.* (mis yōoz') 1. use wrongly. 2. mistreat. —*n.* (mis yōos') 3. wrong use or treatment.

**mit'i·gate'**, *v.t., v.i.* lessen in severity.

**mit'ten**, *n.* glove with only the thumb separate.

**mix**, *v.t.* 1. assemble and make uniform. 2. have together. —*v.i.* 3. be on social terms. —*n.* 4. mixture. —**mix'ture,** *n.*

**mix'up'**, *n.* confusion.

**moan**, *n.* 1. low, sad sound. —*v.i.* 2. make such a sound.

**moat**, *n.* defensive, water-filled ditch.

**mob**, *n.* 1. disorderly or hostile crowd. —*v.t.* 2. attack in a mob.

**mo'bile**, *adj.* movable.

**mo'bi·lize'**, *v.t., v.i.* make ready for war.

**moc'ca·sin**, *n.* soft heelless slipper.

**mock**, *v.t.* 1. ridicule. 2. imitate; mimic. —*adj.* 3. imitation.

**mode**, *n.* 1. manner of doing. 2. fashion. —**mod'ish,** *adj.*

**mod'el**, *n.* 1. small-scale three-dimensional copy. 2. something to imitate. 3. poser for pictures. —*adj.* 4. exemplary. —*v.t.* 5. copy in three dimensions. 6. mold as in making a model. 7. make as a copy.

**mo''dem**, *n.* (computers) device for linking computers via telephone lines.

**mod·er·ate**, *adj.* (mod'ər ət) 1. avoiding extremes. —*n.* 2. moderate person. —*v.t.* (mod'ər āt') 3. make moderate. 4. preside over. —*v.i.* 5. become moderate.

**mod'ern**, *adj.* 1. pertaining to the present. 2. reflecting advance taste, thought, technology, etc.

**mod'est**, *adj.* 1. disliking praise, publicity, etc. 2. avoiding self-exposure. 3. not outstanding.

**mod'i·fy'**, *v.t., v.i.* 1. alter in nature. —*v.t.* 2. limit slightly.

**moist**, *adj.* slightly wet. —**moist'en,** *v.t., v.i.* —**mois'ture,** *n.*

**mo'lar**, *n.* grinding tooth.

**mo·las'ses**, *n.* syrup from sugar refining.

**mold**, *n.* 1. device for forming a casting. 2. model. 3. destructive fungus. —*v.t.* 4. model. 5. cast in a mold. —*v.i.* 6. become moldy. —**mold'y,** *adj.*

**mole**, *n.* 1. spot on the skin. 2. burrowing animal. 3. breakwater.

**mol'e·cule'**, *n.* smallest characteristic particle of an element or compound. —**mo·lec'u·lar,** *adj.*

**mo·lest'**, *v.t.* trouble or interfere with.

**mol'ten**, *adj.* melted.

**mo'ment**, *n.* 1. very brief period. 2. present time. 3. importance.

**mo·men'tous**, *adj.* of great importance.

**mo·men'tum**, *n., pl.* **-tums, -ta.** force of a moving object.

**mon'arch**, *n.* king, queen, etc.

**mon'as·ter'y**, *n., pl.* **-ies.** home of monks or nuns.

**mo·nas'tic**, *adj.* pertaining to monks and nuns.

**mon'ey**, *n., pl.* **-eys, -ies.** paper or metal accepted everywhere in payment of debts. —**mon'eyed,** *adj.* —**mon'e·tar'y,** *adj.*

**mon'i·tor**, *n.* 1. device for checking or supervising. —*v.t.* 2. check or supervise.

**monk**, *n.* member of a religious order.

**mon'key**, *n., pl.* **-keys.** 1. primate

other than a human or lemur. 2. small, long-tailed primate.

**mon·o·cle**, n. corrective lens for one eye.

**mon·o·logue″**, n. uninterrupted speech of one person. Also, **mon′ o·log″**. —**mon′o·log″ist**, n.

**mo·nop′o·ly**, n., pl. **-lies**. exclusive use, control, or possession.

**mon′o·tone″**, n. sound with unvarying pitch.

**mo·not′o·nous**, adj. tediously unvaried.

**mon′ster**, n. 1. frightening legendary creature. 2. grotesque or disgusting person. —**mon′strous**, adj. —**mon·stros′i·ty**, n.

**month**, n. one of the twelve divisions of the year.

**mon′u·ment**, n. something built or put up in remembrance.

**mood**, n. state of mind.

**mood′y**, adj., **-ier**, **-iest**. 1. gloomy. 2. changing mood quickly.

**moon**, n. 1. satellite of the earth. 2. lighted portion of this satellite as seen from the earth. —v.i. 3. be abstracted or sentimental.

**moon′light″ing**, n. holding of a second job.

**moon′struck″**, adj. 1. crazy. 2. dreamy.

**moor**, v.t. tie or anchor.

**moor′ings**, n., pl. 1. tackle for mooring. 2. place to moor.

**moot**, adj. 1. hypothetical. 2. open to question.

**mop**, n. 1. long-handled device for washing or dusting. —v.t. 2. clean with a mop.

**mope**, v.i. brood.

**mor′al**, adj. 1. pertaining to morality. 2. in accord with morality. 3. pertaining to morale. —n. 4. lesson of an experience. ,5. **morals**, moral principles.

**mo·rale′**, n. confidence in oneself, a situation, etc.

**mor′al·ize″**, v.i. discuss morality.

**mor′bid**, adj. 1. pertaining to disease. 2. mentally unhealthy.

**more**, adj. 1. greater in number, amount, etc. 2. additional. —adv. 3. additionally. —n. 4. greater number, amount, etc. 5. something additional.

**more·o′ver**, adv. besides.

**morgue′**, n. place for keeping the unidentified dead.

**morn′ing**, n. early part of the day.

**mo′ron**, n. feeble-minded person.

**mo·rose′**, adj. downhearted or surly.

**mor′phine**, n. analgesic opiate.

**mor′sel**, n. small portion of food.

**mor′tal**, adj. 1. having eventually to die. 2. human. 3. fatal. 4. threatening the soul. —n. 5. human being.

**mor′tar**, n. 1. adhesive for masonry. 2. bowl for grinding. 3. short cannon.

**mort′gage**, n. 1. pledge or property as security for a loan. —v.t. 2. pledge in this way.

**mor·ti′cian**, n. undertaker.

**mor′ti·fy″**, v.t. 1. humiliate. 2. suppress with austerities.

**mor·tu·ar′y**, adj., n., pl. **-ies**. adj. 1. pertaining to death or funerals. —n. 2. place for receiving the dead.

**mo·sa′ic**, n. picture of inlaid pieces.

**mos·qui′to**, n., pl. **-toes**, **-tos**. small blood-sucking insect.

**moss**, n. green, velvety plant.

**most**, adj. 1. greatest in number, amount, etc. 2. in the majority. —adv. 3. to the greatest extent. —n. 4. greatest number, extent, etc.

**most′ly**, adv. in most cases.

**mo·tel′**, n. hotel for motorists.

**moth**, n. nocturnal flying insect.

**moth′er**, n. 1. female parent. —v.t. 2. act as a mother to.

**moth′er-in-law″**, n., pl. **mothers-in-law**. mother of a spouse.

**mo·tif′**, n. basic theme or subject.

**mo′tion**, n. 1. movement. 2. formal proposal.

**motion picture**, series of photographs projected at high speed.

**mo′ti·vate″**, v.t. give desire or incentive.

**mo′tive**, n. 1. desire for action. 2. motif.

**mo′tor**, n. 1. machine providing motive force. —adj. 2. causing motion.

**mo′tor·cade″**, n. procession of automobiles.

**mo′tor·ist**, n. automobile driver.

**mot′to**, n., pl. **-toes**, **-tos**. formal statement of aims or ideals.

**mould**, n., v.t. mold.

**mound**, n., v.t. heap.

**mount**, v.t. 1. climb onto or up. 2. set in place. —v.i. 3. climb. —n. 4. steed. 5. setting or support.

**moun′tain**, n. very high feature of the earth. —**moun′tain·ous**, adj.

**moun''tain·eer'**, *n.* 1. mountain dweller. 2. mountain climber.

**mourn**, *v.t., v.i.* lament. —**mourn'ful**, *adj.* —**mourn'ing**, *n.*

**mouse**, *n., pl.* **mice.** 1. small, timid rodent. 2. (computers) compact device for convenient data manipulation on a monitor.

**mous·tache'**, *n.* mustache.

**mouth**, *n.* 1. orifice used for eating and breathing. 2. opening of a river, etc.

**move**, *v.t.* 1. change the place of. 2. inspire or motivate. 3. propose formally. —*v.i.* 4. change place. 5. change residence or workplace. 6. become in motion. —*n.* 7. act or instance of moving. —**mov'a·ble, move'a·ble**, *adj.*

**move'ment**, *n.* 1. motion. 2. action in a cause.

**mov'ie**, *n.* motion picture.

**mow**, *v.t.*, **mowed, mowed** or **mown, mowing.** 1. cut down, as grass. 2. cut down the plants on.

**Mr.** (mis'tər), title for a man. Also, **Mis'ter.**

**Mrs.** (mis'iz), title for a married woman.

**Ms.** (miz, em'es'), *n.* title for a woman disregarding marital status.

**much**, *adj., adv., n. adj.* 1. in great quantity. —*adv.* 2. to a great extent. 3. about. —*n.* 4. something considerable. 5. a great amount.

**mu'ci·lage,** *n.* liquid glue.

**muck,** *n.* sticky filth.

**mu'cous,** *adj.* 1. having mucus. 2. slimy.

**mu'cus,** *n.* slimy body secretion.

**mud,** *n.* sticky earth. —**mud'dy,** *adj., v.t.*

**mud'dle,** *v.t.* 1. bungle or confuse. —*n.* 2. act or instance of muddling.

**muff,** *n.* 1. cylinder made esp. of fur for keeping the hands warm. —*v.t.* 2. bungle.

**muf'fle,** *v.t.* 1. wrap closely. 2. deaden.

**muf'fler,** *n.* 1. heavy scarf. 2. sound deadener.

**mug,** *n.* 1. cylindrical cup. —*v.t.* 2. attack from behind.

**mu·lat'to,** *n., pl.* **-toes.** person of mixed white and colored blood.

**mule,** *n.* offspring of a donkey and a mare.

**mul''ti·far'i·ous,** *adj.* with many components.

**mul'ti·ple,** *adj.* 1. in a large number. —*n.* 2. number evenly divisible by another.

**mul''ti·pli·cand',** *n. Math.* number to be multiplied.

**mul''ti·plic'i·ty,** *n.* large number or variety.

**mul'ti·ply',** *v.t.* 1. repeat a specified number of times for a final sum. —*v.i.* 2. increase in size or number. —**mul''ti·pli·ca'tion,** *n.*

**mul'ti·tude',** *n.* large number. —**mul''ti·tu'di·nous,** *adj.*

**mum'ble,** *v.i.* say something quietly and indistinctly.

**mum'my,** *n., pl.* **-mies.** preserved dead body. —**mum'mi·fy'',** *v.t., v.i.*

**mumps,** *n.* communicable disease.

**mu·nic'i·pal,** *adj.* pertaining to city government.

**mu·ni'tions,** *n., pl.* military supplies, esp. guns and ammunition.

**mu'ral,** *n.* wall painting.

**mur'der,** *n.* 1. willful unlawful killing. —*v.t.* 2. commit murder against. —**mur'der·er,** *fem.,* **mur'der·ess,** *n.* —**mur'der·ous,** *adj.*

**mur'mur,** *n.* 1. low, indistinct speech or sound. —*v.i.* 2. make a murmur.

**mus'cle,** *n.* body tissue for pulling. —**mus'cu·lar,** *adj.* —**mus'cu·la·ture,** *n.*

**mu·se'um,** *n.* public institution for displaying things of interest.

**mush'room'',** *n.* 1. edible fungus. —*v.i.* 2. grow rapidly.

**mu'sic,** *n.* art of composing series of tones, etc. —**mu·si'cian,** *n.* —**mu'si·col'o·gy,** *n.*

**mu'si·cal,** *adj.* 1. pertaining to music. 2. sweet-sounding. —*n.* 3. Also, **musical comedy,** play with frequent musical numbers.

**mus'ket,** *n.* antique smooth-bored gun.

**mus'lin,** *n.* cotton cloth.

**must,** *v.* 1. have or has to. 2. am, is, or are very probably being or doing as stated.

**mus·tache',** *n.* hair on the upper lip.

**mus'tang,** *n.* wild horse of the Southwest.

**mus'tard,** *n.* condiment made from ground yellow seeds.

**mus'ter,** *v.t.* 1. summon; rally. 2. enlist or discharge. —*n.* 3. gathering.

**L**
**M**

**mus'ty,** *adj.,* **-ier, -iest.** moldy in smell or taste.

**mu·ta'tion,** *n.* **1.** living thing with characteristics not inherited. **2.** change.

**mute,** *adj.* **1.** unable to speak. **2.** not speaking. —*n.* **3.** mute person. —*v.t.* **4.** soften the effect of.

**mu'ti·late'',** *v.t.* injure severely.

**mu'ti·ny,** *n., pl.* **-nies,** *v.i.* revolt against superiors. —**mu''ti·neer',** *n.* —**mu'ti·nous,** *adj.*

**mut'ter,** *v.i.* **1.** speak in a low, indistinct voice. —*n.* **2.** muttering voice.

**mut'ton,** *n.* sheep meat.

**mu'tu·al,** *adj.* affecting one another. —**mu'tu·al·ly,** *adj.*

**muz'zle,** *n.* **1.** nose and jaws of an animal. **2.** device to prevent biting. **3.** end of a gun facing the target. —*v.t.* **4.** put a muzzle on. **5.** keep from talking.

**my,** *pron.* pertaining or belonging to me.

**my·o'pi·a,** *n.* nearsightedness. —**my·op'ic,** *adj.*

**myr'i·ad,** *adj.* **1.** very many. —*n.* **2.** great number.

**my·self',** *pron.,* *pl.* **ourselves. 1.** (intensive and reflexive of *me* ). **2.** my true self.

**mys'ter·y,** *n., pl.* **-ies. 1.** something not readily explained. **2.** secrecy.

**mys'tic,** *adj.* **1.** pertaining to secret rites and teachings. Also, **mys' ti·cal,** of spiritual significance. —*n.* **3.** person having deep spiritual experiences. —**mys'ti·cism,** *n.*

**mys'ti·fy'',** *v.t.* puzzle.

**mys·tique',** *n.* air of mysticism surrounding a person, profession, etc.

**myth,** *n.* **1.** religious legend. **2.** false belief. —**myth'i·cal,** *adj.* —**my·thol'o·gy,** *n.*

# N

**N, n,** *n.* fourteenth letter of the English alphabet.

**nag,** *v.t.* **1.** pester. —*n.* **2.** poor horse.

**nail,** *n.* **1.** pointed, driven fastening.

**2.** horny growth on fingers or toes. —*v.t.* **3.** fasten with nails.

**na·ive'** (nah ēv'), *adj.* simple; unsophisticated. —**na·ive·té',** *n.*

**na'ked,** *adj.* **1.** unclothed; uncon cealed. **2.** unassisted by lenses.

**name,** *n.* **1.** word or words by which a person or thing is recognized. **2.** reputation. **3.** insulting epithet. —*v.t.* **4.** give a name to. **5.** appoint.

**name'ly,** *adv.* that is to say.

**name'sake'',** *n.* person or thing having the same name as another.

**nap,** *n.* **1.** brief sleep. **2.** fuzzy surface. —*v.i.* **3.** have a brief sleep.

**nap'kin,** *n.* cloth covering the lap at meals.

**nar·cot'ic,** *n.* **1.** pain-relieving drug, often addictive. —*adj.* **2.** pertaining to narcotics.

**nar'rate,** *v.t.* tell the story of. —**nar'ra·tor,** *n.*

**nar'ra·tive,** *adj.* **1.** story-telling. —*n.* **2.** story; account.

**nar'row,** *adj.* **1.** not wide. **2.** not ample **3.** illiberal. —*v.t.* **4.** make narrow. —*v.i.* **5.** become narrow.

**na'sal,** *adj.* spoken through the nose.

**nas'ty,** *adj.,* **-tier, -tiest.** revolting; unpleasant.

**na'tion,** *n.* **1.** group with common ancestral and traditional associations. **2.** politically independent state.

**na'tion·al·ism,** *n.* assertion of the rights, cultural values, etc. of a nation.

**na'tion·al·ize'',** *v.t.* put under government ownership.

**na'tive,** *adj.* **1.** born in or characteristic of a certain place. **2.** inborn. —*n.* **3.** native person.

**na·tiv'i·ty,** *n., pl.* **-ties.** birth.

**nat'u·ral,** *adj.* **1.** pertaining to nature. **2.** inborn. **3.** unaffected; easy. **4.** to be expected.

**nat'u·ral·ist,** *n.* student of nature.

**nat'u·ral·ize'',** *v.t.* admit to citizenship.

**na'ture,** *n.* **1.** everything not manmade. **2.** essential quality or composition.

**naugh'ty,** *adj.,* **-tier, -tiest.** ill-behaved. —**naugh'ti·ly,** *adv.*

**nau'se·a,** *n.* sickness at the stomach. —**nau'se·ate'',** *v.t.* —**nau'se·ous,** *adj.*

**nau'ti·cal,** *adj.* pertaining to ships and navigation.

**na'val,** *adj.* 1. pertaining to navies. 2. pertaining to ships.

**na'vel,** *n.* mark where the umbilical cord was attached.

**nav'i·ga·ble,** *adj.* able to be sailed over.

**nav'i·gate',** *v.t.* 1. cross or pass through in a ship or aircraft. 2. determine the position and course of. —*v.i.* 3. direct a ship or aircraft. —**nav'i·ga''tor,** *n.*

**na'vy,** *n., pl.* **-ies.** seagoing fighting force.

**near,** *adj.* 1. short in distance. 2. closely related. —*adv.* 3. at a short distance. —*prep.* 4. close to. —*v.t.* 5. approach.

**near'by',** *adj., adv.* near.

**neat,** *adj.* 1. free of dirt and clutter. 2. finely done.

**neb'u·lous,** *adj.* vague.

**nec'es·sar'y,** *adj.* 1. not to be dispensed with. 2. inevitable. —**nec''es·sar'i·ly,** *adv.*

**ne·ces'si·ty,** *n., pl.* **-ties.** 1. state of needing. 2. something needed.

**neck,** *n.* 1. part of the body which supports the head. 2. narrow feature. —**neck'wear'',** *n.*

**neck'lace,** *n.* chain, string of beads, etc. worn around the neck.

**neck'tie'',** *n.* cloth tied around the neck.

**nec'tar,** *n.* 1. drink of the classical gods. 2. sweetish liquid of flowers.

**need,** *v.t.* 1. be obliged to have or do. —*n.* 2. state of needing. 3. thing needed. 4. poverty or trouble.

**nee'dle,** *n.* 1. sharp object used for passing thread through cloth. —*v.t.* 2. *Informal.* goad; annoy.

**need'y,** *adj.* **-ier, -iest.** in need.

**ne·gate',** *v.t.* 1. deny. 2. render ineffective.

**neg'a·tive,** *adj.* 1. saying or meaning no. 2. opposite to positive. 3. less than zero. —*n.* 4. negative statement or attitude.

**neg·lect',** *v.t.* 1. deny proper care to. 2. disregard. —*n.* 3. state of being neglected. 4. state of neglecting. —**neg·lect'ful,** *adj.*

**neg'li·gent,** *adj.* 1. neglecting responsibilities. —**neg'li·gence,** *n.*

**neg'li·gi·ble,** *adj.* too unimportant to matter.

**ne·go'ti·ate'',** *v.i.* 1. bargain. —*v.t.* 2. establish by bargaining. 3. succeed in passing through. —**ne·go'ti·a''tor,** *n.*

**ne'gro,** *n., pl.* **-groes.** dark-skinned person of African origin. —**Neg'roid,** *adj.*

**neigh'bor,** *n.* 1. person living nearby. 2. fellow human.

**neigh'bor·hood'',** *n.* 1. area within a town. 2. approximate area or range.

**neither,** *adj., pron., conj.* not either.

**ne'on,** *n.* rare gaseous element.

**neph'ew,** *n.* son of a brother, sister, brother-in-law, or sister-in-law.

**nerve,** *n.* 1. fiber carrying signals through the body. 2. courage. 3. insolent boldness. 4. **nerves,** nervousness.

**nerve'less,** *adj.* 1. without strength. 2. not nervous.

**nerv'ous,** *adj.* full of apprehension or restlessness.

**nest,** *n.* 1. place for bearing and sheltering young. —*v.i.* 2. settle in a nest.

**nes'tle,** *v.i.* settle down.

**net,** *n.* 1. open cloth for capturing or supporting. 2. amount after deductions. —*adj.* 3. after deductions. —*v.t.* 4. capture, as in a net.

**net'work'',** *n.* 1. net-like arrangement. 2. system of isolated entities working in coordination.

**neu·ral'gia,** *n.* pain along a nerve.

**neu·rol'o·gy,** *n.* study of nerves.

**neu·ro'sis,** *n., pl.* **-ses.** compulsive mental disorder. —**neu·rot'ic,** *adj., n.*

**neu'ter,** *adj.* 1. without sex. 2. without gender. —*v.t.* 3. remove the sex organs of.

**neu'tral,** *adj.* 1. taking no sides. 2. having no pronounced character. —*n.* 3. neutral person or country.

**nev'er,** *adv.* at no time.

**nev''er·the·less',** *adv.* despite this.

**new,** *adj.* 1. never existing before. 2. unfamiliar. 3. fresh. 4. additional.

**news,** *n., sing.* 1. information of public interest, esp. as published. 2. recent information.

**news'cast'',** *n.* broadcast of news.

**next,** *adj.* 1. directly alongside another. —*adv.* 2. directly afterward.

**nib'ble,** *v.t., v.i.* 1. eat with small bites. —*n.* 2. small bite.

**nice,** *adj.* **nicer, nicest.** 1. agreeable. 2. delicate; subtle.

**N**
**O**

**nick**, n. 1. small notch. —v.t. 2. cut with such a notch.

**nick'el**, n. 1. white metallic element. 2. five-cent piece.

**nick'name''**, n. informal name.

**nic'o·tine''**, n. poisonous extract from tobacco leaves.

**niece**, n. daughter of a brother, sister, brother-in-law, or sister-in-law.

**nig'gard·ly**, adj. stingy.

**night**, n. period when the sun is absent.

**night'mare''**, n. bad dream. —night'mar''ish, adj.

**nim'ble**, adj., -bler, -blest. quick and deft.

**nine**, n. eight plus one. —ninth, adj.

**nine'teen'**, n. ten plus nine. —nine'teenth', adj.

**nine'ty**, adj., n. nine times ten. —nine'ti·eth, adj.

**nip**, v.t. 1. bite or pinch lightly. —n. 2. act or instance of nipping. —nip'per, n.

**nip'ple**, n. 1. small projection from the breast from which milk is sucked. 2. anything resembling this.

**ni'tro·gen**, n. gaseouselement. —ni·trog'e·nous, adj.

**no**, adv., adj., n., pl. noes. adv. 1. it is not so. 2. I will not. 3. do not. 4. not at all. —adj. 5. not any. —n. 6. vote of no.

**no'ble**, adj., -bler, -blest. adj. 1. of high and titled rank. 2. having or revealing a fine character. 3. of high quality. —n. 4. person of noble rank. —no'bly, adv. —no·bil'i·ty, n. —no'ble·man, n.

**no'bod·y**, pron., n., pl. -ies. pron. 1. no person. —n. 2. unimportant person.

**noc·tur'nal**, adj. pertaining to night.

**nod**, v.i. 1. give a quick forward motion of the head. —n. 2. act or instance of nodding.

**noise**, n. loud sound. —nois'y, adj.

**no'mad**, n. wanderer.

**nom'in·al**, adj. 1. in name only. 2. trifling in amount.

**nom'i·nate''**, v.t. 1. appoint. 2. propose for election. —nom''i·nee', n.

**non-**, prefix meaning "not."

**nonce**, n. time being.

**non''cha·lant''**, adj. casual in manner. —non''cha·lance', n.

**non''com·mit'tal**, adj. not committing oneself.

**non''de·script'**, adj. not to be described precisely.

**none**, pron. 1. not one or any. —n. 2. not any amount. —adv. 3. by no means.

**non·en'ti·ty**, n., pl. -ties. very unimportant person or thing.

**none'the·less'**, adv. nevertheless.

**non'plus'**, v.t. baffle into inaction.

**non·prof'it**, adj. not established for profit.

**non'sense**, n. meaningless talk or action. —non·sen'si·cal, adj.

**noo'dle**, n. strip of dough.

**nook**, n. semi-enclosed place.

**noon**, n. twelve o'clock in the daytime.

**no one**, nobody.

**noose**, n. loop made with a knot.

**nor**, conj. and not; and yet not.

**norm**, n. something generally expected.

**nor'mal**, adj. 1. conforming to a norm. 2. average. —nor·mal'i·ty, n. —nor'mal·ize'', v.t.

**north**, n. 1. direction of the north pole. 2. region lying northward. —adv. 3. toward or in the north. —north'ern, adj. —north'ern·er, n. —north'er·ly, adj. —north'ward, adj., adv. —north'wards, adv.

**north''east'**, n. 1. direction halfway between north and east. 2. region lying northeastward. —adj., adv. 3. toward or in the northeast. —north''east'ern, adj. —north''east·ern·er, n.

**north''west'**, n. 1. direction halfway between north and west. 2. region lying northwestward. —adj. 3. toward or in the northwest. —north''west'ern, adj. —north''west·ern·er, n.

**nose**, n. 1. part of the head with nostrils. 2. noselike features. —v.t. 3. nuzzle. —v.i. 4. sniff. 5. advance.

**nose dive**, headlong plunge. —nose'dive'', v.i.

**nos·tal'gia**, n. sentiment over the bygone or remote. —nos·tal'gic, adj.

**nos'tril**, n. one of the openings in the nose for breathing.

**not**, adv. in no way.

**no'ta·ble**, adj. remarkable.

**no·ta'tion**, n. 1. symbol or system of symbols. 2. brief note.

**notch**, n. 1. shallow knife cut. —v.t. 2. make such cuts in.

**note**, n. 1. short message. 2. reminder of something. 3. sound. 4. notice. 5. distinction. 6. feeling; air. —*v.t.* 7. observe. 8. make a note of. —**note'book''**, *n.* —**note'wor''thy**, *adj.*

**not'ed**, *adj.* well-known.

**noth'ing**, *n.* 1. not any thing. 2. something non-existent. 3. something insignificant. —*adv.* 4. in no way. —**noth'ing·ness**, *n.*

**no'tice**, *v.t.* 1. be aware of. —*n.* 2. awareness. 3. announcement or warning.

**no'ti·fy''**, *v.t.* give notice to.

**no'tion**, *n.* 1. idea. 2. vague opinion. 3. whim. —**no'tion·al**, *adj.*

**no·to'ri·ous**, *adj.* unfavorably well-known. —**no''to·ri'e·ty**, *n.*

**nought**, *n.* 1. nothing. 2. zero.

**noun**, *n.* name of a person, place, or thing.

**nour'ish**, *v.t.* feed. —**nour'ish·ment**, *n.*

**nou'veau riche**, *Fr.* person recently acquiring large sums of money.

**nov'el**, *adj.* 1. new; unprecedented. —*n.* 2. long written story. —**nov'el·ty**, *n.*

**nov'ice**, *n.* 1. monk or nun in a religious house who has not yet taken the vow. 2. beginner. —**no·vi'**·ti·ate, *n.*

**now**, *adv.* 1. at present. 2. at some past or future moment. 3. as matters are. —*conj.* 4. inasmuch. —*n.* 5. present moment.

**now'a·days'**, *adv.* at present.

**no'where'**, *adv.* not in any place.

**noz'zle**, *n.* pouring end of a pipe, etc.

**nu'ance**, *n.* slight variation in meaning, etc.

**nu'cle·ar**, *adj.* 1. forming a nucleus. 2. pertaining to atomic nuclei.

**nu'cle·us**, *n., pl.* -**cle·i**, -**cle·uses**. 1. core. 2. center of growth or development. 3. center of an atom.

**nude**, *adj.* 1. naked. —*n.* 2. state of nakedness. —**nu'di·ty**, *n.*

**nudge**, *v.t.* 1. jab with the elbow. —*n.* 2. act or instance of nudging.

**nug'get**, *n.* lump of natural gold.

**nui'sance**, *n.* source of annoyance.

**nul'li·fy''**, *v.t.* invalidate.

**numb**, *adj.* 1. without feeling. —*v.t.* 2. make numb.

**num'ber**, *n.* 1. expression of quantity or order. 2. quantity or order. 3. item on a program of entertainment. 4. establish the number of. 5. include in a group.

—**num'ber·less**, *adj.*

**nu'mer·al**, *n.* symbol for a number.

**nu·mer'i·cal**, *adj.* expressed in numbers.

**nu'mer·ous**, *adj.* in large numbers.

**nu''mis·mat'ics**, *n.* study of money and medals. —**nu·mis'ma·tist**, *n.*

**nun**, *n.* female member of a religious order. —**nun'ner·y**, *n.*

**nup'tial**, *adj.* 1. pertaining to marriage. —*n.* 2. nuptials, wedding.

**nurse**, *n.* 1. attendant of the sick. 2. attendant of children. —*v.t.* 3. suckle. 4. tend in illness. 5. conserve or foster.

**nurs'er·y**, *n., pl.* -**ies.** 1. place for the care of children. 2. place for raising plants.

**nur'ture**, *v.t.* 1. nourish. 2. raise, as a child. —**nur'ner·y**, *n.*

**nut**, *n.* 1. dry seed in a woody husk. 2. threaded block used with a bolt. 3. *Informal.* insane person. —**nut'crack''er**, *n.* —**nut'meat''**, *n.* —**nut'shell''**, *n.* —**nut'ty**, *adj.*

**nu'tri·ent**, *adj.* 1. nourishing. —*n.* 2. Also, **nu'tri·ment**, nourishment.

**nu·tri'tion**, *n.* 1. assimilation of food. 2. food. —**nu·tri'tion·al**, *adj.* —**nu'tri·tive**, *adj.* —**nu·tri'tious**, *adj.*

**ny'lon**, *n.* synthetic material.

**nymph**, *n.* classical nature goddess.

**N O**

# O

**O, o,** *n.* fifteenth letter of the English alphabet.

**oaf**, *n.* clumsy person.

**oak**, *n.* acorn-bearing hardwood tree. —**oak'en**, *adj.*

**oar**, *n.* bladed lever for rowing.

**o·a'sis**, *n., pl.* -**ses.** place in the desert with water.

**oat**, *n.* cereal grass. —**oat'meal''**, *n.*

**oath**, *n., pl.* **oaths.** 1. vow in the name of a god. 2. blasphemous remark.

**o·bey'**, *v.i.* 1. do as told. —*v.t.* 2. perform as told. 3. perform the orders of. —**o·be'di·ent**, *adj.* —**o·be'di·ence**, *n.*

o·bit'u·ar''y, n., pl. -ies. death notice.

ob·ject', n. (ob'jekt) 1. something tangible. 2. something aimed for. —v.i. (ob jekt') 3. protest. —ob·jec'tion, n. —ob·jec'tion·a·ble, adj. —ob·jec'tor, n.

ob·jec'tive, adj. concerned with reality. —ob''jec·tiv'i·ty, n.

ob'li·gate'', v.t. bind with a duty. —ob''li·ga'to·ry, adj.

o·blige', v.t. 1. force. 2. put in one's debt.

o·blig'ing, adj. ready to do favors.

o·blique', adj. indirect.

ob·lit'er·ate'', v.t. efface.

ob·liv'i·on, n. forgetfulness.

ob'long, adj. longer than broad.

ob·nox'ious, adj. offensive.

ob·scene', adj. offensive to decency. —ob·scen'i·ty, n.

ob·scure', adj. 1. indefinite. 2. dark. 3. little-known. —v.t. 4. make obscure. —ob·scu'ri·ty, n. —ob''scu·ra'tion, n.

ob·serv'a·to''ry, n., pl. -ries. place for observing heavenly bodies.

ob·serve', v.t. 1. study with the eye. 2. notice. 3. remark. 4. obey or respect. —ob·serv'ance, n. —ob·serv'ant, adj. —ob''ser·va'tion, n.

ob·sess', v.t. preoccupy constantly. —ob·ses'sive, adj. —ob·ses'sion, n.

ob'so·lete'', adj. out of date.

ob'sta·cle, n. something hindering advance.

ob·stet'rics, n. branch of medicine for pregnancy and childbirth. —ob·stet'ric, ob·stet'ri·cal, adj. —ob''ste·tri'cian, n.

ob'sti·nate, adj. stubborn.

ob·struct', v.t. hinder; thwart.

ob·tain', v.t. 1. get. —v.i. 2. be in effect.

ob'vi·ous, adj. perceived or understood without effort.

oc·ca'sion, n. 1. specific time or event. 2. opportunity. 3. reason; pretext. —v.t. 4. bring about.

oc·ca'sion·al, adj. occurring now and then.

oc·cult', adj. hidden; mystical.

oc''cu·pa'tion, n. 1. type of work. 2. act or instance of occupying.

oc'cu·py'', v.t. 1. be in. 2. be concerned with. 3. take possession of. —oc''cu·pan'cy, n. —oc'cu·pant, n.

oc·cur', v.i. 1. happen. 2. come to mind. —oc·cur'rence, n.

o'cean, n. vast body of salt water. —o·ce·an'ic, adj.

o'clock', adv. by the clock.

oc'ta·gon, n. eight-sided plane figure. —oc·tag'o·nal, adj.

oc'to·pus, n., pl. -puses, -pi. soft mollusk with eight arms.

oc'u·list, n. ophthalmologist.

odd, adj. 1. not evenly divisible by two. 2. peculiar. 3. occasional. 4. remaining. —n. 5. odds, factors for or against. —odd'i·ty, n.

o'di·ous, adj. hateful.

o'dor, n. smell. —o'dor·ous, adj.

of, prep. 1. coming from or produced by. 2. belonging to. 3. owning. 4. regarding. 5. specified as.

off, prep. 1. away or up from. 2. with sustenance from. —adv. 3. away or up. 4. so as not to work or be in effect. —adj. 5. not working or in effect. 6. on one's way. 7. not right.

of·fend', v.i. 1. commit an offense. —v.i. 2. annoy or wound. 3. displease.

of·fense', n. 1. unlawful act. 2. resentment or hurt. 3. cause of this. 4. attack. Also, of'fence'.

of·fen'sive, adj. 1. tending to offend. 2. attacking. —n. 3. attacker's status.

of'fer, v.t. 1. present, as for acceptance or consideration. 2. shown signs of. —v.i. 3. present itself. —n. 4. act or instance of offering.

off'hand', adv. 1. unprepared. —adj. 2. Also, off'hand'ed, casual.

of'fice, n. 1. position of authority. 2. place for work.

of'fi·cer, n. 1. holder of a position of authority. 2. policeman.

of·fi'cial, adj. 1. coming from supreme authority. —n. 2. person in public office.

of·fi'ci·ate'', v.i. perform official or ceremonial duties.

off''-line'', n. not connected to a network or system.

off''-road'', adj. designed to be used in rough terrain, as an off-road vehicle.

off'set'', v.t. compensate for.

off'spring'', n., pl. -spring, -springs. young of a human or animal.

of'ten, adv. many times.

**oil,** *n.* **1.** any of various combustible liquids. **2.** paint with an oil vehicle. —*v.t.* **3.** lubricate with oil. —**oil'y,** *adj.* —**oil'i·ness,** *n.*

**oint'ment,** *n.* fatty salve.

**O.K.,** *interj., adj., adv., v.t.,* **O.K.'d, O.K.'ing.** *interj., adj., adv.* **1.** all right. —*v.t.* **2.** approve.

**old,** *adj.,* **older** or **elder, oldest** or **eldest.** **1.** long in existence. **2.** experienced. **3.** longer in existence than another. **4.** former.

**old'-fash'ioned,** *adj.* **1.** obsolete. **2.** favoring older manners, etc.

**om'e·let,** *n.* fried beaten eggs.

**o'men,** *n.* sign of the future.

**om'i·nous,** *adj.* threatening.

**o·mit',** *v.t.* **1.** leave out. **2.** forget; neglect. —**o·mis'sion,** *n.*

**om'ni·bus,** *n.* **1.** bus. **2.** complete anthology.

**om·nip'o·tent,** *adj.* all-powerful.

**on,** *prep.* **1.** supported by. **2.** down against. **3.** regarding. **4.** with the help or sustenance of. **5.** at the time of. **6.** engaged in. **7.** being part of. —*adv.* **8.** onto oneself or something else. **9.** further; forward. **10.** into operation. —*adj.* **11.** in operation or effect.

**once,** *adv.* **1.** one time. **2.** formerly. **3.** at any time. —*conj.* **4.** when.

**one,** *n.* **1.** lowest whole cardinal number. **2.** person. —*adj.* **3.** being one in number. **4.** identical. **5.** united. —*pron.* **6.** one person or thing.

**one·self',** *pron.* person's own self.

**one'-sid'ed,** *adj.* **1.** involving only one side. **2.** prejudiced.

**on'ion,** *n.* edible bulb of the lily family.

**on''-line',** *n.* connected to a network or system.

**on'ly,** *adj.* **1.** single; sole. —*adv.* **2.** solely. **3.** at last, however. **4.** as lately as.

**on'slaught'n,** *n.* vigorous attack.

**on'to,** *prep.* into a position on.

**on'ward,** *adv.* **1.** Also, **on'wards,** forward. —*adj.* **2.** forward.

**ooze,** *v.i.* **1.** flow slowly. —*v.t.* **2.** emit slowly. —*n.* **3.** slime.

**o·paque',** *adj.* **1.** passing no light. **2.** obscure. —**o·paque'ness,** *o·pac'i·ty,* *n.*

**o'pen,** *adj.* **1.** able to be entered, seen through, etc. **2.** with the inside revealed. **3.** available or ac-

cessible. **4.** candid. —*v.t.* **5.** make open. —*v.i.* **6.** become open. —*v.t., v.i.* **7.** start. —*n.* **8.** open or unconcealed place or state.

**o'pen·ing,** *n.* **1.** perforation. **2.** beginning. **3.** opportunity.

**op'er·a,** *n.* musical drama. —**op'er·at'ic,** *adj.*

**op'er·a·ble,** *adj.* **1.** treatable by surgery. **2.** able to be operated.

**op'er·ate',** *v.t.* **1.** cause to function. **2.** control; manage. —*v.i.* **3.** function; act. **4.** perform surgery. —**op'er·a''tor**n.

**op'er·et'ta,** *n.* light opera.

**oph''thal·mol'o·gy,** *n.* branch of medicine concerning the eye.

**o·pin'ion,** *n.* **1.** personal belief. **2.** personal evaluation.

**o·pin'ion·at''ed,** *adj.* stubborn in one's opinions.

**op·po'nent,** *n.* adversary.

**op'por·tune',** *adj.* occurring when useful.

**op'por·tu'ni·ty,** *n., pl.* **-ties.** favorable occasion.

**op·pose',** *v.t.* **1.** resist; fight. **2.** be in contrast with. —**op'po·si'tion,** *n.*

**op'po·site,** *adj.* **1.** in the other direction from somewhere between. **2.** totally different in nature. —*n.* **3.** something opposite.

**op·press',** *v.t.* **1.** bully or exploit. **2.** worry or make uncomfortable. —**op·pres'sion,** *n.* —**op·pres'sor,** *n.* —**op·pres'sive,** *adj.*

**op'tic,** *adj.* pertaining to sight.

**op'ti·cal,** *adj.* **1.** visual. **2.** pertaining to optics.

**op·ti'cian,** *n.* dealer in aids to eyesight.

**op'ti·mism,** *n.* readiness to see or predict the best.

**op'tion,** *n.* **1.** choice. **2.** right to buy or not buy something.

**op'u·lent,** *adj.* **1.** rich. **2.** lavish. —**op'u·lence,** *n.*

**or,** *conj.* **1.** (indicating alternatives). **2.** (indicating synonyms).

**o'ral,** *adj.* **1.** pertaining to the mouth. **2.** spoken.

**or'ange,** *n.* **1.** mixture of red and yellow. **2.** fruit of this color.

**o·ra'tion,** *n.* formal speech. —**o'rate',** *v.i.* —**o·ra'tor,** *n.*

**or'a·to''ry,** *n.* public speaking. —**or''a·tor'i·cal,** *adj.*

**or'bit,** *n.* **1.** path of a heavenly body. —*v.i.* **2.** be in orbit. —**or'bit·al,** *adj.*

**or'chard,** *n.* grove of fruit trees.

**N**
**O**

**or·ches·tra**, *n.* 1. large, varied musical group. 2. main floor in an auditorium.

**or·chid**, *n.* tropical flowering plant.

**or·dain**, *v.t.* 1. decree; establish. 2. grant the office of clergyman to. —**or·dain'ment**, **or''di·na'tion**, *n.*

**or·deal**, *n.* severe trial.

**or·der**, *n.* 1. proper or meaningful condition. 2. command. 3. request to purchase. 4. group of monks, etc. —*v.t.* 5. make an order for. 6. put in order.

**or·di·nance**, *n.* law.

**or·di·nar''y**, *adj.* 1. usual, customary. —*n.* 2. customary experience.

**or·gan**, *n.* 1. body part performing a specific function. 2. keyboard wind or electronic instrument. 3. institutional periodical. —**or'gan·ist**, *n.*

**or·gan'ic**, *adj.* 1. pertaining to or suggesting organisms. 2. pertaining to bodily organs. 3. containing carbon.

**or'gan·ism**, *n.* living thing.

**or'gan·ize''**, *v.t., v.i.* 1. join in a coordinated group. —*v.t.* 2. coordinate the functioning of. 3. arrange for. 4. cause to join a group.

**or·gy** (or'jē), *n., pl.* **-gies.** wild revelry.

**o'ri·ent**, *v.i.* 1. establish one's location or course. —*v.t.* 2. establish the location or course of. 3. initiate in fundamentals. 4. face in a certain direction. —*n.* 4. **the** Orient, Asia. —**o''ri·en·ta'tion**, *n.* —**O''ri·en'tal**, *adj., n.*

**or'i·fice**, *n.* opening.

**or'i·gin**, *n.* 1. commencement. 2. source.

**o·rig'i·nal**, *adj.* 1. earliest. 2. copied to make others. 3. never before seen. 4. creative. —*n.* 5. original thing. —**o·rig''i·nal'i·ty**, *n.* —**o·rig'i·nate''**, *v.t., v.i.* —**o·rig'i·na''tor**, *n.*

**or·na·ment**, *n.* (or'na ment) 1. decoration. —*v.t.* (or'na ment'') 2. decorate. —**or''na·men'tal**, *adj.* —**or''na·men·ta'tion**, *n.*

**or''ni·thol'o·gy**, *n.* study of birds.

**or'phan**, *n.* 1. child of dead parents. —*v.t.* 2. kill the parents of.

**or'phan·age**, *n.* home for orphans.

**or'tho·dox''**, *adj.* conforming to standard doctrine. —**or'tho·dox''y**, *n.*

**or·thog'ra·phy**, *n., pl.* **-phies.** spelling.

**or''tho·pe'dics**, *n.* surgery of bones and joints.

**os'cil·late''**, *v.t., v.i.* swing back and forth.

**os·mo'sis**, *n.* passage of fluids through membranes. —**os·mot'ic**, *adj.*

**os·ten'si·ble**, *adj.* seeming.

**os''ten·ta'tion**, *n.* great display.

**os'tra·cize''**, *v.t.* expel; exclude. —**os''tra·cism**, *n.*

**oth'er**, *adj.* 1. not yet mentioned. 2. additional; remaining. —*pron.* 3. other one. —*adv.* 4. otherwise.

**oth'er·wise''**, *adv.* 1. in a different way. 2. in other respects. 3. under other conditions.

**ought**, *aux. v.* 1. am, is, or are obligated. 2. will very probably.

**ounce**, *n.* 1. sixteenth of an avoirdupois pound or twelfth of a troy pound. 2. thirty-second of a liquid quart.

**our**, *adj.* pertaining to us.

**ours**, *pron.* our own.

**oust**, *v.t.* expel.

**out**, *adv.* 1. away from inside. 2. away from existence, action, etc. 3. away from a group. 4. away from consciousness. —*adj.* 5. away from one's usual place. 6. out of existence, action, etc. 7. inaccurate. 8. unconscious. 9. **out of,** with no supply of.

**out'break''**, *n.* sudden manifestation.

**out'burst''**, *n.* vigorous outbreak.

**out'cast''**, *adj.* 1. rejected by all. —*n.* 2. outcast person.

**out'come''**, *n.* result.

**out'cry''**, *n., pl.* **-cries.** strong protest.

**out·do'**, *v.t.,* **-did, -done, -doing.** act more effectively than.

**out'doors''**, *adv.* 1. away from the insides of buildings. —*n.* 2. nature.

**out'er**, *adj.* further out. —**out'er·most''**, *adj.*

**out'fit''**, *n.* 1. equipment. 2. ensemble of clothes. —*v.t.* 3. supply with an outfit.

**out'growth''**, *n.* 1. something that grows out. 2. development; consequence.

**out'ing**, *n.* pleasure trip.

**out·land''ish**, *adj.* strange.

**out·law**", *n.* 1. criminal. —*v.t.* 2. forbid by law.

**out·lay**", *n.* expenditure.

**out·let**", *n.* 1. means of emergence. 2. sales market.

**out·line**", *n.* 1. outer edge; silhouette. 2. summary of essentials.

**out·look**", *n.* 1. view. 2. viewing place. 3. prospect.

**out·mod·ed**, *adj.* no longer in use.

**out'-of-date**", *adj.* obsolete.

**out·post**", *n.* remote fort, settlement, etc.

**out·put**", *n.* 1. production. 2. (computers) data sent from a computer after processing.

**out·rage**", *n.* 1. indignation. 2. act causing indignation. —*v.t.* 3. make indignant. —**out·ra'geous**, *adj.*

**out·right**", *adj.* pure and unambiguous.

**out·set**", *n.* beginning.

**out·side**", *n.* 1. exterior. —*adj.* 2. pertaining to an exterior. 3. extreme. 4. remotely possible. —*adv.* 5. to the exterior. —*prep.* 6. away from the interior of.

**out·skirts**", *n.*, *pl.* border areas.

**out·spo·ken**, *adj.* frank.

**out·stand·ing**, *adj.* 1. prominent. 2. unpaid.

**out·ward**, *adj.* 1. outer; exterior. —*adv.* 2. Also, **out'wards**, towards the outside.

**o·val**, *n.* 1. closed curve with a longer and a shorter axis. —*adj.* 2. shaped like such a curve.

**o·va·ry**, *n.*, *pl.* **ries**. female reproductive gland. —**o·var'i·an**, *adj.*

**o·va·tion**, *n.* enthusiastic applause.

**ov·en**, *n.* heating chamber.

**o·ver**, *prep.* 1. above or on. 2. to or on the far side of. 3. superior to. 4. more than. 5. concerning. —*adv.* 6. above. 7. across. 8. more. 9. again. 10. upside down. 11. to a new attitude or belief. 12. to completion. —*adj.* 13. upper. 14. finished.

**o·ver-**, prefix indicating "to excess."

**o'ver·bear·ing**, *adj.* domineering.

**o'ver·cast**", *adj.* cloudy, as the sky.

**o'ver·coat**", *n.* heavy outer coat.

**o'ver·come**", *v.t.*, get the better of.

**o'ver·dose**", *v.* to ingest, with

harmful effect, too much of a drug.

**o·ver·flow**, *v.t.* (o''vər flō') 1. spill over the rim of. —*v.i.* 2. be filled beyond capacity. —*n.* (o'vər flō') 3. act or instance of overflowing. 4. amount that overflows.

**o'ver·haul**", *v.t.* 1. inspect thoroughly. 2. repair.

**o'ver·head**", *adj.*, *adv.* 1. above one's head. —*n.* 2. continuing business costs.

**o'ver·look**", *v.t.* 1. omit by mistake. 2. look out over.

**o'ver·ly**, *adv.* excessively.

**o·ver·night**, *adv.* (ō''vər nīt') 1. during the night. —*adj.* (ō'vər nīt'') 2. from beginning to end of one night. 3. for one night.

**o'ver·pass**", *n.* roadway passing over another, etc.

**o'ver·pow·er**, *v.t.* reduce to helplessness.

**o'ver·ride**", *v.t.* prevail against or nullify.

**o'ver·rule**", *v.t.* nullify with superior authority.

**o'ver·run**", *v.t.* 1. overflow. 2. infest.

**o'ver·see**", *v.t.* supervise.

**o'ver·shoe**", *n.* waterproof shoe covering.

**o'ver·sight**", *n.* mistaken omission.

**o'ver·sleep**", *v.i.* sleep too long.

**o'ver·state**", *v.t.* exaggerate.

**o·vert**, *adj.* 1. unhidden. 2. open and deliberate.

**o'ver·take**", *v.t.* catch up with.

**o''ver-the-coun'ter**, *adj.* (drugs) available without a prescription.

**o·ver·throw**, *v.t.* (ō''vər thrō') 1. cause to fall over. 2. banish from power. —*n.* (ō'vər thrō'') 3. act or instance of overthrowing.

**o'ver·time**", *adj.*, *adv.* 1. beyond regular hours. —*n.* 2. time beyond regular hours. 3. overtime pay.

**o'ver·weight**", *adj.* too heavy.

**o'ver·whelm**", *v.t.* render powerless.

**o'ver·wrought**", *adj.* very nervous.

**o'vum**, *n.*, *pl.* **-va**. female germ cell.

**owe**, *v.t.* 1. be obligated to give or pay. 2. be obligated to. 3. have someone to thank for.

**own**, *v.t.* 1. be the rightful possessor of. —*v.t.*, *v.i.* 2. admit or confess.

—*adj.* **3.** personally or individually possessed. —**own′er·ship**, *n.*

**ox**, *n.*, *pl.* **oxen.** castrated bull.

**ox′y·gen**, *n.* gaseous element needed for breathing and burning.

**ox·y·mor′on**, *n.* figure of speech in which two ideas of opposite meaning are combined to form an expressive phrase.

# P

**P, p**, *n.* sixteenth letter of the English alphabet.

**pace**, *n.* **1.** rate of movement, esp. in walking or running. **2.** an individual step.

**pace″mak·er**, *n.* artificial device to regulate the heartbeat.

**pa·cif′ic**, *adj.* peaceful; calm.

**pac′i·fism**, *n.* opposition to violence and war. —**pac′i·fist**, *n.*

**pac′i·fy″**, *v.t.* quiet or calm. —**pac′i·fi″er**, *n.*

**pack**, *n.* **1.** bundle or package. **2.** group of people, animals, or things. **3.** complete set of. —*v.t.* **4.** make into a bundle.

**pack′age**, *n.* bundle; parcel.

**pact**, *n.* agreement; treaty.

**pad**, *n.* **1.** soft cushion. **2.** tablet of writing paper. —*v.t.* **3.** furnish with pads.

**pad′dle**, *n.* **1.** oar-like implement, esp. for a canoe. —*v.t.* **2.** move with paddles.

**pad′lock**, *n.* portable lock with a shackle.

**pa′gan**, *adj.* heathen; barbaric.

**page**, *n.* **1.** single side of a leaf, as of a book. **2.** young servant. —*v.t.* **3.** hail by naming loudly.

**pag′eant**, *n.* elaborate spectacle.

**pag′er**, *n.* electronic device for remote alerting and communication with a person.

**pail**, *n.* bucket.

**pain**, *n.* **1.** physical or mental suffering. —*v.t.* **3.** hurt; distress. —**pain′ful**, *adj.* —**pain′less**, *adj.*

**pains′tak″ing**, *adj.* careful.

**paint**, *n.* **1.** pigmented liquid used to coat surfaces. —*v.t.* **2.** cover with paint. —**paint′er**, *n.* —**paint′ing**, *n.*

**pair**, *n.*, *pl.* **pairs, pair.** set of two, esp. when matching.

**pa·ja′mas**, *n.*, *pl.* loose, two-piece sleeping clothes.

**pal′ace**, *n.* official residence of a sovereign, etc. —**pa·la′tial**, *adj.*

**pal′at·a·ble**, *adj.* tasty.

**pal′ate**, *n.* roof of the mouth.

**pale**, *adj.*, **paler, palest.** *adj.* lacking intensity of color; whitish.

**pal′ette**, *n.* board on which a painter spreads colors.

**pal′id**, *adj.* pale, drawn. —**pal′lor**, *n.*

**pall′bear″er**, *n.* person who attends or carries the coffin at a funeral.

**palm**, *n.* **1.** soft inner surface of the hand. **2.** tall unbranched tropical tree or shrub topped with large leaves. —*v.t.* **3.** conceal in the hand.

**pal′pa·ble**, *adj.* **1.** tangible. **2.** obvious, clear.

**pal′pi·tate″**, *v.i.* pulsate with unnatural rapidity.

**pam′per**, *v.t.* treat with excessive indulgence; coddle.

**pam′phlet**, *n.* unbound booklet with a paper cover.

**pan**, *n.* broad, shallow metal container.

**pan·a·ce′a** (pan″a sē′a), *n.* cureall.

**pan′cake″**, *n.* flat batter cake fried on both sides.

**pane**, *n.* sheet of glass, esp. for doors and windows.

**pan′el**, *n.* **1.** list of persons called for a special task, e.g. jury duty. **2.** wood filling for a wall or door. **3.** mounting for controls or instruments.

**pang**, *n.* sudden feeling of distress or guilt.

**pan′ic**, *n.* sudden, overpowering fear.

**pan″o·ram′a**, *n.* wide view of a large area.

**pan′sy**, *n.* colorful outdoor flower related to the violet.

**pant**, *v.i.* breathe hard and quickly, as after exercise.

**pan′ther**, *n.* large wild cat, e.g. leopard, cougar, puma.

**pan·to·mime″**, *n.* **1.** expression through movement and gesture only. **2.** drama using movement and no speech.

**pan'try,** *n.,* *pl.* **-tries.** small supply room or closet off a kitchen.

**pants,** *n.,* *pl.* trousers.

**pa'pa·cy,** *n.* office of the Pope. —**pa'pal,** *adj.*

**pa'per,** *n.* **1.** fibrous compound made in sheets to receive writing, etc. **2.** newspaper. **3.** **papers,** documents.

**par,** *n.* **1.** equality in level or value. **2.** accepted standard; average.

**par'a·chute'',** *n.* umbrellalike device used for descents from aircraft.

**pa·rade',** *n.* ceremonial procession or march.

**par·a·digm** (par'a dīm), *n.* ideal; model.

**par'a·dise'',** *n.* **1.** heaven. **2.** Garden of Eden.

**par'a·dox'',** *n.* true statement that seems to contradict itself.

**par'af·fin,** *n.* waxy substance used in candles and to seal jars.

**par'a·graph'',** *n.* subdivision of a writing that contains one or more sentences.

**par'al·lel',** *adj.* **1.** lying or moving in the same direction but equidistant at all points. —*n.* **2.** anything parallel.

**pa·ral'y·sis,** *n.,* *pl.* **-ses,** loss of feeling or voluntary muscular control. —**par'a·lyze',** *v.t.*

**par'a·mount'',** *adj.* superior; predominant.

**par'a·phrase'',** *v.t.* **1.** restate in other words. —*n.* **2.** restatement in different words.

**par'a·site'',** *n.* organism which lives in or on another.

**par'cel,** *n.* wrapped package, esp. for mailing.

**parch,** *v.t.* dry by heat.

**parch'ment,** *n.* skin of sheep or goat prepared for writing on.

**par'don,** *n.* **1.** official release from penalty or punishment. **2.** indulgence, forgiveness. —*v.t.* **3.** grant pardon to.

**pare,** *v.t.* trim off the outside part or skin of.

**par'ent,** *n.* mother or father.

**par'ent·age,** *n.* descent, origin or lineage.

**pa·ren'the·sis,** *n.,* *pl.* **-ses,** punctuation marks, ( or) used to enclose parenthetical material.

**par'ish,** *n.* **1.** ecclesiastical district under one pastor. **2.** local church community. —**pa·rish'ion·er,** *n.*

**par'i·ty,** *n.* equality; equivalence.

**park,** *n.* **1.** land set aside as a recreation area or game preserve. —*v.t.,* *v.i.* **2.** halt for an extended period.

**par'lia·ment,** *n.* national legislative body.

**par'lor,** *n.* room for entertaining.

**pa·ro·chi·al** (pa ro'kē al), *adj.* **1.** pertaining to a parish. **2.** narrow or limited in scope.

**par'o·dy,** *n.,* *pl.* **-dies,** *n.* satiric or humorous imitation.

**pa·role',** *n.* conditional early release from prison.

**par'rot,** *n.* hook-billed tropical bird capable of talking.

**par'si·mo'ny,** *n.* extreme frugality or cheapness.

**pars'ley,** *n.* garden herb used as garnish or seasoning.

**par'son,** *n.* clergyman, esp. Protestant.

**par'son·age,** *n.* house for a parson.

**part,** *n.* **1.** portion or division. **2.** role in drama, etc. —*v.t.* **3.** divide.

**par·take',** *v.i.* **1.** participate. **2.** receive or take a portion.

**par'tial** (par'shal), *adj.* **1.** favoring one over another; biased. **2.** especially fond. **3.** affecting a part only. —**par·tial'i·ty,** *n.*

**par·tic'i·pate'',** *v.i.* take part; share. —**par·tic'i·pant,** *n.* —**par·tic''i·pa'tion,** *n.*

**par'ti·ci·ple,** *n.* adjective based on a verb.

**par'ti·cle,** *n.* very small piece or amount.

**par·tic'u·lar,** *adj.* distinctive, special. —**par·tic'u·lar·ly,** *adv.*

**part'ing,** *n.* departure.

**par'ti·san,** *n.* **1.** person who takes a side in a controversy. **2.** guerrilla.

**par·ti'tion,** *n.* **1.** division into parts. **2.** divider.

**part'ly,** *adv.* in some measure; not fully.

**part'ner,** *n.* **1.** associate, colleague. **2.** spouse. **3.** joint owner.

**par'ty,** *n.,* *pl.* **-ties,** *n.* **1.** social gathering. **2.** group of people with common political interests and opinions.

**pass,** *v.t.* **1.** go past. **2.** hand over; serve. —*n.* **3.** paper granting admission, leave, etc. **4.** route, as between mountains.

**pass'a·ble,** *adj.* **1.** able to be

**P**
**R**

passed or crossed. 2. good enough; tolerable.

**pas´sage**, *n.* 1. right or freedom to pass. 2. means of passing. 3. enactment. —**pas´sage·way´**, *n.*

**pas´sen·ger**, *n.* traveler, esp. on a vehicle.

**pas´sion**, *n.* strong feeling or emotion.

**pas´sive**, *adj.* inactive; not in action.

**pass´port´**, *n.* official document carried by a foreign traveler.

**past**, *adj.* 1. gone by or elapsed. —*n.* 2. time gone by. —*prep.*, *adv.* 3. beyond.

**paste**, *n.* 1. soft mixture, esp. for sticking things together. —*v.t.* 2. fasten with paste.

**pas·tel´**, *n.* 1. light or pale color. 2. drawing or painting in pastel.

**pas´teur·ize´**, *v.t.* heat to destroy harmful bacteria.

**pas´time´**, *n.* diversion; hobby.

**pas´tor**, *n.* clergyman serving a local parish or church.

**pas´to·ral**, *adj.* pertaining to shepherds or the rural life.

**pas´try**, *n.* sweet baked goods.

**pas´ture**, *n.* grassy land used for grazing animals.

**pat**, *n.* 1. light stroke with the flat of the hand. —*v.i.* 2. place the flat of the hand on lightly.

**patch**, *n.* 1. piece used to cover or repair a worn spot. —*v.t.* 2. mend or cover with a patch.

**pat´ent**, *n.* certificate of exclusive rights to an invention.

**pa·ter´nal**, *adj.* fatherly.

**path**, *n.* narrow road.

**pa·thet´ic**, *adj.* 1. evoking pity. 2. miserably inadequate.

**pa·thol´o·gy**, *n.* 1. study of the nature of disease. 2. characteristics of a disease.

**pa´tient**, *n.* 1. person under the care of a doctor. —*adj.* 2. enduring without complaint. —**pa´tience**, *n.*

**pa´ti·o´**, *n.*, *pl.* **patios**, open courtyard.

**pa´tri·arch´**, *n.* father or founder, e.g. of a tribe or institution.

**pa´tri·ot**, *n.* person who loves and supports his country. —**pa´tri·ot´ic**, *adj.* —**pa´tri·ot´ism**, *n.*

**pa·trol´**, *v.t.* 1. guard making a round. —*v.t.* 2. guard with a patrol. —**pa·trol´man**, *n.*

**pa´tron**, *n.* 1. influential or

wealthy supporter. 2. customer or client.

**pa´tron·age**, *n.* support by a patron.

**pa´tron·ize´**, *v.t.* 1. be a customer of. 2. treat with condescension.

**pat´tern**, *n.* 1. decorative design. 2. model for making or copying.

**pau´per**, *n.* poor person.

**pause**, *n.* temporary stop.

**pave**, *v.t.* cover with hard material, as a road. —**pave´ment**, *n.*

**pa·vil´ion**, *n.* light, open structure for entertainment or shelter.

**paw**, *n.* animal foot with nails or claws.

**pawn**, *v.t.* 1. deposit as security for a loan. —*n.* 2. state of being pawned. 3. chess piece of the lowest value.

**pay**, *v.t.* 1. give money to in return for goods or services. —*v.i.* 2. give money in exchange. —*n.* 3. wages or salary.

**pea**, *n.* round, edible vegetable seed.

**peace**, *n.* calm and quiet. —**peace´a·ble**, **peace´ful**, *adj.*

**peach**, *n.* sweet juicy fruit.

**pea´cock´**, *n.* male peafowl with long, brilliant tail feathers.

**peak**, *n.* 1. pointed top. 2. top of a mountain or hill.

**peal**, *n.* 1. loud, prolonged ringing of bells. —*v.i.* 2. sound in a peal.

**pea´nut´**, *n.* pod or edible seed of an annual herb.

**pear**, *n.* fleshy fruit related to the apple.

**pearl**, *n.* hard, lustrous gem formed within the shell of an oyster. —**pearl´y**, *adj.*

**peas´ant**, *n.* poor farm worker.

**peb´ble**, *n.* small stone.

**peck**, *v.t.*, *v.i.* jab repeatedly with a beak.

**pe·cu´liar**, *adj.* strange; odd. —**pe·cu´li·ar´i·ty**, *n.*

**pe·cu´ni·ar´y**, *adj.* pertaining to money; monetary.

**ped´al**, *n.* lever worked by the foot.

**ped´ant**, *n.* person who makes a display of his learning.

**ped´dle**, *v.t.*, *v.i.* sell on the street or road. —**ped´dler**, *n.*

**ped´es·tal**, *n.* base for a statue, etc.

**pe·des´tri·an**, *n.* walker.

**pe˝di·at´rics**, *n.* study of care and diseases of children. —**pe´di·a·tri´cian**, *n.*

**ped´i·gree´**, *n.* 1. certificate of

**ancestry.** 2. ancestry, esp. when distinguished.

**peek,** *v.i.* glance furtively.

**peel,** *v.t.* 1. strip or remove. —*n.* 2. skin of fruit or vegetable.

**peep,** *v.i.* 1. peek. 2. utter a faint, shrill cry.

**peer,** *n.* 1. equal in rank or abilities. 2. nobleman.

**peg,** *n.* small hook, pin or fastener, esp. one fitting into a hole.

**pelt,** *n.* 1. animal hide, esp. with fur. —*v.t.* 2. attack with blows or missiles.

**pel'vis,** *n.* basinlike bone in the lower part of the trunk.

**pen,** *n.* 1. instrument for writing with ink. —*v.t.* 2. write.

**pen'al·ty,** *n., pl.* -ties. punishment.

**pen'chant,** *n.* strong inclination; liking.

**pen'cil,** *n.* cylindrical implement containing graphite for writing, etc.

**pend'ant,** *n.* hanging ornament, e.g. an earring.

**pen'e·trate'',** *v.t.* enter. —**pen''·e·tra'tion,** *n.*

**pen''i·cil'lin,** *n.* antibiotic produced by certain molds.

**pen·in'su·la,** *n.* land body surrounded by water on three sides.

**pen'i·tent,** *adj.* feeling repentance.

**pen''i·ten'tia·ry,** *n.* prison.

**pen'knife'',** *n.* small pocketknife; jackknife.

**pen'ny,** *n., pl.* -nies. smallest denomination of currency. —**pen'ni·less,** *adj.*

**pen'sion,** *n.* fixed, periodic payment to a retiree.

**pen'sive,** *adj.* sadly or dreamily thoughtful; quiet.

**pent'house'',** *n.* habitable structure on the roof of a building.

**peo'ple,** *n.* 1. humanity generally. 2. *pl.* peoples. national, cultural, or racial group.

**pep,** *Informal, n.* energy, vigor.

**pep'per,** *n.* 1. pungent condiment from an East Indian plant. 2. hot or mild fruit used as a condiment vegetable.

**per,** *prep.* through; by means of; according to.

**per·ceive'',** *v.t.* 1. become aware of. 2. apprehend or understand. —**per·ceiv'a·ble,** or **per·cep'ti·ble,** *adj.* —**per·cep'tion,** *n.*

**per·cent',** *n.* part in a hundred.

**per·cent'age,** *n.* proportion per hundred.

**per·cep'tive,** *adj.* understanding; discerning.

**perch,** *n.* 1. roost for birds. 2. fresh-water food fish. —*v.t., v.i.* 3. set or rest as on a perch.

**per'co·late'',** *v.t., v.i.* filter.

**per·emp'to·ry,** *adj.* giving no opportunity to refuse or deny.

**pe·ren'ni·al,** *adj.* 1. enduring. 2. lasting more than two years. —*n.* 3. plant growing every year.

**per'fect,** *adj.* (par'fəkt) 1. flawless and complete. 2. *Grammar.* denoting completed action. —*v.t.* (parfekt') 3. make perfect. —**per·fec'tion,** *n.*

**per'fo·rate'',** *v.t.* pierce through.

**per·form',** *v.t.* 1. carry out; execute. —*v.i.* 2. appear in a play, concert, etc. —**per·form'ance,** *n.* —**per·form'er,** *n.*

**per·fume'** *n.* sweet odor; fragrance.

**per·func'to·ry,** *adj.* routine and unenthusiastic.

**per'haps',** *adv.* maybe, possibly.

**per'il,** *n.* 1. danger. 2. source of danger.

**pe·rim'e·ter,** *n.* outer boundary.

**pe'ri·od,** *n.* 1. division or extent of time. 2. punctuation point at the end of a declarative sentence.

**pe''ri·od'ic,** *adj.* intermittently or regularly recurring.

**pe·riph'er·y,** *n., pl.* -eries. 1. boundary of a rounded figure. 2. outer limits; border.

**per·ish,** *v.i.* 1. die, esp. from privation or violence. 2. decay. —**per'ish·a·ble,** *adj.*

**per'jure,** *v.t.* make guilty of perjury. —**per'jur·er,** *n.* —**per'jured,** *adj.*

**per'ju·ry,** *n., pl.* -ries 1. lying under oath. 2. lie so uttered.

**per'ma·nent,** *adj.* existing always.

**per·mit',** *v.t.* 1. allow. —*n.* (par'mit) 2. written permission; license. —**per·mis'sion,** *n.* —**per·mis'si·ble,** *adj.*

**per'pen·dic'u·lar,** *adj.* vertical.

**per'pe·trate'',** *v.t.* commit; be guilty of.

**per·pet'u·al,** *adj.* permanent.

**per·plex',** *v.t.* bewilder. —**per·plex'i·ty,** *n.*

**per'se·cute'',** *v.t.* continually harass or oppress. —**per''se·cu'tion,** *n.*

**per''se·vere'',** *v.t.* persist in spite of obstacles. —**per''se·ver'ance,** *n.*

**P R**

**per·sist'**, v.i. 1. continue resolutely. 2. last; endure. —**per·sist'ent**, adj.

**per'son**, n. human being; individual.

**per'son·al**, adj. pertaining to one individual.

**per''son·al'i·ty**, n., pl. -ties. distinctive personal character.

**per'son·nel'**, n. employees of an organization.

**per·spec'tive**, n. 1. technique of three-dimensional representation.

**per·spire'**, v.i. sweat.

**per·suade'**, v.t. prevail on by argument. —**per·sua'sive**, adj.

**per·sua'sion**, n. process or act of persuading.

**per·tain'**, v.i. have reference to; relate.

**per'ti·nent**, adj. relevant; applicable.

**per·turb'**, v.t. greatly disturb in mind; upset.

**per·vade'**, v.t. extend or spread throughout; permeate.

**per·verse'**, adj. 1. abnormal; corrupt. 2. stubbornly contrary; obstinate.

**per·vert'**, n. 1. perverted person, esp. sexually. —v.t. 2. deviate from the proper or right course of action. —**per·ver'sion**, n.

**pes'si·mism'**, n. disposition toward the least favorable interpretation or expectation.

**pest**, n. troublesome person or thing; nuisance.

**pes'ter**, v.t. annoy.

**pes'ti·lence**, n. deadly epidemic or disease; plague.

**pet**, n. 1. tamed animal kept for pleasure. 2. darling; favorite. —v.t. 3. stroke or fondle affectionately.

**pet'al**, n. colored leaf of a flower.

**pe·ti'tion**, n. request or entreaty, esp. when written.

**pet'ri·fy'**, v.t. 1. turn into stone; stiffen. 2. paralyze or stupefy with horror, wonder, etc.

**pe·tro'le·um**, n. natural oily liquid found underground.

**pet'ti·coat''**, n. skirt worn under a dress.

**pet'ty**, adj., -tier, -tiest. 1. of little importance; trivial. 2. narrow-minded; mean.

**pet'u·lant**, adj. marked by impatient irritation; irritable, peevish.

**pew**, n. enclosed church bench.

**phan'tom**, n. insubstantial image; dreamlike apparition.

**phar''ma·ceu'ti·cal**, adj. of or pertaining to pharmacy. Also, **phar''ma·ceu'tic**.

**phar'ma·cy**, n., pl. -cies. 1. practice of preparing medicines. 2. drug store. —**phar'ma·cist**, n.

**phase**, n. stage of a process.

**pheas'ant**, n. large, long-tailed, brightly colored game bird.

**phe·nom'e·nal**, adj. amazing.

**phe·nom'e·non**, n., pl. -na, -nons. apparent occurrence, circumstance, or fact.

**phi·lan'thro·py**, n., pl. -pies. 1. love of mankind. 2. charitable act, work, or organization.

**phi·lat'e·ly**, n. collection and study of postage stamps.

**phi·los'o·pher**, n. 1. reflective thinker; 2. scholar trained in philosophy. 3. person who meets difficulties calmly.

**phi·los'o·phy**, n., pl. -hies. study of the fundamental truths of life and the universe. —**phil''o·soph'i·cal, phil''o·soph'ic**, adj.

**phleg·ma'tic**, adj. stolid, impassive; apathetic.

**phlegm**, (flem), n. thick mucus secreted in the nose and throat.

**pho·bi·a**, n. persistent and irrational morbid fear.

**phone**, n. telephone.

**pho·net'ics**, n. study of speech sounds. —**pho·net'ic**, adj.

**pho'no·graph''**, n. machine for playing records.

**pho'ny**, Informal. n. fake person or thing.

**phos'pho·rus**, n. solid nonmetallic element found in bones, nerves, etc.

**pho'to·graph''**, n. picture taken by photography. —**pho·tog'ra·pher**, n.

**pho·tog'ra·phy**, n. process of producing images on treated surfaces by the action of light.

**pho'to·syn'the·sis**, n. process by which chlorophyll-containing plants exposed to sunlight produce carbohydrates.

**phrase**, n. 1. sequence of words conveying a thought. —v.t. 2. express in a certain way.

**phys'i·cal**, adj. 1. pertaining to the body. 2. pertaining to matter or the material world.

**phy·si'cian**, n. medical doctor.

**phys'ics**, *n.* science dealing with motion, matter, energy, and force.

**phys''i·ol'o·gy**, *n.* science of the functioning of living matter and beings.

**phys''i·o·ther'a·py**, *n.* treatment of disease by physical means, e.g. exercise, massage, etc.

**phy·sique'** (fa zēk'), *n.* physical constitution of the body; build.

**pi·an'o**, *n., pl.* **-anos.** percussive, musical keyboard instrument with steel strings struck by hammers. Also, **pi·an''o·for'te.** —**pi·an'ist**, *n.*

**pi·az'za**, *n.* veranda or porch.

**sixth of an inch.**

**pic'co·lo**, *n., pl.* **-los**, small shrill flute.

**pick**, *v.t.* 1. choose or select. 2. gather, e.g. flowers. —*n.* 3. choice; selection. 4. Also, **pick'ax, pick'axe**, sharp tool for breaking rock.

**pick'et**, *n.* 1. protestor stationed by a striking labor union. 2. pointed fence with pickets. —*v.i.* 3. serve as a picket.

**pick'le**, *n.* cucumber cured in spiced vinegar.

**pick'pock''et**, *n.* thief who steals from pockets.

**pic'nic**, *n.* outing with an outdoor meal.

**pic'ture**, *n.* 1. painting, drawing, photograph, etc. —*v.t.* 2. conceive; visualize.

**pic''tur·esque'**, *adj.* 1. charming; quaint. 2. striking; vivid.

**pie**, *n.* baked dish of pastry crust and filling, e.g. meat, fruit, etc.

**piece**, *n.* part or single portion.

**pier**, *n.* 1. massive support. 2. structure loading and unloading vessels.

**pierce**, 1. penetrate into or through. 2. make a hole into.

**pi'e·ty**, *n.* religious dutifulness; devoutness.

**pig**, *n.* swine, esp. young.

**pi'geon**, *n.* short- legged, stout-bodied bird.

**pig'ment**, *n.* coloring matter. —**pig''men·ta'tion**, *n.*

**pile**, *n.* 1. heap. 2. support driven into the ground.

**pil'fer**, *v.i., v.t.* steal.

**pil'grim**, *n.* traveler in foreign lands, esp. to a holy place. —**pil'grim·age**, *n.*

**pill**, *n.* medicine in tablet or capsule form.

**pil'lage**, *v.t.* loot; plunder.

**pil'lar**, *n.* masonry column.

**pil'low**, *n.* cushion filled with feathers, etc. for support, esp. of the head. —**pil'low·case''**, *n.*

**pi'lot**, *n.* person who guides a ship or airplane.

**pim'ple**, *n.* small, inflamed swelling on the skin.

**pin**, *n.* 1. slender, pointed fastener. —*v.t.* 2. fasten with a pin.

**pin'cers**, *n.* gripping tool with two handles.

**pinch**, *v.t.* 1. squeeze, e.g. with the thumb and forefinger. —*n.* 2. act or instance of pinching. 3. tiny amount.

**pine**, *v.i.* 1. yearn, esp. painfully. —*n.* 2. cone-bearing evergreen tree with needle-like leaves.

**pine'ap''ple**, *n.* tropical plant with a juicy, edible fruit.

**pink**, *n.* light red.

**pin'na·cle**, *n.* highest part or position.

**pint**, *n.* 1. unit of liquid measure equal to 16 fluid ounces or half a quart. 2. unit of dry measure equal to half a quart.

**pi''o·neer'**, *n.* early settler or adventurer.

**pi'ous**, *adj.* devout.

**pipe**, *n.* 1. tube for carrying gas, water, etc. 2. tube with a bowl at one end for smoking tobacco.

**pi·quant'** (pē'kant), *adj.* 1. pleasantly sharp; pungent. 2. provocative; charming.

**pique**, *n.* irritation; resentment.

**pi'ra·cy**, *n., pl.* **-cies.** robbery at sea or in the air.

**pis'tol**, *n.* small hand-carried firearm.

**pis'ton**, *n.* reciprocating disk moved by the pressure of steam, combustion gas, etc. in a cylinder.

**pit**, *n.* 1. hole in the ground. 2. stone or seed of a fruit.

**pitch**, *v.t.* 1. set up, as a tent. 2. throw or toss. —*n.* 3. musical tone. 4. sticky substance from coal tar or pine bark. 5. act or instance of pitching.

**pitch'er**, *n.* 1. spouted container for liquids. 2. one who pitches.

**pitch'fork''**, *n.* large, sharp-pointed fork for pitching hay.

**pit'fall''**, *n.* snare; hidden difficulty.

**pit'i·ful**, *adj.* feeling pity.

**pi·tu'i·tar'y**, *n.* pertaining to a gland at the base of the brain.

**P R**

**pity,** n. sympathy for wretchedness. —pit'i·less, adj.

**piv'ot,** n. point or object for turning.

**plac'ard,** n. posted public notice.

**pla'cate,** v.t. appease; pacify.

**place,** n. 1. particular point in space. —v.t. 2. put in a place.

**plac'id,** adj. serene; peaceful.

**pla'gi·a·rize''**, v.t. appropriate wrongly, as another's writings.

**plague,** n. pestilence.

**plain,** adj. 1. evident; obvious. 2. simple, uncomplicated. —n. 3. flat, open area or space of ground. —plain'ly, adv.

**plain'tiff,** n. complaining party in a civil case.

**plain'tive,** adj. melancholy, sad.

**plan,** n. 1. drawing or diagram. 2. intended scheme or method. —v.t. 3. make a plan of.

**plane,** n. 1. flat surface. 2. airplane. 3. bladed tool for smoothing wood. —v.t. 4. smooth or shape with a plane.

**plan'et,** n. solid celestial body that revolves around the sun. —plan'e·tar''y, n.

**plan''e·tar'i·um,** n. optical device which projects images of celestial bodies on a dome.

**plank,** n. long slab of lumber.

**plant,** n. 1. any of the vegetable group of organisms. 2. buildings and equipment of a business. —v.t. 3. put in the ground to grow. 4. put plants in.

**plan·ta'tion,** n. estate esp. for farming, etc.

**plas'ma,** n. liquid element of blood or lymph.

**plas'ter,** n. composition applied to walls, etc.

**plas'tic,** n. molded synthetic material. —adj. 2. capable of being molded.

**plate,** n. 1. thin, flat piece of material. 2. shallow dish from which food is served and eaten.

**pla·teau',** n. large, raised plain.

**plat'form,** n. raised floor area.

**plat'i·num,** n. valuable, silver-white metallic element.

**plat'i·tude'',** n. trite, pompous, or self-righteous remark.

**pla·toon',** n. small military unit.

**plat'ter,** n. large, shallow serving dish.

**plau'si·ble,** adj. seemingly true or believable.

**play,** n. 1. dramatic composition. 2. recreational activity. —v.t. 3. participate in a play or game. —play'er, n. —play'ful, adj.

**play'thing,** n. toy.

**plea,** n. 1. appeal. 2. acknowledgment of denial of guilt.

**plead,** v.i. 1. appeal earnestly. 2. make allegations in court.

**pleas'ant,** adj. agreeable; pleasing.

**pleas'an·try,** n., pl. -tries, humorous or agreeable remark.

**please,** v.t. 1. give satisfaction or pleasure to. —interj. 2. will you kindly? —pleas'ing·ly, adv.

**pleas'ure,** n. enjoyment. —pleas'ur·a·ble, adj.

**pleat,** n. double fold in cloth.

**pleb''i·scite'',** n. direct vote by the people.

**pledge,** n. 1. solemn promise or oath. —v.t. 2. bind or vow by a pledge.

**plen'ty,** n. abundant supply. —plen'te·ous, plen'ti·ful, adj.

**pli'a·ble,** adj. 1. flexible or easily bent. 2. easily influenced; adaptable. —pli''a·bil'i·ty, n.

**pli'ant,** adj. pliable. —pli'an·cy, n.

**pli'ers,** n., pl. small pincers for grabbing, bending, etc.

**plight,** n. predicament.

**plod,** v.i. walk slowly or heavily.

**plot,** n. 1. secret scheme. 2. outline of a novel, etc. 3. piece of land. —v.t. 4. plan secretly.

**plow,** n. 1. implement for dividing soil. —v.t. 2. turn or furrow with or as with a plow. Also, **plough.**

**pluck,** v.t. 1. pull things from. 2. pull suddenly or forcefully. —n. 3. courage.

**plug,** n. 1. object for stopping a hole. —v.t. 2. stop or close with a plug; insert.

**plum,** n. sweet, juicy fruit.

**plum'age,** n. feathers of a bird; finery, esp. in dress.

**plumb'ing,** n. system of water pipes. —plumb'er, n.

**plume,** n. 1. feather, esp. a large, conspicuous one. 2. ornamental tuft.

**plump,** adj. fat; chubby.

**plun'der,** v.t. rob or pillage. —n. 2. act or instance of plundering. 3. loot; spoils.

**plunge,** v.i. 1. rush; dash. 2. pitch forward.

**plu'ral,** adj. denoting more than one.

**plus,** prep. increased by.

**plu·toc'ra·cy**, *n.*, *pl.* -cies, 1. rule by or power of the wealthy. 2. controlling wealthy group. —**plu'to·crat"**, *n.*

**ply'wood**, *n.* sheeting of thin plies of wood glued together.

**pneu·mat'ic** (nōō mat'ik), *adj.* pertaining to, or using air or wind.

**pneu·mo'nia** (nōō mō'nyə), *n.* inflamed lung disease.

**poach**, *v.i.* 1. trespass to hunt or fish illegally. —*v.t.* 2. cook in hot but not boiling water.

**pock'et**, *n.* pouch in a garment.

**pock'et·book"**, *n.* purse; handbag.

**pod**, *n.* vegetable seed covering.

**po·di'a·try**, *n.* medical treatment of the foot. —**po·di'a·trist**, *n.*

**po'di·um**, *n.* small platform.

**po'em**, *n.* composition in verse.

**po'et·ry**, *n.* rhythmical, verse composition. —**po'et**, *fem.*, —**po'et·ess**, *n.* —**po·et'ic**, **po·et'i·cal**, *adj.*

**poign'ant** (poin'yənt), *adj.* deeply moving. —**poign'an·cy**, *n.*

**poin·set'ti·a**, *n.* tropical plant with scarlet flowers.

**point**, *n.* 1. dot. —*v.i.* 2. indicate a direction. —*v.t.* 3. direct or turn. —**point'less**, *adj.*

**point'er**, *n.* 1. something that points or indicates. 2. breed of hunting dog.

**poise**, *n.* balance; composure.

**poi'son**, *n.* 1. substance that kills or harms. —*v.t.* 2. administer poison to. —**poi'son·ous**, *adj.*

**poke**, *v.i.*, *v.t.*, *n.* thrust.

**po'lar**, *adj.* pertaining to a pole of the earth, a magnet, etc.

**pole**, *n.* 1. long, slender, round object. 2. end of an axis. 3. terminal of a battery. 4. areas where magnetism is concentrated.

**pole'cat"**, *n.* skunk.

**po·lem'ics**, *n.* art of argument. —**po·lem'ic**, *adj.*

**po·lice'**, *n.* 1. governmental organization for enforcing the law. —*v.t.* 2. control or regulate. —**po·lice'man**, *fem.*, —**po·lice'wom"an**, *n.*

**pol'i·cy**, *n.*, *pl.* -cies, 1. course of principle action. 2. insurance contract.

**pol'i·o·my"e·li'tis**, *n.* infantile spinal paralysis. Also, **po'li·o**.

**pol'ish**, *v.t.* 1. make smooth and glossy. —*n.* 2. polishing material.

**po·lite'**, *adj.* 1. marked by good

manners. 2. cultivated. —**po·lite'ness**, *n.*

**pol'i·tic**, *adj.* 1. expedient. 2. political.

**pol'i·tics**, *n.* 1. theory and conduct of government. 2. political affairs and methods. —**po·lit'i·cal**, *adj.* —**pol"i·ti'cian**, *n.*

**poll**, *n.* 1. casting of votes. —*v.t.* 2. receive votes. 3. question regarding opinions.

**pol'len**, *n.* spores of a seed plant.

**pol·lute'**, *v.t.* make impure; contaminate. —**pol·lu'tion**, *n.*

**pol'y·an'dry**, *n.* marriage to more than one husband at a time.

**po·lyg'a·my**, *n.* marriage to more than one spouse at a time.

**pol'y·glot"**, *adj.* 1. knowing a number of languages. 2. made up of several languages.

**pol'y·gon"**, *n.* closed plane figures with three or more sides. —**po·lyg'o·nal**, *adj.*

**pol'y·graph**, *n.* a lie detector.

**pol"y·he'dron**, *n.*, *pl.* -drons, -dra, closed solid figure.

**pomp**, *n.* stately display.

**pomp'ous**, *adj.* 1. pretentiously self-important; ostentatious. 2. excessively dignified.

**pon'cho**, *n.*, *pl.* -chos, *n.* blanket-like cloak with an opening for the head.

**pond**, *n.* small body of water.

**pon'der**, *v.t.* consider deeply.

**pon'der·ous**, *adj.* 1. heavy. 2. lacking grace.

**pon'tiff**, *n.* bishop or head priest, esp. a pope. —**pon·tif'i·cal**, *adj.*

**pon·tif'i·cate**, *v.i.* speak dogmatically.

**pon·toon'**, *n.* flat-bottomed boat used esp. in construction.

**po'ny**, *n.*, *pl.* -nies. young horse.

**pool**, *n.* 1. small, still body of fresh water. 2. group of available workers, automobiles, etc. —*v.t.* 3. put into a common fund or effort.

**poor**, *adj.* having little money.

**pop**, *v.i.*, *v.t.* 1. burst with a quick, explosive sound. —*v.i.* 2. bulge, as the eyes. —*n.* 3. sound of popping.

**pope**, *n. Often cap.* head of the Roman Catholic Church.

**pop'lar**, *n.* any of various quick-growing trees.

**pop'u·lace**, *n.* people; general public.

**pop'u·lar**, *adj.* 1. pertaining to

the general public. 2. widely liked or approved.

**pop'u·la'tion**, *n.* 1. number of people. 2. body of inhabitants.

**por'ce·lain**, *n.* shiny ceramic ware.

**porch**, *n.* open, often roofed, appendage to a building; veranda.

**por·cine** (por'sin), *adj.* of or suggesting swine.

**por'cu·pine''**, *n.* rodent covered with stiff, sharp quills.

**pore**, *n.* minute opening in the skin.

**pork**, *n.* flesh of swine used as food.

**por·nog'ra·phy**, *n.* erotic writing or art intended for sexual excitement. —**por''no·graph'ic**, *adj.*

**po'rous**, *adj.* permeable to liquids and air.

**por'ridge**, *n.* cereal boiled in milk or water.

**port**, *n.* 1. loading and unloading place for ships and aircraft. 2. when facing the bow, the left side of a ship. 3. a sweet, red wine. 4. (computers) point at which peripheral components can be connected.

**port'a·ble**, *adj.* easily carried; small.

**por'tal**, *n.* gate or door.

**por·tend'**, *v.t.* 1. indicate in advance. 2. indicate; signify.

**por'tent**, *n.* 1. omen. 2. ominous significance.

**por'ter**, *n.* 1. doorman. 2. baggage carrier.

**port'fo''li·o''**, *n.* portable case for documents.

**port'hole''**, *n.* window, esp. round, in the side of a plane or ship.

**por'ti·co''**, *n., pl.* -coes or -cos. roof supported by a colonnade; porch.

**por'tion**, *n.* part or share.

**port'ly**, *adj.* fat; chubby.

**por'trait**, *n.* picture or description of a person. —**por'trai·ture**, *n.*

**por·tray'**, *v.t.* 1. depict or represent in a portrait. 2. represent dramatically. —**por·tray'al**, *n.*

**pose**, *v.i.* 1. hold a position. 2. assume a character or attitude. —*n.* 3. assumed character. —**pos'er**, *n.*

**po·si'tion**, *n.* location.

**pos'i·tive**, *adj.* affirmative.

**pos·sess'**, *v.t.* 1. have or own. 2. dominate. —**pos·ses'sive**, *adj.* —**pos·ses'sion**, *n.* —**pos·ses'sor**, *n.*

**pos'si·ble**, *adj.* capable of existing or happening.

**post**, *n.* 1. upright column or pole. 2. appointed job, station or task. 3. permanent military station. —*v.t.* 4. put up, as a public announcement. 5. assign to a place. 6. enter in a ledger. 7. mail.

**post'age**, *n.* 1. charge for mailing. 2. stamps, etc. for mailing.

**post'al**, *adj.* pertaining to mail.

**post'card'**, *n.* message card mailed without an envelope.

**post'er**, *n.* public advertisement.

**pos·te'ri·or**, *adj.* 1. situated behind. 2. later in time. —*n.* 3. buttocks, rump.

**pos·ter'i·ty**, *n.* 1. descendants. 2. succeeding or future generations.

**post'mark'**, *n.* postal mark indicating a time and place of reception by a post office.

**post'of''fice**, *n.* government agency that handles mail.

**post'paid'**, *adj., adv.* with postage prepaid.

**post·pone'**, *v.t.* delay, as action.

**post'script'**, *n.* note added to a finished letter.

**pos'ture**, *n.* position of the body.

**pot**, *n.* deep, round container.

**po·tas'si·um**, *n.* silver, metallic, chemical element used in glass, fertilizer, etc.

**po·ta'to**, *n., pl.* -toes. edible tuber of a common vegetable plant.

**po'tent**, *adj.* 1. powerful. 2. sexually capable.

**po·ten'tial**, *adj.* 1. possible; capable of being realized. —*n.* 2. possible ability.

**po'tion**, *n.* drink, esp. a medicinal one.

**pot·pour·ri** (pō''pə rē'), *n.* miscellaneous collection.

**pot'ter·y**, *n.* dishes, pots, mugs, etc. made of baked clay.

**pouch**, *n.* 1. sack or bag. 2. baglike part of a marsupial.

**poul'try**, *n.* domestic fowl, e.g. chicken.

**pounce**, *v.i.* swoop down suddenly.

**pound**, *n.* unit of avoirdupois weight equal to 16 ounces or troy weight equal to 12 ounces.

**pour**, *v.t.* cause to flow.

**pout**, *v.i.* look sullen; act hurt.

**pov'er·ty**, *n.* lack of money.

**pow'der**, *n.* 1. dry substance of very fine particles. —*v.t.* 2. apply powder to. —**pow'der·y**, *adj.*

**pow'er**, *n.* 1. ability to act. 2. personal ability. —**pow'er·ful**, *adj.* —**pow'er·ful·ly**, *adv.* —**pow'er·less**, *adj.*

**prac'ti·ca·ble**, *adj.* feasible.

**prac'ti·cal**, *adj.* 1. pertaining to practice. 2. useful. 3. aware of realities. 4. virtual.

**prac'tice**, *n.* 1. custom. 2. actual performance. 3. repeated exercise. 4. professional activity. —*v.i.*, *v.t.* 5. Also, **prac'tise**, perform habitually or repeatedly.

**prac'ti·tion·er**, *n.* person who practices a profession.

**prai'rie**, *n.* flat, treeless, rolling grassland.

**praise**, *n.* 1. expressed approval. —*v.t.* 2. express approval of.

**prance**, *v.i.* 1. spring on the hind legs. 2. swagger.

**prank**, *n.* mischievous trick.

**pray**, *v.i.* 1. petition or worship a divinity. —*v.t.* 2. implore. 3. ask earnestly for.

**prayer**, *n.* 1. act of addressing a divinity. 2. earnest request.

**preach**, *v.t.* 1. advocate. —*v.i.* 2. give a sermon. —**preach'er**, *n.*

**pre·car'i·ous**, *adj.* risky. —**pre·car'i·ous·ly**, *adv.*

**pre·cau'tion**, *n.* caution beforehand. —**pre·cau'tion·ar'y**, *adj.*

**pre·cede'**, *v.i.*, *v.t.* 1. go before. —**pre·ced'ence**, *n.*

**prec'e·dent**, *n.* past occurrence or principle used as an example or justification.

**pre'cept**, *n.* principle or rule of conduct.

**pre'cinct**, *n.* administrative district.

**pre'cious**, *adj.* 1. valuable. 2. cherished. 3. overly refined.

**prec'i·pice**, *n.* steep cliff.

**pre·cip'i·tate**, *v.t.* 1. throw down violently. 2. hasten in occurring. —*adj.* 3. hasty; rash; headlong. —**pre·cip'i·ta'tion**, *n.*

**pre·cip'i·tous**, *adj.* 1. steep. 2. precipitate.

**pre·cise'**, *adj.* 1. specific. 2. scrupulous; strict. —**pre·ci'sion**, *n.*

**pre·clude'**, *v.t.* exclude the possibility of.

**pre·co'cious**, *adj.* advanced in development, esp. of the mind. —**pre·coc'i·ty**, *n.*

**pre·cur'sor**, *n.* 1. forerunner. 2. harbinger.

**pred''e·ces'sor**, *n.* person or thing that precedes another.

**pre·des''ti·na'tion**, *n.* determination in advance of actions and consequences; fate.

**pre·dic'a·ment**, *n.* difficult or dangerous situation.

**pred·i·cate**, *v.t.* (pred'ə kāt'') 1. declare; assume. 2. base on an assumption. —*n.* (pred'ək ət) 3. *Grammar.* part sentence or clause expressing what is said of its subject.

**pre·dict'**, *v.t.*, tell in advance. —**pre·dic'tion**, *n.*

**pre·dom'i·nate**, *v.i.* 1. be stronger or more numerous. —*v.t.* 2. master. —**pre·dom'i·nance**, *n.* —**pre·dom'i·nant**, *adj.*

**pre·em'i·nent**, *adj.* outstanding; superior.

**pre·fab'ri·cate'**, *v.t.* assemble from large, previously finished, components.

**pre'face**, *n.* introductory text.

**pre·fer'**, *v.t.* like better or favor more than others. —**pref'er·a·ble**, *adj.* —**pref'er·a·bly**, *adv.* —**pref'er·ence**, *n.*

**pre'fix**, *n.* qualifying beginning of a word.

**preg'nant**, *adj.* being with child. —**preg'nan·cy**, *n.*

**pre''his·tor'ic**, *adj.* pertaining to the time before recorded history.

**prej'u·dice**, *n.* 1. opinion without adequate basis. —*v.t.* 2. influence or affect with prejudice. —**prej'u·di'cial**, *adj.*

**pre·lim'i·nar'y**, *adj.* introductory.

**prel'ude**, *n.* preliminary to a larger work.

**pre'ma·ture''**, *adj.* 1. born or happening too early. 2. overly hasty.

**pre·med'i''tate**, *v.i.*, *v.t.* plan or consider beforehand.

**pre·miere** (pri mîr'), *n.* first public performance.

**pre·mier** (pri mîr'), *n.* chief officer, esp. a prime minister.

**prem'ise**, *n.* basis of an argument or conclusion.

**pre'mi·um**, *n.* 1. prize. 2. high evaluation. 3. bonus. 4. cost of an insurance policy.

**pre''mo·ni'tion**, *n.* foreboding; presentiment.

**pre·na'tal**, *adj.* prior to birth.

**pre·oc'cu·pied'**, *adj.* completely engrossed. —**pre·oc'cu·py'**, *v.t.* —**pre·oc''cu·pa'tion**, *n.*

**pre·pare'**, *v.t.* 1. put in readiness.

**P R**

2. manufacture. —*v.i.* 3. get or put oneself in readiness. —**prep′·a·ra′tion**, *n.* —**pre·par′a·to′·ry**, *adj.*

**pre·pon′der·ant**, *adj.* superior in numbers, strength, etc.

**prep′o·si′tion**, *n.* word or words placed before a noun or adjective to form a modifying phrase.

**pre″pos·sess′ing**, *adj.* impressing favorably.

**pre·pos′ter·ous**, *adj.* absurd.

**pre·req′ui·site**, *n.* something required beforehand; condition.

**pre·rog′a·tive**, *n.* special power, right, or privilege.

**pre·scribe′**, *v.t.* order for use or adoption. —**pre·scrip′tion**, *n.*

**pres′ence**, *n.* 1. state of being present. 2. vicinity or view.

**pres·ent**, *adj.* (prez′ənt) 1. being or happening now. —*n.* 2. present time. 3. present tense. 4. gift. —*v.t.* (pri zent′) 5. give, bring, or offer. 6. introduce or make public. —**pres″en·ta′tion**, *n.*

**pre·sent′a·ble**, *adj.* suitable in appearance, manners, etc.

**pres′ent·ly**, *adv.* 1. soon. 2. at present; now.

**pre·serve′**, *v.t.* 1. keep in good condition. 2. prepare for storage, as food. —**pres″er·va′tion**, *n.* —**pre·serv′a·tive**, *n.*

**pre·side′**, *v.i.* act as chairman; be at the head of.

**pres′i·dent**, *n.* 1. chief officer of a corporation. 2. highest elected official. —**pres′i·den·cy**, *n.* —**pres″i·den′tial**, *adj.*

**press**, *v.t.* 1. act against with weight or force. 2. iron, as clothing. —*n.* 3. journalism. 4. machine for printing.

**press′ing**, *adj.* urgent.

**pres′sure**, *n.* 1. exertion of force. 2. compulsion toward a certain action or decision. 3. urgency.

**pres·tige′** (pres tēzh′), *n.* respected standing or reputation.

**pre·sume′**, *v.t.* 1. take for granted. —*v.i.* 2. act with unwarranted boldness.

**pre·sump′tion**, *n.* 1. assumption. 2. unwarranted boldness. —**pre·sump′tu·ous**, *adj.*

**pre″sup·pose′**, *v.t.* 1. suppose beforehand. 2. require beforehand as a condition.

**pre·tend′**, *v.t.* 1. imagine as a fantasy. 2. profess or appear falsely.

**pre·ten′sion**, *n.* 1. ostentation; self-importance. 2. act or instance of alleging or pretending. —**pre·ten′tious·ly**, *adv.*

**pre′text**, *n.* ostensible or false reason; excuse.

**pret′ty**, *adj.* -tier, -tiest, *adj.* 1. pleasingly attractive. —*adv.* 2. moderately. —**pret′ti·fy″**, *v.t.* —**pret′ti·ly**, *adv.* —**pret′ti·ness**, *n.*

**pre·vail′**, *v.i.* 1. be widespread. 2. prove superior in force, etc. 3. succeed in persuasion. —**prev′a·lent**, *adj.*

**pre·vent′**, *v.t.* stop; hinder. —**pre·ven′tion**, *n.* —**pre·ven′tive**, *adj.*

**pre′view″**, *n.* 1. advance showing, as of a motion picture. —*v.t.* 2. show or view in advance.

**pre′vi·ous**, *adj.* happening or going earlier.

**prey**, *n.* 1. animal hunted for food. 2. victim.

**price**, *n.* amount for which something is sold.

**price′less**, *adj.* invaluable; beyond any price.

**prick**, —*v.t.* pierce or stab lightly.

**pride**, *n.* 1. high opinion of one's worth. 2. self-respect.

**priest**, *n.* 1. clergyman; person authorized to perform religious ceremonies. 2. Also, *fem.,* **priest′-ess**, one who performs religious rites.

**prim**, *adj.* rigidly proper.

**pri′ma·ry**, *adj.* 1. first in rank or importance. 2. first in time. —**pri·mar′i·ly**, *adv.*

**prime**, *adj.* 1. first in rank, value, etc. 2. original. —*n.* 3. best part or period.

**prim′i·tive**, *adj.* 1. earliest. 2. simple; crude.

**prince**, *n.* 1. son of royalty. 2. ruler. Also, *fem.,* **prin′cess**.

**prin′ci·pal**, *adj.* 1. most important. —*n.* 2. head of a school.

**prin′ci·ple**, *n.* 1. rule of action, conduct, or belief. 2. adherence to rules of conduct. 3. scientific law.

**print**, *v.t.* 1. reproduce from inked type. —*n.* 2. state of being printed. 3. printed picture. —**print′er**, *n.*

**print′er**, *n.* 1. one who prints. 2. (computers) device for transcribing data to paper.

**print′out**, *n.,v.* (computers) data transcribed onto paper.

**pri′or**, *adj.* 1. earlier. —*adv.* 2. previously. —*n.* 3. Also, *fem.,*

**pri'or·ess**, head of a religious house. —**pri'o·ry**, *n.*

**pri·or'i·ty**, *n., pl.* **-ties.** 1. state of being earlier in time. 2. precedence in order, privilege, etc.

**prism**, *n.* three-sided glass object that breaks light into its spectrum.

**pris'on**, *n.* jail; building for confining criminals. —**pris'on·er**, *n.*

**pri'vate**, *adj.* 1. belonging to a specific person or group. 2. confidential. —*n.* 3. lowest soldier. —**pri'va·cy**, *n.*

**priv'i·lege**, *n.* special advantage.

**priv'y**, *adj.* 1. admitted to a secret. 2. private; personal. —*n.* 3. outhouse; outdoor toilet.

**prize**, *n.* 1. reward for victory. —*v.t.* 2. value or esteem highly.

**prob'a·ble**, *adj.* 1. likely to happen, etc. 2. giving ground for belief. —**prob''a·bil'i·ty**, *n.*

**pro·ba'tion**, *n.* act or instance of testing.

**probe**, *v.t.* search into thoroughly.

**prob'lem**, *n.* question or situation involving difficulty.

**pro·ceed'**, *v.i.* 1. go onward. 2. continue an action. 3. issue forth. —*n.* 4. proceeds, revenue from selling. —**pro·ce'dure**, *n.*

**proc'ess**, *n.* series of actions ending in a result.

**pro·ces'sion**, *n.* parade.

**pro-choice'**, *adj.* supporting legalized abortion.

**pro·claim'**, *v.t.* 1. announce publicly. 2. reveal conspicuously. —**proc''la·ma'tion**, *n.*

**pro·cras'ti·nate''**, *v.i., v.t.* put off to another time. —**pro·cras''ti·na'tion**, *n.*

**pro·cure'**, 1. obtain. 2. bring about.

**prod**, *v.t.* 1. poke; jab. 2. goad; incite.

**prod'i·gy**, *n., pl.* **-gies.** very talented person.

**pro·duce'**, *v.t.* 1. bring into existence. 2. exhibit. —**pro·duc'tion**, *n.* —**pro·duc'tive**, *adj.*

**prod'uct**, *n.* something produced.

**pro-family**, *adj.* antiabortion; prolife.

**pro·fane'**, *adj.* 1. secular. 2. impure; foul. 3. irreverent; disrespectful. —*v.t.* 4. treat with irreverence.

**pro·fan'i·ty**, *n.* 1. sacrilege. 2. cursing.

**pro·fess'**, *v.t.* 1. claim of oneself.

2. affirm allegiance to or faith in.

**pro·fes'sion**, *n.* 1. learned occupation. 2. act or instance of professing.

**pro·fes'sion·al**, *adj.* 1. pursuing a profession. 2. meeting the standards of a profession. —*n.* 3. professional person. —**pro·fes'sion·al·ly**, *adv.* —**pro·fes'sion·al''ism**, *n.*

**pro·fes'sor**, *n.* college teacher of the highest rank. —**pro''fes·sor'i·al**, *adj.*

**pro·fi'cient**, *adj.* skillful; learned.

**pro'file**, *n.* side view.

**prof'it**, *n.* 1. net gain from business. —*v.t.* 2. gain a profit. —**prof'it·a·ble**, *adj.*

**prof'li·gate**, *adj.* 1. licentious. 2. extravagant. —*n.* 3. profligate person. —**prof'li·ga·cy**, *n.*

**pro·found'**, *adj.* 1. characterized by deep thought. 2. deeply felt. 3. deep. —**pro·fun'di·ty**, *n.*

**pro·fuse'**, *adj.* 1. plentiful. 2. lavish.

**prog'e·ny**, *n., pl.* **-nies.** children; descendants.

**pro''gram**, *n.* 1. plan, method. 2. list of subjects or events. 3. (computers) a set of instructions to perform specific operations to data. —*v.* 4. create a computer program. —**pro''gram'ming**, *n.*

**prog'ress**, *n.* (prog'res) advancement. —*v.i.* (pro·gres') 2. advance. —**pro·gres'sive**, *adj.*

**pro·hib'it**, *v.t.* 1. forbid. —**pro''hi·bi'tion**, —**pro''hi·bi'tion·ist**, *n.*

**proj·ect**, *n.* (proj'ekt) 1. plan; scheme. —*v.t.* (prō jekt') 2. plan or intend. —*v.i.* 3. protrude. —**pro·jec'tion**, *n.* —**pro·jec'tor**, *n.*

**pro·jec'tile**, *n.* missile from a gun.

**pro·lif'ic**, *adj.* productive.

**pro'logue**, *n.* introduction to a play, novel, etc. Also, **pro'log.**

**pro·long'**, *v.t.* lengthen, esp. in duration.

**prom'i·nent**, *adj.* 1. conspicuous. 2. distinguished.

**pro·mis'cu·ous**, *adj.* indiscriminate.

**prom'ise**, *n.* 1. assurance to do or not to do something. —*v.t.* 2. make a promise.

**pro·mote'**, *v.t.* 1. advance in rank or position. 2. further the growth or progress of. —**pro·mo'ter**, *n.* —**pro·mo'tion**, *n.*

**P**
**R**

**prompt,** *adj.* **1.** ready to act. **2.** quick or punctual.

**pro·mul'gate,** *v.t.* proclaim publicly.

**pro·noun'',** *n.* word used as a substitute for a noun.

**pro·nounce',** *v.t.* utter; deliver.

**pro·nounced',** *adj.* strongly marked or apparent.

**pro·nun''ci·a'tion,** *n.* act or manner of speaking.

**proof,** *n.* **1.** evidence demonstrating a fact. **2.** preliminary printing for inspection.

**prop,** *n.* **1.** rigid support. —*v.t.* **2.** support; strengthen.

**prop''a·gan'da,** *n.* assertions, etc. intended to help or oppose a cause.

**prop'a·gate'',** *v.t., v.i.* **1.** reproduce; breed. —*v.t.* **2.** transmit, as ideas.

**pro·pel'ler,** *n.* screwlike propelling device.

**pro·pen'si·ty,** *n.* inclination; tendency.

**prop'er,** *adj.* suitable.

**prop'er·ty,** *n., pl.* **-ties.** possessions.

**proph·e·sy** (prof'ǝ sī), *v.t.* foretell; predict. —**proph'e·cy,** *n.*

**proph'et,** *n.* **1.** utterer of divine revelations. **2.** person who prophesies the future. Also, *fem.,* **proph'et·ess.** —**pro·phet'ic,** *adj.*

**pro·pi'ti·ate'',** *v.t.* make favorable; appease.

**pro·pi'tious,** *adj.* favorable; auspicious.

**pro·por'tion,** *n.* **1.** quantitative relation. **2.** due relationship. **3.** proportions, dimensions. —**pro·por'tion·al, pro·por'tion·ate,** *adj.*

**pro·pose',** *v.t.* **1.** suggest or offer. —*v.i.* **2.** suggest marriage. —**prop''o·si'tion,** *n.* —**pro·pos'al,** *n.*

**pro·pri'e·tor,** *n.* manager or owner. —**pro·pri'e·tor·ship'',** *n.*

**pro·pri'e·ty,** *n., pl.* **-ties.** respectability.

**pro·pul'sion,** *n.* propelling force.

**pro·sa'ic,** *adj.* commonplace; dull.

**prose,** *n.* ordinary language of speech and writing.

**pros'e·cute'',** *v.t.* **1.** begin legal proceedings against. **2.** continue to completion.

**pros'pect,** *n.* **1.** likelihood, esp. of success. **2.** view. **3.** potential customer or buyer.

**pros'per,** *v.i.* be successful. —**pros·per'i·ty,** *n.* —**pros'per·ous,** *adj.*

**pros'ti·tute'',** *n.* person who engages in sexual intercourse for pay.

**pros'trate,** *v.t.* **1.** lay flat. —*adj.* **2.** lying.

**pro·tect',** *v.t.* defend or preserve. —**pro·tec'tion,** *n.* —**pro·tec'tive,** *adj.* —**pro·tec'tive·ly,** *adv.* —**pro·tec'tor,** *n.*

**pro·tec'tor·ate,** *n.* protection and partial control of one state by another.

**pro·té·gé** (prō'tǝ zhā''), *n.* person under patronage. Also, *fem.,* **pro''té·gée''.**

**pro'te·in,** *n.* nitrogenous compound essential for life processes present in living matter.

**pro'test,** *n.* **1.** objection. —*v.i., v.t.* **2.** make an objection. —*v.t.* **3.** declare solemnly.

**Prot'es·tant,** *n.* western Christian not belonging to the Roman Catholic Church. —**Prot'es·tant·ism'',** *n.*

**pro'to·col,** *n.* code of etiquette, esp. diplomatic.

**pro·trude',** *v.i.* project.

**pro·tu'ber·ant,** *adj.* bulging out.

**proud,** *adj.* **1.** having self-respect. **2.** feeling honored.

**prove,** *v.t.* establish the truth of.

**prov'erb,** *n.* wise popular saying. —**pro·ver'bi·al,** *adj.*

**pro·vide',** *v.t.* **1.** supply; equip. **2.** yield. —*v.i.* **3.** prepare beforehand. —**pro·vid'er,** *n.*

**pro·vid'ed,** *conj.* if; on condition that.

**prov'i·dence,** *n.* **1.** divine care or guidance. **2.** economy.

**prov'ince,** *n.* **1.** administrative district. **2.** personal area of operations or expertise.

**pro·vin'cial,** *adj.* **1.** of a province. **2.** narrow-mindedly local.

**pro·vi'sion,** *n.* **1.** stipulation. **2.** act or instance of providing. **3.** provisions, food supply; goods.

**pro·voke',** *v.t.* **1.** exasperate. **2.** call into being or effect. —**prov''o·ca'tion,** *n.*

**prow'ess,** *n.* extraordinary ability.

**prowl,** *v.i.* roam about or search stealthily.

**prox·im'i·ty,** *n.* nearness.

**prox'y,** *n., pl.* **proxies.** **1.** agent. **2.** authority to act or vote for another.

**prude,** *n.* extremely modest person.

**pru·dence**, *n.* **1.** caution. **2.** practical wisdom. —**pru′dent**, *adj.*

**prune**, *n.* dried plum.

**pru·ri·ent**, *adj.* having lewd thoughts. —**pru′ri·ence**, *n.*

**pry**, *v.i.* **1.** inquire unjustifiably into another's affairs. —*v.t.* **2.** move by leverage.

**psalm** (sahm), *n.* sacred song or poem.

**pseu·do·nym**, *n.* assumed name.

**pseu·do** (sōō′dō), *adj.* false; spurious.

**psy·che·del·ic** (sī″kə del′ik), *adj.* pertaining to intense hallucinatory effects.

**psy·chi·a·try**, *n.* science of healing mental disorders. —**psy·chi′a·trist,** *n.*

**psy′chic,** *n.* **1.** medium or clairvoyant. —*adj.* Also, **psy′chi·cal.** **2.** pertaining to the psyche. **3.** supernatural.

**psy″cho·a·nal′y·sis,** *n.* detailed study and treatment of neuroses.—**psy″cho·an′a·lyst,** *n.*

**psy·chol·o·gy,** *n.* **1.** study of the mind and behavior. **2.** mental and behavioral constitution. —**psy″cho·log′i·cal,** *adj.* —**psy·chol′o·gist,** *n.*

**psy·cho·sis,** *n., pl.* **-ses,** mental disease marked by loss of contact with reality. —**psy·chot′ic,** *n., adj.*

**pto·maine** (tō′mān), *n.* substance produced by bacteria in decaying matter.

**pu·ber·ty** (pyōō′bər tē), *n.* sexual maturity.

**pub·lic,** *adj.* **1.** of or for all people. **2.** known by or knowable to all. —*n.* **3.** people generally.

**pub″li·ca′tion,** *n.* **1.** act or instance of publishing. **2.** published work.

**pub·lic′i·ty,** *n.* **1.** public attention or notice. **2.** material claiming public attention.

**pub·lish,** *v.t.* **1.** print or issue for distribution. **2.** announce publicly. —**pub′lish·er,** *n.*

**pud·ding,** *n.* soft, sweet dessert.

**pud′dle,** *n.* small pool of water.

**pueb·lo** (pweb′lō), *n.* **1.** adobe Indian village of U.S. Southwest. **2.** *Pueblo,* Southwestern U.S. Indian group.

**puff,** *n.* **1.** short quick gust, e.g. of wind. —*v.i.* **2.** blow or breathe in puffs. —*v.t.* **3.** blow or puff on.

**pull,** *v.t.* **1.** move toward or after one. —*v.i.* **2.** attempt to move toward one. —*n.* **3.** act or instance of pulling. **4.** *Informal.* influence.

**pul·ley,** *n., pl.* **-leys.** wheel with a rim grooved for a rope.

**pul·mo·nar′y,** *adj.* of the lungs.

**pulp,** *n.* soft, fleshy material.

**pul·pit,** *n.* raised platform or lectern used by a clergyman.

**pul′sate,** *v.i.* throb; quiver.

**pulse,** *n.* regular throb of the arteries produced by the heart.

**pul′ver·ize,** *v.t.* reduce to powder or dust.

**pump,** *n.* **1.** device for applying force to liquids and gases. —*v.t.* **2.** move with a pump.

**pump′kin,** *n.* large orange fruit that grows on a vine.

**pun,** *n.* play with similar-sounding words with different meanings.

**punch,** *n.* **1.** quick blow, esp. with the fist. **2.** sweet mixed beverage. —*v.t.* **3.** hit. **4.** perforate.

**punc′tu·al,** *adj.* on time; prompt.

**punc·tu·ate′,** *v.t.* mark with commas, periods, etc. —**punc″tu·a′tion,** *n.*

**punc·ture,** *v.t.* **1.** pierce with a pointed object. —*n.* **2.** act or instance of puncturing.

**pun′gent,** *adj.* sharp of taste.

**pun·ish,** *v.t.* **1.** subject to a penalty or revenge. **2.** inflict a penalty for. —**pun′ish·ment,** *n.*

**pu′ny,** *adj.,* **-nier, -niest.** small; slight; weak.

**pup,** *n.* young dog. Also, **pup′py.**

**pu′pil,** *n.* student.

**pup′pet,** *n.* small figure moved by hand or by wires.

**pur·chase,** *v.t.* **1.** buy. —*n.* **2.** act or instance of purchasing. **3.** thing purchased. **4.** leverage.

**pure,** *adj.,* **purer, purest.** unmixed or unpolluted.

**pu·ree** (pyōō rā′), *n.* cooked and sieved food.

**purge,** *v.t.* **1.** cleanse; purify. —*n.* **2.** act or instance of purging. —**pur·ga′tion,** *n.* —**pur′ga·tive,** *adj., n.*

**pu′ri·fy,** *v.t.* make pure.

**pu′ri·tan,** *n.* **1.** member of a strict religious group. **2.** adherent to an unusually strict moral code. —**puri·tan′i·cal,** *adj.*

**pu′ri·ty,** *n.* quality or condition of being pure.

**pur·loin′,** *v.t.* steal.

**pur′ple,** *n.* **1.** bluish-red color. —*adj.* **2.** of the color purple.

P R

**pur·port**, *v.t.* (par''port') 1. claim or profess. 2. express; imply. —*n.* 3. (pər'port) significance.

**pur·pose**, *n.* 1. intention; object. —*v.t.* 2. intend.

**pur'pose·ly**, *adv.* intentionally.

**purse**, *n.* small bag for money.

**pur·sue'**, *v.t.* 1. chase. 2. proceed with.

**pur·suit'**, *n.* 1. act or instance of pursuing. 2. occupation; calling.

**push**, *v.t.* 1. press against to move. —*n.* 2. act or instance of pushing. —**push'er,** *n.*

**put**, *v.t.* 1. carry to a specified place. 2. cause to be in a specified condition.

**pu'trid**, *adj.* rotten; decayed.

**putt**, *v.t. Golf.* 1. hit gently. —*n.* 2. act or instance of putting.

**put'ty**, *n.* 1. cement of linseed oil and whiting. —*v.t.* 2. secure with putty.

**puz'zle**, *n.* 1. device or problem posing difficulties. —*v.t.* 2. mystify; perplex.

**pyr'a·mid**, *n.* structure or form with triangular sides.

**pyre**, *n.* heap of material for burning a corpse.

**qual'i·ty**, *n., pl.* -ties. 1. essential characteristic. 2. degree of merit. 3. excellence. —**qual'i·ta''tive,** *adj.*

**quan'da·ry**, *n., pl.* -ries. perplexed state.

**quan'ti·ty**, *n., pl.* -ties. 1. amount or number. 2. large or considerable amount.

**quar'an·tine''**, *n.* isolation of suspected disease bearers.

**quar'rel**, *n.* 1. angry argument; fight. —*v.i.* 2. have a quarrel.

**quar'ry**, *n., pl.* -ries, place from which stone is extracted.

**quart**, *n.* unit of measure equal to one fourth of a gallon.

**quar'ter**, *n.* 1. fourth part. —*v.t.* 2. divide into quarters.

**quar'ter·ly**, *adj., n., pl.* -lies. *adj.* 1. ocurring every three months. —*n.* 2. periodical published four times a year.

**quar'ter·mas''ter**, *n.* 1. army officer who oversees supplies, etc. 2. petty officer in charge of a ship's signals, steering, etc.

**quar·tet'**, *n.* group of four, esp. musicians. Also, **quar·tette'**.

**quay** (kē), *n.* pier; wharf.

**quea'sy**, *adj.,* -sier, -siest. 1. nauseous. 2. uneasy.

**queen**, *n.* 1. female sovereign. 2. spouse of a king.

**queer**, *adj.* peculiar.

**quell**, *v.t.* subdue.

**quench**, *v.t.* slake, as thirst.

**que'ry**, *n., pl.* -ries, *n.* 1. question; inquiry. —*v.t.* 2. inquire regarding.

**quest**, *n., v.i.* search.

**ques'tion**, *n.* 1. interrogative sentence. 2. problem or issue. —*v.t.* 3. ask questions of. 4. challenge; doubt. —**ques'tion·a·ble,** *adj.*

**ques''tion·naire'**, *n.* set or list of questions.

**queue** (kyōō), *n.* 1. line of waiting persons. 2. braid of hair at the back of the head. —*v.t., v.i.* 3. form in a line.

**quick**, *adj.* 1. prompt. 2. intelligent. 3. speedy. —**quick'ly,** *adv.* —**quick'ness,** *n.*

**qui'et**, *adj.* 1. at rest. 2. silent. —**qui'e·tude'',** *n.*

**quill**, *n.* 1. large stiff feather. 2. bristle or spine.

**quilt**, *n.* 1. lined and padded bedspread.

**quince**, *n.* hard yellowish fruit.

# Q

**Q, q,** *n.* seventeenth letter of the English alphabet.

**quad·ran'gle**, *n.* 1. closed figure with four angles. 2. enclosed four-sided yard. —**quad·ran'gu·lar,** *adj.*

**quad·ra·phon'ic**, *adj.* of a sound system using four independent speakers.

**quad'ru·ped''**, *n.* animal with four feet.

**quail**, *n., pl.* quails, quail. game bird.

**quaint**, *adj.* pleasingly odd or old-fashioned.

**quake**, *v.i.* 1. tremble or shake. —*n.* 2. earthquake.

**qual'i·fy''**, *v.t.* 1. make eligible or capable. 2. modify. —**qual'i·fi·ca''tion,** *n.* —**qual'i·fied'',** *adj.*

**qui'nine**, *n.* bitter saltlike substance used medically.

**quin'tet'**, *n.* group of five, esp. musicians.

**quip**, *v.i.* 1. sarcastic or clever remark. —*v.i.* 2. make a quip.

**quit**, *v.t.*, *v.i.* 1. discontinue. —*v.t.* 2. leave. 3. abandon. —**quit'ter**, *n.*

**quite**, *adv.* 1. completely. 2. positively.

**quiv'er**, *v.t.*, *v.i.* 1. tremble; shake. —*n.* 2. case for arrows.

**quiz**, *v.t.* 1. give a brief test to. 2. question closely. —*n.* 3. test or questioning.

**quo'rum**, *n.* sufficient number of attending members.

**quo'ta**, *n.* assigned share or number.

**quo·ta'tion**, *n.* 1. word-for-word citation. 2. specified price.

**quo·ta'tion marks**, *n.* pair of punctuation marks, " ", used to mark the beginning and end of a direct quotation.

**quote**, *v.t.* 1. repeat verbatim. 2. cite as evidence. 3. state, as a price. —*n.* 4. quotation. —**quot'a·ble**, *adj.*

# R

**R, r,** *n.* eighteenth letter of the English alphabet.

**rab'bi**, *n.*, *pl.* **-bis**. Jewish preacher. —**rab·bin'ic**, **rab·bin'i·cal**, *adj.*

**rab'bit**, *n.* small long-eared mammal.

**rab'ble**, *n.* mob.

**rab'id**, *adj.* 1. irrationally extreme. 2. having rabies.

**ra'bies**, *n.* infectious disease transmitted by animal bites.

**race**, *n.* 1. contest of speed. 2. group of persons with a common origin. —*v.i.* 3. participate in a race. 4. move quickly. —*v.t.* 5. cause to move quickly.

**ra'cial**, *adj.* concerning race (2), or the differences between races. —**rac'ism**, *n.*

**rack**, *n.* 1. framework for storage.

2. bar-like gear engaging a pinion. —*v.t.* 3. torture. 4. strain.

**rack'et**, *n.* 1. noise; commotion. 2. dishonest or illegal activity. 3. cross-stringed light bat, used esp. in tennis.

**ra'dar**, *n.* device using radio waves to locate objects.

**ra'di·ant**, *adj.* 1. bright; shiny. 2. emitting light. —**ra'di·ance**, *n.*

**ra'di·ate'**, *v.i.* 1. move or spread like rays from a center. —*v.t.* 2. emit, as rays.

**ra'di·a'tor**, *n.* convection heater.

**rad'i·cal**, *adj.* 1. fundamental. 2. favoring drastic or extreme change. —*n.* 3. person with radical ideas.

**ra'di·o'**, *n.* 1. wireless transmission of sound by electromagnetic waves. 2. device for receiving radio transmissions.

**ra'di·um**, *n.* radioactive metallic element.

**ra'di·us**, *n.*, *pl.* **-dii**, **-diuses**. straight line to an arc from its center.

**raft**, *n.* floating platform.

**rag**, *n.* torn or waste piece of cloth. —**rag'ged**, *adj.*

**rage**, *n.* 1. violent anger. 2. popular vogue.

**raid**, *n.* 1. sudden attack. —*v.t.* 2. attack suddenly.

**rail**, *n.* 1. horizontal bar or beam. 2. guide for a wheel of a railroad car.

**rail'ing**, *n.* barrier of uprights and rails.

**rail'road''**, *n.* 1. road of rails on which trains run. —*v.t.* 2. transport by railroad.

**rain**, *n.* 1. condensed water falling in drops from the clouds. 2. rainstorm. —*v.i.* 3. fall as rain. —*v.t.* 4. give abundantly; shower. —**rain'y**, *adj.* —**rain'fall''**, *n.*

**rain'bow''**, *n.* colored arc of sunlight refracted through raindrops.

**raise**, *v.t.* 1. lift. 2. set upright. 3. solicit and collect. 4. grow. 5. bring up. 6. call to attention. —*n.* 7. increase in salary.

**rake**, *n.* 1. pronged implement for collecting leaves, etc. 2. libertine. 3. slope. —*v.t.* 4. smooth, collect, etc. with a rake.

**ral'ly**, *v.*, *n.*, *pl.* **-lies**. *v.t.*, *v.i.* 1. gather. —*v.i.* 2. reorganize. 3. tease. —*v.i.* 4. recover strength. —*n.* 5. gathering. 6. recovery of strength.

**ram**, *n.* 1. male sheep. 2. device for

**ram'ble**, v.i. 1. wander leisurely. 2. talk discursively. —n. 3. leisurely stroll.

**ram'i·fy'**, v.t., v.i. branch out.

**ramp**, n. sloping road or walk.

**ram'page'**, n. 1. violent behavior. —v.i. 2. rush about furiously.

**ram'part**, n. mound of earth erected as a defense; parapet.

**ranch**, n. large stock farm.

**ran·cid** (ran'sid), adj. spoiled.

**ran'cor**, n. resentment.

**ran'dom**, adj. without pattern or aim.

**range**, n. 1. extent. 2. row. 3. mountain chain. 4. grazing area. 5. distance of gunfire, reach, etc. 6. shooting ground. 7. stove. —v.t. 8. put in a row. 9. pass over. —v.i. 10. have a range.

**rank**, n. 1. group, class, or standing. 2. high position. 3. row. 4. **ranks**, ordinary troops. —v.t. 5. arrange in formation. —adj. 6. excessively grown. 7. offensively strong in taste or smell. 8. utter.

**ran'som**, n. 1. price demanded for return of a prisoner. —v.t. 2. redeem for money.

**rap**, v.t. 1. strike sharply. —n. 2. quick, sharp blow.

**rape**, n. 1. forced sexual violation. —v.t. 2. commit rape on. 3. seize and carry off by force. —ra'pist, n.

**rap'id**, adj. speedy.

**rare**, adj., **rarer**, **rarest**. 1. unusual. 2. thin. 3. not completely cooked.

**rash**, adj. 1. unreasonably hasty. —n. 2. skin irritation.

**rate**, n. 1. fixed relation between variables. —v.t. 2. establish a rate for.

**rath'er**, adv. 1. to a certain extent. 2. on the contrary. 3. in preference.

**ra'tion**, n. limited allotment.

**ra'tion·al**, adj. 1. reasonable. 2. sane.

**ra·tio**, (ra'shō) n. relation of quantities.

**rat'tle**, v.t. make successive short sharp noises.

**rave**, v.i. talk wildly.

**raw**, adj. 1. naked. 2. uncooked.

**ray**, n. 1. narrow beam of light. 2. glimpse.

**ra'zor**, n. sharp instrument for shaving.

**re-**, prefix meaning "again."

**reach**, v.t. 1. arrive at. 2. extend. 3. be able to touch. 4. communicate with. —v.i. 5. extend the hand. —n. 6. act, instance, or extent of reaching.

**re·act'**, v.i. 1. act in response. 2. interact.

**re·ac'tion**, n. action in response.

**read'y**, adj. 1. prepared. 2. willing. 3. imminent.

**re'al**, adj. 1. not false; genuine. 2. not imaginary or ideal. —re·al'i·ty, n. —re'al·ly, adv.

**re'al·ize'**, v.t. 1. understand completely. 2. bring into actuality. 3. obtain as a profit. —re''al·i·za'tion, n.

**realm** (relm), n. 1. special field of expertise. 2. kingdom.

**reap**, v.t. 1. harvest. 2. get as a reward. —reap'er, n.

**rear**, n. 1. back part. 2. backside. —adj. 3. pertaining to the rear. —v.t. 4. raise; erect. 5. bring up to maturity. —v.i. 6. rise on the rear legs.

**rea'son**, n. 1. cause or justification. 2. objectivity; logic. 3. sanity. —v.i. 4. think or argue logically. —v.t. 5. infer or conclude. —rea'son·a·ble, adj. —rea'son·a·bly, adv.

**re·as·sure'**, v.t. restore the confidence of.

**re·bel'**, v.i. (rē bel') 1. arise against authority. —n. (reb'əl) 2. person who rebels. —re·bel'lion, n. —re·bel'lious, adj.

**re·buke'**, v.t. reprimand.

**re·but'**, v.t. refute. —re·but'tal, n.

**re·cal·ci·trant** (rē kal'sə trənt), adj. stubborn.

**re·call'**, v.t. 1. remember. 2. withdraw. 3. call or summon back. —n. 4. act or instance of recalling. 5. memory.

**re·cede'**, v.i. 1. move back. 2. diminish.

**re·ceipt'**, n. 1. act or instance of receiving. 2. document acknowledging payment or delivery. 3. **receipts**, income.

**re·ceive'**, v.t. 1. take when offered or sent. 2. sustain; experience. 3. welcome. —re·ceiv'a·ble, adj.

**re'cent**, adj. not long past.

**re·cep'ta·cle**, n. container.

**re·cep'tion**, n. 1. act or instance of receiving. 2. formal social function. 3. quality of radio signals, etc. as received.

**re·cep'tive**, *adj.* 1. ready to consider new ideas. 2. amenable.

**re·cess'**, *n.* 1. pause in work. 2. hollowed-out space. 3. recesses, inner areas.

**rec'i·pe'**, *n.* formula, esp. in cooking.

**re·cip'i·ent**, *n.* receiver.

**re·cip'ro·cal**, *adj.* 1. mutual. —*n.* 2. counterpart.

**re·cip'ro·cate''**, *v.t., v.i.* 1. give, receive, etc. in return. 2. move back and forth. —**rec''i·proc'i·ty,** *n.*

**re·cit'al**, *n.* 1. account or narration. 2. performance of music.

**re·cite'**, *v.t.* 1. repeat from memory. 2. narrate; read aloud.

**reck'less**, *adj.* foolhardy, careless.

**re·cline'**, *v.i., v.t.* lie or lay back.

**rec'og·nize''**, *v.t.* 1. identify from memory. 2. be aware of. 3. acknowledge formally. —**rec''og·ni'tion**, *n.*

**re·coil'**, *v.i.* draw or shrink back.

**rec''ol·lect'**, *v.t., v.i.* remember.

**rec''om·mend'**, *v.t.* 1. speak favorably of. 2. advise. —**rec''om·men·da'tion**, *n.*

**rec''on·cile'**, *v.t.* 1. return to harmony. 2. make compatible. 3. settle amicably. 4. make acquiescent. —**rec''on·cil'a·ble**, *adj.* —**rec''on·cil''i·a'tion**, *n.*

**re·cord'**, *v.t.* (rē kord') 1. make a written account of. 2. put in reproducible form. —*n.* (rek'ərd) 3. written account. 4. disk for sound reproduction. 5. best performance. —*adj.* 6. being the best to date.

**re·cov'er**, *v.t.* 1. get back. 2. salvage. —*v.i.* 3. regain health. 4. regain composure.

**rec''re·a'tion**, *n.* refreshing occupation.

**re·cruit'**, *n.* 1. newly enlisted person. —*v.t.* 2. enlist.

**rec·tan'gle**, *n.* parallelogram with four right angles.

**rec'ti·fy''**, *v.t.* correct.

**rec'tor**, *n.* clergyman in charge of a parish.

**rec'to·ry**, *n.* parsonage.

**rec'tum**, *n.* terminal part of the large intestine. —**rec'tal**, *adj.*

**re·cu'per·ate''**, *v.i.* regain health.

**re·cur'**, *v.i.* 1. occur again or repeatedly. 2. return to one's thoughts. —**re·cur'rence**, *n.* —**re·cur'rent**, *adj.* —**re·cur'rent·ly**, *adv.*

**red**, *n., adj.*, redder, reddest. *n.* color of blood. —**red'den**, *v.t., v.i.*

**re·deem'**, *v.t.* 1. recover. 2. pay off. —**re·demp'tion**, *n.*

**re·duce'**, *v.t.* 1. lessen. 2. alter. 3. lower in rank, etc. 4. subdue. —*v.i.* 5. act so as to lose weight. —**re·duc'i·ble**, *adj.* —**re·duc'tion**, *n.*

**reed**, *n.* 1. tall marsh grass. 2. vibrating part of the mouthpiece on certain wind instruments.

**reef**, *n.* ridge near the surface of a body of water.

**reel**, *n.* 1. revolving drum for winding. 2. lively dance. —*v.t.* 3. wind on a reel. —*v.i.* 4. stagger or sway. 5. whirl.

**re·fer'**, *v.i.* 1. allude. 2. look for information. —*v.t.* 3. direct for help or information. —**ref'er·a·ble**, *adj.* —**re·fer'ral**, *n.*

**ref''er·ee'**, *n.* 1. arbiter. *v.t., v.i.* 2. arbitrate.

**ref'er·ence**, *n.* 1. act or instance of referring. 2. something referred to. 3. recommendation.

**re·fine'**, *v.t.* 1. free from impurities. 2. make cultured.

**re·flect'**, *v.t.* 1. return, as images, light, or sound. 2. give as a result. —*v.i.* 3. think carefully. —**re·flec'tion**, *n.* —**re·flec'tive**, *adj.* —**re·flec'tor**, *n.*

**re'flex**, *adj.* 1. denoting involuntary reaction. —*n.* 2. involuntary reaction.

**re·form'**, *n.* 1. correction of wrongs. —*v.t.* 2. correct the wrongs of. —*v.i.* 3. correct one's wrongdoing. —**ref''or·ma'tion**, *n.*

**re·frig'er·ate''**, keep or make cold. —**re·frig'er·ant**, *n.* —**re·frig'er·a''tor**, *n.*

**ref'uge**, *n.* shelter from danger.

**ref''u·gee'**, *n.* seeker of refuge.

**re·fuse'**, *v.t.* (rē fyōoz') 1. decline. 2. decline to accept. 3. deny, as a request. —*n.* (ref'yōoz). 4. rubbish. —**re·fus'al**, *n.*

**re·fute'**, *v.t.* prove wrong.

**re·gain'**, *v.t.* get again.

**re'gal**, *adj.* royal.

**re·gard'**, *v.t.* 1. look on. 2. consider. 3. concern; relate to. 4. hold in respect. —*n.* 5. look; gaze. 6. relation. 7. affection and respect.

**re·gard'less**, *adj.* 1. careless. —*adv.* 2. anyway.

**reg'i·ment**, *n.* (rej'ə mənt) 1. army unit of two or more battalions. —*v.t.* (rej′ə ment″) 2. subject to strict discipline.

**re′gion,** *n.* part of the earth's surface.

**reg′is·ter,** *n.* 1. written record, list, etc. 2. device for regulating the passage of air. —*v.t., v.i.* 3. enroll. —*v.t.* 4. show, as on the face. —*v.i.* 5. make an impression. —**reg′is·trant,** *n.* —**reg″is·tra′tion,** *n.* —**reg′is·try,** *n.*

**re·gret′,** *v.t.* 1. feel sorry about. —*n.* 2. sorrow or remorse.

**reg′u·lar,** *adj.* 1. customary. 2. consistent. 3. symmetrical. 4. permanent, as an army. 5. *Informal.* a. complete. b. likeable. —*n.* 6. someone regularly seen. 7. regular soldier.

**reg′u·late″,** *v.t.* 1. control by rule. 2. make regular. —**reg″u·la′tor,** *n.* —**reg′u·la·to″ry,** *adj.*

**re·hearse′,** *v.t., v.i.* practice for a performance. —**re·hears′al,** *n.*

**reign** (rān), *n.* 1. royal power. 2. period of rule.

**rein** (rān), strap for controlling a horse.

**re″in·force′,** *v.t.* strengthen.

**re″in·state′,** *v.t.* restore to a former state.

**re·it′er·ate″,** *v.t.* say or do again.

**re·ject′,** *v.t.* (ri jekt′) 1. refuse to accept. 2. discard. —*n.* (rē′jekt) 3. rejected person or thing. —**re·jec′tion,** *n.*

**re·joice′,** *v.t.* 1. gladden. —*v.i.* 2. feel joy.

**re·lapse′,** *v.i.* 1. fall into a former state. —*n.* 2. act or instance of relapsing.

**re·late′,** *v.t.* 1. tell; narrate. 2. connect; associate.

**re·la′tion,** *n.* 1. narrative. 2. connection; association. 3. connection by blood or marriage. —**re·la′tion·ship′,** *n.*

**rel′a·tive,** *adj.* 1. comparative. 2. related to each other. —*n.* 3. person related by blood or marriage.

**re·lax′,** *v.t., v.i.* rest.

**re·lay′** *n.* (rē′lā) 1. relief crew or team. 2. race in which team members run individual portions. —*v.t.* (rē′lā; also ri lā′) 3. send by relay or relays.

**re·lease′,** *v.t.* 1. free. 2. let go of. 3. license for publication. —*n.* 4. act or instance of releasing. 5. communication, etc.

**re·lent′,** *v.i.* become less severe.

**rel′e·vant,** *adj.* relating to the mat-

ter at hand. —**rel′e·vance, rel′e·van·cy,** *n.*

**re·li′a·ble,** *adj.* dependable. —**re·li″a·bil′i·ty,** *n.*

**re·li′ance,** *n.* trust; confidence. —**re·li′ant,** *adj.*

**re·lief′,** *n.* 1. release from pain, discomfort, etc. 2. means of such relief.

**re·lieve′,** *v.t.* 1. ease, as from pain or discomfort. 2. vary. 3. release from duty.

**re·li′gion,** *n.* belief in a divine being or beings. —**re·li′gious,** *adj.*

**re·luc′tant,** *adj.* unwilling. —**re·luc′tance,** *n.*

**re·ly′,** *v.i.* depend; trust.

**re·main′,** *v.i.* 1. stay behind. 2. endure; persist. 3. continue as before. —*n.* 4. remains, a. remainder. b. corpse. —**re·main′der,** *n.*

**re·mark′,** *v.t., v.i., n.* 1. comment. —*v.t., n.* 2. notice.

**rem′e·dy,** *n.* 1. medicine or treatment. 2. something that corrects wrong. —*v.t.* 3. cure; correct. —**re·me′di·al,** *adj.*

**re·mem′ber,** *v.t.* 1. recall to mind. 2. not forget. 3. carry greetings from. —**re·mem′brance,** *n.*

**re·mind′,** *v.t.* cause to remember. —**re·mind′er,** *n.*

**rem″i·nisce′,** *v.i.* discuss or think of the past. —**rem″i·nis′cence,** *n.* —**rem″i·nis′cent,** *adj.*

**rem′nant,** *n.* something left over.

**re·morse′,** *n.* mental anguish from guilt.

**re·mote′,** *adj.,* **-moter, -motest.** 1. distant. 2. slight.

**re·move′,** *v.t.* 1. move from a place. 2. dismiss, as from office. —*v.i.* 3. change residence. —*n.* 4. interval; step. —**re·mov′a·ble,** *adj.*

**rend′,** *v.t., v.i.* split apart by force.

**ren′der,** *v.t.* 1. give in return. 2. submit. 3. state, as a decision.

**ren·dez·vous** (ran′dā voo″), *n., pl.* **-vous.** 1. meeting place. 2. appointment to meet.

**re·nounce′,** *v.t.* give up formally. —**re·nun″ci·a′tion, re·nounce′ment,** *n.*

**re·nown′,** *n.* great reputation. —**re·nowned′,** *adj.*

**rent,** *n.* 1. Also **rent′al,** payment for temporary use. 2. tear; rip. —*v.t.* 3. use by paying. 4. grant temporarily for payment.

**re·pair′,** *v.t.* 1. return to good con-

dition. 2. set right. —v.i. 3. go.
—n. 4. act or instance of repairing. 5. good condition. —**rep'a·
ra·ble**, **re·pair'a·ble**, adj.

**rep"a·ra'tion**, n. 1. amends for
injury. 2. reparations, compensation for war damage.

**re·peat'**, v.t., v.i. 1. say or do
again. —n. 2. act or instance of
repeating. —**rep'e·ti'tion**, n.
—**rep"e·ti'tious**, adj.

**re·pel'**, v.t. 1. drive back. 2. disgust. —**re·pel'lent**, adj., n.

**re·pent'**, v.t., v.i. regret as wrong
or mistaken. —**re·pent'ance**, n.
—**re·pent'ant**, adj.

**rep'er·toire"**, n. stock of songs,
plays, etc. performed. Also, **rep'-
er·to"ry**, n.

**re·place'**, v.t. 1. put back in place.
2. substitute for. —**re·place'a·
ble**, adj. —**re·place'ment**, n.

**re·plen'ish**, v.t. make full again.

**re·ply'**, v., n., pl. **-plies.** v.t., v.i.,
n. answer.

**re·port'**, n. 1. statement. 2. rumor. 3. explosive noise. —v.t. 4.
give an account of. 5. inform
against. —v.i. 6. make a report. 7.
present oneself.

**rep"re·sent'**, v.t. 1. exemplify. 2.
portray. 3. act or speak for.
—**rep"re·sen·ta'tion**, n.

**rep're·sen'ta·tive**, adj. 1. serving as an example. 2. acting or
speaking for others. —n. 3. person who represents. 4. elected leg-
islator.

**re·press'**, v.t. restrain; check.

**re·proach'**, v.t. 1. scold for a
fault; blame. —n. 2. discredit.

**re"pro·duce'**, v.t. 1. copy; duplicate. 2. produce by propagation.
—**re"pro·duc'tion**, n. —**re"-
pro·duc'tive**, adj.

**rep'tile**, n. cold-blooded vertebrate.
—**rep·til'i·an**, n.

**re·pub'lic**, n. state governed by
elected legislators.

**re·pub'li·can**, adj. 1. pertaining
to or favoring a republic. —n. 2.
**Republican**, member of the Republican party. 3. partisan of a
republican form of government.
—**re·pub'li·can·ism**, n.

**re·pu'di·ate"**, v.t. disown.

**re·pulse'**, v.t. 1. drive back, as an
attack. 2. reject; rebuff. —n. 3.
act or instance of repulsing. —**re·
pul'sion**, n.

**re·pul'sive**, adj. disgusting.

**rep'u·ta·ble**, adj. of good reputation.

**rep"u·ta'tion**, n. 1. estimation
of a person or thing. 2. fame.

**re·pute'**, n. 1. reputation. —v.t. 2.
consider or regard.

**re·quest'**, v.t. 1. ask for. —n. 2.
act or instance of requesting. 3.
something requested.

**re·quire'**, v.t. 1. need. 2. demand.

**req"ui·si'tion**, n. 1. act or instance of requiring. 2. formal order for goods, etc. —v.t. 3. take
by authority.

**re·scind'**, v.t. revoke; annul.

**res'cue**, v.t. 1. free or save. —n. 2.
act or instance of rescuing.

**re·search'**, n. 1. careful investigation. —v.t. 2. do research on or
in.

**re·sem'ble**, v.t. be like or similar
to. —**re·sem'blance**, n.

**re·sent'**, v.t. feel indignant at.

**res"er·va'tion**, n. act or instance
of reserving.

**re·serve'**, v.t. 1. keep back; set
aside. —n. 2. something reserved.
3. reticence, as about feelings.

**res'er·voir"**, n. 1. storage place for
water.

**re·side'**, v.i. dwell.

**res'i·dence**, n. 1. dwelling place.
2. act or instance of residing.
—**res'i·dent**, n., adj. —**res"i·
den'tial**, adj.

**res'i·due"**, n. remainder. —**re·sid'
u·al**, adj.

**re·sign'**, v.i. 1. give up a duty.
—v.t. 2. give up.

**res"ig·na'tion**, n. 1. act or instance of resigning. 2. submission.

**re·signed'**, adj. reluctantly submissive.

**re·sist'**, v.t., v.i. withstand; oppose.
—**re·sist'ance**, n.

**res'o·lute"**, adj. firm in purpose;
determined.

**res"o·lu'tion**, n. 1. formal expression of opinion. 2. decision.

**re·solve'**, v.t. 1. decide; determine. —v.t. 2. analyze. 3. solve.
4. dispel, as fear. —n. 5. determination.

**res'o·nant**, adj. 1. resounding. 2.
vibrant; sonorous. —**res'o·nance**,
n. —**res'o·nate"**, v.t., v.i. —**res'-
o·na"tor**, n.

**re·sort'**, v.i. 1. have recourse. —n.
2. public place, as for recreation.
3. recourse.

**re·sound'**, v.i. reverberate.

**re·source'**, n. 1. source of help or

**P
R**

support. 2. resources, money; means.

**re·spect'**, n. 1. esteem; honor. 2. consideration. 3. detail. 4. deference; regard. —v.t. 5. show consideration for.

**re·spec'tive**, adj. relating to each of several.

**res'pite**, n. temporary relief.

**re·spond'**, v.i. 1. answer. 2. react.

**re·sponse'**, n. reply. —**re·spon'sive**, adj.

**re·spon'si·bil'i·ty**, n., pl. —ties. 1. state of being responsible. 2. obligation.

**re·spon'si·ble**, adj. 1. accountable. 2. reliable. 3. distinguishing between right and wrong. —**re·spon'si·bly**, adv.

**rest**, n. 1. sleep; repose. 2. inactivity after work. 3. support; base. 4. Music. silent interval. —v.i. 5. be at rest. 6. lay. 7. lie. —v.t. 8. cause to rest. 9. base.

**res'tau·rant**, n. public eating place.

**res'ti·tu'tion**, n. return of something taken away.

**re·store'**, v.t. 1. return to a former state. 2. give back. —**res'to·ra'tion**, n. —**re·stor'a·tive**, adj.

**re·strain'**, v.t. 1. hold back; check. 2. confine.

**re·straint'**, n. 1. control of emotions, etc. 2. confinement. 3. something that restrains.

**re·strict'**, v.t. limit; confine.

**re·sult'**, n. 1. consequence; outcome. —v.i. 2. follow as a consequence. —**re·sult'ant**, adj., n.

**re·sume'**, v.t. 1. continue. 2. take again. —**re·sump'tion**, n.

**ré·su·mé'**, n. summary, as of work experience.

**res''ur·rect'**, v.t. raise from the dead.

**re·tail'**, n. 1. sale of consumer goods. —v.t., v.i. 2. sell at retail.

**re·tain'**, v.t. 1. keep; hold. 2. hire by a retainer.

**re·tain'er**, n. 1. fee for continuing services. 2. servant.

**re·tal'i·ate'**, v.i. give like for like.

**re·tard'**, v.t. hinder; slow.

**re·ten'tion**, n. act or instance of retaining.

**ret'i·cent**, adj. disposed to silence; taciturn. —**ret'i·cence**, n.

**ret'i·nue'**, n. group of attendants.

**re·tire'**, v.i., v.t. 1. withdraw. 2. withdraw from working life. —v.i. 3. go to bed. —v.t. 4. pay off, as

bonds. —**re·tir''ee'**, n. —**re·tire'ment**, n.

**re·tract'**, v.t., v.i. withdraw.

**re·treat'**, n. 1. withdrawal, as from danger. 2. secluded place. —v.i. 3. withdraw.

**ret''ri·bu'tion**, n. retaliation; punishment. —**re·trib'u·tive**, adj.

**re·trieve'**, v.t. 1. regain. 2. recover. 3. make good, as a mistake. —**re·triev'al**, n.

**ret'ro·ac'tive**, adj. valid for some past period.

**ret'ro·spect'**, n. look to the past.

**re·turn'**, v.i. 1. go back. 2. reply. —v.t. 3. put back. 4. repay. 5. elect or reelect. 6. yield, as a profit. —n. 7. act or instance of returning. 8. recurrence. 9. repayment; yield. 9. report; response. —**re·turn'a·ble**, adj.

**re·veal'**, v.t. 1. disclose. 2. manifest.

**rev'el**, v.i. 1. take great delight. 2. make merry. —n. 3. merrymaking. —**rev'el·ry**, n.

**rev''e·la'tion**, n. act or instance of revealing.

**re·venge'**, n. 1. retaliation. 2. vindictiveness. —v.t. 3. take revenge for.

**rev'e·nue''**, n. income, as from taxes.

**re·ver'ber·ate'**, v.t., v.i. reecho; resound.

**re·vere'**, v.t. regard with deep respect, love, etc.

**rev'er·ence**, n. 1. deep respect. —v.t. 2. revere; honor. —**rev'er·ent, rev''er·en'tial**, adj.

**rev'er·end**, adj. worthy of reverence.

**rev'er·ie**, n., pl. —ies. daydreaming; deep musings. Also, **rev'er·y**.

**re·verse'**, adj. 1. turned backward. 2. making an opposite motion. —n. 3. opposite; contrary. 4. misfortune. —v.t. 5. turn back or in an opposite direction. 6. exchange; transpose. —v.i. 7. move in an opposite direction. —**re·vers'i·ble**, adj.

**re·vert'**, v.i. return as to a former way or state, etc. —**re·ver'sion**, n.

**re·view'**, n. 1. reexamination. 2. general survey or report. 3. critical writing. —v.t. 4. reexamine. 5. look back on. 6. write a review of. 7. inspect formally.

**re·vise'**, *v.t.* amend. —**re·vi'sion**, *n.*

**re·viv'al**, *n.* 1. return to life, use, etc. 2. emotional religious meeting. —**re·viv'al·ist**, *n.*

**re·vive'**, *v.i., v.t.* return to consciousness or effectiveness.

**re·voke'**, *v.t.* repeal or nullify. —**rev'o·ca·ble**, *adj.* —**rev'o·ca'tion**, *n.*

**re·volt'**, *n.* 1. uprising; rebellion. —*v.i.* 2. rebel. —*v.t.* 3. disgust.

**rev'o·lu'tion**, *n.* 1. war against one's government. 2. complete change. 3. rotation. —**rev'o·lu'tion·ar'y**, *adj., n.* —**rev'o·lu'tion·ist**, *n.*

**re·volve'**, *v.t.* 1. cause to rotate. —*v.i.* 2. rotate.

**re·volv'er**, *n.* pistol with a revolving magazine.

**re·vul'sion**, *n.* disgust.

**re·ward'**, *n.* 1. grateful gift or payment. —*v.t.* 2. give a reward to.

**rhet'o·ric**, *n.* art of using language effectively.

**rheu'ma·tism"**, *n.* painful condition of the muscles and joints. —**rheu·mat'ic**, *adj.*

**rhyme**, *n.* 1. similarity of sound at verse ends. 2. poetry with such similarity. —*v.i., v.t.* 3. compose in rhyme.

**rhythm**, *n.* regular recurrence of stress, as in poetry or music. —**rhyth'mic**, *adj.*

**rib**, *n.* one of the curved bones around the chest cavity.

**rib'bon**, *n.* narrow strip of fabric.

**rice**, *n.* edible cereal of warm climates.

**rich**, *adj.* 1. having much wealth. 2. abundant; abounding. 3. full of desirable qualities or resources. 4. appetizing but hard to digest. 5. mellow. —*n.* 6. **the rich**, people of wealth. 7. **riches**, wealth. —**rich'ly**, *adv.* —**rich'ness**, *n.*

**rick'et·y**, *adj.* shaky; feeble.

**ric·o·chet** (rik'ə shā"), *v.i.* rebound.

**rid**, *v.t.* free; clear. —**rid'dance**, *n.*

**rid'dle**, *n.* 1. puzzle; enigma. 2. —*v.t.* pierce with holes.

**ride**, *v.,* **rode, rid·den, rid·ing,** —*v.t.* 1. be carried on or within. 2. be carried over or through. —*v.i.* 3. be carried. 4. depend (on). 5. be at anchor. —*n.* 6. act or instance of riding.

**rid'er**, *n.* 1. person who rides. 2. addition to a document.

**ridge**, *n.* 1. narrow, raised edge. 2. sharp crest or elevation of land. —*v.t., v.i.* 3. form into a ridge.

**rid'i·cule"**, *n.* 1. derision. —*v.t.* 2. make fun of; mock. —**ri·dic'u·lous**, *adj.*

**ri'fle**, *n.* 1. shoulder gun with a long barrel. —*v.t.* 2. ransack and rob.

**rig**, *v.t.* 1. equip, as for sailing. 2. manipulate. —*n.* 3. arrangement of the sails, etc. on a ship. 4. equipment. 5. tractor-trailer.

**right**, *adj.* 1. good; virtuous. 2. correct. 3. suitable. 4. opposite to left. 5. straight. —*n.* 6. what is right, just, etc. 7. lawful power or privilege. 8. *Politics.* conservative. —*adv.* 9. properly. 10. correct; put in order. 11. set upright.

**right'eous**, *adj.* 1. virtuous; blameless. 2. just; worthy.

**rig'id**, *adj.* 1. stiff; unyielding. 2. strict. —**rig'id·ness**, **ri·gid'i·ty**, *n.*

**rig'or**, *n.* 1. strictness. 2. hardship.

**rim**, *n.* 1. edge; border; margin. —*v.t.* 2. furnish with a rim.

**rind**, *n.* hard outer coating, as of cheese or fruit.

**ring**, *n., v.,* **rang, rung, ring·ing.** *n.* 1. sound of a bell. 2. finger band. 3. circular object or area. 4. group of conspirators. 5. telephone call. —*v.t.* 6. sound, as a bell. 7. call by telephone. 8. encircle. —*v.i.* 9. resound. 10. sound clearly. 11. seem to be true or false.

**rink**, *n.* area for skating.

**rinse**, *v.t.* 1. wash lightly, as to remove soap. —*n.* 2. act or instance of rinsing. 3. solution for rinsing.

**ri'ot**, *n.* act of mob violence.

**rip**, *v.i., v.t.* tear apart.

**ripe**, *adj.,* **rip·er, rip·est.** fully aged or developed. —**rip'en**, *v.i., v.t.*

**rip'ple**, *v.i., v.t.* 1. form in little waves. —*n.* 2. little wave.

**rise**, *v.i.,* **rose, ris·en, ris·ing,** 1. get up. 2. rebel. 3. ascend. 4. begin. 5. increase in amount, degree, etc. 6. originate. —*n.* 7. act or instance of rising. 8. small hill. 9. increase. 10. advance in rank, power, etc.

**risk**, *n.* 1. chance of defeat, injury, loss, etc. —*v.t.* 2. expose to loss. 3. incur the risk of. —**risk'y**, *adj.*

**rite**, *n.* ceremonial act.

**rit'u·al**, *n.* 1. set form for rites.

**P**
**R**

—*adj.* **2.** according to a ritual. —**rit′u·al·is′tic,** *adj.*

**ri′val,** *n.* **1.** competitor. **2.** equal. —*adj.* **3.** competing. —*v.t.* **4.** compete with. **5.** equal. —**ri′val·ry,** *n.*

**riv′er,** *n.* large natural stream of water.

**riv′et,** *n.* **1.** metal bolt forged tight after insertion. —*v.t.* **2.** fasten with rivets.

**road,** *n.* way for travel.

**roam,** *v.i.* wander.

**roar,** *v.i.* emit a bellow.

**roast,** *v.t.* cook with dry heat.

**rob,** *v.t.* take from without right. —**rob′ber·y,** *n.*

**robe,** *n.* **1.** long, loose piece of clothing. —*v.t.* **2.** clothe in a robe.

**ro′bot,** *n.* man-like machine.

**ro·bust′,** *adj.* vigorous.

**rock,** *n.* **1.** piece of stone. —*v.i.,* *v.t.* **2.** swing back and forth. —**rock′y,** *adj.*

**rock′et,** *n.* object propelled by reactive thrust. —**rock′et·ry,** *n.*

**rock ′n′ roll,** *n., adj.* a form of popular music originating in the U.S. and characterized by a distinct beat. Also, **rock.**

**rod,** *n.* **1.** round, slender object. **2.** five-and-a-half linear yards.

**ro′dent,** *n.* gnawing mammal.

**ro·de′o′′,** *n., pl.* **-os.** cowboy show.

**roe,** *n.* fish eggs.

**rogue,** *n.* rascal. —**ro′guish,** *adj.* —**ro′guer·y,** *n.*

**role,** *n.* character assumed.

**roll,** *v.i.* **1.** move like a ball, or as if on wheels. **2.** revolve; turn over and over. **3.** move like waves; billow. —*v.t.* **4.** cause to roll. **5.** move on wheels. **6.** shape into a round or cylindrical form. **7.** smooth or flatten with a cylinder, as metal. —*n.* **8.** act or instance of rolling. **9.** a cylinder, as of paper, wire, etc. **10.** list of names. **11.** small loaf of bread.

**ro·man′ à clef′′,** *n.* novel that disguises real people and events.

**ro·mance′,** *n.* **1.** love affair. **2.** fanciful story. **3.** realm of fantasy. —**ro·man′tic,** *adj.* —**ro·man′ti·cal·ly,** *adv.*

**romp,** *v.i.* **1.** play boisterously. —*n.* **2.** act or instance of romping.

**roof,** *n., pl.* **roofs.** **1.** covering for a building. —*v.t.* **2.** furnish with a roof.

**rook′ie,** *n.* raw recruit.

**room,** *n.* **1.** space. **2.** fully enclosed space in a building. —*v.i.* **3.** lodge.

**roost,** *n., v.i.* perch.

**roost′er,** *n.* male chicken.

**root,** *n.* **1.** buried part of a plant. **2.** similar part of a tooth, hair, etc. **3.** basic cause. —*v.t.* **4.** plant. **5.** dig. —*v.i.* **6.** grow roots. **7.** cheer.

**rope,** *n.* **1.** length composed of strands used for pulling or binding. —*v.t.* **2.** tie with rope.

**ro′sa·ry,** *n., pl.* **-ries.** **1.** chain of beads used by Roman Catholics to count prayers said. **2.** series of prayers.

**rose,** *n.* pink or yellow scented flower.

**ros′ter,** *n.* list.

**ros′trum,** *n., pl.* **-trums, -tra.** speaker's platform.

**ros′y,** *adj.* **-ier, -iest.** **1.** pink. **2.** optimistic; promising. —**ros′i·ly,** *adv.*

**rot,** *v.t., v.i., n.* decay. —**rot′ten,** *adj.*

**ro′ta·ry,** *adj.* rotating as a whole or in part.

**ro′tate′,** *v.t., v.i.* **1.** turn around a point. —*v.t.* **2.** assign regular turns to. —**ro·ta′to′′ry,** *adj.*

**rote,** *n.* memorization.

**ro′tor,** *n.* rotating part of a machine.

**ro·tund′,** *adj.* plump. —**ro·tun′di·ty,** *n.*

**rough,** *adj.* **1.** unfinished. **2.** violent. —**rough′en,** *v.t., v.i.*

**rough′age,** *n.* coarse food.

**round,** *adj.* **1.** curved, or with a curved exterior. **2.** approximate. —*n.* **3.** repeated series. **4.** single shot. —*adv., prep.* **5.** around. —*v.t.* **6.** make round. **7.** go around.

**round′a·bout′′,** *adj.* indirect.

**round′up′′,** *n.* **1.** gathering of cattle. **2.** summary.

**rouse,** *v.t., v.i.* **1.** awaken. —*v.t.* **2.** excite.

**rout,** *n.* **1.** put to flight. **2.** gouge. —*n.* **3.** disorderly flight.

**route,** *n.* course of travel.

**rou·tine′,** *n.* **1.** standard course of action. —*adj.* **2.** ordinary; customary.

**rove,** *v.i.* wander.

**row,** *v.t., v.i.* (rō) **1.** move with oars. —*n.* **2.** group in a line. **3.** (row) fight; quarrel. —**row′boat′′,** *n.*

**row'dy**, *adj.*, **-dier**, **-diest**, *n.*, *pl.* **-dies**. *adj.* **1.** boisterous or violent. —*n.* **2.** rowdy person.

**roy'al**, *adj.* **1.** pertaining to kings or queens. —*n.* **2.** sail above a top gallant. —**roy'al·ist**, *n.*

**roy'al·ty**, *n.*, *pl.* **-ties**. **1.** kings and queens. **2.** fee to an author, patentee, etc.

**rub**, *v.t.*, *v.i.*, *n.* **1.** apply friction to. **2.** apply with friction. —*v.i.* **3.** apply friction. —*n.* **4.** act or instance of rubbing. **5.** source of difficulty.

**rub'ber**, *n.* **1.** resilient substance. **2.** decisive game. —**rub'ber·ize'**, *v.t.* —**rub'ber·y**, *adj.*

**rub'bish**, *n.* **1.** cast-off material. **2.** worthless speech, etc.

**rub'ble**, *n.* broken stone or masonry.

**rud'der**, *n.* steering device.

**rude**, *adj.* **ruder**, **rudest**. **1.** offensive in manner. **2.** rough; rugged.

**ru'di·ment**, *n.* basic principle, etc. —**ru''di·men'ta·ry**, *adj.*

**rue**, *v.t.* feel remorse or regret for.

**ruf'fi·an**, *n.* hoodlum.

**ruf'fle**, *v.t.* **1.** disturb the surface of. **2.** disturb the calm of.

**rug**, *n.* floor cloth.

**rug'ged**, *adj.* **1.** rough in surface or outline. **2.** harsh.

**ruin**, *n.* **1.** Also, **ruins**, remains of something destroyed or injured. **2.** downfall. **3.** source of one's downfall. —*v.t.* **4.** bring to ruin. —**ru''in·a'tion**, *n.* —**ru'in·ous**, *adj.*

**rule**, *n.* **1.** principle or law. **2.** government; dominion. **3.** measuring stick. —*v.t.*, *v.i.* **4.** govern.

**rul'er**, *n.* **1.** sovereign. **2.** measuring stick.

**rum**, *n.* alcoholic liquor made from sugar.

**rum'ble**, *v.i.* **1.** dull continuous noise. —*n.* **2.** act or instance of rumbling.

**rum'mage**, *v.t.*, *v.i.* search thoroughly.

**ru'mor**, *n.* **1.** unconfirmed popular report. —*v.t.* **2.** tell in a rumor.

**rump**, *n.* hindquarters.

**run**, *v.*, **ran**, **run**, **running**, —*v.i.* **1.** move quickly on the feet. **2.** be in motion; operate. **3.** flow. —*v.t.* **4.** operate or manage. **5.** drive. —*n.* **6.** act or instance of running. **7.** route or journey. **8.** series. **9.** brook.

**run'down''**, *n.* summary.

**rung**, *n.* rodlike crosspiece.

**run'ner-up'**, *n.*, *pl.* **-ners-up**. second-best racer or performer.

**runt**, *n.* stunted creature. —**runt'y**, *adj.*

**rup'ture**, *n.* **1.** hernia. **2.** break. —*v.t.* **3.** cause a rupture. —*v.i.* **4.** undergo a rupture.

**ru'ral**, *adj.* pertaining to the country.

**rush**, *v.t.*, *v.i.*, *n.* **1.** hurry. —*v.t.* **2.** charge; attack with speed. —*n.* **3.** hurry. **4.** grasslike marsh plant.

**rust**, *n.* **1.** coating of oxidized iron or steel. **2.** plant fungus disease. —*v.i.* **3.** have rust. —*v.t.* **4.** cause to rust. —**rust'y**, *adj.*

**rus'tic**, *adj.* **1.** rural. —*n.* **2.** rural person.

**rus'tle**, *v.i.* **1.** make a soft, whispering sound. —*v.t.* **2.** steal, as cattle. —*n.* **3.** rustling sound.

**rut**, *n.* **1.** worn track. **2.** fixed routine. —*v.t.* **3.** make ruts in. —**rut'ty**, *adj.*

**ruth'less**, *adj.* without compunction or compassion.

**rye**, *n.* edible grain.

# S

**S, s**, *n.* nineteenth letter of the English alphabet.

**Sab'bath**, *n.* day of worship and rest.

**sa'ber**, *n.* single-edged curved sword. Also, **sa'bre**.

**sa'ble**, *n.* weasel-like mammal with dark-brown fur.

**sab'o·tage''**, *n.* **1.** intentional damage to equipment. —*v.t.* **2.** damage intentionally. —**sab'o·teur''**, *n.*

**sac**, *n.* baglike part of the body.

**sac'cha·rine**, *adj.* **1.** too sweet, as in manner. —*n.* **2.** saccharin.

**sac'cha·rin** (sak'kə rin), *n.* sugar substitute.

**sack**, *n.* **1.** bag, esp. a large, strong one. —*v.t.* **2.** put into a sack or sacks. **3.** plunder.

**sac'ra·ment**, *n.* **1.** ceremony or act regarded as sacred. **2. Sacraments**, Eucharist. —**sac''ra·men'tal**, *adj.*

S
T

**sa'cred,** *adj.* holy.

**sac'ri·fice,** *n.* **1.** offer of something valuable to a deity. —*v.t.* **2.** offer or lose in a sacrifice. —**sac''ri·fi'cial,** *adj.*

**sac'ri·lege,** *n.* violation or mockery of something sacred. —**sac''ri·le'gious,** *adj.*

**sac'ro·sanct,** *adj.* sacred.

**sad,** *adj.*, **sadder, saddest.** low in spirits; melancholy. —**sad'den,** *v.t., v.i.*

**sad'dle,** *n.* **1.** seat for the rider of a horse, bicycle, etc. —*v.t.* **2.** put a saddle on.

**sad'ism,** *n.* practice of cruelty for pleasure. —**sad'ist,** *n.* —**sa·dis'tic,** *adj.*

**safe,** *adj.*, **safer, safest, n.** *adj.* **1.** free from danger or risk. —*n.* **2.** container protecting against theft, fire, etc. —**safe'ty,** *n.*

**safe'guard,** *v.t.* **1.** protect from danger. —*n.* **2.** something protective.

**sag,** *v.i.* **1.** bend or hang downwards where not supported; droop. —*n.* **2.** distortion caused by sagging.

**sa'ga,** *n.* Nordic heroic legend.

**sa·gac'i·ty,** *n.* wisdom.

**sage,** *n., adj.*, **sager, sagest.** *n.* **1.** wise and learned person. —*adj.* **2.** wise.

**said,** *adj.* previously mentioned.

**sail,** *n.* **1.** area of cloth used to drive a ship or boat by the force of moving air. —*v.i.* **2.** depart in a ship.

**sail'boat'',** *n.* boat moved by sails.

**sail'or,** *n.* member of a ship's crew.

**saint,** *n.* person officially venerated by a church. —**saint'hood,** *n.* —**saint'ly,** *adj.*

**sake,** *n.* (sāk) benefit.

**sal'a·ble,** *adj.* able to be sold. Also, **sale'a·ble.**

**sa·la'cious,** *adj.* obscene; lewd.

**sal'ad,** *n.* dish mainly of raw vegetables or fruits.

**sal'a·ry,** *n., pl.* **-ries.** regular payment for a permanent employee.

**sale,** *n.* act or occasion of selling.

**sales'man,** *n.* man who sells merchandise, etc. Also, *fem.*, **sales'wom''an, sales'la''dy, sales'girl''.**

**sa'lient,** *adj.* **1.** outstanding. **2.** projecting.

**sa·li'va,** *n.* fluid secreted in mouth by glands to aid digestion.

**sal'low,** *adj.* with a sickly, yellowish complexion.

**sal'mon,** *n.* edible fish with pink flesh.

**sa·lon',** *n.* **1.** room for conversation. **2.** art gallery.

**sa·loon',** *n.* place where liquor is served and drunk.

**salt,** *n.* **1.** sodium chloride. —*v.t.* **2.** treat with salt. —**salt'y,** *adj.* —**salt'shak''er,** *n.*

**sa·lu'bri·ous,** *adj.* promoting health.

**sal'u·tar''y,** *adj.* beneficial.

**sal''u·ta'tion,** *n.* **1.** greeting. **2.** opening phrase of a letter, naming the addressee.

**sa·lute',** *n.* **1.** act expressing respect or attention in military etiquette. —*v.t.* **2.** recognize with a salute.

**sal'vage,** *v.t.* **1.** rescue from loss, as a ship. **2.** gather for reuse, as discarded material. —*n.* **3.** salvaged material.

**sal·va'tion,** *n.* act of saving or state of being saved, as from damnation or destruction.

**salve** (sav), *n.* soothing or healing ointment.

**same,** *adj.* **1.** identical. **2.** without change.

**sam'ple,** *n.* **1.** something representing more or others of its kind. —*v.t.* **2.** take a sample of.

**sam'pler,** *n.* piece of needlework demonstrating skill.

**san''a·to'ri·um,** *n.* sanitarium.

**sanc'ti·fy,** *v.t.* make sacred.

**sanc'ti·mo''ny,** *n.* showy or false piety. —**sanc''ti·mo'ni·ous,** *adj.*

**sanc'tion,** *n.* **1.** permission or support. —*v.t.* **2.** authorize.

**sanc'ti·ty,** *n.* holiness or sacredness.

**sanc'tu·ar''y,** *n., pl.* **-aries. 1.** consecrated place. **2.** place of refuge.

**sand,** *n.* fine pieces of rock.

**san'dal,** *n.* open shoe secured by straps.

**sand'pa''per,** *n.* **1.** sand-coated paper for smoothing or reducing surfaces. —*v.t.* **2.** rub with sandpaper.

**sand'wich,** *n.* bread, roll, etc. in two slices with meat, etc. between them.

**sand'y,** *adj.*, **-ier, -iest.** abounding in sand.

**sane,** *adj.*, **saner, sanest.** mentally sound.

**san'guine,** *adj.* optimistic.

**san''i·tar''i·um,** *n.* place for the recovery of health.

**san'i·tar''y,** *adj.* **1.** free of harmful bacteria, etc. **2.** pertaining to health.

**san''i·ta'tion,** *n.* provisions against disease.

**san'i·ty,** *n.* mental soundness.

**sap,** *n.* **1.** juice of a tree, etc. —*v.t.* **2.** weaken.

**sap'ling,** *n.* young tree.

**sap'phire,** *n.* blue gemstone.

**sar'casm,** *n.* making of agreeably worded but harshly intended remarks. —**sar·cas'tic,** *adj.*

**sar·dine',** *n.* trade name for a small canned ocean fish.

**sar·don'ic,** *adj.* bitterly sarcastic.

**sash,** *n.* **1.** cloth band worn over the upper part of the body or around the waist. **2.** frame for window glass.

**Sa'tan,** *n.* the Devil. —**sa·tan'ic,** *adj.*

**satch'el,** *n.* small cloth suitcase or bag.

**sat'el·lite,** *n.* heavenly body moving around a planet.

**sa·ti·ate** (sā'shē āt), *v.t.* glut. —**sa''ti·a'tion, sa·ti'e·ty,** *n.*

**sat'in,** *n.* glossy fabric or silk or a silk substitute.

**sat'ire,** *n.* **1.** sarcasm or ridicule in the exposure of wrongful actions or attitudes. **2.** story, etc. using these means. —**sa·tir'i·cal, sa·tir'ic,** *adj.* —**sa'tir·ist,** *n.*

**sat'ir·ize,** *v.t.* portray satirically.

**sat'is·fy,** *v.t.* **1.** fulfill the wishes or needs of. **2.** convince. —**sat''is·fac'tion,** *n.* —**sat''is·fac'to·ry,** *adj.*

**sat'u·rate,** *v.t.* cause complete absorption by. —**sat''u·ra'tion,** *n.*

**sauce,** *n.* **1.** liquid for flavoring or cooking. **2.** semiliquid stewed fruit.

**sau'cer,** *n.* small dish.

**sau'cy,** *adj.,* **-cier, -ciest.** impudent. —**sau'ci·ly,** *adv.* —**sau'ci·ness,** *n.*

**saun'ter,** *v.i., n.* stroll.

**sau'sage,** *n.* minced and seasoned meat, often in a casing.

**sav'age,** *adj.* uncivilized. —*n.* **2.** uncivilized person.

**save,** *v.t.* **1.** keep from harm. **2.** keep for future use. **3.** keep from being wasted. —*prep., conj.* **4.** except.

**sav'ings,** money saved.

**sav'ior,** **1.** rescuer. **2.** the Savior, Christ.

**sa·voir-faire** (sav'wahr fâr'), *n.* skill in human relations.

**sa'vor,** *n., v.t.* taste or smell.

**saw,** *n.* **1.** cutting tool with a row of teeth. **2.** saying or proverb. —*v.t.* **3.** cut with a saw.

**sax'o·phone,** *n.* keyed metal reed instrument.

**say,** *v.t.* speak.

**say'ing,** *n.* proverb.

**scab,** *n.* **1.** crust over a healing wound or sore. **2.** worker who replaces a striking worker.

**scab'bard,** *n.* sword sheath.

**scaf'fold,** *n.* **1.** Also, **scaf'fold·ing,** temporary platform. **2.** platform for execution of condemned persons.

**scald,** *v.t.* burn with hot fluid.

**scale,** *n.* **1.** platelike portion of the covering of a fish, snake, etc. **2.** Also, **scales,** weighing device. **3.** range of musical tones. **4.** system of relations, as of actual size to represented size or of different degrees of a thing. —*v.t.* **5.** climb.

**scalp,** *n.* **1.** hair and skin covering the top of the head. —*v.t.* **2.** take a scalp from, esp. as a trophy.

**scam,** *n.* con game; deception practiced to defraud.

**scamp,** *n.* rascal; imp.

**scam'per,** *v.i.* run quickly.

**scan,** *v.t.* **1.** examine in detail. **2.** analyze the rhythmic pattern of.

**scan'dal,** *n.* **1.** malicious gossip. **2.** disgraceful occurrence or situation. —**scan'dal·ous,** *adj.*

**scan'dal·ize,** *v.t.* shock with a scandal.

**scant,** *adj.* scarcely sufficient. Also, **scant'y.**

**scape'goat,** *n.* person blamed for the misdeeds of others.

**scar,** *n.* mark left by a cut.

**scarce,** *adj.,* **scarcer, scarcest.** not plentiful or common. —**scarc'i·ty, scarce'ness,** *n.*

**scarce'ly,** *adv.* **1.** only just; barely. **2.** hardly.

**scare,** *n., v., v.t.* **1.** frighten. —*v.i.* **2.** become frightened. —*n.* **3.** frightening occurrence.

**scarf,** *n., pl.* **scarfs, scarves.** length of cloth for warming the neck and chest.

**scar'let,** *n.* bright red.

**scath'ing,** *adj.* bitterly harsh, as something said or written.

**scat'ter,** *v.t.* throw in all directions.

**scav'enge,** *v.t.* **1.** clean out. —*v.i.*

2. search for refuse that can be eaten or reused.

**scene**, *n.* 1. what is seen from a certain place. 2. location of an action. —**scen'ic**, *adj.*

**scen'er·y**, *n.* 1. pleasant outdoor scene. 2. painted canvases, etc. representing the scene of a dramatic action.

**scent**, *n.* 1. distinctive smell. 2. trail left by something with such a smell.

**scep·ter** (sep'tər), *n.* short staff symbolizing royal power.

**sched'ule**, *n.* 1. list of the times of planned actions or events. 2. any orderly list. —*v.t.* 3. put on a schedule.

**scheme**, *n.* 1. plan or design. 2. plot; intrigue. —*v.i.* 3. plot to do or attain something.

**schol'ar**, *n.* 1. person who studies to acquire knowledge. 2. school pupil.

**schol'ar·ly**, *adj.* pertaining to or in the manner of scholars.

**schol'ar·ship**, *n.* 1. activities and accomplishments of scholars. 2. grant of money to make school attendance possible.

**scho·las'tic**, *adj.* pertaining to education.

**school**, *n.* 1. place or institution for education or training. 2. group with a common set of beliefs or practices.

**schoon'er**, *n.* fore-and-aft rigged sailing vessel with two or more masts, including a foremast.

**sci'ence**, *n.* 1. systematic acquisition of knowledge, esp. knowledge that can be measured precisely. 2. precise method or skill. —**sci''en·tif'ic**, *adj.* —**sci'en·tist**, *n.*

**scin·til·late** (sin'təl lāt), *v.i.* sparkle.

**scis'sors**, *n.* instrument for cutting by means of two moving blades.

**scoff**, *n.*, *v.i.*, jeer.

**scold**, *v.t.* reproach at length.

**scoop**, *n.* 1. device for digging deeply. 2. *Informal.* prior publication of news. —*v.t.* 3. remove or empty with a scoop.

**scope**, *n.* range of responsibility or possibility for action.

**scorch**, *v.t.* burn on the surface.

**score**, *n.* 1. total, as of points in a game. 2. musical arrangement. —*v.t.* 3. add, as points in a game. 4. mark with a long, shallow cut.

**scorn**, *n.* 1. contempt. 2. derision.

—*v.t.* 3. treat with scorn. —**scorn'ful**, *adj.*

**scor·pi·on**, *n.* poisonous, long-tailed eight-legged animal.

**Scotch**, *n.* malted-barley whisky made in Scotland.

**scoun'drel**, *n.* rascal.

**scour**, *v.t.* clean with a steady rubbing action.

**scout**, *n.* 1. person sent to explore or search. —*v.t.* 2. reject as absurd. —*v.i.* 3. act as a scout.

**scowl**, *v.i.* frown angrily.

**scram'ble**, *v.t.* 1. mix up; confuse. —*v.i.* 2. move in short, rapid steps. —*n.* 3. undignified struggle, as for something of value.

**scrap**, *n.* 1. small piece. 2. refuse material, esp. when reclaimable. 3. *Informal.* fight. —*v.t.* 4. make into scrap. —**scrap'heap**, *n.*

**scrape**, *v.t.* rub against roughly.

**scratch**, *v.t.* 1. make a long, shallow cut in. —*n.* 2. long, shallow cut. 3. **from scratch**, from the beginning.

**scratch'y**, *adj.*, **-ier, -iest.** suggesting scratching, esp. in sound.

**scrawl**, *v.t.*, *v.i.* 1. write with a bad hand. —*n.* 2. writing in a bad hand.

**scrawn'y**, *adj.*, **-nier, -niest.** disagreeably thin.

**scream**, *n.* 1. loud, high-pitched cry.—*v.i.* 2. utter such a cry.

**screech**, *n.* 1. harsh screamlike sound. —*v.i.* 2. utter such sounds.

**screen**, *n.* 1. flat object or surface for division, protection, or concealment. 2. surface on which motion pictures, television programs, etc. are projected. —*v.t.* 3. enclose or protect with or as if with a screen.

**screw**, *n.* 1. simple machine for fastening, moving, etc., in the form of an inclined plane wound around an axis. —*v.t.* 2. fasten with screws. —**screw'driv''er**, *n.*

**scrib'ble**, *v.t.*, *v.i.* write hastily and carelessly.

**script**, *n.* 1. handwriting. 2. manuscript, esp. of a play, etc.

**Scrip'ture**, *n.* 1. portion or portions of the Bible. 2. **the Scriptures,** the Bible.

**scroll**, *n.* 1. roll of paper, etc. bearing writing or print. 2. spiral ornamental motif. —*v.* 3. (computers) to move the display on a monitor so that other data can be read.

**scrub,** *v.t.* wash with a vigorous rubbing action.

**scru'ple,** *n.* prompting of the conscience.

**scru'pu·lous,** *adj.* 1. conscientious. 2. careful.

**scru'ti·nize,** *v.t.* examine carefully. —**scru'ti·ny,** *n.*

**scuf'fle,** *v.i.* 1. fight confusedly at close quarters. —*n.* 2. confused fight at close quarters.

**sculp'ture,** *n.* 1. art of composing in three dimensions. 2. example of this art. —**sculp'tor,** *n.,* *fem.,* **sculp'tress.**

**scythe,** *n.* mowing instrument with curved blade and long handle.

**sea,** *n.* 1. part of an ocean, esp. one partly bounded by land. 2. relative turbulence of ocean water at a given time.

**seal,** *n.* 1. device for giving official character to or preventing tampering with a document, locked space, etc. 2. four-flippered sea mammal. —*v.t.* 3. put a seal on.

**seam,** *n.* 1. line of junction. —*v.t.* 2. join at or with a seam.

**sea'man,** *n.,* *pl.* **-men.** sailor

**sea'port',** *n.* port fronting on an ocean.

**sear,** *v.t.* 1. burn the surface of. 2. wither.

**search,** *n.* 1. methodical attempt to find something. —*v.t.* 2. examine in making a search. —*v.i.* 3. hunt.

**search'ing,** *adj.* deep and perceptive, as an investigation.

**sea'shore'',** *n.* shore of an ocean. Also, **sea'side''.**

**sea'sick'',** *adj.* sick from the motion of a ship. —**sea'sick''ness,** *n.*

**sea'son,** *n.* 1. quarter of the year beginning at a solstice or equinox. —*v.t.* 2. flavor with salt, spices, herbs, etc. —**sea'son·al,** *adj.*

**sea'son·ing,** *n.* flavoring of salt, spices, herbs, etc.

**seat,** *n.* 1. place for sitting. 2. place of governmental activities, residence, etc. —*v.t.* 3. put onto a seat.

**se·cede',** *v.i.* withdraw from a political state, etc. —**se·ces'sion,** *n.*

**se·clude',** *v.t.,* isolate, esp. from society or activity. —**se·clu'sion,** *n.*

**sec'ond,** *adj.* 1. next after the first. —*n.* 2. sixtieth of a minute. 3. approve.

**sec'ond·ar·y,** *adv.* forming a second stage or phase.

**se'cret,** *n.* 1. something not to be known by everyone. —*adj.* 2. hidden or not to be known by everyone. —**se'cre·cy,** *n.*

**sec're·tar''y,** *n.,* *pl.* **-taries.** 1. assistant to a businessman, official, etc. 2. head of a government department.

**se·crete',** *v.t.* produce and release substances, as a gland.

**se'cre·tive,** *adj.* 1. reluctant to reveal information. 2. pertaining to secretion.

**sect,** *n.* religious group.

**sec'tion,** *n.* 1. separate part. 2. act or instance of dividing. —**sec'tion·al,** *adj.*

**sec'u·lar,** *adj.* not religious.

**se·cure',** *adj.* 1. safe or certain. 2. firmly in place. —*v.t.* 3. make secure.

**se·cu'ri·ty,** *n.,* *pl.* **-ties.** state of being secure.

**se·date',** *n.* 1. quiet in manner.

**sed'a·tive,** *n.* 1. medicine to relieve pain or nervousness. —*adj.* 2. relieving pain or nervousness.

**sed'en·tar''y,** *adj.* not physically active.

**sed'i·ment,** *n.* matter falling to the bottom of a body of liquid.

**se·duce',** *v.t.* tempt or induce to commit a wrong. —**se·duc'tion,** *n.*

**se·duc'tive,** *adj.* tempting; attractive.

**see,** *v.,* **saw, seen, seeing,** *n.* *v.t.* 1. sense with the eyes. 2. realize or understand. —*v.i.* 3. have use of the eyes.

**seed,** *n.,* *pl.* **seeds, seed.** 1. thing from which a plant grows. 2. offspring. —**seed'less,** *adj.*

**seek,** *v.t.,* **sought, seeking.** look for.

**seem,** *v.t.,* *v.i.* give the effect of being or acting in some specified way.

**seem'ly,** *adj.,* **-lier, -liest.** proper in appearance or effect.

**seep,** *v.i.* ooze.

**seethe,** *v.t.,* *v.i.* boil.

**seg'ment,** *n.* portion.

**seg're·gate,** *v.t.* keep apart from others.

**seize,** *v.t.* 1. take by authority or force. 2. grasp, as an idea.

**sel'dom,** *adv.* rarely.

**se·lect',** *v.t.* 1. choose. —*adj.* 2. selected; choice. —**se·lec'tion,** *n.*

**S**
**T**

**se·lec'tive**, *adj.* 1. pertaining to selection. 2. careful in selecting.

**self**, *n.* 1. one's own person. 2. one's own well-being. —*adj.* 3. of the same kind.

**self''-as·sur'ance**, *n.* self-confidence. —**self''-as·sured'**, *adj.*

**self''-cen'tered**, *adj.* seeing all things in reference to one's self or self-interest.

**self''-con'fi·dence**, *n.* confidence in one's own ability, rightness, etc. —**self''-con'fi·dent**, *adj.*

**self''-con'scious**, *adj.* excessively aware of the impression one may be making.

**self''-con·tained'**, *adj.* 1. complete in itself. 2. reserved in manner.

**self''-con·trol'**, *n.* ability to restrain one's impulses or expressions of emotion.

**self''-de·ni'al**, *n.* readiness to forgo gratifications. —**self''-de·ny'ing**, *adj.*

**self'-es·teem'**, *n.* good opinion of one's self.

**self'-ev'i·dent**, *adj.* evident without further proof or explanation.

**self''-im·por'tant**, *adj.* seeming to have an excessive idea of one's own importance.

**self''-in'ter·est**, *n.* concern for one's own well-being.

**self'ish**, *adj.* acting for or thinking of one's own well-being alone. —**self'ish·ness**, *n.*

**self'less**, *n.* self-sacrificing.

**self'-re·spect'**, *n.* respect for one's own dignity, rights, etc. —**self'—re·spect'ing**, *adj.*

**self''-right'eous**, *adj.* conceitedly sure of one's righteousness.

**self'-styled'**, *adj.* thus named by the one so named.

**self''-suf·fi'cient**, *adj.* able to depend on one's own resources.

**sell**, *v.t.,* sold, selling. 1. exchange for money. 2. offer for sale.

**sem'blance**, *n.* 1. seeming state. 2. resemblance.

**se·mes'ter**, *n.* unit consisting of half a school year.

**se'mi·cir'cle**, *n.* half a circle. —**se''mi·cir'cu·lar**, *adj.*

**sem'i·col''on**, *n.* punctuation mark of the form; that is used to divide clauses of a sentence.

**sem''i·con·duc'tor**, *n.* a material used to modify electrical current, used in solid-state circuitry.

**sem'i·nar''**, *n.* academic class with a format of discussion or research.

**sem'i·nar''y**, *n.,* pl. **-naries.** 1. school for divinity students. 2. school for young women.

**sen'ate**, *n.* senior legislative body. —**sen'a·tor**, *n.*

**send**, *v.t.* cause to go.

**se·nile'** (sē'nīl), *adj.* decrepit, esp. mentally, in old age.

**sen'ior**, *adj.* 1. older. 2. higher in authority.

**sen·sa'tion**, *n.* 1. use of the senses. 2. experience obtained through the senses.

**sen·sa'tion·al**, *adj.* causing or intended to cause excited public interest.

**sense**, *n.* 1. sight, hearing, touch, taste, or smell. 2. meaning. —*v.t.* 3. perceive by or as if by one of the senses.

**sense'less**, *adj.* 1. unreasonable. 2. unconscious.

**sen'si·ble**, *n.* 1. reasonable. 2. perceptible through the senses. 3. aware.

**sen'si·tive**, *n.* 1. able to sense or register obects, data, etc. in small amounts. 2. easily disturbed.

**sen'su·al**, *adj.* 1. given to the pleasures of the senses. 2. pertaining to such pleasure. —**sen'su·al·ism**, *n.* —**sen'su·al·ist**, *n.*

**sen'su·ous**, *adj.* pertaining to the senses.

**sen'tence**, *n.* 1. unit of prose writing expressing one thought. 2. legal decision, esp. regarding a punishment. —*v.t.* 3. determine the punishment of.

**sen·ten'tious**, *adj.* tiresomely opinionated or voluble on matters of right and wrong.

**sen'ti·ment**, *n.* personal feeling.

**sen'ti·men'tal**, *adj.* characterized by love, pity, etc., esp. to an unreasonable extent.

**sep·a·rate**, *v.t., v.i.* (sep'ə rāt) 1. part. —*adj.* (sep'ə rət) 2. unconnected; individual. —**sep''a·ra'tion**, *n.*

**sep·ul'cher** (sep'əl kər), *n.* tomb. Also, **sep'ul·chre.**

**se'quel**, *n.* 1. event that follows. 2. story continuing the subject of a previous one.

**se'quence**, *n.* succession or series.

**ser'e·nade''**, *n.* 1. musical composition for outdoor evening performance. —*v.t.* 2. perform a serenade for.

**se·rene'**, *adj.* 1. calm. 2. fair, as the weather. —**se·ren'i·ty**, *n.*

**ser'geant**, *n.* highest noncommissioned army officer.

**se'ri·al**, *adj.* 1. forming part of a series. —*n.* 2. story appearing in installments.

**se'ries**, *n.*, *pl.* **-ries**. group of things coming one after the other.

**se'ri·ous**, *adj.* 1. solemn. 2. important. —**se'ri·ous·ly**, *adv.* —**se'ri·ous·ness**, *n.*

**ser'mon**, *n.* speech to a religious congregation.

**ser'pent**, *n.* any large snake.

**ser'rat·ed**, *adj.* resembling sawteeth in outline.

**se'rum**, *n.* liquid part of the blood, sometimes used in inoculation.

**serv'ant**, *n.* person hired to work in a household.

**serve**, *v.t.* 1. act in the service of. 2. be of use to. 3. present for consumption, as food or drink. —*v.i.* 4. act in the service of a person, organization, or cause.

**serv'ice**, *n.* 1. activity on behalf of a person, organization, or cause. 2. military organization or the military. 3. session of public worship. 4. set of matched dishes, eating implements, etc.

**serv'ice·a·ble**, *adj.* useful.

**ser·vile'** (sər'vĭl), *adj.* slavelike; obsequious.

**ser'vi·tude**, *n.* bondage.

**ses'sion**, *n.* occasion of the gathering of members of a group.

**set**, *v.t.* 1. place or put. —*v.i.* 2. become fixed or firm. 3. go below the horizon, as a star or planet. —*n.* 4. apparatus. 5. complete group or collection. —*adj.* 6. firm or fixed.

**set'ting**, *n.* environment.

**set'tle**, *v.t.* 1. resolve, as a dispute. —*v.i.* 2. fall gently into a position of rest. 3. take up residence. —**set'tler**, *n.* —**set'tle·ment**, *n.*

**sev'en**, *n.*, *adj.* one more than six.

**sev'en·teen'**, *n.*, *adj.* seven more than ten. —**sev''en·teenth'**, *adj.*

**sev'en·ty**, *n.*, *adj.* seven times ten. —**sev''en·ti'eth**, *adj.*

**sev'er**, *v.t.* cut off or separate. —**sev'er·ance**, *n.*

**sev'er·al**, *adj.* a few.

**se·vere'**, *adj.* 1. sternly demanding. 2. harsh or violent. —**se·ver'i·ty**, *n.*

**sew**, *v.t.* join with thread.

**sew'age**, *n.* waste material in sewers.

**sew'er**, *n.* covered channel for waste.

**sex**, *n.* 1. individual nature as determined by the reproductive system. 2. either of two divisions of a species as so determined. —**sex'u·al**, *adj.*

**sex'is·m**, *n.* discrimination on the basis of sex.

**sex·tet'**, *n.* group of six, esp. musicians. Also, **sex·tette'.**

**sex'ton**, *n.* caretaker of a church.

**shab'by**, *adj.*, **-bier, -biest,** 1. worn and untidy-looking. 2. mean.

**shack**, *n.* shanty.

**shack'les**, *n.* chains for binding prisoners.

**shade**, *n.* 1. area sheltered from direct light. 2. device for cutting off direct light. 3. variety of color or tone. 4. slight degree. 5. soul of a dead person. —*v.t.* 6. shelter from direct light. 7. vary, as a color or tone.

**shad'ow**, *n.* darkness of a shaded area.

**shad'y**, *adj.* 1. in the shade. 2. *Informal.* to be suspected.

**shaft**, *n.* 1. long, cylindrical object for support, rotation, etc. 2. beam of light. 3. narrow vertical space.

**shag**, *n.* long, rough hair, fur, or nap. —**shag'gy**, *adj.*

**shake**, *v.t.* 1. cause to move rapidly back and forth. —*v.i.* 2. move rapidly back and forth. —*n.* 3. act or instance of shaking.

**shak'er**, *n.* device for sprinkling seasoning.

**shak'y**, *adj.*, **-kier, -kiest.** unstable.

**shall**, *v.* am, is, or are going to.

**shal'low**, *adj.* not deep.

**sham**, *adj.* 1. false; imitation. —*n.* 2. something false or imitative. —*v.t.* 3. pretend; feign.

**sham'ble**, *v.i.* 1. walk draggingly or awkwardly. —*n.* 2. **shambles,** a. scene of disorder. b. slaughterhouse.

**shame**, *n.* 1. painful sense of guilt or inadequacy. 2. deplorable situation. —*v.t.* 3. put to shame. —**shame'ful**, *adj.* —**shame'less**, *adj.*

**shame'faced**, *adj.* showing embarrassment.

**sham·poo'**, *v.t.* 1. wash with soap, as the hair or a carpet. —*n.* 2. soap, etc. used for shampooing.

**S
T**

**sham'rock**, *n.* cloverlike plant with a triple leaf: symbol of Ireland.

**shank**, *n.* lower leg above the ankle.

**shan'ty**, *n., pl.* **-ties.** roughly built wooden house.

**shape**, *n.* 1. form. —*v.t.* 2. give form to.

**shape'ly**, *adj.* handsome in form.

**share**, *n.* 1. rightful or predetermined portion. —*v.t.* 2. divide into such portions. 3. use or experience together.

**shark**, *n.* large predatory fish.

**sharp**, *adj.* 1. having or as if having a cutting point or edge. 2. shrewd. 3. *Music.* raised in pitch. —*n.* 4. a semitone higher than a stated tone. —**sharp'en**, *v.t.*

**shat'ter**, *v.t., v.i.* break in small pieces.

**shave**, *v.t.* 1. cut the hair off with a razor. —*n.* 2. act or instance of being shaved.

**shav'ing**, *n.* thin layer of material shaved from a larger piece.

**she**, *pron.* woman or female previously mentioned.

**sheaf**, *n., pl.* **sheaves.** bundle.

**shear**, *v.t.* divide as with the motion of one blade across another.

**shears**, *n. pl.* large scissors.

**sheath**, *n., pl.* **sheaths.** closely fitting case or cover.

**sheathe**, *v.t.* put into a sheath.

**shed**, *v.t.* 1. leave or cast off. 2. pour forth, as light. —*n.* 3. rough shelter.

**sheen**, *n.* dull reflection.

**sheep**, *n., pl.* **sheep.** mammal yielding fleece and mutton.

**sheer**, *adj.* 1. absolute; utter. 2. very steep or perpendicular. —*v.i.* 3. swerve.

**sheet**, *n.* 1. broad, thin piece of material. 2. cloth used to cover a mattress or a sleeper.

**shelf**, *n., pl.* **shelves.** horizontal ledge or slab for supporting objects.

**shell**, *n.* 1. hard outer covering. 2. shotgun cartridge. 3. explosive artillery missile. —*v.t.* 4. bombard with shells.

**shell'fish''**, *n.* any aquatic animal with a shell.

**shel'ter**, *n.* 1. something serving as a protection, as against the weather. —*v.t.* 2. protect. —*v.i.* 3. take shelter.

**shelve**, *v.t.* put on a shelf.

**shep'herd**, *n.* person who leads

and guards sheep. Also, *fem.,* **shep'herd·ess.**

**sher'bet**, *n.* frozen dessert of water, gelatin, flavoring, and sometimes milk.

**sher'iff**, *n.* county police officer.

**shield**, *n.* 1. piece of armor worn on the arm. —*v.t.* 2. protect or hide.

**shift**, *v.t., v.i.* 1. move from place to place. 2. change, as one's place. —*n.* 3. act or instance of shifting. 4. daily period of labor.

**shift'less**, *adj.* lazy or feeble.

**shim'mer**, *v.i.* glow or appear in a flickering, unsteady way.

**shin**, *n.* front of the shank of the leg.

**shine**, *v.i.* 1. emit or reflect strong light. —*v.t.* 2. polish to a high gloss. —**shin'y**, *adj.*

**shin'gle**, *n.* thin plate of wood or other material used in courses as a roof covering or siding.

**ship**, *n.* 1. large ocean-going vessel. —*v.t.* 2. send by a freight carrier. —**ship'mate''**, *n.* —**ship'ment**, *n.*

**ship'ping**, *n.* vessels, esp. merchant ships.

**ship'shape''**, *adj., adv.* in good order.

**ship'wreck''**, *n.* destruction of a ship from running aground.

**ship'yard''**, *n.* place for building or repairing ships.

**shirk**, *v.t.* evade, as an obligation.

**shirt**, *n.* a long- or short-sleeved upper garment usually having a front opening, collar and cuffs, worn esp. by men.

**shiv'er**, *v.i.* 1. tremble. —*n.* 2. trembling movement.

**shock**, *n.* 1. violent impact. 2. violent emotional disturbance. —*v.t.* 3. disturb with a shock.

**shod'dy**, *adj.* poor in quality.

**shoe**, *n.* 1. protective covering for the foot. —*v.t.* 2. provide with shoes.

**shoot**, *v.t.* 1. send a missile from. 2. hit with a missile. —*v.i.* 3. use a gun, bow, etc.

**shop**, *n.* 1. store, esp. a small specialized one. 2. industrial workroom. —*v.i.* 3. look for or make purchases.

**shore**, *n.* 1. land bordering a body of water. —*v.t.* 2. prop.

**short**, *adj.* 1. not tall or long. 2. scanty, as a supply. —*n.* 3. **shorts,** shortlegged pants or underpants. —**short'en**, *v.t.*

**short'age**, *n.* short supply.

**short'com''ing,** *n.* fault or inadequacy.

**short'cut'',** *n.* shorter way than the usual.

**short'hand'',** *n.* system of writing for fast note-taking.

**short-lived** (short'līvd'), *adj.* not living or existing long.

**shot,** *n., pl.* **shots** or (for 2) **shot.** 1. discharge of a missile. 2. *Often pl.* missiles, esp. shotgun pellets or cannonballs.

**shot'gun,** *n.* gun firing shells filled with metal pellets.

**should,** *v.* 1. ought to. 2. were to. 3. past tense of **shall**.

**shoul'der,** *n.* 1. part of the human body between the upper arms and neck. —*v.t.* 2. take up and carry.

**shout,** *n.* 1. very loud call or voice. —*v.i.* 2. give such a call.

**shove,** *v.t., v.i.* push vigorously.

**shov'el,** *n.* hand tool or machine for scooping up material.

**show,** *v.t.* 1. display. 2. prove or demonstrate. —*v.i.* 3. be visible or apparent. —*n.* 4. entertainment.

**show'down'',** *n.* confrontation, as between enemies.

**show'er,** *n.* 1. brief rainstorm. 2. bath in which water is sprayed from above.

**show'off'',** *n.* vain, ostentatious person.

**show'y,** *adj.,* **-ier, -iest.** attracting attention, esp. through gaudiness.

**shrap'nel,** *n.* small missiles hurled by the bursting of an artillery shell.

**shred,** *n.* torn strip.

**shrewd,** *adj.* clever in dealing with or understanding others.

**shriek,** *n.* 1. loud, shrill cry. —*v.i.* 2. utter such a cry.

**shrill,** *adj.* high-pitched.

**shrimp,** *n.* small, long-tailed shellfish.

**shrine,** *n.* sacred place.

**shrink,** *v.i.* 1. become smaller. —*v.t.* 2. cause to shrink.

**shrivel,** *v.i.* shrink and become wrinkled.

**shrub,** *n.* small, treelike plant. —**shrub'ber·y,** *n.*

**shrug,** *v.t.* 1. movement of raising both shoulders. —*v.i.* 2. make such a movement.

**shud'der,** *v.i.* tremble violently and briefly.

**shuf'fle,** *v.i.* walk with feet scraping the ground.

**shut,** *v.t.* 1. close. 2. keep in or out.

—*v.i.* 3. be closed. —*n.* 4. closed.

**shut'ter,** *n.* 1. cover for a window opening. 2. device for timed exposure of film in a camera.

**shut'tle,** *v.i.* 1. go short distances back and forth. —*n.* 2. device on a loom for moving warp thread back and forth.

**shy,** *adj.,* **shier, shiest.** 1. timid in the presence of others. 2. lacking by a specified number.

**sib'ling,** *n.* brother or sister.

**sick,** *adj.* 1. not in health. —*n.* 2. sick people. —**sick'ness,** *n.* —**sick'en,** *v.t., v.i.*

**sick'ly,** *adj.,* **-lier, -liest.** not healthy or robust.

**side,** *n.* 1. area of someone or something to the right or left of the face or front. 2. aspect. 3. person or group in a dispute or conflict. —*v.i.* 4. ally oneself.

**side'walk'',** *n.* walk beside a roadway.

**side'ways'',** *adv., adj.* 1. with a side foremost. 2. to or from one side. Also, **side'wise''.**

**SIDS,** sudden infant death syndrome, unexplained death of baby while asleep.

**si·dle,** *v.i.* move sideways.

**siege,** *n.* prolonged attack on a fortified place.

**si·es'ta,** *n.* brief daytime nap.

**sieve,** *n.* strainer of wire mesh.

**sift,** *v.t.* separate with a sieve.

**sigh,** *v.i.* 1. release pent-up breath in reaction to grief, annoyance, etc. —*n.* 2. such a release of breath.

**sight,** *n.* 1. something perceived by the eyes. 2. something remarkable to see. 3. range of distances one's eyes can see clearly. —*v.t.* 4. discover with the eye.

**sight'ly,** *adj.,* **-lier, -liest.** pleasing to see.

**sign,** *n.* 1. indication. 2. written, printed, or hand-given symbol. 3. display surface containing such symbols or writing. —*v.t.* 4. put a signature on.

**sig'nal,** *n.* 1. device presenting a message in symbols. —*v.t.* 2. communicate through a signal.

**sig'na·ture,** *n.* one's name in one's handwriting.

**sig·nif'i·cance,** *n.* 1. meaning. 2. importance. —**sig·nif'i·cant,** *adj.*

**s'g'ni·fy'',** *v.t.* 1. mean. 2. indicate.

**si'lence,** *n.* 1. absence of noise,

**S**
**T**

conversation, or sound. —*v.t.* **2.** make silent. —**si'lent,** *adj.*

**sil·hou·ette** (sil″ŏŏ et′), *n.* outline figure, usually filled in with black.

**silk,** *n.* cloth made of fiber spun by silkworms.

**silk'en,** *adj.* **1.** made of silk. **2.** suggesting silk in smoothness. Also, **silk'y.**

**sill,** *n.* horizontal structural member, esp. below a wall or opening.

**sil'ly,** *adj.,* **-lier, -liest.** foolish or stupid.

**si'lo,** *n.* airtight place for storing fodder.

**silt,** *n.* fine earth, etc. deposited by running water.

**sil'ver,** *n.* **1.** white noble metallic element. **2.** coins, utensils, etc. customarily made of silver. —*adj.* **3.** made of or colored silver.

**sil'ver·ware″,** *n.* tableware traditionally made of silver.

**sim'i·an,** *adj.* pertaining to or suggesting apes and monkeys.

**sim'i·lar,** *adj.* of the same sort. —**sim″i·lar'i·ty,** *n.*

**sim'i·le″,** *n.* expression comparing one thing to another.

**si·mil'i·tude″,** *n.* likeness.

**sim'mer,** *v.t., v.i.* almost boil.

**sim'per,** *v.i.* smile foolishly or affectedly.

**sim'ple,** *adj.,* **-pler, -plest. 1.** of the most basic kind. **2.** readily understood or mastered. —**sim·plic'i·ty,** *n.*

**sim'ple-mind'ed,** *adj.* foolish; low in intelligence.

**sim'ple·ton,** *n.* foolish or naive person.

**sim·pli'fy,** *v.t.* make easier to understand or master.

**sim'u·late,** *v.t.* pretend; feign.

**si″mul·ta'ne·ous,** *adj.* at the very same time. —**si″mul·ta'ne·ous·ly,** *adv.*

**sin,** *n.* **1.** violation of religious law. —*v.i.* **2.** commit such a violation. —**sin'ful,** *adj.*

**since,** *conj.* **1.** during the time after. **2.** because or inasmuch as. —*adv.* **3.** from that time on. **4.** at some time afterwards.

**sin·cere',** *adj.,* **-cerer, -cerest.** genuine; honest and unaffected. —**sin·cer'i·ty,** *n.*

**sin'ew,** *n.* **1.** tendon. **2.** muscular strength.

**sing,** *v.i.* **1.** make musical sounds with the voice. —*v.t.* **2.** render by

singing.

**singe,** *v.t.* burn on the surface.

**sin'gle,** *adj.* **1.** alone or unique. **2.** unmarried. —**sin'gly,** *adv.*

**sin'gu·lar,** *adj.* **1.** peculiar or extra-ordinary. **2.** unique. —*n.* **3.** *Grammar.* singular number of a word. —**sin″gu·lar'i·ty,** *n.*

**sin'is·ter,** *adj.* evilly threatening.

**sink,** *v.i.* **1.** descend beneath a surface. —*v.t.* **2.** cause to descend or penetrate beneath a surface. —*n.* **3.** basin with a drain. —**sink'er,** *n.*

**sin'u·ous,** *adj.* meandering; serpentine.

**si'nus,** *n.* cavity, esp. one in the skull opening into the nasal passages.

**sip,** *v.t.* **1.** drink in tiny amounts. —*n.* **2.** act or instance of sipping.

**si'phon,** *n.* curved tube for sucking liquids automatically from place to place.

**sir,** *n.* formal term used in addressing a man.

**si'ren,** *n.* **1.** mythical sea nymph luring sailors with singing to shipwreck. **2.** horn with a wavering tone used on emergency vehicles.

**sir'loin,** *n.* cut of beef at the loin end by the rump.

**sis'ter,** *n.* daughter of one's own parents.

**sis'ter·hood″,** *n.* **1.** organization of nuns. **2.** condition of being a sister.

**sis'ter-in-law″,** *n., pl.* **sisters-in-law. 1.** sister of a spouse. **2.** wife of a brother.

**sit,** *v.i.* rest on the behind.

**site,** *n.* location, as of a building.

**sit'ting,** *n.* session.

**sit'u·ate″,** *v.t.* place or locate.

**sit″u·a'tion,** *n.* **1.** location. **2.** condition or predicament.

**six,** *n., adj.* one more than five. —**sixth,** *adj.*

**six'teen′,** *n., adj.* six more than ten. —**six'teenth′,** *adj.*

**six'ty,** *n., adj.* six times ten. —**six'ti·eth,** *adj.*

**siz'a·ble,** *adj.* fairly large. Also, **size'a·ble.**

**size,** *n.* area, volume, number, etc. by which something is measured or graded.

**siz'zle,** *v.i.* hiss or crackle, as from being fried.

**skate,** *n.* **1.** piece of footwear for gliding across ice. —*v.i.* **2.** go on skates.

**skel'e·ton**, *n.* bone structure of an animal. —**skel'e·tal**, *adj.*

**skep'tic**, *n.* doubter. —**skep'ti·cal**, *adj.* —**skep'ti·cism'**, *n.*

**sketch**, *n.* **1.** rough drawing. —*v.t.* **2.** make a sketch of.

**sketch'y**, *adj.* vague or without detail.

**ski**, *n.*, *pl.* **skis**, *v.i.*, *n.* **1.** long, flat runner for gliding or walking on snow. —*v.i.* **2.** glide on skis. —**ski'er**, *n.*

**skid**, *v.i.*, *v.t.* **1.** slide. —*n.* **2.** skidding motion.

**skill**, *n.* practised ability. —**skill'ful**, *adj.*

**skim**, *v.t.* **1.** remove from a liquid surface. —*v.i.* **2.** move lightly across a surface.

**skimp**, *v.i.* economize; scrimp.

**skimp'y**, *adj.*, **skimpier**, **skimpiest.** scant.

**skin**, *n.* **1.** outer covering of an animal body. —*v.t.* **2.** remove skin or hide from.

**skin'ny**, *adj.* thin of body.

**skip**, *v.i.* **1.** jump lightly. —*v.t.* **2.** omit.

**skir'mish**, *n.* brief, minor battle.

**skirt**, *n.* **1.** open-bottomed garment fastened around the waist. —*v.t.* **2.** pass around the border of.

**skit'tish**, *adj.* readily excited or frightened.

**skulk**, *v.i.* lurk.

**skull**, *n.* bony shell of a head.

**skunk**, *n.* small mammal defending itself with foul-smelling liquid.

**sky**, *n.*, *pl.* **skies.** **1.** part of the atmosphere visible from the earth. **2.** condition of this at a certain place and time.

**sky'line''**, *n.* silhouette against the horizon.

**sky'scrap''er**, *n.* very tall building, esp. one for offices.

**slab**, *n.* flat, fairly thick piece of material.

**slack**, *adj.* **1.** loose. **2.** inactive.

**slack'en**, *v.t.*, *v.i.* **1.** make or become slack. **2.** lessen in intensity or vigor.

**slacks**, *n.*, *pl.* loosely fitting trousers.

**slake**, *v.t.* quench.

**slam**, *v.t.* push violently and noisily into place.

**slan'der**, *n.* **1.** maliciously untrue statement or statements about someone. —*v.t.* **2.** utter such statements about. —**slan'der·ous**, *adj.*

**slang**, *n.* highly informal speech.

**slant**, *v.t.*, *v.i.* **1.** move or head diagonally. —*n.* **2.** diagonal movement or heading.

**slap**, *v.t.* **1.** hit with a flat object, esp. the hand. —*n.* **2.** act or instance of slapping.

**slash**, *v.t.* **1.** cut deeply with a long, sweeping motion. —*n.* **2.** long, deep cut.

**slat**, *n.* thin board.

**slate**, *n.* **1.** stone that can be cleaved into thin pieces. **2.** list of candidates.

**slaugh'ter**, *n.* **1.** mass killing; massacre. **2.** killing of animals for meat. —*v.t.* **3.** submit to slaughter.

**slave**, *n.* **1.** person treated as the property of another. —*v.i.* **2.** drudge. —**slav'er·y**, *n.*

**slav'ish**, *adj.* in the manner of a slave, esp. in lacking originality or initiative.

**slea'zy**, *adj.*, **-zier**, **ziest.** shoddy

**sled**, *n.* **1.** vehicle for gliding across snow or ice. —*v.i.* **2.** travel by sled.

**sledge**, *n.* **1.** sledlike vehicle. **2.** Also, **sledge'ham·mer**, heavy hammer.

**sleek**, *adj.* smooth or glossy.

**sleep**, *n.* **1.** periodic state of unconscious rest. —*v.i.* **2.** be in such a state. —**sleep'y**, *adj.*

**sleep'er**, *n.* **1.** sleeping person. **2.** railroad car with berths.

**sleet**, *n.* rain frozen in fine particles.

**sleeve**, *n.* part of a shirt or coat covering an arm.

**sleigh**, *n.* horse-drawn light sled.

**slen'der**, *adj.* **1.** attractively thin. **2.** meager, as means of livelihood.

**sleuth**, *n. Informal.* detective.

**slice**, *n.* **1.** thin piece cut from a larger one. —*v.t.* **2.** cut as a slice.

**slick**, *adj.* **1.** smooth or slippery. **2.** cunning.

**slide**, *v.t.*, *v.i.* move with surface contact between the object moving and something else.

**slight**, *adj.* **1.** unimportantly little. **2.** slender. —*v.t.*, *n.* **3.** snub.

**slim**, *adj.*, **slimmer**, **slimmest.** **1.** slender. **2.** small in amount or size.

**slime**, *n.* semi-liquid, sticky matter.

**slim'y**, *adj.*, **slimier**, **slimiest.** of the nature of slime.

**sling**, *n.* **1.** flexible device for hurl-

**S**
**T**

ing missiles. **2.** suspended cloth support. —*v.t.* **3.** hurl or shy.

**slip,** *v.t., v.i.* **1.** slide smoothly. —*v.i.* **2.** loose grip or footing. —*n.* **3.** act or instance of slipping.

**slip′per,** *n.* soft, unlaced shoe for household wear.

**slip′per·y,** *adj.,* **-ier, -iest.** allowing slipping.

**slip′shod″,** *adj.* careless.

**slit,** *n.* **1.** long, deep opening. —*v.t.* **2.** cut with slits.

**sliv′er,** *n., v.t.* splinter.

**slo′gan,** *n.* motto.

**slop,** *v.t., v.i.* spill or toss carelessly, as a liquid.

**slope,** *n.* **1.** angled rise or descent. —*v.i.* **2.** form a slope.

**slop′py,** *adj.* **1.** untidy. **2.** carelessly done.

**slot,** *n.* narrow opening.

**slouch,** *v.i.* **1.** have a drooping posture. —*n.* **2.** drooping posture.

**slov·en** (sluv′ən), *n.* untidy or careless person. —**slov·en·ly,** *adj.*

**slow,** *adj.* **1.** moving or acting without speed. **2.** behind the correct or appointed time. —*v.t.* **3.** cause to move or act slowly. —*v.i.* **4.** move or act slowly.

**slug′gish,** *adj.* abnormally slow or lacking in vigor.

**sluice,** *n.* artificial channel controlled by a gate.

**slum,** *n.* squalid home or residential area.

**slum′ber,** *v.i.* **1.** sleep deeply. —*n.* **2.** deep sleep.

**slump,** *v.i.* drop or sag heavily.

**slur,** *v.t.* **1.** say indistinctly. —*n.* **2.** disparaging remark.

**slush,** *n.* melting snow.

**slut,** *n.* immoral or slatternly woman.

**sly,** *adj.,* **slyer or slier, slyest or sliest.** cunning; tricky.

**smack,** *v.t.* **1.** separate noisily, as the lips. **2.** slap.

**small,** *adj.* **1.** little. —*n.* **2.** narrow part, esp. of the back.

**small′pox″,** *n.* contagious disease with fever and pustules as symptoms.

**smart,** *adj.* **1.** intelligent or clever. **2.** in style. —*n.* **3.** sharp, stinging pain. —*v.i.* **4.** feel such a pain. —**smart′en,** *v.t.*

**smash,** *v.t.* break into fragments.

**smat·ter·ing,** *n.* slight knowledge.

**smear,** *v.t.* rub with greasy clinging material.

**smell,** *n.* **1.** sense perceived by the nose and olfactory organs. **2.** odor. —*v.t.* **3.** sense with the nose and olfactory organs.

**smelt,** *v.t.* extract from ore by melting or fusing.

**smile,** *v.i.* **1.** assume a look of pleasure, etc., by upturning the corners of the mouth. —*n.* **2.** smiling appearance.

**smirk,** *v.i.* have an affected or self-satisfied smile.

**smith,** *n.* metalworker.

**smith′y,** *n., pl.* **smithies.** blacksmith's shop.

**smock,** *n.* loose garment covering the whole body.

**smog,** *n.* fog with smoke.

**smoke,** *n.* **1.** unconsumed material emitted by a fire. —*v.i.* **2.** inhale and exhale smoke from smoldering tobacco, etc.

**smol′der,** *v.i.* burn flamelessly.

**smooth,** *adj.* **1.** without unevenness. **2.** without harsh or disturbing qualities. —*v.t.* **3.** make smooth.

**smoth′er,** *v.t.* **1.** suffocate. **2.** cover completely.

**smudge,** *n.* spot of smoke, dirt, ink, etc.

**smug,** *adj.* excessively self-satisfied.

**smug′gle,** *v.t.* bring in or out secretly in violation of laws or regulations.

**smut,** *n.* soot or smudge.

**snack,** *n.* small meal.

**snag,** *n.* **1.** projection that catches or tears. —*v.t.* **2.** catch or damage, as with a snag.

**snail,** *n.* crawling mollusk with a shell.

**snake,** *n.* scaly reptile without limbs.

**snap,** *v.i.* **1.** make a sharp clicking sound. **2.** break abruptly. —*n.* **3.** act or instance of snapping.

**snap′shot″,** *n.* uncomposed photograph from a small, hand-held camera.

**snare,** *n., v.t.* trap.

**snarl,** *v.i.* **1.** growl. —*v.t.* **2.** tangle.

**snatch,** *v.t.* **1.** grab. —*v.i.* **2.** reach suddenly or eagerly.

**sneak,** *v.i.* **1.** go furtively. —*n.* **2.** furtive, dishonest person.

**sneer,** *v.i.* **1.** express contempt. —*n.* **2.** expression of contempt.

**sneeze,** *v.i.* expel breath explosively and involuntarily.

**sniff,** *v.i.* **1.** inhale quickly through the nose. —*n.* **2.** act or instance of sniffing.

**snip**, *v.t.* cut, as with scissors.

**sniv'el**, *v.i.* plead, complain, etc. in a whining tone.

**snob**, *n.* person with ostentatious likes and dislikes based on pretentious standards of excellence.

**snoop**, *Informal. v.i.* seek information furtively.

**snooze**, *v.i., n.* nap.

**snore**, *v.i.* breathe noisily while sleeping. —*n.* 2. sound of such breathing.

**snort**, *n.* 1. loud exhalation through the nose. 2. give such an exhalation.

**snout**, *n.* protruding front of an animal head.

**snow**, *n.* 1. precipitation frozen in crystalline flakes. —*v.i.* 2. precipitate snow. —**snow'y**, *adj.*

**snub**, *v.t.* 1. refuse attention or respect to. —*n.* 2. act or instance of snubbing.

**snug**, *adj.*, **snugger**, **snuggest.** 1. cozy. 2. neat.

**so**, *adv.* 1. as stated or indicated. 2. to such an extent. —*conj.* 3. therefore. —*adj.* 4. true.

**soak**, *v.t.* 1. put into and cover with liquid. —*v.i.* 2. become absorbed.

**soap**, *n.* substance used in washing.

**soar**, *v.i.* 1. rise into the air. 2. glide or hover in the air.

**sob**, *v.i.* 1. weep convulsively. —*n.* 2. sound of sobbing.

**so'ber**, *adj.* 1. not drunk. 2. serious or quiet. —**so'bri'e·ty**, *n.*

**so'cia·ble**, *adj.* friendly; gregarious.

**so'cial**, *adj.* 1. pertaining to society. 2. sociable.

**so'cial·ism**, *n.* theory advocating public ownership of means of production, with work and products shared. —**so'cial·ist**, *n.* —**so'cial·ize''**, *v.t.*

**so·ci'e·ty**, *n., pl.* **-ties.** 1. human beings, in their relations with one another. 2. organization, esp. a professional or public-service one.

**so'ci·ol'o·gy**, *n.* study of society.

**sock**, *n.* 1. short stocking. —*v.t.* 2. *Informal.* hit.

**sock'et**, *n.* a hollow part in which something is inserted and held.

**sod**, *n.* earth with growing grass.

**so'da**, *n.* 1. drink with soda water. 2. chemical containing sodium.

**so'fa**, *n.* wide, upholstered seat with a back and arms.

**soft**, *adj.* 1. yielding readily to pressure. 2. gentle. —**soft'en**, *v.t., v.i.*

**soft'ball''**, *n.* baseball-like game using a softer ball.

**soft'ware**, *n.* (computers) programming enabling a system to function.

**sog'gy**, *adj.* moist and heavy with absorbed liquid.

**soil**, *v.t.* 1. dirty. —*n.* 2. earth. 3. sewage.

**so'journ**, *v.i.* 1. stay briefly. —*n.* 2. brief stay.

**sol'ace** (sol'əs), *n.* comfort in unhappiness.

**so'lar**, *adj.* pertaining to the sun.

**sol'der** (sod'ər), *n.* alloy with low melting point for joining or patching metal.

**sol'dier**, *n.* member of an army.

**sole**, *n.* 1. salt-water flatfish. 2. wearing surface on the bottom of a shoe. —*adj.* 3. single; only.

**sol'emn**, *adj.* 1. serious; earnest. 2. formal.

**so·lic'i·tous**, *adj.* showing friendly concern.

**so·lic'it** (sə lis'ət), *v.t.* 1. request. 2. canvass for.

**sol'id**, *adj.* 1. pertaining to or existing in three dimensions. 2. firm; substantial. —*n.* 3. three-dimensional object. 4. non-fluid material. —**so·lid'i·ty**, *n.* —**so·lid'i·fy''**, *v.t., v.i.*

**sol'id-state'**, *adj.* designating electronic circuitry that uses solid semiconductors, as transistors, to control current.

**sol'i·tar''y**, *adj.* 1. single. 2. alone. 3. isolated.

**sol'i·tude**, *n.* state of being alone or isolated.

**so'lo**, *n.* performance by one person, esp. in music or aviation. —**so'lo·ist**, *n.*

**sol'stice**, *n.* point when the sun is furthest from the equator; beginning of summer or winter.

**sol'u·ble**, *adj.* able to be dissolved.

**so·lu'tion**, *n.* 1. means of solving a problem. 2. dispersal of one material in another.

**solve**, *v.t.* explain or find means to overcome, as a problem.

**sol'vent**, *n.* 1. material that dissolves another. —*adj.* 2. able to meet one's debts. —**sol'ven·cy**, *n.*

**som'ber**, *adj.* gloomy. Also, **som'bre.**

**some**, *adj.* 1. indefinite amount or

S  
T

number of. **2.** certain unknown or unspecified. —*pron.* **3.** unknown or unspecified number.

**some'bod'y**, *pron.* unspecified person. Also, **some'one''**.

**some'how''**, *adv.* in some way. Also, **some'way''**.

**some'thing**, *n.* thing not specified.

**some'time''**, *adv.* at an indefinite time.

**some'times''**, *adv.* now and then.

**some'what''**, *adv.* to some extent.

**some'where''**, *adv.* at or to an unspecified place.

**son**, *n.* male offspring.

**so·na'ta**, *n.* instrumental musical composition.

**song**, *n.* vocal musical composition.

**son'ic**, *adj.* pertaining to sound.

**son'-in-law''**, *n.*, *pl.* **sons-in-law.** husband of one's daughter.

**son'net**, *n.* poem with one eight-line and one six-line part.

**so·no'rous**, *adj.* deep or rich in sound.

**soon**, *adv.* after a short time.

**soot**, *n.* black particles in smoke.

**soothe**, *v.t.* **1.** free of agitation or annoyance. **2.** relieve, as pain.

**so·phis'ti·cate**, *v.t.* **1.** (sō fis'tə kāt'') make sophisticated. —*n.* **2.** (sō fis'tə kət) sophisticated person.

**so·phis'ti·cat''ed**, *adj.* acquainted with the ways of society. —**so·phis''ti·ca'tion**, *n.*

**soph'is·try**, *n.* specious, unsound reasoning. —**soph'ist**, *n.*

**soph'o·more''**, *n.* second-year secondary or college student.

**soph'o·mor'ic**, *adj.* intellectually immature.

**so·pran'o**, *n.* singer in the highest vocal range.

**sor'cer·er**, *n.* magician. Also, *fem.,* **sor'cer·ess.** —**sor'cer·y**, *n.*

**sor'did**, *adj.* disgustingly mean or ignoble.

**sore**, *adj.,* **sorer, sorest,** *n. adj.* **1.** aching or tender. **2.** *Informal.* angry. —*n.* **3.** sore place on the body.

**so·ror'i·ty**, *n.,* *pl.* **-ties.** women's organization, esp. in a college.

**sor'row**, *n.* **1.** great unhappiness or regret. —*v.i.* **2.** feel sorrow. —**sor'row·ful**, *adj.*

**sor'ry**, *adj.* **1.** feeling regret. **2.** feeling pity.

**sort**, *n.* **1.** type; classification. **2.** quality. —*v.t.* **3.** arrange by type.

**SOS**, call for help.

**souf·flé**, *n.* light, puffy baked dish.

**soul**, *n.* **1.** non-material aspect of a person. **2.** feeling or sensitivity. —**soul'ful**, *adj.*

**sound**, *n.* **1.** air vibrations perceptible in part to the ear. **2.** inlet or channel of sea water. —*v.t.* **3.** cause to make a sound. **4.** measure the depth of. —*v.i.* **5.** make a sound. —*adj.* **6.** healthy.

**soup**, *n.* savory, mainly liquid food.

**sour**, *adj.* **1.** acid-tasting. —*v.i.* **2.** become sour.

**source**, *n.* origin.

**south**, *n.* **1.** direction of the South Pole. **2.** region located in this direction. —**south'ern**, *adj.*

**south''east''**, *n.* direction halfway between south and east.

**south''west''**, *n.* direction halfway between south and west.

**sou·ve·nir** (sōō'və nēr), *n.* thing to remember a place, event, etc. by.

**sov·er·eign** (sov'rən), *n.* **1.** monarch. —*adj.* **2.** having supreme political power. **3.** politically independent. —**sov'er·eign·ty**, *n.*

**so'vi·et'**, *adj.* **1.** Soviet, pertaining to the Soviet Union. —*n.* **2.** Russian governmental council.

**sow**, *v.t.* **1.** (sō) plant, as seed. —*n.* **2.** (sow) female hog.

**space**, *n.* **1.** limitless three-dimensional expanse. **2.** specific area within this. —*v.t.* **3.** separate, esp. as regular intervals.

**space'craft''**, *n.* vehicle for exploration of outer space.

**space'ship''**, *n.* vehicle for travel in outer space.

**spa'cious**, *adj.* amply extensive.

**spade**, *n.* **1.** shovel with long shaft-like handle. **2. spades,** black suit of playing cards.

**spa·ghet'ti**, *n.* stringy pasta, usually served with a sauce.

**span**, *n.* **1.** something between two supports. —*v.t.* **2.** cross.

**spank**, *v.t.* slap on the behind.

**spar**, *v.i.* **1.** box with the fists. —*n.* **2.** pole.

**spare**, *v.t.,* *adj.,* **sparer, sparest.** *v.t.* **1.** use or spend with restraint. **2.** give without inconvenience. —*adj.* **3.** in reserve; extra. **4.** gaunt; lean.

**spark**, *n.* **1.** glowing, burning piece of matter from a fire. **2.** electric flash.

**spar·kle**, v.i. emit or reflect small flashes of light.

**spar·row**, n. bird of the finch family.

**sparse**, adj., **sparser**, **sparsest**. 1. scattered. 2. scanty.

**Spar·tan**, adj. austere; disciplined.

**spasm**, n. sudden and involuntary contraction of the muscles.

**spas·mod·ic**, adj. 1. in spasms. 2. at unpredictable intervals.

**spa·tial**, adj. pertaining to space.

**spat·ter**, v.t. splash, esp. in small amounts over a wide area.

**speak**, v.i. 1. communicate with the voice. —v.t. 2. use in speaking, as a language.

**speak·er**, n. 1. person who speaks. 2. president of a legislature.

**spear**, n. long-handled, pointed weapon for hurling or thrusting.

**spe·cial**, adj. 1. distinct from all others. 2. remarkable.

**spe·cial·ize**, v.i. study, work, or trade in a special area. —**spe·cial·ist**, n.

**spe·cial·ty**, n., pl. **-ties**. area of specialization.

**spe·cies**, n. group of fundamentally identical plants or animals.

**spe·cif·ic**, adj. 1. detailed. 2. exact.

**spe·ci·fy**, v.t. state or demand specifically.

**spec·i·men**, n. typical example.

**spe·cious**, adj. falsely seeming good or valid.

**speck**, n. 1. small particle or spot.

**spec·ta·cle**, n. 1. marvelous event or sight. 2. **spectacles**, eyeglasses.

**spec·tac·u·lar**, adj. marvelous or grandiose in appearance, etc.

**spec·ta·tor**, n. person who sees an event or view.

**spec·ter**, n. ghost; apparition. Also, **spec·tre**.

**spec·trum**, n., pl. **-tra**, **-trums**. group of color bands produced when light is dispersed by a prism.

**spec·u·late**, v.i. 1. think contemplatively. 2. undertake a business risk in the hope of large profits. —**spec·u·la·tor**, n.

**speech**, n. 1. ability to speak. 2. talk to an audience. —**speech·less**, adj.

**speed**, n. 1. swiftness of motion or action. 2. rate of motion or action. —v.t. 3. increase the speed of. —v.i. 4. move swiftly. 5. drive with excessive speed. —**speed·y**, adj.

**spell**, v.t. 1. name the letters of. 2. comprise the letters of. —n. 3. enchantment.

**spend**, v.t. 1. pay. 2. pass, as a period of time.

**spend·thrift**, n. spender to excess.

**spent**, adj. exhausted.

**spew**, v.t., v.i. vomit or pour with force.

**sphere**, n. 1. round solid with all radii equal; ball. —**spher·i·cal**, adj.

**sphinx**, n. Classical mythology. creature with a human head and the body of a lion.

**spice**, n. 1. aromatic plant substance for seasoning, preservation, etc. —v.t. 2. season or treat with spice.

**spi·der**, n. eight-legged predatory animal that captures insects in a web.

**spig·ot**, n. faucet.

**spike**, n. 1. large hammer-driven fastener. —v.t. 2. fasten with spikes.

**spill**, v.t. 1. lose, as from the tipping of a container. —v.i. 2. be lost, as over the rim of a container.

**spin**, v.t. 1. make from twisted yarn. —v.t., v.i. 2. whirl. —**spin·ner**, n.

**spin·ach**, n. plant with dark-green edible leaves.

**spin·dle**, n. 1. rod used in spinning thread. 2. any slender round rod.

**spine**, n. backbone; vertebrae. Also called **spinal column**. —**spin·al**, adj.

**spin·ster**, n. unmarried woman past the normal marriageable age.

**spi·ral**, n. 1. flat curve with steadily increasing radius. —adj. 2. formed along such a curve.

**spire**, n. tall pyramidal structure forming the roof of a tower.

**spir·it**, n. 1. spiritual part of a person; soul. 2. ghost. 3. mood, sentiment, or intent.

**spir·it·u·al**, adj. 1. pertaining to religion. 2. pertaining to the soul. —n. 3. Negro religious song.

**spir·it·u·al·ism**, n. belief that the living and the dead can communicate.

**spir·it·u·ous**, adj. alcoholic and distilled.

**spit**, v.t. 1. eject from the mouth. —v.i. 2. eject saliva from the mouth. —n. 3. long skewer.

**spite**, n. 1. small-minded hostility or vengefulness. 2. **in spite of**, notwithstanding. —*v.t.* **3.** offend or hurt out of spite. —**spite'ful**, *adj.*

**splash**, *v.t.* cause to fly in various directions, as a liquid.

**splat'ter**, *v.i.* be splashed.

**splay**, *v.t., v.i.* **1.** spread apart. —*adj.* **2.** spreading apart.

**splen'did**, *adj.* **1.** magnificent. **2.** excellent. —**splen'dor**, *n.*

**splice**, *v.t.* join into a single piece.

**splint**, *n.* temporary reinforcement for a broken bone.

**splin'ter**, *n.* **1.** sharp, broken fragment. —*v.t., v.i.* **2.** break into splinters.

**split**, *v.t., v.i.* **1.** break or pull in two. —*v.t.* **2.** share or divide.

**splurge**, *v.i.* spend money lavishly and showily.

**spoil**, *v.t.* **1.** ruin. —*v.i.* **2.** become unfit to eat, drink, or use. —**spoil'age,** *n.*

**spoke**, *n.* shaft between the hub and rim of a wheel.

**spokes'man**, *n.* person who speaks for a group.

**sponge**, *n.* **1.** marine animal. **2.** skeleton of this animal used to absorb water. —*v.t.* **3.** wipe with a sponge.

**spon'sor**, *n.* **1.** person who undertakes responsibility for another. **2.** advertiser who buys television or radio time. —*v.t.* **3.** act as sponsor for.

**spon·ta'ne·ous**, *adj.* occuring without an external cause. —**spon''ta·ne'i·ty,** *n.*

**spool**, *n.* small drum on which thread, film, recording tape, etc. is wound.

**spoon**, *n.* utensil for handling or stirring liquids or food.

**spo·rad'ic**, *adj.* occasional.

**spore**, *n.* seedlike body from which fungi, mosses, etc. grow.

**sport**, *n.* **1.** recreation involving bodily activity. —**sports'man,** *n.*

**spor'tive**, *adj.* playful.

**spot**, *n.* **1.** round mark. **2.** place. —*v.t.* **3.** mark with spots. **4.** notice. —**spot'ty,** *adj.*

**spouse**, *n.* husband or wife.

**spout**, *n.* **1.** channel for discharging liquids, grain, etc. —*v.t.* **2.** emit with force.

**sprain**, *v.t.* **1.** injure by wrenching muscles or ligaments. —*n.* **2.** injury so produced.

**sprawl**, *v.i.* stretch out in an ungraceful way.

**spray**, *n.* **1.** liquid driven in fine particles. —*v.t.* **2.** drive as a spray.

**spread**, *v.t., v.i.* **1.** extend. **2.** scatter or disperse. —*v.t.* **3.** cover or apply thinly. —*n.* **4.** soft food eaten with breadstuffs.

**spree**, *n.* occasion of uninhibited activity.

**sprig**, *n.* twig or spray.

**spright'ly**, *adj.*, **-lier, -liest,** lively

**spring**, *n.* **1.** season between winter and summer. **2.** stream emerging from the earth. **3.** resilient elastic device, e.g. a wire coil. —*v.i.* **4.** jump.

**sprin'kle**, *v.t.* **1.** scatter thinly. —*v.i.* **2.** rain lightly. —*n.* **3.** act or instance of sprinkling.

**sprint**, *n.* **1.** short run. —*v.i.* **2.** make a short run.

**sprout**, *v.i.* **1.** begin to grow or send forth shoots. —*n.* **2.** shoot that has sprouted.

**spruce**, *n.* coniferous evergreen.

**spry**, *adj.*, **sprier** or **spryer, spriest** or **spryest.** active; lively.

**spur**, *n.* **1.** sharp device for urging on a horse. **2.** short extension. —*v.t.* **3.** urge on.

**spur·i·ous** (spyŏŏr'ē əs), *adj.* false; fraudulent.

**spurn**, *v.t.* reject with scorn.

**spurt**, *v.t., v.i.* **1.** shoot forth, as a liquid. —*n.* **2.** act or instance of spurting.

**sput'ter**, *v.t.* **1.** eject in drops or particles. —*v.i.* **2.** splutter.

**spy**, *n., pl.* **spies**, *v. n.* **1.** person who attempts to obtain secret information. —*v.t.* **2.** notice, esp. at a distance. —*v.i.* **3.** act as a spy.

**squab'ble**, *n., v.i.* quarrel over trifles.

**squad**, *n.* small group, as of soldiers.

**squad'ron**, *n.* military unit of airplanes, ships, or cavalry.

**squal'id**, *adj.* dirty or nasty. —**squal'or,** *n.*

**squall**, *n.* strong, brief storm or gust of wind.

**squan'der**, *v.t.* spend or use up wastefully.

**square**, *n., adj.*, **squarer, squarest,** *v.t. n.* **1.** right-angled figure with four equal sides. **2.** paved public area. **3.** *Math.* product of a number multiplied by itself. —*adj.* **4.** formed like a square. —*adv.* **5.** fairly; straightforwardly. —*v.t.* **6.** make square.

**squash**, *v.t.* **1.** crush. —*n.* **2.** gourdlike fruit.

**squat**, *v.i.* **1.** crouch with the legs doubled under the body. —*adj.* **2.** Also, **squat′ty**, short and broad of figure.

**squaw**, *n.* American Indian woman.

**squawk**, *n.* loud, harsh cry.

**squeak**, *n.* shrill noise.

**squeal**, *n.* shrill cry.

**squeam′ish**, *adj.* **1.** easily disgusted. **2.** prudish.

**squeeze**, *v.t.* **1.** press from both sides. **2.** cram.

**squelch**, *v.t.* silence with a crushing remark.

**squint**, *v.i.* **1.** see through partly-closed eyes. **2.** be crosseyed.

**squirm**, *v.i.*, *v.* wriggle.

**squir′rel**, *n.* bushy-tailed rodent living in trees.

**squirt**, *v.t.*, *v.i.* shoot, as a liquid.

**stab**, *v.t.* **1.** wound with a knife, etc. —*n.* **2.** wound or thrust from such a weapon.

**sta′bil·ize**, *v.t.* cause to be or remain stable.

**sta′ble**, *n.* **1.** Also, **stables**, accomodation for animals, esp. horses. —*v.t.* **2.** put into a stable, as a horse. —*adj.* **3.** resistant to displacement or change. —**sta·bil′i·ty**, *n.*

**stack**, *n.* **1.** orderly pile. —*v.t.* **2.** gather into stacks.

**sta′di·um**, *n.*, *pl.* **-diums, -dia.** outdoor arena for spectator sports.

**staff**, *n.*, *pl.* **staves** or **staffs** (for 1), **staffs** (for 2), *v.t.* *n.* **1.** stick carried in the hand. **2.** group of employees, esp. in administrative jobs. —*v.t.* **3.** provide or work as a staff for.

**stag**, *n.* adult male deer.

**stage**, *n.* **1.** distinct phase. **2.** performers' platform. —*v.t.* **3.** present on a stage.

**stage′coach″**, *n.* horse-drawn coach for long-distance travel.

**stag′ger**, *v.i.* **1.** walk or stand unsteadily. —*v.t.* **2.** schedule over a range of times.

**stag′nant**, *adj.* not flowing, as a body of water. —**stag′nate**, *v.i.*

**staid**, *adj.* sober and quiet; sedate.

**stain**, *n.* **1.** discoloration. **2.** dye applied to wood or other materials. —*v.t.* **3.** discolor. **4.** apply dye to.

**stair**, *n.* tall flight of steps. Also, **stairs**, **stair′way″**.

**stair′case″**, *n.* interior stair.

**stake**, *n.* **1.** upright post. **2.** some-

thing wagered. —*v.t.* **3.** mark or secure with a stake.

**stale**, *adj.*, **staler, stalest.** no longer fresh.

**stale′mate″**, *n.* *Chess.* situation making a move impossible.

**stalk**, *v.t.* **1.** pursue stealthily. —*v.i.* **2.** walk proudly or deliberately. —*n.* **3.** plant stem.

**stall**, *n.* **1.** compartment. —*v.t.* **2.** *Informal.* delay or keep waiting. —*v.i.* **3.** stop because of malfunctioning.

**stal′wart**, *adj.* reliable through bravery, vigor, or faithfulness.

**stam′i·na**, *n.* enduring vigor.

**stam′mer**, *v.i.* speak with involuntary repetitions or pauses.

**stamp**, *v.t.* **1.** step on forcefully. **2.** form or print with a stamp. —*n.* **3.** act or instance of stamping. **4.** adhesive paper proving payment of postage, etc.

**stam·pede′**, *n.* mass flight, as of frightened cattle.

**stance**, *n.* **1.** position of a standing person. **2.** attitude or policy.

**stanch**, *adj.* **1.** (stonch) stalwart. —*v.t.* **2.** (stanch) stop from bleeding.

**stand**, *v.i.* **1.** be or become upright on the feet. —*v.t.* **2.** endure or tolerate. —*n.* **3.** small platform or table.

**stand′ard**, *n.* **1.** basis for evaluation or measurement. **2.** upright support. —*adj.* **3.** of the normal or typical sort.

**stand′ard·ize**, *v.t.*, *v.i.* conform to a standard.

**stand′ing**, *n.* **1.** status. **2.** duration.

**stand′point″**, *n.* viewpoint.

**sta′ple**, *n.* **1.** fastener of bent wire or bar stock. —*adj.* **2.** main or standard.

**star**, *n.* **1.** heavenly body of incandescent gas. **2.** figure with radiating points. **3.** prominent or leading performer or player.

**star′board″**, *Nautical.* *n.* right-hand side, facing forward.

**starch**, *n.* **1.** tasteless vegetable substance.

**stare**, *v.i.* gaze with fixed, open eyes.

**stark**, *adj.* **1.** outright. **2.** bleak.

**star′ling**, *n.* small bird of European origin.

**start**, *v.t.*, *v.i.* **1.** begin. —*n.* **2.** beginning.

**star′tle**, *v.t.* disturb with sudden surprise.

**starve**, v.t. 1. kill or trouble with hunger. —v.i. 2. die or be troubled from hunger. —**star'va'tion**, n.

**state**, n. 1. condition. 2. politically autonomous or semi-autonomous region. —v.t. 3. declare.

**state'house''**, n. U.S. state capitol.

**state'ly**, adj., -lier, -liest. dignified.

**state'ment**, n. declaration.

**state-of-the-art'**, adj. of or pertaining to the highest level of technological achievement to date.

**states'man**, n. person wise in government.

**stat'ic**, adj. 1. not moving. —n. 2. unmoving electrical charges.

**sta'tion**, n. 1. building where a train, bus, etc. stops or originates. 2. place of duty. —v.t. 3. assign to a place.

**sta'tion·ar''y**, adj. not in motion.

**sta'tion·er**, n. seller of paper and writing materials. —**sta'tion·er''y**, n.

**sta·tis'tics**, n. collection and analysis of numerical data. —**sta·tis'ti·cal**, adj. —**stat''tis·ti'cian**, n.

**stat'ue**, n. three-dimensional sculpture of a human or animal.

**stat'ure**, n. 1. tallness. 2. eminence or achievement.

**sta·tus** (stā'təs, sta'təs), n. state or condition.

**stat'ute**, n. law; ordinance. —**stat'u·to''ry**, adj.

**staunch**, n., adj. stanch.

**stave**, n. 1. curved board forming part of a barrel side. —v.t. 2. repel.

**stay**, v.i. 1. remain or continue. —v.t. 2. support or prop. —n. 3. halt or delay.

**stead**, n. in one's stead, in place of one.

**stead'fast'**, adj. 1. unchanging. 2. loyal or determined.

**stead'y**, adj., steadier, steadiest, v. adj. 1. firm; unwavering. 2. regular; unvarying. —v.t., v.i. 3. make or become steady. —**stead'i·ly**, adv.

**steak**, n. slice of meat or fish for broiling or frying.

**steal**, v.t. take without right.

**stealth**, n. secret activity. —**stealth'y**, adj.

**steam**, n. 1. gaseous or vaporized water. —v.t. 2. treat with steam. —**steam'y**, adj. —**steam'boat'**, n. —**steam'ship'**, n.

**steam'er**, n. 1. vehicle operated by steam. 2. device for treating with steam.

**steed**, n. riding horse.

**steel**, n. iron alloyed with carbon.

**steep**, adj. 1. far from horizontal. —v.t. 2. soak.

**steep'le**, n. tall tower with a spire.

**steer**, v.t. direct or guide.

**stel'lar**, adj. pertaining to or suggesting stars.

**stem**, n. 1. support of a plant, leaf, or fruit. —v.t. 2. check, as liquid.

**stench**, n. stink.

**sten'cil**, n. pierced sheet allowing paint or ink to mark an underlying surface.

**ste·nog'ra·phy**, n. shorthand writing. —**sten''o·graph'ic**, adj. —**ste·nog'ra·pher**, n.

**step**, n. 1. movement of the walking foot. 2. raised surface on which one walks upwards. 3. stage of a process. —v.i. 4. walk.

**step-**, by the remarriage of a parent: a prefix.

**step'lad''der**, n. ladder with steps.

**ster'e·o''**, n. device for playing recorded or broadcast music in stereophonic sound.

**ster''e·o·phon'ic**, adj. pertaining to realistic sound reproduction through two or more loudspeakers.

**ster'e·o·type''**, n. 1. process for casting printing plates. 2. unimaginative or oversimplified conception.

**ster'ile**, adj. 1. free of microbes. 2. barren. —**ster·il'i·ty**, n.

**ster'i·lize''**, v.t. make sterile.

**ster'ling**, adj. composed of 92.5° silver.

**stern**, adj. 1. grimly strict. —n. 2. after end of a ship.

**steth'o·scope''**, n. instrument for listening to body sounds.

**stew**, n. 1. dish of simmered food. —v.t. 2. simmer to cook.

**stew'ard**, n. 1. person in charge of food, supplies, and services. 2. attendant. Also, fem., **stew'ard·ess**.

**stick**, v.t. 1. thrust. 2. cause to adhere. —v.i. 3. fail to move properly. 4. project. —n. 5. length of wood.

**stick'er**, n. adhesive label.

**stick'ler**, n. person who insists on something.

**stick'y,** *adj.,* stickier, stickiest. adhesive.

**stiff,** *adj.* unbending. —**stiff'en,** *v.t., v.i.*

**sti'fle,** *v.t.* 1. smother. 2. suppress.

**stig'ma,** *n., pl.* stigmata, stigmas. mark or indication of disrepute.

**still,** *adj.* 1. motionless or silent. —*adv.* 2. up to an indicated time. —*adv., conj.* 3. nevertheless. —*v.t., v.i.* 4. make or become still. —*n.* 5. distillation apparatus.

**stim'u·late,** *v.t.* cause to be active or more active. —**stim'u·la'tion,** *n.* —**stim'u·la·tive,** *adj.* —**stim'u·lant,** *n.*

**stim'u·lus,** *n., pl.* -li. something stimulating.

**sting,** *v.t.,* stung, -ing. *n., v.t.* 1. inflict a small, painful wound or blow. 2. annoy or goad severely. —*n.* 3. wound from stinging. 4. sharp part for stinging. 5. undercover operation run by a law enforcement agency to catch suspected criminals.

**stin'gy,** *adj.* characteristic of or suggesting miserliness.

**stink,** *v.i.* have a bad smell.

**sti'pend,** *n.* regular payment.

**stip'u·late,** *v.t.* require as a condition.

**stir,** *v.t.* 1. mix by moving. —*n.* 2. public excitement or commotion.

**stir'ring,** *adj.* exciting.

**stitch,** *n.* 1. single repeated operation in sewing, knitting, etc. 2. sharp pain. —*v.t.* 3. sew.

**stock,** *n.* 1. goods, materials, etc. on hand. 2. cattle. 3. any of various parts of guns, implements, etc. 4. ancestry. —*v.t.* 5. keep for sale or use.

**stock·ade',** *n.* barrier of upright stakes.

**stock'ing,** *n.* clothing for the foot and lower parts of the leg.

**stock'y,** *adj.* broad and short of figure.

**stodg'y,** *adj.,* stodgier, stodgiest. heavy and boring.

**sto'ic,** *n.* 1. person who maintains indifference to pain or sorrow. —*adj.* 2. Also, **sto'i·cal,** characteristic of a stoic.

**stoke,** *v.t.* keep burning by adding fuel.

**stol'id,** *adj.* showing no liveliness.

**stom'ach,** *n.* organ of digestion.

**stone,** *n., pl.* stones, *adj., v.t. n.* 1.

hard mineral substance. 2. pit of a fruit. —*v.t.* 3. attack with stones.

**stool,** *n.* armless, backless seat.

**stoop,** *v.i.* 1. bend forward. 2. demean oneself. —*n.* 3. bent posture.

**stop,** *v.t.* 1. prevent from starting or going on. —*v.i.* 2. act or move no further or not at all. —*n.* 3. act, instance or place of stopping. —**stop'page,** *n.*

**stop'per,** *n.* plug, as for a bottle.

**stor'age,** *n.* 1. act or instance of storing. 2. condition of being stored.

**store,** *n.* 1. place for the sale of goods. 2. place of storage. 3. **stores,** supplies. 4. **in store,** waiting in the future. 5. accumulate and save. 6. put away for future use.

**stork,** *n.* long-billed, long-legged wading bird.

**storm,** *n.* 1. high wind, often with rain, snow, etc. —*v.t.* 2. attack suddenly and violently.

**stor'y,** *n., pl.* -ries. 1. account of events, often fictitious. 2. level in a building.

**stout,** *adj.* 1. sturdy. 2. heavy-set.

**stove,** *n.* device for heating or cooking.

**stow,** *v.t.* 1. put in storage, as on a ship. —*v.i.* 2. **stow away,** hide on a ship for a free passage.

**strad'dle,** *v.t.* stand over or mount with a leg on each side.

**strag'gle,** *v.i.* stray or fall behind.

**straight,** *adj.* 1. from point to point in the shortest way; direct. 2. honest or unevasive. —*adv.* 3. directly. —**straight'en,** *v.t., v.i.*

**straight'for'ward,** *adj.* unevasive; honest.

**strain,** *v.t.* 1. tax the strength of. 2. run through a filter or sieve. —*n.* 3. major effort or burden.

**strait,** *n.* 1. narrow natural waterway. 2. **straits,** difficulties.

**strand,** *n.* 1. length of fiber for twisting into rope. —*v.t.* 2. put in a helpless position.

**strange,** *adj.,* stranger, strangest. strikingly unfamiliar; odd.

**stran'ger,** *n.* unfamiliar person.

**stran'gle,** *v.t.* kill by choking. —**stran'gu·la'tion,** *n.*

**strap,** *n.* 1. band for fastening. —*v.t.* 2. fasten with a strap.

**strat'e·gy,** *n., pl.* -gies. art of planning military operations.

**strat'o·sphere",** *n.* atmospheric

zone 6 to 15 miles above the earth. —**strat'o·spher'ic**, *adj.*

**stra'tum**, *n., pl.* **strata, stratums.** layers, as of rock.

**straw**, *n.* 1. stalk of threshed grain. 2. tube for sucking liquids.

**straw'ber'ry**, *n., pl.* **-ries.** red fruit of a vinelike plant.

**stray**, *v.i.* 1. wander aimlessly. 2. wander away. —*adj.* 3. passing or occurring by chance.

**streak**, *n.* 1. long mark. 2. trait of character. 3. brief period, as of luck. —*v.t.* 4. mark with streaks. —*v.i.* 5. move swiftly. 6. run naked through a public place. —**ing,** *n.*

**stream**, *n.* body of running water.

**stream'line''**, *v.t.* 1. make with a form minimizing air or water resistance. 2. purge of unnecessary elements.

**street**, *n.* road in an urban area.

**street'car''**, *n.* rail car for transportation along streets.

**strength**, *n.* 1. power of the muscles. 2. resistance to force.

**strength'en**, *v.t., v.i.* make or become stronger.

**stren'u·ous**, *adj.* 1. involving great effort. 2. vigorous.

**stress**, *n.* 1. emphasis. 2. difficulties. —*v.t.* 3. put a stress on.

**stretch**, *v.t., v.i.* 1. extend or spread. —*n.* 2. unbroken extent.

**stretch'er**, *n.* 1. device for carrying a sick person lying down. 2. device for stretching.

**strew**, *v.t.* scatter.

**strict**, *adj.* 1. demanding exact conformity. 2. conforming exactly.

**stride**, *v.i.* 1. walk with long steps. —*n.* 2. long step.

**stri'dent**, *adj.* loud and harsh.

**strife**, *n.* conflict.

**strike**, *v.t.* 1. hit. —*v.i.* 2. stop work to enforce demands. —*n.* 3. act or instance of striking.

**strik'ing**, *adj.* remarkable.

**string**, *n.* 1. thin cord. —*v.t.* 2. set in a series or row.

**strin'gent**, *adj.* very strict. —**strin'gen·cy,** *n.*

**strip**, *n.* 1. long, narrow piece. —*v.t.* 2. remove the clothing or covering from.

**stripe**, *n.* long, broad mark.

**strive**, *v.i.* try hard; strain.

**stroke**, *v.t.* 1. rub or graze gently. —*n.* 2. act or instance of stroking. 3. blow. 4. sudden attack of illness, esp. apoplexy. 5. line made by a pen or pencil.

**stroll**, *v.i.* 1. walk idly. 2. wander.

**strong**, *adj.* having strength.

**strong'hold''**, *n.* place secure against attack.

**struc'ture**, *n.* 1. something built. 2. basic form.

**strug'gle**, *v.i.* 1. strive. —*n.* 2. strenuous effort.

**strut**, *v.i.* walk affectedly.

**stub**, *n.* 1. short remnant. —*v.t.* 2. ram against something, esp. a toe.

**stub'ble**, *n.* 1. plant stalks mown short. 2. short growth of beard.

**stub'born**, *adj.* refusing to obey, give up, etc.

**stud**, *n.* 1. projecting feature. 2. male animal, esp. a horse, for breeding.

**stu'dent**, *n.* person who studies.

**stud'ied**, *adj.* intentional.

**stu'di·o**, *n.* artist's workplace.

**stu'di·ous**, *adj.* studying diligently.

**study**, *n., pl.* **studies,** *v.t., v.i.* 1. methodical acquisition of skill or knowledge. 2. room for reading or writing. —*v.t.* 3. make a subject of study.

**stuff**, *n.* 1. material. —*v.t.* 2. fill under pressure.

**stuff'ing**, *n.* material stuffed into a hollow object.

**stuff'y**, *adj.,* **stuffier, stuffiest.** 1. dull and formal. 2. lacking fresh air.

**stum'ble**, *v.i.* trip and begin to fall.

**stump**, *n.* 1. remnant of something cut off. —*v.t.* 2. baffle.

**stun**, *v.t.,* **stunned, stunning.** 1. halt with amazement. 2. knock unconscious.

**stunt**, *n.* 1. act displaying skill. —*v.t.* 2. hinder in growing.

**stu·pe·fy**, *v.t.* 1. put in a stupor. 2. amaze.

**stu·pen'dous**, *adj.* astounding.

**stu'pid**, *adj.* 1. low in intelligence. 2. pointless.

**stu'por**, *n.* unconscious or semiconscious state.

**stur'dy**, *adj.* 1. strong. 2. vigorous.

**stut'ter**, *v.i., n.* stammer.

**sty**, *n., pl.* **sties.** 1. pig shelter. 2. swollen inflammation of the eyelid.

**style**, *n.* 1. manner of artistic composition, writing, living, etc. 2. elegance.

**styl'ish**, *adj.* in style; elegant.

**suave** (swahv), *adj.* smoothly polite.

**sub·con·scious**, *n.* 1. part of the mind beyond consciousness. —*adj.* 2. pertaining to this part of the mind.

**sub·di·vide''**, *v.t.* divide still further. —**sub'di·vi'sion**, *n.*

**sub·due'**, *v.t.* overcome.

**sub·ject**, *n.* (sub'jekt) 1. thing thought, written, etc. about. 2. person ruled by a government. —*adj.* 3. exposed to a specified treatment. —*v.t.* (sub jekt') 4. submit to a specified treatment.

**sub·jec'tive**, *adj.* existing or originating in one's person's mind.

**sub'ju·gate''**, *v.t.* conquer.

**sub·junc'tive**, *Grammar. adj.* 1. pertaining to a verbal mode of possibility, etc. —*n.* 2. subjunctive mode.

**sub·lime'**, *adj.* 1. noble and exalted. —*n.* 2. realm of sublime things. —**sub·lim'i·ty**, *n.*

**sub·ma·rine'**, *n.* (sub'mə rēn), 1. underwater vessel. —*adj.* (sub mə rēn') 2. undersea.

**sub·merge'**, *v.t., v.i.* sink into a liquid.

**sub·mit'**, *v.t.* 1. offer, as in surrender. 2. offer for consideration. 3. subject to a specified treatment. —*v.i.* 4. surrender or yield oneself. —**sub·mis'sion**, *n.* —**sub·mis'sive**, *adj.*

**sub·or'di·nate**, *adj.* 1. lower in rank or importance. —*n.* 2. someone or something subordinate. —**sub·or'di·na'tion**, *n.*

**sub·scribe'**, *v.i.* 1. pay for continued supply of a periodical, service, etc. 2. promise to contribute money. 3. agree. —**sub·scrip'tion**, *n.*

**sub'se·quent**, *adj.* occurring after.

**sub·side'**, *v.i.* 1. settle or sink. 2. die down. —**sub·sid'ence**, *n.*

**sub·sid'i·ar''y**, *adj., n., pl.* -ries. *adj.* 1. subordinate or auxiliary. —*n.* 2. subsidiary entity.

**sub'si·dize''**, *v.t., n., pl.* -dies. monetary aid, esp. from a government. —**sub'si·dize''**, *v.t.*

**sub'stance**, *n.* 1. material. 2. essential part or aspect.

**sub·stan'tial**, *adj.* 1. material. 2. essential.

**sub'sti·tute**, *v.t., v.i.* 1. put or act in another's place. —*n.* 2. person or thing that substitutes. —**sub''sti·tu'tion**, *n.*

**sub'ter·fuge''**, *n.* evasive trick or trickery.

**sub''ter·ra'ne·an**, *adj.* underground.

**sub·tle**, (sut'əl), *adj.* 1. highly sensitive. 2. scarcely perceived. —**sub'tle·ty**, *n.*

**sub·tract'**, *v.t.* remove, as one quantity from another.

**sub'urb**, *n.* community adjoining or dependent on a city. —**sub·ur'ban**, *adj.*

**sub·vert'**, *v.t.* undermine or corrupt. —**sub·ver'sive**, *adj., n.*

**sub'way''**, *n.* underground railroad.

**suc·ceed'**, *v.i.* 1. obtain good results. —*v.t.* 2. follow in an office, inheritance, etc.

**suc·cess'**, *n.* 1. favorable outcome of an attempt. 2. commonly sought goals. 3. person or thing that attains success. —**suc·cess'ful**, *adj.*

**suc·ces'sion**, *n.* 1. sequential order of things. 2. act of succeeding another. —**suc·ces'sive**, *adj.* —**suc·ces'sor**, *n.*

**suc·cinct'**, (suk sinkt'), *adj.* restricted to essential information. —**suc·cinct'ly**, *adv.* —**suc·cinct'ness**, *n.*

**suc'cu·lent**, *adj.* juicy.

**suc·cumb'**, *v.i.* 1. yield. 2. die.

**such**, *adj.* 1. of the kind mentioned. 2. so much of. —*adv.* 3. so greatly. —*pron.* 4. the kind mentioned.

**suck**, *v.t.* 1. draw by suction. 2. absorb by capillarity.

**suck'er**, *n.* 1. person or thing that sucks. 2. lollipop. 3. *Informal.* person easily cheated.

**suc'tion**, *n.* forcing of a fluid into a vacuum by atmospheric pressure.

**sud'den**, *adj.* quick and unexpected.

**suds**, *n., pl.* 1. fine soap bubbles. 2. soapy water.

**sue**, *v.t.,* 1. claim damages from in court. —*v.i.* 2. make an appeal.

**suf'fer**, *v.t.* 1. undergo. 2. permit or tolerate.

**suf·fice'**, *v.i.* be enough.

**suf·fi'cient**, *adj.* enough. —**suf·fi'cien·cy**, *n.*

**suf'fo·cate**, *v.t., v.i.* 1. cut off or be without air for breathing. —**suf''fo·ca'tion**, *n.*

**suf'frage**, *n.* right to vote.

**suf·fuse'**, *v.t.* spread light, color, etc. over.

**sug'ar**, *n.* 1. sweet carbohydrate. —*v.t.* 2. add sugar to.

**sug·gest'**, *v.t.* 1. offer as advice. 2.

**ST**

propose. 3. imply. —**sug·ges'·tion,** *n.*

**sug·ges'tive,** *adj.* full of implication, esp. of impropriety.

**su·i·cide",** *n.* 1. willful killing of oneself. 2. person who kills himself willfully. —**su''i·cid'al,** *adj.*

**suit,** *n.* 1. complete set of clothes. 2. lawsuit. —*v.t.* 3. satisfy; please. 4. adapt.

**suit'a·ble,** *adj.* right; appropriate.

**suit'case",** *n.* travel case for clothes, etc.

**suite** (swēt), *n.* 1. apartment of connected rooms. 2. set of musical compositions.

**suit'or,** *n.* wooer.

**sulk,** *v.i.* 1. be angry and aloof. —*n.* 2. fit of sulking.

**sul'len,** *adj.* 1. quietly resentful. 2. gloomy.

**sul'try,** *adj.,* -**tri·er,** -**tri·est.** 1. hot and humid. 2. sexually inviting.

**sum,** *n.* 1. number obtained by addition. —*v.t.* 2. add up.

**sum'ma·rize,** *v.t.* present in a summary.

**sum'ma·ry,** *n.,* *pl.* -**ries,** *adj.* *n.* 1. presentation of essential information only. —*adj.* 2. without formalities or preliminaries.

**sum'mer,** *n.* season between spring and autumn.

**sum'mit,** *n.* highest point.

**sum'mon,** *v.t.* order or ask to come.

**sum'mons,** *n.* order or request to come.

**sump'tu·ous,** *adj.* costly and luxurious.

**sun,** *n.* 1. star of the solar system. 2. rays from this star. —**sun'light",** *n.* —**sun'lit",** *adj.*

**sun'burn",** *n.,* *v.t.* burn from or with the rays of the sun.

**sun'di'al,** *n.* instrument telling time by the shadow of a pointer.

**sun·dry** (sun'drē), *adj.* various.

**sun'glas'ses,** *n.,* *pl.* spectacles tinted to weaken the sun's rays.

**sun'rise",** *n.* rise of the sun above the horizon.

**sun'set",** *n.* descent of the sun below the horizon.

**sun'shine",** *n.* rays of the sun.

**su·perb',** *adj.* admirably excellent.

**su''per·fi'cial,** *adj.* 1. on the surface only. 2. lacking depth of thought or feeling.

**su·per'flu·ous,** *adj.* 1. more than is useful. 2. redundant; useless.

**su''per·hu'man,** *adj.* beyond ordinary human limitations.

**su''per·im·pose',** *v.t.* place over something else.

**su''per·in·tend',** *v.t.* supervise. —**su''per·in·ten'dent,** *n.,* *adj.*

**su·pe'ri·or,** *adj.* 1. better. 2. excellent. —*n.* 3. superior person. —**su·pe''ri·or'i·ty,** *n.*

**su·per'la·tive,** *adj.* 1. *Grammar.* denoting the extreme in a comparison. —*n.* 2. something superlative.

**su''per·nat'u·ral,** *adj.* 1. outside the laws of nature. —*n.* 2. realm of things outside such laws.

**su''per·sede',** *v.t.* replace, esp. in importance or function.

**su''per·son'ic,** *adj.* pertaining to speeds faster than that of sound.

**su''per·sti'tion,** *n.* unconfirmed belief, esp. in the supernatural. —**su''per·sti'tious,** *adj.*

**su'per·vise',** *v.t.* direct and inspect. —**su'per·vis'or,** *n.*

**sup'per,** *n.* late dinner.

**sup·plant',** *v.t.* replace, as in favor or function.

**sup'ple,** *adj.,* -**pler,** -**plest.** flexible.

**sup'ple·ment,** *n.* (sup'plə mənt) 1. desirable addition. —*v.t.* (sup'plə ment'') 2. give a supplement to.

**sup'pli·cate",** *v.t.* implore. —**sup'pli·cant,** *n.*

**sup·ply',** *v.t., n., pl.* -**plies.** *v.t.* 1. provide, as goods. —*n.* 2. something supplied.

**sup·port',** *v.t.* 1. hold up. 2. provide a livelihood for. 3. endure. —*n.* 4. someone or something that supports.

**sup·pose',** *v.t.* 1. assume as true. 2. expect to act as stated. —**suppo·si'tion,** *n.*

**sup·press',** *v.t.* 1. force into inaction. 2. kept from being known or apparent.

**su·preme',** *adj.* highest or greatest. —**su·prem'a·cy,** *n.*

**sure** (shoŏr), *adj.,* -**surer,** -**surest.** 1. convinced; positive. 2. reliant. 3. reliable.

**sure'ty** (shoŏr'i tē, shoŏr'tē), *n.,* *pl.* -**ties.** 1. certainty. 2. security against risk.

**surf,** *n.* waves breaking against land, shoals, etc.

**sur'face,** *n.* 1. outer area. 2. outer appearance. —*v.t.* 3. finish the surface of.

**surge,** *v.i.* gather volume or force suddenly.

**sur'geon,** *n.* practitioner of surgery.

**sur'ger·y,** *n., pl.* **-ries. 1.** treatment of illness by physical rather than chemical means. **2.** place where such treatment is given. **—sur'gi·cal,** *adj.*

**sur'ly,** *adj.,* **-lier, -liest.** sullenly illtempered.

**sur·mise',** *v.t.* **1.** guess.

**sur·mount',** *v.t.* overcome, as an obstacle. **—sur·mount'a·ble,** *adj.*

**sur'name'',** *n.* last personal name.

**sur·pass',** *v.t.* **1.** be superior to. **2.** exceed.

**sur'plus,** *adj.* **1.** beyond the needed amount. **—n. 2.** surplus amount.

**sur·prise',** *n.* **1.** emotion on encountering the unexpected. **2.** unexpected occurrence. **—v.t. 3.** fill with surprise. **4.** attack, etc. when not expected.

**sur·ren'der,** *v.t.* **1.** give up. **—n. 2.** act or instance of surrendering.

**sur''rep·ti'tious,** *adj.* stealthy.

**sur·round',** *v.t.* enclose or be close to on all sides.

**sur·round'ings,** *n., pl.* things all around; environment.

**sur·veil'lance,** *n.* close observation.

**sur·vey',** *v.t., v.i., pl.* **-veys.** *v.t.* (sərvā') **1.** measure or evaluate precisely. **2.** view. **—n.** (sər'vā) **3.** act or instance of surveying. **—sur·vey'or,** *n.*

**sur·vive',** *v.i.* **1.** remain alive. **—v.t. 2.** outlive. **—sur·vi'vor,** *n.* **—sur·viv'al,** *n.*

**sus·cep'ti·ble** (sus sep'tə bəl), *adj.* easily affected.

**sus·pect',** *v.t.* (səs pekt') **1.** regard without trust. **2.** guess. **—n.** (sus' pekt) **3.** suspected person.

**sus·pend',** *v.t.* **1.** hang. **2.** postpone.

**sus·pense',** *n.* anxiety due to uncertainty.

**sus·pen'sion,** *n.* act or instance of suspending.

**sus·pi'cion,** *n.* **1.** feeling of one who suspects. **2.** state of being suspected.

**sus·pi'cious,** *adj.* **1.** having suspicions. **2.** arousing suspicion.

**sus·tain',** *v.t.* **1.** maintain; continue. **2.** suffer.

**sus'te·nance,** *n.* means of existence.

**swag'ger,** *v.i.* walk arrogantly.

**swal'low,** *v.t.* **1.** take down the throat. **—n. 2.** small, forked-tailed bird. **3.** act or instance of swallowing.

**swamp,** *n.* **1.** area of wet land and water vegetation. **—v.t. 2.** drench.

**swan,** *n.* large, long-necked water bird.

**swap,** *v.t., v.i. Informal.* exchange.

**swarm,** *n.* **1.** large, unorganized group. **—v.i. 2.** move in a swarm.

**swarth'y,** *adj.,* **-ier, -iest.** rather dark-skinned.

**swas'ti·ka,** *n.* cross with end pieces forming right angles.

**swat,** *v.t. Informal,* hit sharply.

**sway,** *v.i.* **1.** move unsteadily from side to side. **—v.t. 2.** influence through argument.

**swear,** *v.t.* **1.** affirm with an oath. **—v.i. 2.** utter profanity.

**sweat,** *v.i.* **1.** pass moisture through the pores. **—n. 2.** sweated body moisture.

**sweat'er,** *n.* knitted garment covering the area from waist to neck.

**sweep,** *v.t.* **1.** free of loose dirt, etc., esp. with brushing motions. **—v.i. 2.** move swiftly and continuously.

**sweet,** *adj.* **1.** somewhat sugarlike in taste. **2.** agreeable, esp. to the senses. **—sweet'en,** *v.t., v.i.*

**sweet'heart'',** *n.* loved one.

**swell,** *v.t., v.i.* **1.** expand beyond natural size from pressure. **—adj. 2.** *Informal.* excellent.

**swerve,** *v.t., v.i.* turn suddenly aside.

**swift,** *adj.* **1.** quick or prompt. **2.** fast.

**swim,** *v.i.* **1.** move through water by actions of the body. **—n. 2.** occasion of swimming.

**swin'dle,** *v.t.* **1.** cheat. **2.** fraud.

**swine,** *n., pl.* **swine.** pig or hog.

**swing,** *v.t., v.i.* **1.** move back and forth through part of a circle. **—n. 2.** suspended seat for swinging.

**swirl,** *v.t., v.i., n.* whirl.

**swish,** *v.t., v.i.* whirl through the air with a sound.

**switch,** *n.* **1.** change. **2.** device for controlling electric current. **—v.t. 3.** change or exchange. **4.** control or direct with a switch. **—switch'-board'',** *n.*

**swiv'el,** *n.* **1.** rotating support.

**S**
**T**

—*v.t., v.i.* **2.** turn on or as if on a swivel.

**swoop**, *v.i.* descend speedily, as a bird of prey.

**sword** (sôrd), *n.* long, sharp-pointed or -bladed weapon.

**syl'la·ble**, *n.* individual sound that is part of a spoken word. —**syl·lab'ic**, *adj.*

**sym'bol**, *n.* something representing another thing. —**sym·bol'ic, sym·bol'i·cal**, *adj.* —**sym'bol·ize''**, *v.t.*

**sym'bol·ism**, *n.* group of symbols.

**sym'me·try**, *n., pl.* **-tries. 1.** mirror-image uniformity on opposite sides. **2.** harmony of arrangement. —**sym·met'ri·cal**, *adj.*

**sym'pa·thize''**, *v.i.* be in sympathy.

**sym'pa·thy**, *n., pl.* **-thies. 1.** oneness of feeling or opinion. **2.** regret for another's unhappiness. —**sym''pa·thet'ic**, *adj.*

**sym'pho·ny**, *n., pl.* **-nies.** major orchestral composition. —**sym·phon'ic**, *adj.*

**symp'tom**, *n.* characteristic indication, esp. of an illness. —**symp''to·mat'ic**, *adj.*

**syn'a·gogue''**, *n.* congregation or house of Jewish worship.

**syn'chro·nize''**, *v.t.* cause to occur at the same time or rate of speed.

**syn'di·cate**, *n.* organization of independent organizations for a major effort.

**syn''fuel**, *n.* synthetic fuel.

**syn'o·nym**, *n.* different word of similar meaning. —**syn·on'y·mous**, *adj.*

**syn·op'sis**, *n., pl.* **-ses.** summary; brief outline.

**syn'the·sis**, *n., pl.* **-ses.** combination of different parts.

**syn·thet'ic**, *adj.* **1.** imitating a natural material, esp. in composition. **2.** pertaining to synthesis.

**syph'i·lis**, *n.* a venereal disease. —**syph''i·lit'ic**, *adj., n.*

**sy·ringe'**, *n.* plunger-operated device for drawing up and ejecting fluids.

**syr'up**, *n.* heavy, sweet liquid, esp. one of sugar and water.

**sys'tem**, *n.* **1.** order or method. **2.** coordinated arrangement of working elements. —**sys''tem·at'ic**, *adj.*

# T

**T, t**, *n.* twentieth letter of the English alphabet.

**ta'ble**, *n.* **1.** piece of furniture with a broad horizontal surface. **2.** orderly arrangement of data. —*v.t.* **3.** postpone, as legislation. —**ta'ble·ware''**, *n.*

**ta'ble·cloth''**, *n.* —**ta'ble·ware''**, *n.*

**ta'ble·spoon''**, *n.* spoon of one half a fluid ounce.

**tab'let**, *n.* **1.** slab for writing or lettering. **2.** pill. **3.** pad of paper.

**tack**, *n.* **1.** short, pointed fastener. **2.** change of course. —*v.t.* **3.** fasten with tacks. **4.** cause to change course. —*v.i.* **5.** change course.

**tact**, *n.* sense of how not to offend. —**tact'less**, *adj.*

**tac'tics**, *n.* **1.** science of maneuvering armed forces. **2.** connivance; artifice.

**tag**, *n.* **1.** label attached with a cord. **2.** chasing game. —*v.t.* **3.** apply a tag to. —*v.i.* **4.** follow closely.

**tail**, *n.* **1.** distinct hindmost extremity of an animal. **2.** feature similar in shape or location, as on a vehicle.

**tail'or**, *n.* **1.** maker of clothes. —*v.t.* **2.** make as a tailor does.

**take**, *v.*, **took, taken, taking.** *v.t.* **1.** carry. **2.** escort. **3.** accept. **4.** seize. **5.** make use of. **6.** select. **7.** require. **8.** react to. **9.** assume. **1·0** engage in. —*v.i.* **1.** be effective.

**tale**, *n.* **1.** narrative. **2.** piece of gossip. **3.** lie. —**tale'bear''er**, *n.*

**tal'ent**, *n.* **1.** personal ability. **2.** person or persons of talent. —**tal'ent·ed**, *adj.*

**talk**, *v.i.* **1.** speak words. **2.** confer. **3.** gossip. —*v.t.* **4.** persuade. —*n.* **5.** conversation. **6.** speech. **7.** gossip or rumor.

**tall**, *adj.* **1.** very high. **2.** of a specified height.

**tame**, *adj.*, **tamer, tamest**, *v.t. adj.* **1.** obedient to a master. **2.** without spirit. —*v.t.* **3.** make tame. —**tame'ly**, *adv.* —**tame'ness**, *n.*

—tam′a·ble, tame′a·ble, adj.
—tam′er, n.

tan, n., adj., tanner, tannest, v.t.
1. yellow-brown. 2. suntan
—adj. 3. yellow-brown. —v.t. 4.
convert into leather.

tan′dem, adv., adj. with one behind the other.

tan′gi·ble, adj. 1. able to be touched. 2. able to be defined.

tan′gle, v.t. 1. intertwine in a disorderly way. —n. 2. tangled state.

tank, n. 1. container for fluids. 2. armored fighting vehicle.

tan′ta·lize″, v.t. torment with gratification withheld.

tap, v.t., v.i. 1. strike lightly. —v.t. 2. draw off or upon. —n. 3. light blow. 4. valve or plug.

tape, n. 1. thin, flat, long strip. —v.t. 2. bind with tape.

tap′es·try, n., pl. -tries. n. woven decorative panel.

tar, n. 1. thick black liquid distilled from wood, coal, etc. —v.t. 2. coat with tar.

tar′dy, adj., -dier, -diest. behind the expected time. —tar′di·ly, adv. —tar′di·ness, n.

tar′get, n. something aimed at.

tar′iff, n. 1. tax on imports or exports. 2. price or charge.

tar′nish, v.t. 1. spoil the luster of. —v.i. 2. become tarnished. —n. 3. tarnished state.

tart, adj. 1. acid. —n. 2. small pie.

task, n. 1. something to be done. —v.t. 2. burden.

taste, v.t. 1. sense with the tongue. 2. experience. —v.i. 3. have a specific flavor. —n. 4. sense operating through the tongue. 5. flavor. 6. sense of what is appropriate or seemly. 7. liking. —tast′er, n.

tast′y, adj., -ier, -iest. good-tasting.

tat′ter, n. 1. ragged fragment. —v.t. 2. reduce to tatters. —tat′tered, adj.

tat′tle, v.i. gossip.

tat·too′, v.t., n., pl. -toos. v.t. 1. mark with pigments under the skin. —n. 2. tattooed design. 3. military drum or bugle signal.

taunt, v.t. 1. mock. —n. 2. mocking remark.

taut, adj. tight or tense. —taut′ly, adv. —taut′ness, n.

tav′ern, n. public drinking place.

tax, n. 1. money exacted by a government. 2. demand on resources.
—v.t. 3. exact a tax on or from. 4. accuse. —tax′a·ble, adj. —tax′a′tion, n. —tax′pay″er, n.

tax′i, n. hired vehicle with metered charges. Also, tax′i·cab″.

tea, n. drink made from the dried leaves of a shrub grown in Asia.

teach, v., taught, teaching. v.t. 1. inform on a subject. 2. inform students regarding. —v.i. 3. be a teacher. —teach′a·ble, adj. —teach′er, n.

team, n. 1. group of animals or persons acting together. —v.i. 2. join or act in a team. —team′mate″, n. —team′work″, n.

tear, v., tore, torn, tearing, n. v.t. (ter) 1. pull apart by force. 2. make by piercing or rending. 3. lacerate or harass. —v.i. 4. be torn. 5. hurry. —n. 6. torn place. 7. (tēr) liquid from the weeping eye. —tear′drop″, n. —tear′ful, adj.

tease, v.t. 1. bother with gentle malice. 2. comb.

teat, n. nipple.

tech′ni·cal, n. 1. pertaining to technology. 2. pertaining to technique. 3. pertaining to specific details. —tech′ni·cal·ly, adv. —tech″ni·cal′i·ty, n. —tech·ni′cian, n.

tech·nique′, n. 1. working method. 2. proficiency. Also, tech′nic.

tech·noc′ra·cy, n. government by technical experts.

tech·nol′o·gy, n., pl. -gies. application of science, esp. to industry.

te′di·um, n. wearisome or boring quality or state. —te′di·ous, adj.

tel′e·graph″, n. 1. apparatus sending messages in code by electrical impulses. —v.t. 2. reach by telegraph. 3. send by telegraph. —tel″e·graph′ic, adj. —te·leg′ra·phy, n. —te·leg′ra·pher, n. —tel″e·gram″, n.

tel′e·phone″, n. 1. device for transmitting personal spoken messages. —v.t. 2. reach by telephone. 3. transmit by telephone. —tel″e·phon′ic, adj.

tel′e·scope″, n. 1. device for magnifying distant images. —v.t., v.i. 2. slide lengthwise into one another. —tel″e·scop′ic, adj.

tel′e·vise″, v.t. transmit by television.

tel′e·vi″sion, n. method of trans-

**S T**

mitting images by radio waves and electrical impulses.

**tell,** v., **told, telling.** v.t. 1. inform. 2. recount. 3. order. 4. distinguish; recognize. —v.i. 5. give a narrative. 6. have an effect. —**tel´ling,** adj. —**tel´ling·ly,** adv.

**tem´per,** n. 1. mood. 2. anger. 3. control of one's anger. 4. hardness and flexibility, as of steel. —v.t. 5. moderate. 6. give toughness to.

**tem´per·a·ment,** n. natural mental disposition. —**tem´per·a·men´tal,** adj.

**tem´per·ate,** adj. moderate.

**tem´per·a·ture,** n. 1. relative heat. 2. condition of excessive body heat.

**tem´pest,** n. violent storm. —**tem·pes´tu·ous,** adj.

**tem´ple,** n. 1. place of worship. 2. area to either side of the brow.

**tem´po·rar´y,** adj. for a limited time. —**tem´po·rar´i·ly,** adv.

**tempt,** v.t. create an appetite or inclination in. —**temp·ta´tion,** n. —**tempt´er,** fem., **tempt´ress,** n.

**ten,** n. nine plus one.

**ten´ant,** n. renter of building space or land. —**ten´an·cy,** n.

**tend,** v.i. 1. have a tendency. —v.t. 2. manage or care for.

**ten´den·cy,** n., pl. **-cies.** mild predominance of a certain result, preference, etc.

**ten´der,** adj. 1. soft. 2. warmly affectionate. 3. feeling pain readily. —n. 4. person who tends. 5. railroad car for fuel. 6. something offered in payment. —v.t. 7. offer. —**ten´der·ly,** adv. —**ten´der·ness,** n. —**ten´der·heart´ed,** adj. —**ten´der·ize´´,** v.t.

**ten´don,** n. muscle attachment.

**tennis,** n. game played with rackets and a ball.

**ten´or,** n. highest male singing voice.

**tense,** adj., **tenser, tensest,** v., n. adj. 1. staut. 2. nervous; strained. —v.t. 3. make tense. —v.i. 4. become tense. —n. 5. Grammar. expression of past, present, future, etc. —**tense´ly,** adv. —**ten´sion, tense´ness, ten´si·ty** n.

**tent,** n. fabric shelter spread over poles.

**ten´ta·tive,** adj. done as a trial.

**tenth,** adj. 1. following nine others. —n. 2. one of ten equal parts.

**term,** n. 1. word with a specific

meaning. 2. period of activity. 3. **terms, a.** requirements of an agreement. **b.** basis of a relationship.

**ter´min·al,** n. 1. station at the end of a railroad, etc. 2. electrical connecting point. 3. (computers) work station for data processing. —adj. 4. coming at the end. 5. causing death. —**ter´min·al·ly,** adv.

**ter´mi·nate´´,** v.t., v.i. finish. —**ter´mi·na·ble,** adj. —**ter´mi·na´tion,** n.

**ter´race,** n. 1. raised outdoor platform. —v.t. 2. form in terraces.

**ter·res´tri·al,** adj. pertaining to the earth.

**ter´ri·ble,** adj. 1. bad; poor. 2. awesome.

**ter·rif´ic,** adj. awesome in force.

**ter´ri·fy,** v.t. fill with terror.

**ter´ri·to´´ry,** n., pl. **-ries.** 1. region without full political status. 2. distinct area of land. —**ter´ri·to´ri·al,** adj.

**ter´ror,** n. 1. great fear. 2. cause of such fear.

**terse,** adj., **terser, tersest.** short-spoken; concise. —**terse´ly,** adv. —**terse´ness,** n.

**test,** n. 1. act or event that reveals qualities, accomplishments, illnesses, etc. —v.t. 2. subject to a test. —v.i. 3. perform a test. —**test´er,** n.

**tes´ti·fy,** v.t., v.i. bear witness.

**tes´ti·mo´´ny,** n., pl. **-nies.** declaration.

**text,** n. 1. written matter. 2. textbook. —**text´u·al,** adj.

**tex´tile,** n. cloth.

**tex´ture,** n. surface quality. —**tex´tur·al,** adj.

**than,** conj. (introduces a basis of comparison).

**thank,** v.t. express gratitude to.

**that,** pron., adj., pl. **those,** conj. pron., adj. 1. the one. 2. the other. —pron. 3. which. —conj. 4. (used to introduce noun and adverbial clauses). —adv. 5. to such an extent.

**the,** def. article. (refers to a particular person, thing, or type).

**the´a·ter,** n. 1. place for plays, etc. 2. theatrical profession. Also, **the´a·tre.** —**the·at´ri·cal,** adj. —**the·at´ri·cal·ly,** adv.

**theft,** n. stealing.

**their,** adj. pertaining to them.

**theirs,** *pron.* something pertaining to them.

**them,** *pron.* (objective of *they*).

**theme,** *n.* 1. subject. 2. basic melody. —**the·mat'ic,** *adj.*

**them·selves',** *pron.* 1. (intensive and reflexive of *they*). 2. their true selves.

**then,** *adv.* 1. at that time. 2. and after. 3. in that case. —*n.* 4. that time.

**thence,** *adv.* from there or then.

**thence''forth',** *adv.* from then on.

**the·ol'o·gy,** *n.*, *pl.* **-gies.** study of religious doctrine.

**the'o·ry,** *n.*, *pl.* **-ries.** 1. statement of a possible truth. 2. untried assumption. —**the''o·ret'i·cal,** *adj.* —**the''o·ret'i·cal·ly,** *adv.* —**the'o·rize'',** *v.i.* —**the'o·rist,** *n.*

**ther'a·py,** *n.*, *pl.* **-pies.** healing process. —**ther'a·pist,** *n.*

**there,** *adv.* 1. at or to that place. 2. in that respect. 3. (used to introduce expressions of existence or non-existence).

**there·af'ter,** *adv.* from then on.

**there'by',** *adv.* in connection with that.

**there'fore'',** *adj.* for this reason.

**there·in',** *adv.* in that.

**there·of',** *adv.* of that.

**there·on',** *adv.* 1. on that. 2. just afterward.

**there'up·on',** *adv.* 1. just afterward. 2. in consequence.

**ther·mom'e·ter,** *n.* heat-measuring device.

**ther''mo·nu'cle·ar,** *adj.* pertaining to atomic fusion at high heat.

**ther'mo·stat'',** *n.* heating control.

**they,** *n.* (plural of *he, she,* or *it.* )

**thick,** *n.* 1. deep from front to back. 2. dense. —**thick'ly,** *adv.* —**thick'ness,** *n.* —**thick'en,** *v.t., v.i.*

**thief,** *n.*, *pl.* **thieves.** person who steals. —**thiev'er·y,** *n.* —**thiev'ish,** *adj.*

**thigh,** *n.* upper leg.

**thim'ble,** *n.* fingertip protector.

**thin,** *adj.* **thinner, thinnest,** *v.t. adj.* 1. shallow from front to back. 2. not dense; meager. —*v.t.* 3. make thin. —**thin'ly,** *adv.* —**thin'ness,** *n.* —**thin'ner,** *n.*

**thing,** *n.* inanimate entity.

**think,** *v.*, **thought, thinking.** *v.t.* 1. have in the mind. 2. believe. —*v.i.*

3. employ the mind. —**think'er,** *n.*

**third,** *adj.* 1. being number three. —*n.* 2. one of three equal parts.

**thirst,** *n.* desire to absorb liquids. —**thirst'y,** *adj.* —**thirst'i·ly,** *adv.*

**thir·teen',** *adj., n.* ten plus three. —**thir·teenth',** *adj.*

**thir'ty,** *adj., n.* three times ten. —**thir'ti·eth,** *adj., n.*

**this,** *pron., adj., pl.* **these.** *pron., adj.* 1. (designating something near at hand). —*adv.* 2. to this extent.

**thor'ough,** *adj.* complete in every detail.

**thou,** *pron. Archaic.* you.

**though,** *conj.* 1. despite the fact that. —*adv.* 2. however.

**thought,** *n.* 1. thinking process. 2. something thought. 3. something to consider.

**thou'sand,** *adj., n.* ten times one hundred. —**thou'sandth,** *adj., n.*

**thread,** *n.* 1. length of spun fiber. 2. ridge on a screw. —*v.t.* 3. put a thread through.

**threat,** *n.* warning of revenge or danger.

**threat'en,** *v.t.* make or constitute a threat against.

**three,** *n.* two plus one.

**thrice,** *adv.* three times.

**thrift,** *n.* saving of money, etc.

**thrill,** *v.t.* 1. excite emotionally. —*v.i.* 2. be excited emotionally. —*n.* 3. act or instance of thrilling.

**thrive,** *v.i.*, **thrived.** or **throve, thrived** or **thriven, thriving.** be prosperous or healthy.

**throat,** *n.* interior of the neck.

**throb,** *v.i.* 1. beat, as the heart or pulse, with more than usual force. —*n.* 2. act or instance of throbbing.

**throne,** *n.* chair of state.

**throng,** *n., v.i.* crowd.

**through,** *prep.* 1. from end to end of. 2. by means of. —*adv.* 3. from end to end. —*adj.* 4. from end to end. 5. finished.

**through·out',** *prep.* 1. in every part of. —*adv.* 2. in every part.

**throw,** *v.t.*, **threw, thrown,** *n. v.t.* 1. propel unsupported. 2. send forcefully. —*n.* 3. act or instance of throwing. 4. distance of throwing. —**throw'er,** *n.*

**thrust,** *v.t., v.i.* push.

**thumb,** *n.* 1. innermost hand digit. —*v.t.* 2. move with the thumb.

**S**
**T**

**thun'der**, *n.* 1. sound following lightning. —*v.t.* 2. say loudly or vehemently. —**thun'der·ous**, *adj.* —**thun'der·bolt''**, *n.* —**thun'der·clap''**, *n.* —**thun'der·cloud''**, *n.* —**thun'der·show''er**, *n.* —**thun'der·storm''**, *n.*

**thus**, *adv.* 1. in this way. 2. to this extent. 3. therefore.

**thy**, *adj. Archaic.* your.

**tick**, *n.* 1. sound of a mechanical clock. 2. bloodsucking insect. 3. mattress cloth. —*v.i.* 4. make a ticking sound. —**tick'er**, *n.*

**tick'et**, *n.* 1. paper giving admission. 2. list of candidates.

**tick'le**, *v.t.* 1. cause to twitch by light stroking. 2. amuse. —*v.i.* 3. cause tickling.

**tick'lish**, *adj.* 1. susceptible to tickling. 2. needing caution.

**tide**, *n.* periodic fluctuation of sea level. —**tid'al**, *adj.* —**tide'wa''ter**, *n.*, *adj.*

**ti'dings**, *n., pl.* news.

**ti'dy**, *adj.*, **-dier, -diest**, *v.t.* *adj.* 1. orderly. —*v.t.* 2. make orderly. —**ti'di·ness**, *n.* —**ti'di·ly**, *adv.*

**tie**, *v.t.*, **tied, ty·ing**, *n.* *v.t.* 1. fasten with ropes, etc. 2. equal in scoring. —*n.* 3. something that ties. 4. something that prevents spreading. 5. equal score. 6. necktie.

**ti'ger**, *n.* large catlike animal.

**tight**, *adj.* 1. preventing movement. 2. fully stretched. —*adv.* 3. securely. —*n.* 4. tights, tight-fitting trousers. —**tight'ly**, *adv.* —**tight'ness**, *n.* —**tight'en**, *v.t.*, *v.i.* —**tight'-fit''ting**, *adj.*

**tile**, *n.* 1. thin piece of material, originally baked earth. —*v.t.* 2. furnish with tiles. —**til'ing**, *n.*

**till**, *prep.*, *conj.* 1. until. —*v.t.* 2. prepare for growing crops. —*n.* 3. money drawer.

**tilt**, *v.t.*, *v.i.* 1. slant from an upright position. —*n.* 2. act or instance of tilting.

**tim'ber**, *n.* 1. cut wood. 2. trees collectively. —**tim'bered**, *adj.*

**time**, *n.* 1. past, present, and future. 2. Often, **times**, period of occurrence. 3. instance. —*prep.* 4. **times**, multiplied by. —*v.t.* 5. determine the time or duration of. —**tim'er**, *n.*

**time'ly**, *adj.*, **-lier, -liest** coming at the right time.

**time'piece''**, *n.* clock or watch.

**time'ta''ble**, *n.* schedule of times.

**tim'id**, *adj.* lacking self-confidence.

**tin**, *n.* 1. white metallic element. —*v.t.* 2. plate with tin. —**tin'foil''**, *n.* —**tin'smith''**, *n.*

**tinge**, *n.* 1. slight color or trace. —*v.t.* 2. give a tinge to.

**tint**, *n.* 1. light color or shade. —*v.t.* 2. give a tint to.

**ti'ny**, *adj.*, **-nier, -niest.** very small.

**tip**, *n.* 1. outermost point. 2. reward for a service. —*v.i.* 3. overturn. —*v.t.* 4. give a tip to. —**tip'per**, *n.*

**ti'rade**, *n.* vehement speech.

**tire**, *v.t.* 1. make tired. —*v.i.* 2. become tired. —*n.* 3. wearing surface of a wheel.

**tired**, *adj.* without strength because of exertion.

**tis'sue**, *n.* 1. thin cloth or paper. 2. organic matter.

**ti'tle**, *n.* 1. formal name. 2. right of ownership. —*v.t.* 3. give a title to. —**ti'tled**, *adj.*

**to**, *prep.* 1. as far as. 2. in the direction of. 3. until; before. 4. being supported or held by. 5. along with. 6. in comparison or equivalence with.

**toast**, *n.* 1. browned sliced bread. 2. drink in honor of someone. —*v.t.* 3. brown with heat. 4. drink in honor of.

**to·bac'co**, *n., pl.* **-cos** leaves prepared for smoking, chewing, etc.

**to·day'**, *adv.* 1. on the present day. —*n.* 2. present day. 3. modern times.

**toe**, *n.* foot digit. —**toed**, *adj.* —**toe'nail''**, *n.*

**to·geth'er**, *adv.* one with another.

**toil**, *n.*, *v.i.* labor. —**toil'er**, *n.* —**toil'some**, *adj.*

**toi'let**, *n.* 1. dress and grooming. 2. place or fixture for excretion.

**to'ken**, *n.* 1. souvenir. 2. indication. 3. metal disk used in payment. —*adj.* 4. intended as a gesture.

**tol'er·ance**, *n.* 1. patience or understanding. 2. permissible deviation. 3. resistance to poison, etc. —**tol'er·ant**, *adj.*

**tol'er·ate''**, *v.t.* 1. be patient with. 2. endure. —**tol''er·a'tion**, *n.* —**tol'er·a·ble**, *adj.* —**tol'er·a·bly**, *adv.*

**toll**, *n.* 1. tariff. —*v.t.*, *v.i.* 2. ring solemnly.

**tomb**, *n.* burial place. —**tomb'stone''**, *n.*

**to·mor'row**, *n.*, *adv.* day after this.

**ton,** *n.* U.S. unit of 2,000 pounds.

**tone,** *n.* 1. sound of a certain pitch. 2. shade of color. 3. air or appearance. —**ton'al,** *adj.* —**to·nal'i·ty,** *n.* —**tone'-deaf',** *adj.*

**tongue,** *n.* 1. flexible licking and tasting organ in the mouth. 2. language.

**ton'ic,** *n.* 1. invigorating medicine. 2. *Music.* keynote.

**to·night',** *n., adv.* this night.

**ton'sil,** *n.* oval growth at the back of the throat. —**ton'sil·li'tis,** *n.*

**too,** *adv.* 1. also. 2. excessively.

**tool,** *n.* 1. object for shaping, fastening, etc. 2. something or someone used.

**tooth,** *n., pl.* **teeth.** 1. hard white growth used for biting. 2. similar object in a gear, etc. —**tooth'ache'',** *n.* —**tooth'brush'',** *n.* —**toothed,** *adj.* —**tooth'less,** *adj.* —**tooth'pick'',** *n.* —**tooth'y,** *adj.*

**top,** *n.* 1. uppermost point or part. 2. spinning toy. —*v.t.* 3. put a top on. 4. remove a top from. 5. surpass.

**top'ic,** *n.* subject of discussion. —**top'i·cal,** *adj.*

**torch,** *n.* flame-bearing object.

**tor·ment,** *v.t.* (tor ment') 1. harass or torture. —*n.* (tor'ment) 2. tormented state. 3. something that torments. —**tor·men'tor, tor'men·ter,** *n.*

**tor·na'do,** *n., pl.* **-does, -dos.** violent whirlwind.

**tor'rent,** *n.* rush of fluid. —**tor·ren'tial,** *adj.*

**tor'rid,** *adj.* hot.

**tor'so,** *n., pl.* **-sos.** trunk of the human body.

**tor'ture,** *n.* 1. application of severe pain, etc. —*v.t.* 2. subject to torture. —**tor'tur·er,** *n.*

**toss,** *v.t.* 1. throw lightly. 2. jerk upward. —*n.* 3. act or instance of tossing.

**to'tal,** *adj.* 1. being a sum. 2. complete. —*n.* 3. sum. —**to'tal·ly,** *adv.* —**to·tal'i·ty,** *n.*

**touch,** *v.t.* 1. tap, pat, or feel. 2. move emotionally. —*n.* 3. act or instance of touching. 4. distinctive manner. 5. slight amount.

**tough,** *adj.* 1. resistant to injury. 2. enduring. 3. brutal. 4. difficult. —**tough'ness,** *n.* —**tough'en,** *v.t., v.i.*

**tour,** *n.* 1. trip with many stops. —*v.t.* 2. make a tour through.

**tour'ist,** *n.* person on a pleasure tour. —**tour'ism,** *n.*

**tour'na·ment,** *n.* 1. knightly contest. 2. series of athletic contests.

**tow,** *v.t.* 1. pull with a line. —*n.* 2. act or instance of towing. —**tow'line'', tow'rope'',** *n.* —**tow'path'',** *n.*

**to·ward',** *prep.* in the direction of. Also, **to·wards'.**

**tow'el,** *n.* drying cloth.

**tow'er,** *n.* 1. tall construction. —*v.i.* 2. stand high.

**town,** *n.* 1. large community. 2. urban center. —**towns'man,** *n.* —**towns'peo''ple,** *n., pl.*

**toy,** *n.* 1. something to play with. —*v.i.* 2. play; trifle.

**trace,** *n.* 1. faint sign or trail. —*v.t.* 2. follow the trail of. 3. copy by following the lines of. —**trace'a·ble,** *adj.* —**trac'er,** *n.* —**trac'ing,** *n.*

**track,** *n.* 1. trail or trace. 2. pair of rails, etc. used as a guide. —*v.t.* 3. follow or trace.

**tract,** *n.* 1. expanse of land. 2. series of bodily organs. 3. religious leaflet.

**trac'tion,** *n.* 1. pulling effort. 2. friction between a foot or wheel and a surface.

**trac'tor,** *n.* pulling vehicle.

**trade,** *v.t.* 1. exchange. —*v.i.* 2. have business dealings. 3. make an exchange. —*n.* 4. buying and selling. 5. skilled occupation. 6. swap. —**trad'er,** *n.*

**tra·di'tion,** *n.* long-accepted custom or belief.

**traf'fic,** *n., v.i.* **-ficked, -ficking.** *n.* 1. movement along roadways. 2. commerce. —*v.i.* 3. have dealings. —**traf'fick·er,** *n.*

**trag·e·dy,** *n., pl.* **-ies.** 1. drama ending unhappily. 2. disastrous event. —**tra·ge'di·an,** *n., fem.,* **tra·ge'di·enne'',** *n.* —**trag'ic, trag'i·cal,** *adj.* —**trag'i·cal·ly,** *adv.*

**trail,** *n.* 1. mark left in passing. 2. route, esp. in wild country. —*v.t.* 3. trace. 4. drag. —*v.i.* 5. drag or grow along the ground.

**train,** *n.* 1. string of railroad cars. 2. trailing skirt or cape. 3. connected series. 4. procession. —*v.t.* 5. educate for a purpose. 6. exercise for sports. —**train·ee',** *n.* —**train'er,** *n.* —**train'ing,** *n.*

**trait,** *n.* distinctive quality.

**trai'tor,** *n.* betrayer of one's country.

S
T

**tramp**, *v.i.* 1. walk heavily. 2. travel on foot. —*n.* 3. vagrant. 4. hike.

**trance**, *n.* sleeplike or abstracted state.

**tran'quil**, *adj.* serene; relaxed.

**trans·act'**, *v.t.* complete, as a business deal. —**trans·ac'tion**, *n.* —**trans·ac'tor**, *n.*

**tran·scend'**, *v.t.* 1. go outside the limits of. 2. surpass. —**tran'scend'ent**, *adj.*

**trans·fer'**, *v.t., v.i.* (trans fər') 1. move to another place. —*n.* (trans'fər) 2. act or instance of transferring. 3. authorization for transferring. —**trans·fer'a·ble**, *adj.* —**trans'fer·ence**, *n.*

**trans·form'**, *v.t., v.i.* change in nature.

**tran·si'tion**, *n.* gradual change of nature or condition.

**trans·late'**, *v.t.* 1. alter in language. 2. alter in condition. —**trans·la'tion**, *n.* —**trans·la'tor**, *n.* —**trans·lat'a·ble**, *adj.*

**trans·lu'cent**, *adj.* passing light but not images.

**trans·mis'sion**, *n.* 1. act or instance of transmitting. 2. something transmitted. 3. gear assembly.

**trans·mit'**, *v.t.* 1. convey through a medium. 2. send out in radio waves. 3. hand down, as to a new generation. —**trans·mit'tal**, **trans·mit'tance**, *n.* —**trans·mit'ter**, *n.*

**trans·par'ent**, *adj.* 1. passing light and images. 2. obvious. —**trans·par'ent·ly**, *adv.* —**trans·par'en·cy**, *n.*

**trans·plant'**, *v.t.* 1. plant in a new place. 2. graft surgically. —*n.* 3. act of transplanting. —**trans'·plan·ta'tion**, *n.*

**trans·port'**, *v.t.* (trans port') 1. carry. —*n.* (trans'port) 2. transportation. 3. state of rapture. 4. carrier for troops. —**trans''por·ta'tion**, *n.*

**trans·verse'**, *adj.* crosswise. —**trans·verse'ly**, *adv.*

**trap**, *n.* 1. device for catching animals. 2. trick for detection or capture. —*v.t.* 3. catch. 4. adorn. —**trap'per**, *n.* —**trap'pings**, *n., pl.*

**trash**, *n.* discarded matter. —**trash'y**, *adj.*

**trav'el**, *v.i.* 1. go on a journey.

—*n.* 2. traveling, esp. for pleasure. —**trav'el·er, trav'el·ler**, *n.*

**trav·erse'**, *v.t.* pass across.

**tray**, *n.* shallow, broad receptacle.

**treach'er·y**, *n., pl.* -ies. betrayal of trust. —**treach'er·ous**, *adj.*

**tread**, *v.*, **trod, trod·den, tread·ing.** *v.i.* 1. walk deliberately. —*v.t.* 2. press, make, etc. by treading. —*n.* 3. manner of treading. 4. step. 5. surface of a wheel, tire, etc. that touches the ground.

**trea'son**, *n.* betrayal of one's country.

**treas'ure**, *n.* 1. precious possession. —*v.t.* 2. regard as a treasure.

**treas'ur·y**, *n., pl.* -ies. department or place for storing money.

**treat**, *v.t.* 1. act toward as specified. 2. handle as specified. 3. give medical care to. 4. have as a guest. —*n.* 5. something offered a guest. 6. source of pleasure. —**treat'ment**, *n.*

**trea'ty**, *n., pl.* -ties. agreement between nations.

**tree**, *n., v.t.,* **treed, tree·ing.** *n.* 1. tall plant with a woody stem and branches. —*v.t.* 2. chase up a tree.

**trem'ble**, *v.i.* 1. shiver. 2. be in fear or awe.

**tre·men'dous**, *adj.* huge. —**tre·men'dous·ly**, *adv.*

**trench**, *n.* deep, narrow ditch.

**trend**, *n.* current style or tendency.

**tres'pass**, *v.i.* 1. enter property without right. —*n.* 2. sin. —**tres'pas·ser**, *n.*

**tri'al**, *n.* 1. test, as for value. 2. annoyance or source of annoyance. 3. examination in a law court.

**tri'an·gle**, *n.* three-sided figure. —**tri·an'gu·lar**, *adj.*

**tribe**, *n.* group of related persons under one leader. —**trib'al**, *adj.* —**tribes'man**, *n.*

**trib'ute**, *n.* 1. compulsory payment. 2. expression of gratitude or honor.

**trick**, *n.* 1. cunning or treacherous act. —*v.t.* 2. cheat. —**trick'er·y**, *n.* —**trick'ster**, *n.*

**trick'y**, *adj.,* **-ier, -iest.** 1. treacherous; wily. 2. challenging the skill or cunning.

**tri'fle**, *n.* 1. something of little importance. —*v.i.* 2. talk or act frivolously.

**trig'ger**, *n.* 1. lever for firing a

gun. —v.t. 2. precipitate; cause to happen.

**trim**, v.t., n., adj., trimmer, trimmest. v.t. 1. make neat. 2. decorate. 3. balance. —n. 4. good condition. —adj. 5. neat. —**trim'ly**, adv. —**trim'mer**, n.

**tri·o** (trē'ō), n., pl. -os. group of three.

**trip**, v.i. 1. stumble and lose balance. —v.t. 2. cause to stumble. 3. set in motion. —n. 4. act or instance of tripping. 5. journey.

**tri'ple**, adj. 1. in three parts. 2. three times normal size. —v.t., v.i. 3. multiply three times. —**tri'ply**, adv.

**tri'plet**, n. one of three siblings born at the same time.

**trite**, adj., triter, tritest. overly familiar.

**tri'umph**, n. 1. victory. 2. delight in victory. —v.i. 3. be victorious. —**tri·um'phal**. adj. —**tri·um'phant**, adj.

**triv'i·al**, adj. petty and unimportant.

**troop**, n. 1. uniformed group. —v.i. 2. move in a group. —**troop'er**, n.

**tro'phy**, n., pl. -phies. memento of victory.

**trop'ic**, n. 1. boundary of the Torrid Zone 2. tropics, Torried Zone or nearby areas. —adj. 3. Also, **trop'i·cal**, pertaining to the Torrid Zone.

**trot**, v.i. 1. run at moderate speed. —n. 2. trotting gait. —**trot'ter**, n.

**trou'ble**, n. 1. worry or exertion. 2. source of these. —v.t. 3. cause trouble to. —v.i. 4. go to trouble.

**trough**, n. long, open container.

**trounce**, v.t. beat.

**trou'sers**, n., pl. pants.

**truce**, n. temporary suspension of hostilities.

**truck**, n. 1. freight motor vehicle. 2. hand cart for loads. —v.t. 3. carry by truck. —**truck'er**, n.

**true**, adj., truer, truest. adj. 1. according with truth. 2. faithful. —**tru'ly**, adv. —**true'ness**, n.

**trunk**, n. 1. large piece of luggage. 2. main stem of a tree. 3. body apart from head and limbs.

**trust**, n. 1. reliance; faith. 2. custody. 3. monopolistic combination. —v.t. 4. have reliance or faith in. —**trust'ful**, **trust'ing**, adj. —**trust'worth'y**, **trust'y**, adj.

**truth**, n. 1. that which is actually so. 2. accuracy. —**truth'ful**, adj. —**truth'ful·ly**, adv. —**truth'fulness**, n.

**try**, v.t., tried, trying, n. v.t. 1. attempt. 2. test. 3. examine in a court of law. 4. annoy or afflict. —n. 5. attempt or test. —**try'ing**, adj.

**tub**, n. broad, deep vessel.

**tube**, n. hollow cylinder. —**tub'ing**, n. —**tub'u·lar**, adj.

**tu·ber''cu·lo'sis**, n. illness with swelling lesions. —**tu·ber'cu·lar**, **tu·ber'cu·lous**, adj.

**tuck**, v.t. insert by pressing.

**tuft**, n. cluster of fibers, threads, etc.

**tug**, v.t. 1. pull forcefully. —n. 2. act or instance of tugging. —**tug'boat''**, n.

**tu·i'tion**, n. fee for teaching.

**tu'mor**, n. abnormal growth.

**tu'mult**, n. commotion. —**tu·mul'tu·ous**, adj.

**tune**, n. 1. melody. 2. harmony. —v.t. 3. put in tune. —**tune'ful**, adj. —**tune'less**, adj.

**tun'nel**, n. 1. route cut underground. —v.i. 2. dig a route.

**tur'bine**, n. rotary engine driven by the passing of a fluid.

**tur'bu·lent**, adj. in disturbed motion. —**tur'bu·lence**, n.

**turf**, n. earth held by grass roots. —**turf'y**, adj.

**tur'moil**, n. confused activity.

**turn**, v.t., v.i. 1. change in direction. 2. change in nature. —n. 3. curve. 4. loop. 5. place in a sequence. 6. act toward another. —**turn'ing**, n.

**tur'ret**, n. 1. small tower. 2. housing for cannon.

**tur'tle**, n. shell-encased reptile.

**tusk**, n. long, projecting tooth.

**tus'sle**, n., v.i. struggle.

**tu'tor**, n. 1. private teacher. —v.t. 2. teach privately. —**tu·to'ri·al**, adj., n.

**TV**, television.

**twelve**, n., adj. ten plus two. —**twelfth**, adj., n.

**twen'ty**, adj., n. two times ten. —**twen'ti·eth**, adj., n.

**twice**, adv. two times.

**twig**, n. tiny plant branch.

**twi'light''**, n. half-light, as between day and night.

**twin**, n. 1. one of two siblings born at the same time. 2. exact match. —adj. 3. matching another or each other exactly.

**S**
**T**

**twine**, *n.* 1. string. —*v.t.*, *v.i.* 2. twist together.

**twinge**, *n.* stab of pain.

**twirl**, *v.t.*, *v.i.* rotate rapidly.

**twist**, *v.t.* 1. wind around, rotate, or bend into a helical form. 2. distort the actuality of. —*v.i.* 3. assume a twisted form. 4. squirm. —*n.* 5. act or instance of twisting.

**twitch**, *v.i.* 1. jerk spasmodically. 2. pluck. —*n.* 3. spasmodic jerk.

**two**, *n.*, *adj.* one plus one. —**two″fold″**, *adj.*, *adv.* —**two′some**, *n.*

**ty·coon′**, *n.* man of great wealth and power.

**type**, *n.* 1. variety; sort. 2. reproducible characters used in printing. —*v.t.* 3. classify. 4. produce with a typewriter.

**type′writ″er**, *n.* machine for producing letters by mechanical means.

**ty′phoid**, *n.* acute infectious disease.

**ty·phoon′**, *n.* violent storm of the west Pacific Ocean.

**typ′i·cal**, *adj.* 1. representative of a type. 2. customary. —**typ′i·cal·ly**, *adv.*

**ty·pog′ra·phy**, *n.* art of composing and printing with type. —**ty″po·graph′ic**, *adj.* —**ty·pog′ra·pher**, *n.*

**ty′rant**, *n.* harsh, arbitrary ruler. —**tyr′an·ny**, *n.* —**ty·ran′ni·cal**, *adj.* —**tyr′an·nize″**, *v.i.*, *v.t.*

# U

**U, u**, *n.* twenty-first letter of the English alphabet.

**ud′der**, *n.* mammary gland of a cow.

**ug′ly**, *adj.*, **-lier**, **-liest**. 1. unattractive. 2. discomfiting; difficult. —**ug′li·ness**, *n.*

**u·kase′**, *n.* arbitrary command.

**ul′cer**, *n.* open break in tissue. —**ul′cer·ous**, *adj.* —**ul′cer·ate″**, *v.i.*, *v.t.*

**ul·te′ri·or**, *adj.* 1. further; beyond. 2. concealed; disguised.

**ul′ti·mate**, *adj.* 1. final; conclu-

sive. 2. fundamental; basic. —**ul′ti·mate·ly**, *adv.*

**ul″tra·light**, *n.* miniature aircraft for solo, powered flight.

**um·brel′la**, *n.* collapsible device with a fabric-covered frame, carried for protection against the weather.

**um′pire**, *n.* 1. final authority; judge. —*v.t.* 2. to serve as umpire for.

**un-**, prefix indicating "not."

**u″nan′i·mous**, *adj.* totally agreed. —**u·na·nim′i·ty**, *n.* —**u″nan′i·mous·ly**, *adv.*

**un′cle**, *n.* brother of one's mother or father, or husband of one's aunt.

**un′der**, *prep.*, *adj.*, *adv.* 1. below; beneath. 2. less than. —*adj.* 3. lower.

**un·der·grad′u·ate**, *n.* college student working toward a bachelor's degree.

**un′der·ground″**, *adj.* 1. below the ground. 2. secret; confidential. —*adv.* 3. below the ground. —*n.* 4. secret army of resistance.

**un·der·mine′**, *v.t.* weaken; sabotage.

**un·der·neath′**, *prep.*, *adv.* beneath.

**un·der·stand′**, *v.t.* 1. comprehend; take the meaning of. —*v.i.* 2. sympathize. —**un·der·stand′ing**, *n.*, *adj.*

**un·der·take′**, *v.t.* 1. set about; enter upon. 2. accept as an obligation.

**un′der·tak″er**, *n.* director of funerals.

**un′du·late″**, *v.t.*, *v.i.* 1. move or form in waves. 2. fluctuate in pitch and cadence. —**un″du·la′tion**, *n.*

**u′ni·form″**, *adj.* 1. alike; similar. —*n.* 2. distinctive or stylized dress for a particular group. —*v.t.* 3. clothe with a uniform. —**u·ni·form′i·ty**, *n.*

**un′ion**, *n.* 1. act or instance of uniting. 2. labor group organized for mutual aid. —**un′ion·ize″**, *v.t.*, *v.i.*

**u″nique′**, *adj.* 1. single; only. 2. rare; unusual.

**u′nit**, *n.* single amount, item, etc.

**u·nite′**, *v.t.*, *v.i.* join into one group or entity.

**u′ni·ty**, *n.* 1. state of being united; oneness. 2. agreement.

**u″ni·ver′sal**, *adj.* including all.

**u'ni·verse'**, *n.* entirety of physical creation.

**u''ni·ver'si·ty**, *n., pl.* **-ties.** large institution of higher learning.

**un·less'**, *conj., prep.* if not; except.

**un·til'**, *conj., prep.* 1. up to the time when. 2. before.

**un'to**, *prep.* to.

**un·to·ward'**, *adj.* 1. improper. 2. adverse.

**up**, *adv., adj., prep., v.t.,* **-ped., -ping.** *adv.* 1. to a higher level or location. 2. straight; erectly. 3. at bat. 4. awake; out of bed. 5. (computers) operating. —*prep.* 6. to a higher level or place in or on. —*v.t.* 7. increase.

**up·braid'**, *v.t.* scold; chide.

**up·heav'al**, *n.* turmoil; unrest; agitation.

**up·hol'ster**, *v.t.* furnish with padding and fabric covering. —**up·hol'ster·er**, *n.*

**up·on'**, *prep.* on; onto.

**up'per**, *adj.* higher. —**up'per·most''**, *adj.*

**up'roar''**, *n.* tumult; din.

**up·root''**, *v.t.* 1. to pull up by the roots. 2. displace from a home or homeland.

**up·set'**, *v.t.* (up set') 1. overturn. 2. defeat. 3. put in confusion or distress. —*v.i.* 4. be overturned. —*adj.* 5. distressed in mind. —*n.* (up'set'') 6. act or instance of upsetting.

**up''stairs'**, *adj.* 1. situated on an upper floor. —*adv.* 2. to or on an upper floor. —*n.* 3. floor above a ground floor.

**up'ward**, *adv.* 1. Also, **up'wards.** to a higher level or place. —*adj.* 2. toward a higher level or place.

**u·ra'ni·um**, *n.* radioactive metallic element used as a source for atomic energy.

**ur'ban**, *adj.* pertaining to cities.

**urge**, *v.t.* 1. advocate. 2. implore. —*n.* 3. impulse; desire; longing.

**ur'gent**, *adj.* pressing; vital; crucial. —**ur'gen·cy**, *n.* —**ur'gent·ly**, *adv.*

**u'rine**, *n.* fluid waste from kidneys.

**us**, *pron.* objective case of we.

**us'age**, *n.* 1. custom. 2. treatment; handling.

**use**, *v.t.* (yōōz) 1. employ or engage for a purpose. 2. expend; consume. 3. behave toward; treat. 4. do regularly. 5. accustom; habitu-

ate. —*n.* (yōōs) 6. application; employment. 7. value; service.

**us''er-friend''ly**, *adj.* (computers) designed for ease of use.

**u'su·al**, *adj.* 1. habitual; customary. 2. ordinary; common. —**u'su·al·ly**, *adv.*

**u·ten'sil**, *n.* implement or vessel useful esp. in the kitchen.

**u'ter·us**, *n.* female bodily organ in which fetuses develop.

**u·til'i·ty**, *n., pl.* **-ties.** 1. usefulness; function. 2. service provided for public use.

**u'ti·lize**, *v.t.* make use of. —**u''ti·li·za'tion**, *n.*

**ut'most''**, *adj.* 1. furthest. 2. greatest.

**ut'ter**, *v.t.* 1. say; speak; enunciate. —*adj.* 2. total; complete. —**ut'ter·ance**, *n.* —**ut'ter·ly**, *adv.*

# V

**V, v,** *n.* twenty-second letter of the English alphabet.

**va'can·cy**, *n., pl.* **-cies.** 1. state of being vacant. 2. void. 3. available rental space.

**va'cant''**, *adj.* empty; uninhabited.

**va'cate''**, *v.t.* 1. deprive of an occupant or incumbent. 2. leave.

**va·ca'tion**, *n.* respite from duty or occupation.

**vac'ci·nate''**, *v.t.* inoculate with cowpox virus for immunity to smallpox. —**vac''ci·na'tion**, *n.*

**vac'u·um**, *n.* space devoid of matter.

**va·gin·a** (və jī'nə), *n.* canal in the female from the vulva to the uterus. —**vag'i·nal**, *adj.*

**va'grant**, *n.* 1. wanderer. —*adj.* 2. wandering; itinerant.

**vague**, *adj.,* **vaguer, vaguest.** not definite; imprecise.

**vain**, *adj.* 1. futile. 2. conceited. —**vain'ly**, *adv.*

**val'iant**, *adj.* courageous.

**val'id**, *adj.* reasonable.

**va·lise** (və lēs'), *n.* traveling bag; suitcase.

U
Z

**val′ley**, *n.* long depression between mountains, plateaus, etc.

**val′or**, *n.* courage; bravery.

**val′u·a·ble**, *adj.* having worth or usefulness.

**val′ue**, *n.* **1.** importance; worth. **2.** relative worth. **3.** basic principle. —*v.t.* **4.** estimate the worth of. **5.** prize; esteem. —**val′ue·less**, *n.*

**valve**, *n.* device for regulating the flow of a fluid.

**van**, *n.* enclosed truck.

**van′dal**, *n.* person who willfully damages property. —**van′dal·ism**, *n.* —**van′dal·ize**, *v.t.*

**van′guard′′**, *n.* **1.** advance troops. **2.** forefront of an action, movement, or cause.

**va·nil′la**, *n.* extract of a tropical American orchid used in cookery.

**van′ish**, *v.i.* disappear.

**van′i·ty**, *n.*, *pl.* **-ties.** inflated pride; conceit.

**va′por**, *n.* gaseous substance.

**var′i·ance**, *n.* **1.** divergence. **2.** disagreement.

**var′i·ant**, *adj.* **1.** varying. **2.** altered in form. —*n.* **3.** variant form or structure.

**var′′i·a′tion**, *n.* change; alteration.

**va·ri′e·ty**, *n.*, *pl.* **-ties. 1.** diversity. **2.** assortment. **3.** category; kind; type. —**va·ri′e·tal**, *adj.*

**var′i·ous**, *adj.* **1.** several. **2.** diverse; different. —**var′i·ous·ly**, *adv.*

**var′nish**, *n.* **1.** resinous liquid preparation drying to a hard, glossy surface. **2.** outward appearance; gloss. —*v.t.* **3.** apply varnish to. **4.** gloss over; conceal.

**var′y**, *v.t.*, *v.i.* **1.** change; fluctuate. **2.** differ. —**var′i·ance**, *n.*

**vase**, *n.* ornamental vessel.

**vast**, *adj.* enormous; huge; immense.

**vat**, *n.* large vessel for holding fluids.

**vault**, *n.* **1.** arched structure forming a ceiling. **2.** space covered by such a structure. **3.** burial chamber. **4.** room or container for valuables. —*v.t.* **5.** form or cover with a vault. **6.** leap over. —*v.i.* **7.** perform a leap; jump.

**VCR**, video cassette recorder.

**veal**, *n.* flesh of a young calf.

**veg′e·ta·ble**, *n.* **1.** partly edible plant. —*adj.* *Also,* **veg′e·tal. 2.** being a vegetable. **3.** pertaining to plants.

**ve·he′ment**, *adj.* **1.** passionate;

emotional; fervid. **2.** violent. —**ve′he·ment·ly**, *adj.* —**ve′he·mence**, *n.*

**ve′hi·cle**, *n.* means of transporting or conveying. —**ve·hic′u·lar**, *adj.*

**veil**, *n.* net-like cloth for covering the face.

**vein**, *n.* **1.** tubular vessel conveying blood within the body. **2.** tubular thickening in an insect wing or a leaf. **3.** stratum of mineral, ore, or ice. **4.** spirit; mood. —*v.t.* **5.** pattern with or as if with veins.

**ve·loc′i·ty**, *n.*, *pl.* **-ties.** speed

**venge′ance**, *n.* retaliation; retribution.

**ven′om**, *n.* **1.** poisonous secretion. **2.** malice; spite. —**ven′om·ous**, *adj.*

**vent**, *n.* **1.** means of outlet or escape. —*v.t.* **2.** provide or serve as a vent. **3.** give free expression to.

**ven′ti·late**, *v.t.* provide with or expose to fresh air.

**ven′ture**, *v.t.* **1.** expose to hazard; risk. **2.** offer at risk of rejection. —*n.* **3.** challenging or risky undertaking. —**ven′ture·some, ven′tur·ous**, *adj.*

**verb**, *n. Grammar.* part of speech indicating action, occurrence, being, etc.

**ver′bal**, *adj.* **1.** relating to or formed of words. **2.** oral; spoken. **3.** relating to or constituting a verb or form of a verb. —**ver′bal·ly**, *adv.*

**ver′dict**, *n.* decision.

**verge**, *n.* **1.** margin; edge. —*v.i.* **2.** border; surround. **3.** tend; incline.

**ver′i·fy**, *v.t.* prove or ascertain the correctness of. —**ver·i·fi′a·ble**, *adj.* —**ver·i·fi·ca′tion**, *n.*

**ver′sa·tile**, *adj.* changing tasks or activities easily. —**ver·sa·til′i·ty**, *n.*

**verse**, *n.* **1.** poetry. **2.** part of a poem, esp. when rhymed. **3.** passage from the Bible.

**ver′sion**, *n.* **1.** account. **2.** translation.

**ver′ti·cal**, *adj.* **1.** perpendicular to the horizon. —*n.* **2.** vertical plane, line, etc. —**ver′ti·cal·ly**, *adv.*

**ver′y**, *adj.*, **-i·er, -i·est.** *adv.* **1.** to a great extent. —*adj.* **2.** identical; actual. **3.** absolute.

**ves′sel**, *n.* **1.** ship, boat, etc. **2.** container for fluid. **3.** channel for blood.

**vest,** *n.* sleeveless garment worn under a coat or jacket.

**ves'tige,** *n.* remnant; trace. —**ves·tig'i·al,** *adj.*

**vest-pocket,** *adj.* small enough for a pocket.

**vet'er·an,** *n.* **1.** person who has served, esp. in the military forces. —*adj.* **2.** greatly experienced.

**vet'er·i·nar'y,** *adj., n., pl.* **-ies.** *adj.* **1.** pertaining to the healing of animals. —*n.* **2.** Also, **vet'er·i·nar'i·an,** doctor for animals.

**ve'to,** *n., pl.* **-toes,** *n.* **1.** power to reject, prohibit, or ignore. **2.** prohibition. —*v.t.* **3.** reject or prohibit by veto.

**vex,** *v.t.* irritate. **2.** trouble.

**vi·a** (vī'ə, vē'ə), *prep.* by way of.

**vi'brant,** *adj.* **1.** oscillating; fluctuating. **2.** vigorous; energetic. —**vi'brant·ly,** *adj.* —**vi'bran·cy,** *n.*

**vi'brate,** *v.i., v.i.* **1.** move rapidly back and forth. —*v.i.* **2.** shiver. **3.** resound. —**vi·bra'tion,** *n.* —**vi'bra·to'ry,** *adj.* —**vi·bra'tor,** *n.*

**vice,** *n.* **1.** moral depravity. **2.** habitual personal shortcoming.

**vice-pres'i·dent,** *n.* official next in rank below president.

**vi·ce ver'sa,** with the order changed; conversely.

**vi·cin'i·ty,** *n., pl.* **-ties.** local area; neighborhood.

**vi'cious,** *adj.* **1.** depraved; immoral. **2.** spiteful; malicious. **3.** evil.

**vic'tim,** *n.* **1.** sufferer from a force or action. **2.** dupe. —**vic'tim·ize,** *v.t.*

**vic'tor,** *n.* winner; conqueror.

**vic·to'ry,** *n., pl.* **-ries.** success in a contest; triumph. —**vic·to'ri·ous,** *adj.* —**vic·to'ri·ous·ly,** *adv.*

**vid'e·o,** *n., adj.* **1.** television. **2.** a short, visual performance featuring a rock music soundtrack.

**vid'e·o·tape',** *n.* electromagnetic tape for recording visual images.

**vie,** *v.i.* **vied, vy'ing.** contend; complete.

**view,** *n.* **1.** seeing; beholding. **2.** area or range of vision. **3.** landscape. **4.** purpose. **5.** opinion; attitude. —*v.t.* **6.** look at; regard. —**view'er,** *n.* —**view'less,** *adj.*

**vig'il,** *n.* act of keeping awake and alert.

**vig'i·lant,** *adj.* alert; keenly aware. —**vig'i·lant·ly,** *adv.* —**vig'i·lance,** *n.*

**vig'or,** *n.* robust health, energy, or strength.

**vile,** *adj.,* **viler, vilest. 1.** of little account; mean. **2.** nasty; contemptible. —**vile'ly,** *adv.* —**vile'ness,** *n.*

**vil'lage,** *n.* small town; hamlet. —**vil'lag·er,** *n.*

**vil'lain,** *n.* wicked person; scoundrel. —**vil'lain·ous,** *adj.* —**vil'lain·y,** *n.*

**vin'di·cate',** *v.t.* absolve from suspicion or doubt.

**vin·dic'tive,** *adj.* holding a grudge.

**vine,** *n.* slender, creeping or climbing plant.

**vin'e·gar,** *n.* sour fermented liquid. —**vin'e·gar·y,** *adj.*

**vine'yard** (vin'yərd), *n.* garden or plantation for the growth of vines.

**vin'tage,** *n.* **1.** wine extracted from a single harvest of grapes. **2.** harvest of grapes.

**vi'o·late',** *v.t.* **1.** break; transgress. **2.** desecrate. **3.** rape. —**vi'o·la'tion,** *n.* —**vi'o·la'tor,** *n.*

**vi'o·lent,** *adj.* **1.** physically aggressive. **2.** severe; turbulent. —**vi'o·lent·ly,** *adv.* —**vi'o·lence,** *n.*

**vi'o·let,** *n.* **1.** low-growing herb bearing purplish or bluish blossoms. —*adj.* **2.** bluish purple.

**vi'o·lin',** *n.* bowed musical instrument. —**vi''o·lin'ist,** *n.*

**vir'gin,** *n.* **1.** sexually inexperienced person. —*adj.* **2.** being a virgin. **3.** unexplored, unexploited, etc. —**vir'gin·al,** *adj.*

**vir'ile,** *adj.* **1.** capable of siring offspring. **2.** vigorous; manly; potent. —**vi·ril'i·ty,** *n.*

**vir'tu·al,** *adj.* so in effect. —**vir'tu·al·ly,** *adv.*

**vir'tue,** *n.* **1.** morality. **2.** chastity. **3.** merit. —**vir'tu·ous,** *adj.* —**vir'tu·ous·ly,** *adv.* —**vir'tu·ous·ness,** *n.*

**vir'u·lent,** *adj.* **1.** poisonous; deadly. **2.** hostile. —**vir'u·lence,** *n.* —**vir'u·len·cy,** *n.* —**vir'u·lent·ly,** *adv.*

**vi'rus,** *adj.* infectious agency. —**vi'ral,** *adj.* —**vi'ral·ly,** *adv.*

**vis·cer·a** (vi'sər ə), *n., pl.* internal bodily organs. —**vis'cer·al,** *adj.*

**vise,** *n.* holding tool attached to a work bench, etc.

**vis'i·ble,** *adj.* **1.** capable of being seen. **2.** perceptible. —**vis'i·bly,** *adv.* —**vis·i·bil'i·ty,** *n.*

**vi'sion,** *n.* **1.** sense of sight. **2.** supernatural apprehension. **3.** foresight. —**vi′sion·al,** *adj.*

**vi′sit,** *v.t.* **1.** go to and stay briefly at. **2.** afflict. —*n.* **3.** brief stay, esp. as a guest. —**vis′i·tor,** *n.* —**vis′i·tant,** *n.* —**vis′i·ta′tion,** *n.*

**vi′sor,** *n.* forward projecting part, as of a helmet or cap.

**vis′u·al,** *adj.* pertaining to sight. —**vis′u·al·ly** *adj.*

**vis′u·a·lize′,** *v.t.* obtain or create a picture or conception of. —**vis′u·al·i·za′tion,** *n.*

**vi′tal,** *adj.* **1.** pertaining to life or existence. **2.** extremely important. **3.** full of exuberance, creativity, etc. —**vi′tal·ly,** *adv.* —**vi·tal′i·ty,** *n.*

**vi′ta·min,** *n.* organic substance vital in small quantities to proper nutrition. —**vi′ta·min′ic,** *adj.*

**vi·va′cious,** *adj.* animated; lively. —**vi·va′cious·ly,** *adj.* —**vi·va′ci·ty, vi·va′cious·ness,** *n.*

**viv′id,** *adj.* **1.** bright; brilliant. **2.** intense. —**viv′id·ly,** *adj.* —**viv′id·ness,** *n.*

**viv′i·sect′,** *v.t.* dissect while alive. —**viv′′i·sec′tion,** *n.* —**viv′′i·sec′tion·ist,** *n.*

**vo·cab′u·lar′y,** *n., pl.* **-ies.** **1.** stock of words used by a person, people, or group. **2.** collection of words in alphabetical order.

**vo′cal,** *adj.* **1.** pertaining to the voice. **2.** pertaining to singing. **3.** articulate; outspoken. —**vo′cal·ly,** *adj.* —**vo′cal·ize,** *v.t., v.i.* —**vo′′cal·i·za′tion,** *n.*

**vo·ca′tion,** *n.* profession; occupation. —**vo·ca′tion·al,** *adj.*

**vogue,** *n.* **1.** fashion; trend. **2.** popular favor or approval.

**voice,** *n.* **1.** sound uttered through the mouth. **2.** singing or speaking voice. **3.** expression. **4.** choice. **5.** right to express one's opinion. —*v.t.* **6.** *Grammar.* verbal inflection indicating whether subject is acting or acted upon. —*v.t.* **7.** express; declare. —**voice′less,** *adj.*

**void,** *adj.* **1.** without legal power. **2.** useless; fruitless. **3.** empty; hollow. —*n.* **4.** empty or hollow space. —*v.t.* **5.** cancel; invalidate. —**void′a·ble,** *adj.* —**void′ance,** *n.*

**vol·ca′no,** *n., pl.* **-noes, -nos.** mountain that ejects molten lava, rock, and steam. —**vol·can′ic,** *adj.* —**vol·can′i·cal·ly,** *adv.*

**vo·li′tion,** *n.* **1.** power of choosing or determining; will. **2.** act of willing. —**vo·li′tion·al,** *adj.*

**volt,** *n.* unit of electromotive force.

**vol′ume,** *n.* **1.** size in three dimensions. **2.** quantity; mass. **3.** degree of loudness. **4.** book.

**vo·lu′mi·nous,** *adj.* **1.** great in size or degree. **2.** consisting of or filling many books. —**vo·lu′min·ous·ly,** *adv.*

**vol′un·tar′y,** *adj.* **1.** performed or acted on by choice. **2.** controlled by the will. —**vol′un·tar′i·ly,** *adv.*

**vol′un·teer′,** *v.t.* **1.** offer freely or spontaneously. —*v.i.* **2.** volunteer oneself. —*n.* **3.** person who volunteers.

**vo·lup′tu·ous,** *adj.* sensuous; sensual; luxurious.

**vom′it,** *v.i.* **1.** disgorge the contents of the stomach through the mouth. —*v.t.* **2.** eject with force. —*n.* **3.** matter ejected by vomiting.

**vote,** *n.* **1.** formal expression of opinion or choice, as by ballot. **2.** right to such opinion or choice. **3.** votes collectively. —*v.t.* **4.** express or endorse by vote. —*v.i.* **5.** cast one's vote. —**vot′er,** *n.*

**vouch,** *v.i.* **1.** give a guarantee or surety. **2.** give personal assurance.

**vouch′er,** *n.* **1.** person who vouches. **2.** document certifying the occurrence of a transaction.

**vow,** *n.* **1.** pledge; solemn promise. —*v.t.* **2.** promise solemnly; swear. —*v.i.* **3.** make a vow.

**vow′el,** *n.* **1.** speech sound made with the central part of the breath channel unblocked. **2.** letter representing a vowel: *a, e, i, o, u* and sometimes *y.*

**voy′age,** *n.* **1.** an extended journey, esp. by sea. —*v.i.* **2.** make a journey; travel. —*v.t.* **3.** traverse; sail. —**voy′ag·er** *n.*

**vul′gar,** *adj.* **1.** lacking taste or breeding; unrefined. **2.** ordinary; plebian. **3.** ostentatiously showy. **4.** indecent; obscene. **5.** vernacular. —**vul′gar·ly,** *adv.* —**vul·gar′i·ty, vul′gar·ness,** *n.*

**vul′ner·a·ble,** *adj.* **1.** capable of being physically or emotionally wounded. **2.** open to damage or attack. —**vul′ner·a·bly,** *adv.* —**vul′′ner·a·bil′i·ty,** *n.*

**vul′ture,** *n.* **1.** large bird subsisting chiefly on carrion. **2.** predatory or rapacious person. —**vul'tur·ous**, *adj.*

**vul'va**, *n., pl.* **-vas, -vae.** external female genital organs. —**vul'val**, **vul'var**, *adj.*

# W

**W, w,** *n.* 23rd letter of the Englis alphabet.

**wade**, *v.i.* 1. walk through water. —*v.t.* 2. cross by wading. —**wad'er**, *n.*

**wag**, *v.t., v.i.* 1. shake in an arc. —*n.* 2. wit, joker. —**wag'ger·y**, *n.* —**wag'gish**, *adj.*

**wage**, *n., pl.* **wages.** *n.* 1. pay. —*v.t.* 2. carry on, as war.

**wa'ger**, *n., v.t., v.i.* bet.

**wag'on**, *n.* four-wheeled draft freight vehicle.

**waist**, *n.* part of the body between ribs and hips.

**wait**, *v.i.* 1. stop briefly; pause. 2. be in expectation. 3. be patient. 4. remain undone. 5. serve food, etc. —*n.* 6. act, instance, or period of waiting. 7. **in wait**, in ambush.

**wake**, *v.,* **waked** or **woke, woked** or **woken, waking,** *v.i.* 1. awake. 2. be alert. —*v.t.* 3. arouse. —*n.* 4. vigil, as over a corpse.

**walk**, *v.i.* 1. go on foot. —*v.t.* 2. cause to walk. 3. accompany on foot. —*n.* 4. act or instance of walking. 5. place for walking. —**walk'er**, *n.*

**wall**, *n.* 1. upright enclosure. —*v.t.* 2. enclose or separate.

**wal'nut''**, *n.* edible nut from a northern tree.

**wal'rus**, *n.* large sea mammal with two tusks.

**waltz**, *n.* 1. dance in three-quarter time. —*v.i.* 2. dance a waltz. —*v.t.* 3. *Informal.* lead briskly. —**waltz'er**, *n.*

**wand**, *n.* rod with supposed magical power.

**wan'der**, *v.i.* 1. move about aimlessly. 2. stray. —*v.t.* 3. travel over. —**wan'der·er**, *n.*

**wane**, *v.i.* 1. grow dim. 2. decline

in strength or power. —*n.* 3. decrease.

**want**, *v.t.* 1. wish for. 2. desire, crave, demand. —*v.i.* 3. be lacking or deficient. —*n.* 4. something needed. 5. deficiency or lack. —**want'ing**, *adj., prep.*

**war**, *n.* 1. armed conflict, as between nations. 2. hostility or struggle. —*v.i.* 3. be in conflict. —**war'fare'**, *n.* —**war'like**, *adj.*

**ward**, *n.* 1. administrative division of a city. 2. division of a hospital. 3. person under the care of a guardian. —*v.t.* 4. repel or avert.

**war'den**, *n.* chief officer of a prison.

**ware**, *n.* goods for sale.

**warm**, *adj.* 1. having or giving moderate heat. 2. friendly or affectionate. 3. irritated or angry. —*v.i., v.t.* 4. heat moderately. —**warm'ly**, *adv.* —**warmth**, **warm'ness**, *n.* —**warm'ish**, *adj.*

**warn**, *v.t.* give notice of danger; caution. —**warn'ing**, *n., adj.*

**warp**, *n.* 1. distortion. 2. lengthwise threads in cloth. —*v.t., v.i.* 3. distort.

**war'rant**, *n.* 1. authorization, as by law. 2. guarantee.

**war'ri·or**, *n.* soldier.

**wart**, *n.* small hard protuberance on the skin. —**wart'y**, *adj.*

**war'y**, *adj.,* **warier, wariest.** cautious; watchful. —**war'i·ly**, *adv.* —**war'i·ness**, *n.*

**was**, *v.* 1st and 3rd person singular, past indicative of *be.*

**wash**, *v.t.* 1. clean with or in water or a solution. 2. flow over. —*v.i.* 3. wash oneself. 4. undergo washing.

**wasp**, *n.* stinging insect.

**waste**, *v.t.* 1. use up needlessly. 2. ruin. —*v.i.* 3. be used up gradually. —*n.* 4. needless consumption or expenditure. 5. unused remains. 6. neglect. 7. ruin. —*adj.* 8. unused.

**watch**, *v.i.* 1. observe; be on the alert. —*v.t.* 2. observe. 3. guard or tend. —*n.* 4. period of watching; observation. 5. small timepiece worn on the person.

**wa'ter**, *n.* 1. colorless, odorless liquid forming rain, rivers, etc. —*v.t.* 2. supply with water. —*v.i.* 3. discharge water or tears. —**wa'ter·y**, *adj.*

**wa'ter·fall''**, *n.* steep fall of water, as over a precipice.

**U  
Z**

**wa·ter·proof**'', *adj.* 1. impervious to water. —*v.t.* 2. make waterproof.

**watt**, *n.* unit of electric power. —**watt'age**, *n.*

**wave**, *n.* 1. ridge along the ocean's surface. 2. undulation. 3. movement back and forth, as of a hand or flag. —*v.i.*, *v.t.*, 4. move to and fro. —*v.i.* 5. signal with the hand. —**wav'y**, *adj.*

**wa'ver**, *v.i.* 1. hesitate. 2. sway. —*n.* 3. wavering.

**wax**, *n.* 1. readily melted, molded, and burned substance. —*v.t.* 2. treat with wax. —*v.i.* 3. increase, as the moon. 4. *Archaic.* become. —**wax'en**, *adj.* —**wax'er**, *n.* —**wax'y**, *adj.*

**way**, *n.* 1. manner, custom, or fashion. 2. plan. 3. direction or route.

**way'ward**, *adj.* 1. willful. 2. capricious. —**way'ward·ness**, *n.*

**we**, *pron.* nominative plural of *I.*

**weak**, *adj.* 1. not strong physically. 2. lacking moral or mental strength. 3. easily broken. —**weak'ly**, *adj.*, *adv.* —**weak'en**, *v.t.*, *v.i.* —**weak'ling**, *n.* —**weak'ness**, *n.*

**wealth**, *n.* 1. abundance of money or property. 2. large and valuable amount. —**wealth'y**, *adj.*

**wean**, *v.t.* accustom to food other than mother's milk.

**weap'on**, *n.* instrument for fighting. —**weap'on·ry**, *n.*

**wear**, *v.*, **wore**, **worn**, **wearing**. *v.t.* 1. have on the body, as clothing. 2. diminish by use. —*v.i.* 3. deteriorate as through use. —*n.* 4. diminution or impairment through use. 5. clothing. —**wear'a·ble**, *adj.* —**wear'er**, *n.*

**wea'ri·some**, *adj.* tiresome.

**wea'ry**, *adj.*, **-rier**, **-riest**, *v.t.* *adj.* 1. very tired. 2. causing fatigue. —*v.t.* 3. tire. —**wear'i·ly**, *adv.* —**wear'i·ness**, *n.*

**weath'er**, *n.* 1. condition of the sky. 2. storms, rains, etc. —*v.t.* 3. withstand. 4. expose to the weather.

**weave**, *v.*, **wove**, **woven**. or **weaved**, **weaving**. *n.* *v.t.* 1. interlace threads, etc., as on a loom. 2. construct, as in the mind. —*v.i.* 3. become interlaced. —*n.* 4. type of weaving. —**weav'er**, *n.*

**web**, *n.* 1. something woven. 2. network spun by spiders. 3. trap. —*v.t.* 4. join or cover, as by or

with a web. —**webbed**, *adj.* —**web'bing**, *n.*

**web'foot**'', *n.*, *pl.* **-feet.** foot with webbed toes. —**web'foot''ed**, **web'-toed**'', *adj.*

**wed**, *v.*, **wedded**, **wedded** or **wed**, **wedding**. *v.t.*, *v.i.* 1. marry. 2. join. —**wed'ding**, *n.*

**wedge**, *n.* 1. object with two faces meeting at a sharp angle. —*v.t.* 2. force or fix with a wedge. —*v.i.* 3. become wedged.

**weed**, *n.* 1. useless plant. —*v.i.* 2. free from weeds. —**weed'er**, *n.* —**weed'y**, *adj.*

**week**, *n.* 1. period of seven days, esp. starting from Sunday. 2. working days of the week.

**week'day**'', *n.* any day except Saturday or Sunday.

**week'end**'', *n.* Saturday and Sunday.

**week'ly**, *adj.*, *adv.*, *n.*, *pl.* **-lies.** *adj.* 1. appearing or occurring once a week. 2. lasting a week. —*adv.* 3. every week. —*n.* 4. weekly periodical.

**weep**, *v.i.*, **wept**, **weeping**. mourn or shed tears. —**weep'er**, *n.*

**weigh**, *v.t.* 1. measure the heaviness of. 2. consider carefully. —*v.i.* 3. have significance. 4. be a burden. —**weigh'er**, *n.*

**weight**, *n.* 1. heaviness or pressure. 2. burden, influence, or importance. —*v.t.* 3. burden. —**weight'y**, *adj.* —**weight'i·ness**, *n.*

**weird**, *adj.* strange.

**wel'come**, *n.* 1. friendly greeting. —*v.t.* 2. greet with pleasure. —*adj.* 3. happily or readily received. 4. freely permitted.

**weld**, *v.t.* 1. unite, as by heat or pressure. —*n.* 2. welded joint. —**weld'er**, *n.*

**wel'fare**'', *n.* 1. well-being. 2. aid for the poor.

**well**, *adv.*, **better**, **best**, *adj.*, *n.*, *v.i.*, *interj.* *adv.* 1. in a benevolent, good, or thorough manner. —*adj.* 2. in good health. 3. suitable. —*n.* 4. opening in the earth as a source of water, oil, etc. —*v.i.* 5. flow or gush. —*interj.* 6. (exclamation denoting surprise or introducing a sentence).

**well-** prefix meaning "in a good or thorough manner."

**well'-nigh'**, *adv.* almost.

**well'-off'**, *adj.* 1. in a good condition. 2. prosperous.

**well'-pre·served'**, *adj.* 1. in good

condition. 2. youthful for one's age.

**well'-round·ed,** adj. 1. having varied abilities. 2. well-diversified.

**welt,** n. 1. ridge or wale on the body from a blow. 2. leather strip on the seam of a shoe.

**welt'er,** v.i. 1. roll or heave, as waves. 2. wallow. —n. 3. jumble or muddle.

**went,** v.i. past form of *go.*

**were,** v. past plural form of *be.*

**west,** n. 1. compass point to the left of north. 2. direction of such point. 3. Also, **West,** the Occident. —adj., adv. 4. toward or from the west. —**west'ern,** adj. —**west'ern·er,** n.

**west·er·ly,** adj., adv. 1. from the west, as wind. 2. toward the west.

**west'ern·ize'',** v.t. make Occidental in culture.

**west'ward,** adj. 1. toward the west. —adv. 2. Also, **west'wards,** toward the west. —n. 3. westward direction.

**wet,** adj., wetter, wettest, n., v. adj. 1. covered with water or liquid. —n. 2. water or moisture. —v.t. 3. make wet. —v.i. 4. become wet. —**wet'ness,** n.

**whale,** n. 1. large sea mammal. —v.i. 2. hunt whales. —**whal'er,** n.

**wharf,** n., pl. wharves. pier or quay.

**what,** pron., pl. what, adj., adv., interj. pron. 1. which one? 2. that which. —adj. 3. which kind of. —adv. 4. how? 5. partly. —interj. 6. (exclamation of surprise).

**what·ev'er,** pron. 1. anything that. —adj. 2. of any kind.

**wheat,** n. cereal grass used in flour, etc.

**wheel,** n. 1. rotating disk that transmits power or facilitates movement. —v.t., v.i. 2. move on wheels. 3. revolve.

**when,** adv. 1. at what time? —conj. 2. at the time that. —pron. 3. what or which time.

**whence,** adv. from what place, cause, etc.

**when·ev'er,** adv. 1. when. —conj. 2. at whatever time.

**where,** adv. 1. at what place? 2. in what way? —conj. 3. at which place; wherever. —pron. 4. the place at which.

**where'a·bouts'',** adv. 1. where. —n. 2. location.

**where·as',** conj. 1. considering that. 2. on the contrary.

**where·in',** conj. in which.

**where·with·al',** n. means.

**whet,** v.t. 1. sharpen. 2. stimulate, as the appetite. —**whet'stone',** n.

**wheth'er,** conj. 1. .if it is so that. 2. if either.

**whey,** n. water part of curdled milk.

**which,** pron. 1. what one? 2. that. —adj. 3. what one.

**which·ev'er,** pron., adj. 1. any. 2. regardless of which.

**whiff,** n. light odor or puff.

**while,** n. 1. time. —conj. 2. during the time that. 3. although. —v.t. 4. spend pleasantly, as time.

**whim,** n. sudden fancy; caprice. —**whim'si·cal,** adj. —**whim'sy,** n.

**whine,** v.i. 1. complain childishly. 2. make a high-pitched, nasal sound. —**whin'ing·ly,** adv. —**whin'y,** adj.

**whip,** v.t. 1. strike or lash. —v.i. 2. move quickly. —n. 3. instrument for whipping.

**whirl,** v.i., v.t. 1. move or revolve rapidly. —n. 2. whirling movement. 3. uproar or confusion.

**whirl'pool',** n. whirling current of water.

**whirl'wind'',** n. whirling current of air.

**whisk,** v.t., v.i. 1. brush with a quick motion. —n. 2. act or instance of whisking. —**whisk'-broom',** n.

**whisk'er,** n. 1. a facial hair. 2. long bristle, as on a cat.

**whis'key,** n., pl. -keys, -kies. liquor distilled from fermented grain. Also, **whis'ky.**

**whis'per,** v.i., v.t. 1. speak softly. 2. make a low rustling. —n. 3. act or instance of whispering.

**whis'tle,** v.i. 1. make a high-pitched sound through pursed lips. —n. 2. act or instance of whistling. 3. noise-making device using steam or air.

**white,** adj. 1. of the color of snow. 2. pale. 3. pure. —n. 4. opposite to black. 5. Caucasoid. —**white'ness,** n. —**whit'ish,** adj. —**whit'en,** v.t., v.i.

**white'wash'',** n. 1. mixture for whitening walls. —v.t. 2. apply whitewash to. 3. *Informal.* conceal the guilt of.

**whith'er,** adv., conj. *Archaic.* to what place.

**U Z**

**whit'tle,** v.t., v.i. 1. cut or carve, as from wood. —v.t. 2. reduce the amount of.

**who,** pron. 1. which person? 2. person that.

**who·ev'er,** pron. anyone that.

**whole,** adj. 1. entire. 2. intact. 3. Math. not a fraction. —n. 4. all the amount. —**whole'ly,** adv. —**whole'ness,** n.

**whole'sale',** n. 1. sale of goods in quantity, as to retailers. —adj. 2. selling by wholesale. —v.t., v.i. 3. sell wholesale. —**whole'sal'er,** n.

**whole'some,** adj. healthful, salutary. —**whole'some·ly,** adv. —**whole'some·ness,** n.

**whom,** pron. Grammar. objective case of who.

**whore,** n. 1. prostitute. —v.i. 2. consort with whores. —**whor'ish,** adj.

**whose,** pron. Grammar. possessive case of who.

**why,** adv., n., pl. **whys,** interj. adv. 1. for what reason or cause. —n. 2. reason, cause, or purpose. —interj. 3. exclamation of surprise.

**wick'ed,** adj. 1. bad, evil. 2. mischievous.

**wide,** adj., **wider, widest.** adj. 1. broad. —adv. 2. far. —**wide'ly,** adv. —**wide'ness,** n. —**wid'en,** v.t., v.i. —**wide'spread',** adj.

**wid'ow,** n. 1. unmarried woman whose husband has died. —v.t. 2. make into a widow. Also, masc., **wid'ow·er.** —**wid'ow·hood',** n.

**width,** n. breadth.

**wield,** v.t. 1. handle or manage. 2. exercise, as authority or power. —**wield'er,** n.

**wife,** n., pl. **wives.** married woman. —**wifes'less,** adj. —**wife'ly,** adj.

**wig,** n. 1. artificial hair piece. —v.t. 2. furnish with a wig.

**wild,** adj. 1. uncivilized. 2. uncontrollable. 3. lacking restraint; dissolute. —n. 4. desolate region. —**wild'ly,** adv. —**wild'ness,** n.

**wild'cat',** n. 1. large, fierce feline. 2. savage person. 3. exploratory oil or gas well. —v.i., v.t. 4. search for oil or gas.

**wil'der·ness,** n. uninhabited region.

**wile,** n. 1. sly trick. —v.t. 2. beguile. 3. **wile away,** pass leisurely, as time.

**will,** n. 1. power of conscious choice or action. 2. determination. 3.

disposition toward another. 4. legal document of one's wishes after death. —v.i., v.t. 5. desire, wish, or want. 6. bequeath by a will. —auxiliary v. 7. am, is, or are about to. 8. am, is, or are willing to. 9. am, is, or are expected to. —**will·a·ble,** adj.

**will'ful,** adj. 1. intentional. 2. stubborn. Also, **wil'ful.** —**will'ful·ly,** adv. —**will'ful·ness,** n.

**wilt,** v.i. 1. become limp or weak; droop. —v.t. 2. cause to wilt. —n. 3. wilted state.

**wil'y,** adj., **-lier, -liest.** sly. —**wi'li·ness,** n.

**win,** v.i. 1. succeed. —v.t. 2. gain, as a victory, favor, etc. 3. influence. —n. 4. victory.

**wince,** v.i. 1. shrink, as from a blow or pain. —n. 2. act or instance of wincing.

**winch,** n. 1. crank. 2. windlass. —v.t. 3. hoist or haul by a winch.

**wind** v., **wound, winding,** n. v.t. (wind) 1. turn. —v.i. 2. coil. 3. make one's way, as along a path. —n. (wind) 4. air in motion, as a gale. 5. breath. 6. intestinal gas. —**wind'er,** n. —**wind'y,** adj.

**wind'mill'',** n. wind-driven machine.

**win'dow,** n. opening in a wall for light, air, etc. —**win'dow·pane',** n. —**win'dow·sill',** n. —window shade.

**wind'pipe'',** n. trachea.

**wind'shield'',** n. glass above and across a car's dashboard.

**wind'up'',** n. 1. conclusion or end. 2. Baseball. pitcher's arm and body movements before throwing.

**wind'ward,** n. 1. direction from which the wind blows. —adj. 2. moving to windward. —adv. 3. toward the wind.

**wine,** n. 1. fermented juice from grapes, other fruits, or plants. —v.i., v.t. 2. entertain with wine. —**win'y,** adj.

**wing,** n. 1. organ for flight of birds, insects, bats, etc. 2. supporting surface of an airplane. 3. distinct section. —v.t. 4. shoot in an arm or wing. —v.i. 5. travel on wings.

**wink,** v.i., v.t. 1. close and open quickly, as one eye. 2. signal by winking. —v.i. 3. shine or twinkle. —n. 4. winking, as a signal. 5. instant.

**win'ner,** n. person or thing that wins.

**win'ning,** adj. 1. pleasing; charming. 2. victorious. —n. 3. Often **winnings,** something won, as money. —**win'ning·ly,** adv.

**win'ter,** n. 1. cold season between autumn and spring. 2. time like winter, as of decline, cold, etc. —v.i. 3. spend the winter. —**win'ter·time''**, n. —**win'try, win'ter·y,** adj.

**win'ter·green''**, n. small evergreen aromatic shrub with white flowers.

**wipe,** v.t. 1. clean or rub. —n. 2. act or instance of wiping. —**wip'er,** n.

**wire,** n. 1. stringlike piece of metal. 2. Informal. telegram. —v.t. 3. install or bind with wire. —v.i. 4. telegraph.

**wire'tap''ping,** n. listening secretly to the telephone calls of others.

**wir'y,** adj., **-ier, -iest.** lean and tough.

**wis'dom,** n. 1. knowledge and good judgment. 2. wise teachings.

**wise,** adj., **wiser, wisest.** adj. 1. showing knowledge and judgment. 2. erudite or informed. 3. Informal. insolent. —**wise'ly,** adv.

**wish,** v.t. 1. want or desire. —v.i. 2. yearn. —n. 3. desire; longing. —**wish'er,** n. —**wish'ful,** adj. —**wish'ful·ly,** adv. —**wish'ful·ness,** n.

**wisp,** n. thin film or strand. —**wisp'y,** adj.

**wist'ful,** adj. longing or yearning. —**wist'ful·ly,** adv. —**wist'ful·ness,** n.

**wit,** n. 1. intelligence. 2. cleverness of expression. 3. person clever with words. —**wit'less,** adj. —**wit'less·ly,** adv. —**wit'ty,** adj. —**wit'ti·ly,** adv.

**witch,** n. 1. woman with supposed supernatural power. 2. ugly woman. —**witch'craft'',** n. —**witch'er·y,** n.

**with,** prep. 1. accompanied by. 2. characterized by. 3. against. 4. in regard to.

**with·draw',** v.t. 1. take back. 2. retract as a statement, etc. —v.i. 3. remove oneself. —**with·draw'al,** n.

**with'er,** v.t., v.i. 1. shrive. —n. 2. confuse and humiliate. —**with'er·ing·ly,** adv.

**with'ers,** n. pl. lower nape of the neck of a sheep, horse, etc.

**with·hold',** v.t. 1. hold back. 2. deduct, as taxes.

**with·in',** adv. 1. inside; indoors. —prep. 2. inside. 3. in the area of.

**with·out',** prep. 1. lacking; not with. 2. outside. —adv. 3. outside; externally.

**with·stand',** v.t. resist or oppose.

**wit'ness,** n. 1. person who sees. 2. testimony. —v.t. 3. see. 4. attest.

**wiz'ard,** n. 1. magician; sorcerer. —**wiz'ard·ry,** n.

**wob'ble,** v.i., v.t. 1. shake. —n. 2. wobbling motion. —**wob'bly,** adj. —**wob'bli·ness,** n.

**woe,** n. 1. grief. 2. trouble. —interj. 3. alas! —**woe'ful,** adj. —**woe'ful·ly,** adv. —**woe'ful·ness,** n.

**wolf,** n., pl. **wolves.** 1. wild, doglike mammal. 2. Informal. man who flirts with women. 3. cruel person. —v.t. 4. devour greedily. —**wolf'hound'',** n. —**wolf'ish,** adj. —**wolf'like'',** adj.

**wom'an,** n., pl. **women.** female human being. —**wom'an·hood'',** n. —**wom'an·ish,** adj. —**wom'an·like'',** adj. —**wom'an·ly,** adj. —**wom'an·li·ness,** n.

**womb,** n. 1. uterus. 2. source of being.

**won'der,** n. 1. awe or amazement. 2. source of such an emotion. —v.i. 3. be curious. 4. be filled with wonder. —**won'der·ful,** adj. —**won'der·ful·ly,** adv. —**won'der·ing·ly,** adv. —**won'der·ment,** n. —**won'drous,** adj. —**won'drous·ly,** adv.

**wont,** adj. 1. Also, **won'ted,** accustomed. n. 2. habit.

**won't,** v. contraction of **will not.**

**wood,** n. 1. hard substance beneath the bark of trees. 2. Also, **woods,** forest. 3. lumber. —adj. 4. wooden; made of wood. —**wood'ed,** adj. —**wood'en,** adj. —**wood'y,** adj.

**wood'cut'',** n. 1. carved block of wood. 2. print from this block.

**wood'en,** adj. 1. made of wood. 2. without natural feeling or expression. —**wood'en·ly,** adv.

**wood'work'',** n. 1. objects made of wood. 2. wooden fittings of a house, as doors, moldings, etc. —**wood'work''er,** n. —**wood'work''ing,** n.

**woof'er,** n. loud speaker for reproducing low frequencies.

**wool,** *n.* **1.** soft, curly hair, as from sheep, goats, etc. **2.** yarn or garments made from such. —**wool'len, wool'len,** *adj.* —**wool'y, wool'ly,** *adj.* —**wool'i·ness, wool'li·ness,** *n.*

**word,** *n.* **1.** spoken or written sounds with meaning as a unit of language. **2.** words, speech or talk. **3.** promise or assurance. **4.** news or information. **5.** (computers) several bits of data treated as a unit. —*v.t.* **6.** express in words —**word''age,** *n.* —**word'ing,** *n.* —**word'less,** *adj.* —**word'y,** *adj.* —**word'i·ness,** *n.*

**work,** *n., v.,* **worked** or **wrought, working.** *n.* **1.** labor or toil. **2.** occupation. **3.** something on which one is working. —*v.i.* **4.** do work. **5.** act or operate. —*v.t.* **6.** manage or manipulate. **7.** solve. **8.** cultivate, as the soil. **9.** provoke or excite. —**work'a·ble,** *adj.* —**work'bench'',** *n.* —**work'book'',** *n.* —**work'er,** *n.* —**work' day'',** *n.* —**work'ing·man'',** *n.* —**work'man,** *n.* —**work'shop'',** *n.* —**work'week'',** *n.*

**work'a·day'',** *adj.* **1.** ordinary; humdrum. **2.** characteristic of a workday.

**work'man·ship'',** *n.* **1.** workman's art or skill. **2.** quality of work.

**work'out'',** *n.* practice athletic session.

**world,** *n.* **1.** earth; universe. **2.** people; mankind. **3.** part of the earth. **4.** great quantity or extent. —**world'wide',** *adj.*

**worm,** *n.* **1.** long, soft, legless, creeping animal. **2.** something like this creature. **3.** *Informal.* contemptible person. **4.** worms, intestinal disease from parasitic worms. —*v.i.* **5.** move or act stealthily. —*v.t.* **6.** get by insidious efforts. **7.** free from worms.

**worn,** *adj.* **1.** used by wear, handling, etc. **2.** exhausted; tired. —**worn'out',** *adj.*

**wor'ry,** *v., n., pl.* **-ies.** *v.i.* **1.** feel anxious. —*v.t.* **2.** make anxious —*n.* **3.** anxiety. **4.** cause of anxiety. —**wor'ri·er,** *n.* —**wor'ri·some,** *adj.*

**worse,** *adj.* **1.** bad in a greater or higher degree. **2.** in poorer health. —*n.* **3.** that which is worse. —*adv.* **4.** in a worse manner. —**wors'en,** *v.t., v.i.*

**wor'ship,** *n.* **1.** reverence for a deity. **2.** admiration or love. —*v.t., v.i.* **3.** show religious reverence. —**wor'ship·er, wor'ship·per,** *n.* —**wor'ship·ful,** *adj.*

**worst,** *adj.* **1.** bad in the highest degree. **2.** least well. —*n.* **3.** that which is worst. —*adv.* **4.** in the worst manner. —*v.t.* **5.** beat; defeat.

**worth,** *n.* **1.** material value, as in money. **2.** importance; value. —*adj.* **3.** worthy of; justifying. **4.** having equal value. —**worth'less,** *adj.* —**worth'less·ness,** *n.*

**worth'while',** *adj.* worthy of doing, etc.

**worth'y,** *adj.,* **-i·er, -iest.** deserving. —**worth'i·ly,** *adv.* —**worth'i·ness,** *n.*

**would,** *auxiliary v.* (expressing condition, futurity, habitual action, or request).

**wound,** *n.* **1.** physical injury. **2.** injury to feelings, sensibilities, etc. —*v.t.* **3.** injure. —**wound'ed,** *adj., n., pl.*

**wrap,** *v.t., v.i.* **1.** wind or fold, as around something. —*n.* **2.** enclose or envelop. —*n.* **3.** outer garment wrapped around the body. —**wrap'ping,** *n.*

**wrap'per,** *n.* **1.** person who wraps. **2.** something wrapped around as a cover.

**wrath,** *n.* **1.** anger; rage. **2.** vengeance. —**wrath'ful,** *adj.* —**wrath'ful·ly,** *adv.*

**wreath,** *n., pl.* **wreaths.** circular formation, as of flowers, etc.

**wreck,** *n.* **1.** structure or object in ruins. **2.** run-down person. —*v.t.* **3.** tear down or destroy. —**wreck'age,** *n.* —**wreck'er,** *n.*

**wrench,** *n.* **1.** sudden twist or pull, as to the back, etc. **2.** sudden emotional strain. **3.** tool for turning bolts, etc. —*v.t.* **4.** turn suddenly. —*v.t.* **5.** overstrain or injure.

**wrest,** *v.t.* **1.** pull violently. **2.** usurp. —*n.* **3.** twist.

**wres'tle,** *v.t.* **1.** grapple and attempt to throw down. —*v.i.* **2.** engage in wrestling. **3.** struggle. —**wrest'ler,** *n.*

**wretch'ed,** *adj.* **1.** pitiful. **2.** contemptible. **3.** worthless. —**wretch'ed·ly** *adv.* —**wretch'ed·ness,** *n.*

**wring,** *v.t.* **1.** twist; press; squeeze. —*n.* **2.** act or instance of wringing. —**wring'er,** *n.*

**wrin'kle,** n. 1. ridge or furrow on a surface. 2. ingenious trick or device. —v.t., v.i. 3. crease or furrow. —**wrin'kly,** adj.

**wrist,** n. joint between the hand and forearm. —**wrist'band'',** n. —**wrist'watch',** n.

**write,** v. wrote, written, writing. v.i. 1. form letters, words. etc., as with a pen, pencil, etc. —v.t. 2. compose. 3. communicate with. —**writ'er,** n.

**writhe,** v.t., v.i. 1. squirm, twist, or bend, as in pain. —n. 2. act or instance of writhing.

**wrong,** adj. 1. not right or good. 2. not truthful or factual. 3. inappropriate. —n. 4. injustice; evil. —v.t. 5. do wrong to. —**wrong'ly,** adv. —**wrong'ness,** n. —**wrong'do'er,** n. —**wrong'do'ing,** n. —**wrong'ful,** adj. —**wrong'ful·ly,** adv.

**wry,** adj., wrier, wriest. 1. distorted or lopsided. 2. misdirected or perverse. 3. bitterly ironic.

# X

**X, x,** n. twenty-fourth letter of the English alphabet.

**x'-ray,** n. 1. electromagnetic radiation which penetrates solids. 2. picture made by x-rays. —v.t. 3. treat or photograph with x-rays.

# Y

**Y, y,** n. twenty-fifth letter of the English alphabet.

**yacht,** n. pleasure ship. —**yachts'man,** n.

**yank,** v.t., v.i. pull strongly and abruptly.

**yap,** v.i. yelp; bark shrilly.

**yard,** n. 1. linear unit of measure equal to 3 feet. 2. open area.

**yard'stick'',** n. one-yard measuring stick.

**yarn,** n. 1. multi-stranded thread for sweaters, etc. 2. story; tall tale.

**yawn,** v.i. 1. involuntarily open the mouth wide as from drowsiness. —n. 2. act or instance of yawning.

**year,** n. time period equal to 365 or 366 days. —**year'ly,** adv., adj.

**yearn,** v.i. 1. desire earnestly or strongly. 2. feel affection or tenderness. —**yearn'ing,** n., adj.

**yeast,** n. fungous substance used to leaven bread, etc.

**yell,** v.i., n. cry; shout.

**yel'low,** n. 1. bright color of butter, etc. —adj. 2. of the color yellow.

**yelp,** v.i. 1. cry quickly or shrilly like a dog. —n. 2. quick, sharp bark.

**yen,** n. Informal, desire; urge.

**yes,** adv., n. (expression of assent, agreement or affirmation).

**yes'ter·day,** adv., n. day before today.

**yet,** adv. 1. up to now. 2. besides. 3. nevertheless. 4. eventually. —conj. 5. but; still.

**yield,** v.t., v.i. 1. produce. 2. surrender. 3. concede. —v.i. 4. give way to force. —n. 5. amount produced.

**yo·del** (yōd'əl), v.t., v.i. shout or sing alternating falsetto with chest voice.

**yo'ga,** n. system of exercises for total bodily control.

**yo'gurt,** n. fermented milk food.

**yoke,** n. 1. device for joining oxen. 2. something oppressive. —v.t. 3. put a yoke on.

**yolk,** n. yellow part of the egg.

**yon'der,** adj., adv. over there.

**you,** pron. 1. person or persons addressed. 2. any person.

**young,** adj. 1. in the early stages of life, etc. 2. pertaining to youth. —n. 3. children; young people.

**young'ster,** n. child; youth.

**your,** adj. pertaining to you.

**yours,** pron., belonging to you.

**your·self',** pron., pl. -selves. 1. form of you used reflexively or emphatically. 2. your true self.

**youth,** n. 1. young state. 2. child; young person. —**youth'ful,** adj.

**yule,** n. Christmas.

U Z

# Z

**Z, z,** *n.* twenty-sixth letter of the English alphabet.

**za′ny,** *n., pl.* **-nies,** *adj.* **n. 1.** clown. **2.** silly person. —*adj.* **3.** crazy; foolish.

**zeal,** *n.* intense or eager interest. —**zeal′ous,** *adj.*

**zeal·ot** (zel′ot) *n.* enthusiast; fanatic.

**ze′bra,** *n.* black and white striped horselike African mammal.

**ze′nith,** *n.* **1.** celestial point directly overhead. **2.** highest point.

**ze′ro,** *n.* **1.** numerical symbol, 0, denoting the absence of quantity. **2.** nothing.

**zest,** *n.* **1.** something enhancing enjoyment. **2.** enjoyment.

**zig′zag″,** *n.* **1.** short sharp alternations in a line. —*v.i.* **2.** proceed in a zigzag.

**zip,** *v.i.* **1.** act or move speedily or energetically. —*v.t.* **2.** fasten with a zipper. —*n.* **3.** energy.

**zip′per,** *n.* slide fastener with interlocking teeth.

**zo′di·ac,** *n.* imaginary heavenly region including the paths of all planets except Pluto, with divisions for the twelve constellations.

**zone,** *n.* **1.** special area or region. —*v.t.* **2.** mark off or arrange in zones.

**zoo,** *n.* park where animals are exhibited.

**zo·ol′o·gy,** *n.* study of animals.

**zy·gote′,** *n.* fertilized egg cell.

# FOR GIFT GIVING

## WEDDING
## ANNIVERSARY SYMBOLS

|  | TRADITIONAL | MODERN |
|---|---|---|
| 1st | paper | clocks |
| 2nd | cotton | china |
| 3rd | leather | crystal, glass |
| 4th | books | electrical appliances |
| 5th | wood | silverware |
| 6th | sugar, candy | wood |
| 7th | wool, copper | desk sets |
| 8th | bronze, pottery | linens, laces |
| 9th | pottery, willow | leather |
| 10th | tin, aluminum | diamond jewelry |
| 11th | steel | fashion jewelry |
| 12th | silk, linen | pearls, colored gems |
| 13th | lace | textiles, furs |
| 14th | ivory | gold jewelry |
| 15th | crystal | watches |
| 20th | china | platinum |
| 25th | silver | silver |
| 30th | pearl | diamond |
| 35th | coral | jade |
| 40th | ruby | ruby |
| 45th | sapphire | sapphire |
| 50th | gold | gold |
| 55th | emerald | emerald |
| 60th | diamond | diamond |
| 75th | diamond | diamond |

## BIRTHSTONES

| January | Garnet |
|---|---|
| February | Amethyst |
| March | Bloodstone or Aquamarine |
| April | Diamond |
| May | Emerald |
| June | Pearl or Alexandrite |
| July | Ruby |
| August | Sardonyx or Peridot |
| September | Sapphire |
| October | Opal or Tourmaline |
| November | Topaz |
| December | Turquoise or Zircon |

# METRIC EQUIVALENTS
## Linear Measure

| | | |
|---|---|---|
| 1 centimeter | | 0.3937 inches |
| 1 inch | | 2.54 centimeters |
| 1 decimeter | 3.937 inch | 0.328 foot |
| 1 foot | | 3.048 decimeters |
| 1 meter | 39.37 inches | 1.0936 yards |
| 1 yard | | 0.9144 meter |
| 1 dekameter | | 1.9684 rods |
| 1 rod | | 0.5029 dekameter |
| 1 kilometer | | 0.621 mile |
| 1 mile | | 1.609 kilometers |

## Square Measure

| | | |
|---|---|---|
| 1 square centimeter | | 0.1550 square inches |
| 1 square inch | | 6.452 square centimeters |
| 1 square decimeter | | 0.1076 square foot |
| 1 square foot | | 9.2903 square decimeters |
| 1 square meter | | 1.196 square yards |
| 1 square yard | | 0.8361 square meter |
| 1 acre | | 160 square rods |
| 1 square rod | | 0.00625 acre |
| 1 hectare | | 2.47 acres |
| 1 acre | | 0.4047 hectare |
| 1 square kilometer | | 0.386 square mile |
| 1 square mile | | 2.59 square kilometers |

## Measure of Volume

| | | |
|---|---|---|
| 1 cubic centimeter | | 0.061 cubic inch |
| 1 cubic inch | | 16.39 cubic centimeters |
| 1 cubic decimeter | | 0.0353 cubic foot |
| 1 cubic foot | | 28.317 cubic decimeters |
| 1 cubic meter | | 1.308 cubic yards |
| 1 cubic yard | | 0.7646 cubic meter |
| 1 stere | | 0.2759 cord |
| 1 cord | | 3.624 steres |
| 1 liter | 0.908 dry quart | 1.0567 liquid quarts |
| 1 quart dry | | 1.101 liters |
| 1 quart liquid | | 0.9463 liter |
| 1 dekaliter | 2.6417 gallons | 1.135 pecks |
| 1 gallon | | 0.3785 dekaliter |
| 1 peck | | 0.881 dekaliter |
| 1 hektoliter | | 2.8375 bushels |
| 1 bushel | | 0.3524 hektoliter |

## Weights

| | |
|---|---|
| 1 gram | 0.03527 ounce |
| 1 ounce | 28.35 grams |
| 1 kilogram | 2.2046 pounds |
| 1 pound | 0.4536 kilogram |
| 1 metric ton | 0.98421 English ton |
| 1 English ton | 1.016 metric tons |

# APPROXIMATE METRIC EQUIVALENTS

| | | |
|---|---|---|
| 1 decimeter | | 4 inches |
| 1 liter | 1.06 quarts liquid | 0.9 quart dry |
| 1 meter | | 1.1 yards |
| 1 kilometer | | ⅝ of a mile |
| 1 hektoliter | | 2⅘ bushels |
| 1 hectare | | 2½ acres |
| 1 kilogram | | 2⅕ pounds |
| 1 stere, or cubic meter | | ¼ of a cord |
| 1 metric ton | | 2,204.6 pounds |

# WEIGHTS AND MEASURES

## CUBIC MEASURE

| | |
|---|---|
| 1,728 cubic inches | 1 cubic foot |
| 27 cubic feet | 1 cubic yard |
| 128 cubic feet | 1 cord (wood) |
| 40 cubic feet | 1 ton (shipping) |
| 2,150.42 cubic inches | 1 standard bushel |
| 231 cubic inches | 1 U.S. standard gallon |
| 1 cubic foot | about 4/5 of a bushel |

## DRY MEASURE

| | |
|---|---|
| 2 pints | 1 quart |
| 8 quarts | 1 peck |
| 4 pecks | 1 bushel |

## LIQUID MEASURE

| | |
|---|---|
| 4 gills | 1 pint |
| 2 pints | 1 quart |
| 4 quarts | 1 gallon |
| 31½ gallons | 1 barrel |

## IMPERIAL LIQUID MEASURE

| | |
|---|---|
| 1 U.S. gallon | 0.833 Imperial gallon |
| 1 U.S. gallon | 3.785 liters |
| 1 Imperial gallon | 1.201 U.S. gallons |
| 1 Imperial gallon | 4.546 liters |
| 1 liter | 0.264 U.S. gallon |
| 1 liter | 0.220 Imperial gallon |

## LONG MEASURE

| | |
|---|---|
| 12 inches | 1 foot |
| 3 feet | 1 yard |
| 5½ yards | 1 rod |
| 40 rods | 1 furlong |
| 8 furlongs | 1 sta. mile |
| 3 miles | 1 league |

## MARINER'S MEASURE

| | |
|---|---|
| 6 feet | 1 fathom |
| 120 fathoms | 1 cable length |
| 7½ cable lengths | 1 mile |
| 5,280 feet | 1 staute mile |
| 6,080.2 feet | 1 nautical mile |

## SQUARE MILE

| | |
|---|---|
| 144 square inches | 1 square foot |
| 9 square feet | 1 square yard |
| 30¼ square yards | 1 square rod |
| 40 square rods | 1 rood |
| 4 roods | 1 acre |
| 640 acres | 1 square mile |

## AVOIRDUPOIS WEIGHT

| | |
|---|---|
| 27-11/32 grains | 1 dram |
| 16 drams | 1 ounce |
| 16 ounces | 1 pound |
| 25 pounds | 1 quarter |
| 4 quarters | 1 cwt |
| 2,000 pounds | 1 short ton |
| 2,240 pounds | 1 long ton |

## TROY WEIGHT

| | |
|---|---|
| 24 grains | 1 pwt |
| 20 pwt | 1 ounce |
| 12 ounces | 1 pound |

Used for weighing gold, silver and jewels